THE

Secret Tradition in Alchemy

Its Development and Records

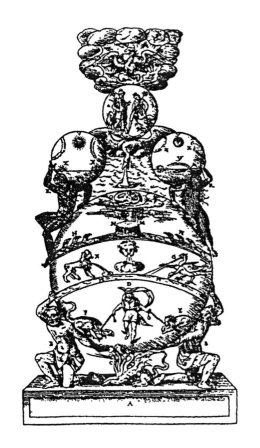

Arthur Edward Waite

ISBN 0-922802-83-1

THE SECRET TRADITION
IN ALCHEMY

Royal 8vo, pp. viii + 334

LAMPS OF WESTERN MYSTICISM

Essays on the Life of the Soul in God

By Arthur Edward Waite

" Representative of Mr. Waite's long apprenticeship and devotion to the study of the greater and lesser lights of Western Christian mysticism and of his insight in differentiating the essentials and inmost ground of truly spiritual mystical experience from so much that is called by the name. . . . The latest and ripest of Mr. Waite's meditations on this great theme."—*The Quest.*

" Throbbing with the vitality of ' experience ' on the part of the writer, and deepening in interior significance as it proceeds. . . . This ennobling work."—*Theosophy.*

" Written by one of the greatest of living scholars in these realms.

. . He ranks with Dean Inge in his knowledge of Mysticism, and need fear no comparison as a stylist."—*The Herald of the Star.*

" A volume of deeply spiritual philosophical essays expounding the experiences of the life of the soul in God."—*Scotsman.*

" Many shrewd and admirable directions for the development of the contemplative life and learned expositions of its literature."—*Westminster Gazette.*

" An introduction and guide-book to this momentous literature. Mr. Waite has written many valuable and important works ; this book is by no means least among them."—*Bookman.*

" Mr. Waite's great range of reading and his power of analysis . . must command universal respect."—*Sunday Times.*

CONTENTS

CHAPTER III

FURTHER SPECULATIONS ON PHILOSOPHICAL GOLD

CHAPTER IV

ANCIENT HERMETIC BOOKS AND THE WAY OF THE SOUL THEREIN

CHAPTER V

CHAPTER VI

CHAPTER VII

CHAPTER VIII

THE EARLY LATIN LITERATURE

CHAPTER IX

THE LATER CHAIN OF HERMES

CHAPTER X

THE MYTH OF FLAMEL

CHAPTER XI

THE CHARIOT OF BASIL VALENTINE

CHAPTER XII

PARACELSUS

CHAPTER XIII

DENYS ZACHAIRE AND OTHERS

CHAPTER XIV

FAMOUS ENGLISH PHILOSOPHERS

CHAPTER XV

CHAPTER XVI

CHAPTER XVII

CHAPTER XVIII

Thomas Vaughan

CHAPTER XIX

The Cosmopolite

CONTENTS

CONTENTS

APPENDICES

PREFACE

FROM Holy Scripture to the *Quest of the Holy Graal*, and thence onward to a comparatively recent epoch in the stream of time, it can be said of many great books that they are "written within and without". In alternative words, they suggest meanings within them which do not appear on their surface ; and it may happen that some which are presented obviously as allegorical—for example, the *Pilgrim's Progress* —are not so deep in their intimations as are others with an interior significance less consciously, or openly at least, designed by their writers. The *Romance of the Rose* is an allegory, and Jean de Meung—who completed it—took care that its whole significance should be manifest in the text itself, while the intention, as it happens, conveys nothing that matters. The second part of *Faust* has meaning within meaning, and though its design emerges, the picture-symbolism exceeds allegorical measures. There must be, however, still a few persons—perhaps many—who are unaware of large literatures which depend for their assumed importance solely on an inner meaning that differs from their outward sense, the latter in certain cases being unintelligible in the absence of a key. One of these literatures is that which was concerned in the past with the supposed trans-mutation of metals, and for many past generations enlisted the interest as it commanded also the convictions of notable persons throughout western Europe. Setting aside the question of possibility—whether, that is to say, metallic conversions were accomplished as a result of any process or by any accident in the past, and whether they will be per-formed in the future—there is no more singular literature than that of Alchemy, and even at the present day it offers material for speculation to persons who, without any predisposition towards so-called secret sciences, and believing most probably that no such sciences exist, are yet not wholly disassociated from an interest in old-world curiosities of experiment and its records in book-writing.

The secret theosophies, like Kabalism, and one at least of the secret sciences were perpetuated *ex hypothesi* by reception, in other words, by transmission from one person and generation to another. They suppose therefore custodians, without which such transmission would be impossible. On the face of alchemical literature the claim of this custody is plainly written : possibly it is the only thing which is plain or demonstrable concerning it. It forms part of a considerable body of evidence that certain knowledge—whether actual or fanciful does not signify at the moment—was handed down from an early period and through the Middle Ages to later times. Such knowledge was sometimes concerned with matters of research belonging to the domain of physics, as in the case of Alchemy ; at others it transmitted old ideas of philosophy : Cornelius Agrippa had claims on the past in this respect and even Paracelsus—great innovator as he was, and notwithstanding his favourite motto[1] —confesses to something brought down.[2] In yet other cases religious practices, connoting religious beliefs of antiquity, under one or other guise and amidst inevitable mutations, have been apparently handed on.

So far as the West is concerned, the literature of Alchemy is in the main a Latin literature, and it rose up in Europe about the beginning of the tenth century. It was by no means to be regarded as new, for, setting China aside, we shall see that it had Greek, Arabian and Syriac antecedents which take the subject back some few centuries further, though by no means into proximity with the beginnings of Christianity. But it assumed certain new and more methodical characteristics when it put on a Latin garb, so that we get into closer

---

[1] See page 177 of the present work : it is the inscription written about the portrait which appears in the great Geneva edition of his collected works.

[2] It is in part by way of appeal to the philosophers and Kabalists who preceded him, to the old "spagyrists" and "the good arts which existed in the first age," as in *The Book Concerning the Tincture of Philosophers*—and in part by reference to a hidden knowledge coming down from the prediluvian past. See my *Hermetic and Alchemical Writings of Paracelsus*, 1894, Vol. I, pp. 19 *et seq.*

touch with its claim and have a better knowledge of those
concerned in its production. From the tenth century to the
end of the seventeenth and even later this literature was
carried on without any interruption, using the same symbolical
style, preferring the same pretensions and being then, as it
remains still, without any real meaning for the general
world. No critical writers have ever taken hold of the gross
fact of this literature and succeeded in explaining it on any
principle of mere crass imposition or forgery of the ordinary
kind. They have seized on it at certain late periods—
notably at the end of the sixteenth century and in the
decades which followed thereon ; they have tried to shew
that the ignorance and credulity then prevalent on physical
subjects created a demand for such books and that booksellers supplied it then as they might do now if the com-
modity were marketable. There is obvious truth in this
impeachment, and it accounts for many spurious tracts on
Alchemy which were produced then and later. But it does
not account for Greek, Arabian, Syriac and Hebrew or
Aramaic texts which did not see print for centuries, which
were put upon no market. It does not account for obscure
alchemical poems containing the memorials and note-books
of obscure and often unknown workers which did not emerge
into daylight till they were brought forth by Ashmole, the
antiquary. It does not account for four centuries of production, and more even than this, between the period of the
Latin Geber and that of Caxton, when there was no printing
and no ready method of circulating manuscripts so that
profit could be assured to their authors.

The same quality of criticism might point to the wider fact
that alchemists, for obvious reasons, were often popular
with princes, were honoured guests at their courts, and that
illusory pretensions arose in this manner ; but such persons—
a few well known exceptions set apart—Edward Kelley is
an instance—were not the alchemists who created or contributed materially to the literature of metallic transmutation. Few cycles of book production have been more independent of patronage. Many of the works in question were
either anonymous or passed under names which were
obviously not those of their real authors. When a courtly
connection existed it tended to produce the opposite effect

to that which such criticism would suggest. There is Arnoldus
de Villa Nova, once a respected royal physician, who—according to one story—lost position, home, personal security and
in the end life itself, because of his devotion to a problematical
art. There is Raymund Lully, the so-called Jewish neophyte,
not the *doctor illuminatus* of *Ars Magna* but that obscure and
indeed unknown master about whom we know only on his
proper testimony what he suffered at the hands of royal
avarice. Passing to later times, there is here the gentleman
from Scotland who was imprisoned and racked, suffering all
martyrdom except its crown, because of the alleged knowledge
which he refused. Again there is the English adept whose
name has never transpired, who describes himself as a
wanderer upon the face of the earth, set apart by his secret
from all common familiarity with men and ever occupied
in eluding his enemies. Later still there is the so-called
Greek Archimandrite who—as if possessed by some missionary
fever—travelled from place to place, exhibiting a mysterious
gift about which we know only that he gained nothing by
dispensing it, while it brought misery on those who received.

If we take the palpable fact of this strange literature of the
centuries and suppose for a moment, in accordance with their
recurring claim, that the men who wrote these books were
members of some Secret Fraternity, speaking a common
language by which at any time and in any place they could
understand one another, then the mere existence of the
literature may seem comparatively intelligible. On the
surface it pretended to afford an instruction which could be
grasped by the uninitiated if he gave himself utterly to their
subject, and if his intent above all were so worthy that he
might win help from God ; but actually it may have registered
—for those who also knew—the individual paths followed in
the course of attainment by each as he worked alone. I am
not putting forward a personal hypothesis but looking at a
possible way of understanding a claim made and the texts
in which it is enshrined. From this point of view, if only in a
vague and general sense, we can get a certain light of purpose
in which to regard the literature—whether the transmutation
of metals was actually the object in view or whether this
ostensible design covered a different purpose, being precisely
that question which it is the proposal of the present volume

to investigate. But it will by no means prove explanatory along the whole line, and it offers nothing which can be said to account for itself. There is very little to shew why the alchemists—if they were at work in physics—should have recourse to such a device, why it was necessary or desirable that they should communicate for each other's benefit that which they had performed, working with more or less agreed formulæ on things put into their hands.

On the other hand, if—as it has been advanced—they were recording the results of explorations in the spiritual nature of man, there is no assignable reason on the surface why they should have adopted the veil of *Chemia*. Moreover, and in either case, there is not only nothing to indicate the existence of any method by which it was possible to reach those who were addressed, but there was almost certainly none. On the hypothesis of initiation, it lay between individual master and apprentice or pupil. It is not until the seventeenth century, and then in the most dubious manner, that we hear of adepts assembled, of their palaces, temples or houses, under the denomination of the Rosy Cross. That there was finally no distribution of manuscripts among persons concerned seems proved by the fact of important typical texts, like the *Ordinal* of Thomas Norton, remaining entombed for generations. In so far therefore as the speculation seems tolerable it means only that people who performed the work of Alchemy —whatever it happened to be—were prompted to record their achievement and did it in such a manner that they might be understood by other masters, and by those only. By a bare possibility they may have written in order that, from age to age, there might be always a witness in the world.

It has been implied that the texts on their surface—and, so to speak, in the book-aspects of their history—are against this view, though it offers a certain indication of purpose going on from century to century, ever saying the same thing, yet ever saying it differently, and at the same time revealing nothing that was intelligible to the unversed mind. On the surface the literature of Alchemy existed to teach the Art, to awaken those who were prepared, the supposition being apparently that students who had fitting dedications would be enabled to interpret the cryptic writing, while it would remain dark to others. There has also to be registered, as further points against it, (1) that a few of the accepted witnesses affirm their attainment of the secret by reading and comparing the best texts, from which it would follow that they were self-initiated and bound by no undertaking ; (2) that yet a few others while making this claim refer also to pledges, initiation in the first case being reduced automatically and at best to a possibly shorter way, while in the second it figures as something imposed presumably from time to time on persons who had bought their knowledge by individual toil, and it seems then to intervene for no other purpose that that of insuring secrecy. It follows that there is not so much help from the consideration here elaborated as might appear *prima facie* and that from whatever point of view we approach the alchemical subject our path is strewn with difficulties. For example, it is paraded everywhere that no writer has ever revealed the First Matter of the Work, in which case it seems idle to suggest that any one could get to know it by a comparison of different texts. There is no answer to this, unless any one elects to think that the grand desideratum is really hidden in the records, for those who are skilled to find it. As to this there is no evidence ; and did it happen to be true, the class of people who would discover the Great Secret would be comparable to those who are found now among us winning prizes in cross-word puzzles and other competitive exercises : in other words, they would be in possession of a faculty which by no means connotes the high qualities that all alchemical masters declare essential, namely, love of God, unselfishness, charity, detachment from earthly interests—including material wealth—and dedication to eternal things.

To enumerate such stipulations suggests that every succeeding sentence in these prefatory words serves mainly to bring forth a new problem : conditions, dedications, warranties of this kind are out of all proportion to anything offered by Alchemy on its serious side, speaking within the measures of its literal sense. If we separate lying texts, like that which passes under the name of Artephius, those who accomplish the *Magnum Opus* can prolong their life, if they choose, to the fullest limit permitted by God and Nature, because the Medicine of Metals is a Medicine also of Man. There is no question, moreover, that the successful alchemist had the key of wealth in his hands, by the hypothesis of the Art, though the only supposed adept who left great treasures behind him was Pope John XXII, and his legend is fraudulent—like the tract ascribed to him. Now, natural longevity—not that there is evidence of its attainment by the aid of any elixir—and as much or as little of precious metal as Alchemy could produce in crucibles, according to its own shewing, are no adequate ground for postulating signal virtues as a prime condition in those who would attain the Art.

On considerations like these the surface claim of the literature has an air of colossal pretence or alternatively conveys the suggestion that it is talking about one thing in the terms of another; and this is precisely what has been advanced concerning it. Out of this possibility also the present work arises. The transmutation of metals *per se* is no concern of mine; but it has been said that great secrets of the soul are hidden under veils of *Chemia*; that they are of a kind which called for concealment in those persecuting days when the literature came into being; and that even now—when things are proclaimed on the housetops which used to be whispered in crypts—it is impermissible to speak of them openly because they are liable to abuse. There is nothing in the last suggestion to inspire a moment's confidence, but it can be left to stand at its value because of the major claim, which is not of to-day altogether, of this or the last century. And when a question of the soul arises—whatever the issue may prove—it is not of my concern only but my part of life and its province. I have set myself therefore to collect and estimate such evidence—if any—as it may be possible to ascertain of that which lies behind the surface sense of alchemical literature through the ages of Christendom. To examine such a scheme of cryptology is no easy task, but it is also no excursion through a realm of fantasy, for there is at least a surface suggestion in the long succession of texts that they are not what they seem—at least always and only. If we can find out that which they are I shall not have undertaken in vain this further journey in research. It may be said by way of conclusion to these prefatory words that the present volume completes my examination of the Secret Tradition transmitted through Christian Times,

Alchemy being the one branch so far unexplored of that which has claimed to constitute Theosophy in Christ, illustrated in experience rather than by formal doctrine. If I am spared for further efforts in these directions, they will belong to the work of revision, when the series at large may come to be drawn together into a collected form.

A. E. WAITE.

CHAPTER I

ALCHEMY AND SUPERNATURAL LIFE

WHILE the explorations and discoveries of science grow from more to more and are offering us at this time not all uncertain suggestions of still untrodden fields, on the threshold of which we stand, there are moments also when apparently quixotic quests, beliefs and hopes of a nearer or further past appear to us less extravagant than they did a few decades ago. Among several illustrations the most obvious perhaps is found in the changes of radium, which have reminded every one about the old dream of the alchemists concerning the transmutation of metals, though offering otherwise little to the elucidation of its cryptic records. Between the new demonstrated facts and the untutored experiments promoted by free imagination in the dark of things, there may be nothing better than a surface analogy; but behind these latter there was the faith of the alchemists, howsoever grounded, on the root-unity of such elements as came within their purview, and this also seems passing from realms of speculation towards those of workable hypothesis. Now, it happens that for the majority at this day, Alchemy is little more than a name and a name also are certain books, if indeed any, which have been heard of as devoted to its subject. It is realised very little at least that the old Art, setting China aside, as a world beyond the ken in this particular respect, is represented by a literature which began about the fourth or fifth century of the Christian era, and continued till late in the eighteenth; that a bibliography of the subject would fill a very large volume; that it is in Greek, Syriac, Arabic, Latin, and in the vernaculars of various countries of western Europe—especially German, French, English and even Italian. From beginning to end the texts are written in a strange symbolical language for the express purpose of concealment, so that they are to all intents and purposes unintelligible, in the absence of a Key, and although there

B

are several lexicons of Alchemy [1] such a Key is wanting. Were it otherwise, it seems certain that long since there would have been a serious examination of the literature, to see what experiments are recorded and for what in reality they stand. All difficulties notwithstanding, some attempts of the kind have been made, but among those which rank as serious it seems necessary at the moment to particularise only those of Berthelot, the distinguished French chemist, on the group of Byzantine texts and on Arabian and Syriac Alchemy. We shall meet with occasional critical opinions in the course of the present inquiry and shall learn what is needful concerning the elucidations offered by various students of the literature and its problems.

It should be understood that on my part I am offering no contribution to the early history of chemistry, nor a canon of criticism in respect of physical experiments couched in evasive terms. My concern in alchemical literature has its point of departure from a very different ground, and the textual examination proposed in the present work is based upon considerations which are of no physical kind. I am well aware that this statement will appear very strange to those who are unversed, and that to investigate the books of alleged processes for transmuting metals from a non-physical point of view must seem a distracted undertaking. Let as much be granted out of hand on the simple surface of things ; but in respect of my personal sanity be it understood further that I am engaged in the criticism of certain views on the literature which do not happen to be of my own invention. For the rest I have intimated that it is written in symbolical language, and it may be thought colourable that the pretence of expounding alleged methods for transmuting

---

[1] There is, for example, that of Johnson, among things that are ready to the hand, being available in English, and there is the large *Lexicon Alchimiæ* of Martinus Rulandus, 1612, which also has appeared in translation together with a supplement, only six copies being printed *circa* 1892. The most interesting of all is the *Dictionnaire Mytho-Hermétique* of Antoine Joseph Pernety. Paracelsus has had his own vocabulary explained in alphabetical order, and I appended something of the kind to my edition of his *Hermetic and Alchemical Writings* long years ago. I have even met in manuscript with a similar list of so-called " hard words " in the writings of Dr. Dee. This passed under the name of Dr. Rudd, and had nothing in reality to do with the learned mathematician of Mortlake: it was borrowed matter—I think, from Johnson and others. Finally the compilation of Johnson was reproduced in the *Bibliotheca Chemica Curiosa* of Mangetus, 1702. The list is by no means exhausted, but it would serve little purpose to carry the enumeration further.

putative metals may after all be part of the veils and the figurative sense of terms.[1] If it has so been regarded for a considerable period of time by persons who count as serious, it is not an insensate inquiry, and may prove to be in a different category from the " mysteries of platonic love in the middle ages ", from the consideration of Dante as " arch heretic and revolutionary ", or from the supposed concealed authorship of the Shakespeare plays—subjects which in themselves are not of necessity distracted but tend so to become in the hands of those who treat them.

There has grown up in mystical circles, more especially of recent years, and there has been reflected thence among persons outside the circles, even in the secular press,[2] a feeling that Alchemy was in reality a spiritual experiment, connoting spiritual attainments, " veiled in allegory and illustrated by symbols," and neither a dark groping in mere physics nor a successful attempt to transmute metals, literally understood. Those who have met with alchemical texts seem to

---

[1] It is a question of logic to place this point on record, but it should be understood that the voice of the literature on *Secretum Artis* is not as to the end and object of experiment but as to materials and procedure. The end was a Medicine of Metals, though in one of its forms it could prolong human life. Now, a literature which claims to communicate—under veils or otherwise—the secret of metallic transmutation must be held to deal therewith unless there is full evidence to the contrary. The " philosophers " may affirm that they are most deceptive when on the surface they are most clear, but it must not be inferred from a suggestion of this kind that when they are dealing obviously with things belonging to the mineral world they are concerned in reality, and under heavy veils, with a subject or subjects at some opposite pole of thought. There is no indication throughout the entire literature that its authors were deceptive in respect of universals but of particulars only. These willing misdirections, moreover, are to be distinguished from things that are admittedly hidden. It is an open secret that the First Matter is called by many names and that all are veils, the *Secretum Artis*, as we have seen, having been declared by none. There is one point more : supposing for a moment an array of textual evidence against metallic transmutation as the real end in view, it does not follow that the alchemical concern was spiritual. Spiritual intimations—if any—discerned throughout the literature may be assuredly another veil. If William Shakespeare did not write the plays which pass under his name, the fact does not signify that of necessity they were the work of Francis Bacon. So also, if Alchemy is not that which it claims, a mystery of the mineral kingdom, the sole alternative is not that it is a mystery of the human soul. Its records may be cryptic manifestoes of some Secret Order which from time immemorial has prepared a political transformation of the world. They may have told those who knew how it was faring with the scheme at one and another time, among these and those persons, and in that or this place and country of the world.

[2] As, for example, in *The Spectator* of June 14, 1924, reviewing my book on *The Brotherhood of the Rosy Cross*, it is proposed that the formulæ of Alchemy were " used in parable "; that Salt, Sulphur and Mercury seem to be spiritual principles ; that the secret purpose was to analyse, rectify, integrate, the human spirit ; and to produce the perfect man.

find such a notion confirmed by the deep religious fervour displayed in many and the suggestion there and here of Spiritual Mysteries which are analogous to the Hermetic Work : some of the latter have been accepted as seemingly accidental but really purposed hints about the nature of the hidden subject.

So much and very shortly of present impressions and dreams which do not arise from knowledge, or in most cases even from passing acquaintance.   Behind them, however, are certain facts in the records, and behind these are others of an earlier period, from both of which something has filtered through and accounts for the persistent and indeed recurring rumours.   Between 1850 and 1858 there were published three obscure works—in England and America—by two authors who knew nothing of one another but who wrote for the purpose of shewing that Alchemy, represented by its literature, all claims and material objects on the surface notwithstanding, was an experimental art or science practised in the soul and mind, instead of a work on metals ; that only in a figurative and emblematic sense was lead transmuted into gold ; and that the alleged elixir of life was not contained in vials or made in stills.[1]   Two centuries and more behind these modern explanations there were men in Germany and England who spoke of Philosophical Gold and used other terms of the Art, to indicate that it had no place in physics and that the true *Alchemia* was a practice of Divine Knowledge.

It follows that there is a problem offered to consideration, that there is a concern of the past and present therein, while it is barely possible that there is something behind it which has the suggestion of a provisional warrant.   My proposition therefore is to survey alchemical literature and

---

[1] We shall see that when the proposed allegorical understanding of Alchemy arose in the nineteenth century, it had from the beginning one fatal and seemingly indelible mark scored against it, being that of unacquaintance with the literature at its fountain-sources.   These were not only unprinted and in Greek, Arabic or Syriac, but were available for the most part to palæographers alone.   They are fortunately in our hands now, the texts edited and printed by the care of scholars, while they have been translated, moreover, into French.   It must be added that if such a mark against the interpreters mentioned disqualified them utterly there would be no need for the present work ; but while it happens that their individual speculations will be set aside in the end they have opened a way to another view of the subject in connection with later characteristics and developments of alchemical texts.

its history, to ascertain what evidence—if indeed any—it may offer thereupon, but perhaps especially whether we can trace from the beginning the presence of any spiritual intent in the literature at large. It should be understood that so formulated the design is to proceed on the evidence offered by the records, for the reason that there is none other, unless it be those occasional lights afforded, so commonly in all subjects, by the lives of their authors, to the extent that they may prove available. It is obvious that the views of those who preceded me in the attempt to fix a spiritual and mystical significance on that which the alchemists themselves were accustomed to term the Work of Philosophy, are of my concern in the sense that to their intimations and unfoldings I owe my whole subject, since it is not to be assumed—either by myself or others—that in the absence of specific leading I should have done more than investigate the external history of Alchemy in connection with other occult studies, undertaken for definite reasons in the course of my literary life. Having registered this position on the score of sincerity, it remains to say that the inquiry which follows after the early chapters will be a first-hand survey of the subject for the purpose of answering in the only valid manner a postulated question whether there is in fact, not in hypothesis or reverie, (1) a spiritual aspect of alchemical literature at large, or alternatively (2) whether the authentic texts call to be regarded altogether from a standpoint of spiritual purpose. As preliminary hereunto it is desirable in this first chapter to say something briefly of what has been done by early antecedent expositors in dealing with this twofold question, leaving the evidence—if any—of professed alchemists to a later stage.[1]

We are taken back in this manner to the first decades of the seventeenth century and to the " deep searchings " of Jacob Böhme, the Teutonic Theosopher, on all things relative to God, man and the universe, but especially the great subject of all his writings, which is Man in the Christ-State. It is to be observed on his own authority that he was not an alchemist, as this class of researcher was understood at the period : he was an expositor who stood apart and, on the faith of other knowledge—received by what must be

[1] The chief among these and the earliest is Heinrich Khunrath.

called revelation—was in a position—*ex hypothesi sua*—
to unfold the true nature of the Great Work and the qualifications essential to its performance. His position is defined
when he says : " I have it not in the *praxis*," [1] and again,
speaking of the Stone : " I cannot yet make it myself,
albeit I know something." [2] He is the first who affirms

[1] " Also concerning the Philosophical Work of the Tincture, its progress is
not so bluntly and plainly to be described ; albeit I have it not in the *Praxis*,
the Seal of God lieth before it to conceal the true ground of the same, upon pain
of eternal punishment, unless a man knew for certain that it might not be misused.
There is also no power to attain unto it, unless a man first become that himself
which he seeketh therein : no skill or art availeth ; unless one give the tincture
into the hands of another, he cannot prepare it unless he be certainly in the New
Birth."—*The Epistles of Jacob Behmen, aliter Teutonicus Philosophus*. Translated out of the German language, 1649. 23rd Epistle, p. 171.

[2] He speaks also of two central fires, affirming that they are a chief part of
the Mystery, that "the might of all things consists therein", and that they are
easy of attainment by those who are fitted, adding, however, as follows : " It
behoves us not to break the Seal of God, for a fiery mountain lieth before it, at
which I am myself amazed and must wait whether it be God's will. How should
I teach others expressly thereof ? I cannot yet make it myself, albeit I know
somewhat. And let no man seek more of me than I have."—*Ibid*. Compare
the *Third Epistle*, p. 44. " I see it well enough, but I have no manual operation,
instigation, or art unto it ; but I only set forth an open Mystery, whereunto
God shall stir up labourers of his own. Let no man seek the Work from me, or
think to get the knowledge and operation of the Philosopher's Stone [or Universal
Tincture from me]. And though it is known clearly and might be opened more
clearly, yet I have broken my will and will write nothing, but as it is given to me,
that so it may not be my work, lest I should be imprisoned in the *Turba* "—
described elsewhere as that which accomplishes the anger of God.

With these citations we may compare what is said in *Aurora*, the first of Böhme's
writings, according to Sparrow's translation. The thesis is that gold and silver
cannot be made " pure or fine " unless they are " melted seven times in the fire ".
When that is done gold or silver " remaineth in the middle or central seat in the
heart of nature, which is the water, sitting in its own quality and colour ".
Whether this obscure statement can have any reference to ordinary refining
processes must be left open, and the same observation may apply to the " sixth
melting ", which is said to be " the greatest danger for chemists " in the
preparation of their silver and gold, because it demands a very subtle fire which
may burn or kill, while the metals become " very dim " when the fire is too cold.
The further explanation of this point is worded as follows, and shall be left to
those who are instructed on the metallurgy of gold : " If the fire be too hot in
the fifth and sixth meltings then the new life, which hath generated itself in the
rising up of the light's power out of the water, is kindled again in the fierceness
in the wrath-fire, and the mineral ore becomes a burnt scum and dross, and the
alchemist hath dirt instead of gold." When the metal is melted for the seventh
time " the life riseth up and rejoiceth in the love, and will shew forth itself in
infinity ". At the end of all these processes, and after the attainment of true
virtue and colour, there is one thing wanting only : " the spirit cannot elevate
itself with its body into the light, but must remain to be a dead stone ; and though
indeed it be of greater virtue than other stones, yet the body remaineth in death."
This is said to be " the earthly god of blind men ", otherwise a dead god and of
such a kind " as hath thrown many into hell ". Thereafter Böhme exhorts his
reader not to take him for an alchemist, because he writes only " in the knowledge
of the spirit and not from experience ". At the same time he could shew something
else, or " in how many days and in what hours these things must be prepared ;
for gold cannot be made in one day, but a whole month is requisite for it ". He

that the gift of Alchemy is the gift of supernatural life and that the Stone is Christ—that is to say, Christ the Spirit. " This is the noble precious Stone—*Lapis Philosophorum*—the Philosopher's Stone, which the Magi do find, which tinctureth Nature and generateth a new Son in the old." It is at once manifest and hidden : it is hidden in this world and yet may be had everywhere. " And this Stone is Christ, the Son of the Living God, Which discovereth Itself in all those that seek and find it." The apostles " went about with this Stone, in power and doing miracles ", but it has been persecuted always by the schools of the worldly wise. It is offered by God and bestowed on man ; it is to be had by those who desire it ; and the power of the whole Deity lies therein.[1]

Whether it can be accommodated or not to the subject-matter of alchemical symbolism and its literature, we cannot affirm that there is anything remote or unlikely in an attempt to understand the Stone of Philosophy in the sense of that Stone which is Christ : on the contrary, it is the institution of an analogy which is a little of the obvious order, since it is written at large in Scripture. That Blessed Stone which is the desire of the eyes in Alchemy could do no otherwise than recall the " Living Stone ",[2] the head in chief of the corner, elect and precious,[3] the Spiritual Rock.[4] And because according to the alchemists the matter of their Stone is common and mean of price, while the Stone itself is *Lapis*

confesses that he does not know "how to manage the fire" : "neither do I know the colours or tinctures of the qualifying or fountain spirits in their outermost birth or geniture, which are two great defects." He adds that he is acquainted with them acccording to the regenerate man, " which standeth not in the palpability." See *Aurora*, edited by C. T. Barker, 1914, *cap.* xxii.

[1] See *The Threefold Life of Man*, Englished by J. Sparrow, 1650, c. vi, v. 98, p. 101 ; v. 100, p. 102 ; c. vii, v. 14, p. 105 ; v. 26, p. 107 ; v. 40, 41, p. 109 ; c. xii, v. 1, p. 207.

[2] The Stone of which there is no end to the virtue and glory.—*Ibid.*, c. vii, v, 100, p. 102.

[3] " He who hath it and knoweth it, if he seek, he may find all things whatsoever [which] are in heaven and in earth. It is the Stone which is rejected of the builders and is the Chief Corner Stone. Upon whatsoever it falleth it grindeth it to powder and kindleth a fire therein. All universities seek it but find it not by their seeking : sometimes it is found by one that seeketh it rightly. But others [that seek it in self and for their own gain] despise it and cast it away ; and so it remaineth hidden still."—*Ibid.*, v, 102. Compare c. vii, v, 9, p. 104, concerning the Garland of Pearl, adorned with the noble and highly precious Stone, that *Lapis Philoch. Angularis, sive Philosophorum*.

[4] Compare the " Spiritual Ground " and what is said of its six properties.—*Epistles*, as *ante*, p. 164, v. 8.

exillis and as Böhme plainly describes it, " a very dark disesteemed Stone, of a grey colour," [1] it is inevitable that it should be compared in the mind—whether versed or not in the labyrinth of the Hermetic subject—with that Stone rejected of the builders,[2] which is a Stone of stumbling and a Rock of offence.[3] But as Christ is also the Stone of Salvation,[4] so is the Philosophical Stone that in which " lieth the highest tincture ".[5] If there is anything valid in analogies it will be seen, I think, that no other can be more exact and catholic after its own kind. But I am concerned at the present stage only with the fact of the comparison so formulated and not with its inherent value.

Having obtained in this manner what may be termed a clear issue, an unthinkable proposition remains. If the Stone of Alchemy is Christ, it is to be understood spiritually ; [6] and if Alchemy itself is a doctrine and practice, as I have intimated, of supernatural life according to Jacob Böhme, we should suppose it to be at the poles asunder from any material workings. On the contrary, those who understand the symbolism in this high sense and have attained the

[1] *Ibid.*, p. 65. Compare also the Ninth Epistle, p. 106, concerning precious gold growing in a "rough stone". There is a variant in the *Threefold Life of Man*, c. vi, v. 100, p. 102, as follows : " It is accounted the meanest of all Stones in the Adamical eyes and is trodden underfoot, for it affordeth no lustre to the sight. If a man light upon it he casteth it away as an unprofitable thing: none inquire for it, though it be so very much sought for in this world. There is none on earth but desireth it. All the great ones and the wise seek it : indeed they find one and think it is the right, but they miss it. They ascribe power and virtue to it, and think they have it and will keep it, but it is not that : it needeth no virtue to be ascribed to it." According to *ibid.*, v. 41, 42, p. 109, the false Stone is " glistering, with a pleasant outside or sound." But it belongs to " the wall of the great building of this world, in which the seven seals accomplish their wonders, and under which the Seven Spirits of the anger of God pour forth their vials of wrath."

[2] Ps. cxviii, 22. See also I St. Peter, ii, 4, 6.

[3] Is. viii, 14.

[4] Acts, iv, 12.

[5] Böhme's Fourth Epistle, v, 111, p. 65.

[6] It is to be understood also in the sense of the Christ within, for Böhme says: " Among many thousand in this world, Thou art scarce rightly known of any one ; and yet Thou art carried in many that know Thee not," the invocation being addressed to *Lapis Philosophorum. Threefold Life of Man*, c. vi, v. 99, p. 101. It was found by Abel and Jacob ; Isaac attained it in his mother's womb ; it was loved by David, and Solomon had it in his heart. Moses and all the prophets worked their miracles by it ; and this Stone " discovereth itself in all those that seek it ". *Ibid.*, c. vii, v. 36–40, pp. 108, 109. " Christ hath put into us the Noble Stone, namely, the Water of Eternal Life." *Ibid.*, v. 50, p. 110. " It is hidden to us men, unless a man have attained the Stone upon the Cross, and then he findeth where reason saith there is nothing," Ibid., c.x. v. 9, p. 152. " In this Stone there lieth hidden whatsoever God and the eternity . . . contain . . . " *Ibid.*, c. xiii, v. 1, p. 207.

spiritual estate which is connoted by supernatural life are those only who are qualified to perform the work of physical transmutation ; [1] and I see no warrant for assuming that the Teutonic Theosophist is here testifying otherwise than at the literal and face value of his words. The thesis is that by Divine knowledge and understanding " all the metals of the earth may be brought to the highest degree of perfection, yet only by the Children of the Divine Magia who have the revelation—or experimental science—of the same ".[2]   It is said also that " the Holy Ghost is the Key to it " ; [3] and he that understands rightly the Centre of Nature " may well find it in metals ".[4]   So also in respect of the Tincture, neither doctor nor alchemist has the true ground thereof " unless he be born again in the spirit ".[5]   On this understanding, according to Böhme, " the work is easy and the Art is simple : a boy of ten years might make it," though " the wisdom is great therein " and it is " the greatest mystery ".   It is said further that " every one must seek it himself ".[6]

[1] It is to be observed that neither Jacob Böhme nor any one or other of his peers and coheirs suggested that Alchemy was not concerned in its past with metallic transmutation.   They set forth a Higher Alchemy, while admitting the possibility of that which was sought in crucibles.

[2] Böhme's *Third Epistle*, v. 33, p. 44.   Compare *Fourth Epistle*, v. iii, p. 65 : " Would you search out the *Mysterium Magnum*, then take before you only the earth with its metals, and so you may well find what the magical or kabalistical ground is."

[3] *Fourth Epistle*, v. 110, pp. 64, 65, addressed to a correspondent who has " undertaken a very hard labour "—namely Vaughan's " blind work on metals "—and yet it is wholly needless.   " He that findeth and knoweth the Great Mystery, he findeth all things therein.   There needs no literal demonstration : God, Christ, and the eternity—with all wonders—do lie therein."   Also v. iii : " Searching only doth nothing."

[4] *Threefold Life of Man*, c. ix, v. 8, p. 129.   It is added that it is not difficult : " if he learn but the right entrance, he hath the end at hand."   Compare, however, the *Twenty-third Epistle*, v. 16, p. 171 : " Therefore, Sir, do not trouble and toil yourself . . . with any gold or minerals : it is all false "—the nearest approach to a condemnation of past procedure which is found in Böhme anywhere.

[5] Ibid., v. 15, p. 171.

[6] *Twenty-third Epistle*, v. 18, p. 171.   It has been affirmed previously—v. 16— that it is far off and nigh at hand, that " the place is everywhere, where it may be had ; but every one is not fit and prepared for it.   Neither doth it cost any money, but what is spent upon the time and bodily maintenance : else it might be prepared with two florins and less ".   The same testimony in almost the same words is borne by Heinrich Khunrath in *Amphitheatrum Sapientiæ Æternæ*, 1609, a work with which Jacob Böhme may have been acquainted.   It is added in this connection —v. 17—as follows : " The world must be made heaven, and heaven the world. It is not of earth, stones, or metals, and yet it is of the ground of all metals."   It is " a spiritual being which is environed with the four elements, which also changeth the four elements into one, a doubled Mercury, yet not quicksilver, or any other mineral or metal ".   With reference to Khunrath it should be said that he was a practical alchemist and that his testimony is therefore reserved.

We have heard of " astrology theologised ", otherwise an art in ruling the stars by a law of grace, and this is within comprehension, on the hypothesis, since it is the government of influence according to one kind by another and higher influence; but the annals of sanctity and of the attainments reached therein may be searched through East and West before and after the Teutonic Theosopher, and in no other quarter shall we find it on record or claimed that the second birth of the mystic gives the power to elevate so-called base metals into the " perfect form " of gold. I conceive therefore that the notion originated at his time in Germany, in the main with him, and although it is put forward in dogmatic terms as part of his revelations, that it belonged to the region of reverie. In this connection he reaffirms indeed expressly : " I cannot yet make it myself," nor does he suggest that there is any authority behind him derived from those who could.[1] It may be thought that I am dwelling over seriously on an ultra-fantastic dream ; but in the first place it belongs to the exegesis of that subject into the validity of which we are inquiring, while in the second we shall meet with it again among modern expositors. At the moment it will be sufficient to add that in the midst of his own experiences and at his day in the world it was not possible for the mind which was Böhme to challenge, in the face of its literature, the claims on material transmutation. I have shewn elsewhere and recently [2] that Alchemy was followed in Germany at that period with perfervid zeal ; the testimonies to the fact of transmutation were everywhere—real or alleged ; he explained therefore to himself and from himself to others his view of the conditions on which the things that were affirmed to be actual lay within the possibility of attainment.

The second witness on Alchemy, understood spiritually, was contemporary in England with Jacob Böhme in the Teutonic Fatherland. This was Robert Fludd, to whom I have devoted a considerable chapter in my work already

---

[1] Jacob Böhme seldom appealed to authorities outside Holy Scripture. In all his alchemical expositions he mentions one tract only, and that is the *Water-Stone of the Wise*, of which he says : " Therein is much truth ; and it is, moreover, clear."

[2] *The Brotherhood of the Rosy Cross*, c. iii.

mentioned,[1] and may reasonably refer thereto, even while I extend therefrom. The Kentish Theosophist's disposition towards a mystical understanding of the Hermetic subject is found early in his literary life; he distinguishes in his second publication between those who possess the true Alchemy and the false operators who seek to make " metallic gold ", caring nothing for the treasures of heaven, " the spiritual splendour and light." [2]   A work which he translated into Latin, being the production of a friend who wrote it in his defence, which he also prepared for press and which represents on all points his own views and principles, devotes an entire section to the same contrast, namely, spurious chemistry, working vainly on tinctures and striving to turn White into Red, and the true gold, which is not that of the vulgar but living " gold of God ".[3] This is life communicated by Christ, the very Word of Jehovah. It works transmutations as by a spiritual chemistry, but they are performed on the subject Man, whom It sublimates by virtues and adorns with sacramental graces, so that he attains a perfection which is comparable in analogy to purest gold and becomes truly the House of God. So far in respect of the inward nature or part of soul in man. But Spiritual Alchemy can transmute also the body[4]—as it is said—into the Divine

---

[1] *Ibid.*, c. x.

[2] *Tractatus Theologo-Philosophicus, in Libros Tres distributos, quorum* I *De Vita*, II *De morte*, III *De Resurrectione*, etc. Oppenheim, 1617.

[3] *Summum Bonum, quod est verum Subjectum veræ Magiæ, Cabalæ, Alchymiæ verorum Fratrum Roseæ Crucis.* Frankfurt, 1629. A careful consideration of things cited in my text above will suggest to those who are acquainted with Christian mystical literature that albeit Robert Fludd and he who was his *alter ego* and apologist in *Summum Bonum* by no means belonged to the great tradition of Latin Catholicism, they had not only derived therefrom but may have also attained a certain inward realisation as to its term of quest. The first point seems to me beyond question, meaning that it is an irresistible inference, and it should be remembered in this connection that Fludd was neither Puritan nor Protestant of his period. The second is subject to a certain qualification, for it seems to me that he had realised by the normal processes of thought and intellectual dedication but not by the way of the mystics, in the still contemplation of the soul.

[4] Compare *Tractatus Theologo-Philosophicus* on the body of resurrection, which the Eternal Spirit shall make like unto that of Enoch and Elias. Such a renovation is for those who die in Christ and are raised also by Him. The inspiration comes obviously from St. Paul and is like an elaborate unfoldment of the thesis that " it is sown a natural body, it is raised a spiritual body "; but the " glorious resurrection " of the Christian Funerary Service is not regarded as reserved to a postulated General Judgment, approximate or remote. In writers like Thomas Vaughan, if not in Robert Fludd—but inferentially, I think, also in him—the transfiguration of Tabor was an exemplary manifested in advance of the " robe of glory ", the radiance of immortal vesture. So also was the face of Moses descending from Sinai,

Image, and we make contact here with what I have found to be a recurring *Theosophia Hermetica* concerning the body of adeptship. From this point of view the true gold is also a true elixir, a Cup of Wisdom, life and food from God, bread and water of life. It is that which sustained Elias in the desert, Moses on Mount Horeb and Christ in the forty days' fast.[1] With this kind of Alchemy Fludd held that Holy Scripture is concerned throughout. The Stone of Philosophy, Stone of Wisdom, the Corner Stone is the Word of God before the beginning of things, and this Stone or Word is Christ, by Whose Divine Alchemy the world was made.[2] By this same Alchemy and by this Divine Alchemist the true is separated from the false, pure from impure, light from darkness, good also from evil, or in the symbolism of spiritual chemistry authentic gold and silver are set apart from the things of this world. From another point of view, and so far as man is concerned, the Stone which tinges and transmutes is the Blood of Christ; those who have been redeemed therein become alchemists on their own part [3] and enter into very life immortal of the soul. This is the Stone, tried and precious, which was laid for a foundation in Zion, and in man himself it is comparable to a " fixed gold ".[4] It enables the soul to contemplate God clearly and

according to *Anthroposophia Theomagica*, and so was the state of Enoch in translation, according to *Cœlum Terræ*. But this " spiritual and heavenly body " was brought forth in the work of adeptship, according to the same text. See my *Works of Thomas Vaughan*, pp. xxxi, xxxii.

[1] It follows according to Fludd and his *alter ego* that there is attainable by man and unto him communicated a Divine Nutriment, of which material Bread is the symbol, and an Arch-Natural Elixir, represented Sacramentally by Wine. They are administered to those who seek and find the Tree of Life, the White Stone, the New Name, and that garment of " fine linen " which is " the righteousness of saints."

[2] Hence one of the charges preferred against Fludd by Petrus Gassendus in his *Epistolica Exercitatio*. Parisiis, 1630 : *Totam scripturam sacram referri ad alchymiam, et principia alchymistica. Sensum scripturæ mysticum non esse alium, quam explicatum per alchymiam et philosophicum lapidem. Non interesse ad illum habendum cujus religionis sis, Romanæ, Lutheranæ, aut alterius. Catholicum ille solum esse qui credit in Lapidem Catholicum, hoc est Philosophicum, cujus ope homines dæmonia ejiciant,* etc. The position of the Kentish theosophist is summarised with perfect accuracy in these lines, and when Fludd answered the French theologian his task was one of defence and further exposition.

[3] Compare the further charge of Gassendus : *Hominem justum esse alchymistam, qui Philosophico Lapide invento, illius usu immortalis fiat. Mori tamen dici, cum partes corruptibiles abjicit ; resurgere, cum fit incorruptibilis ; glorificari, cum proinde easdem dotes assequitur, quæ tribuuntur corporibus gloriosis . . . Moysen cum creationem mundi descripsit fuisse alchymistam, itemque Davidem, Salomonem, Jacob, Job et omnes alios.*

[4] It is that also which transforms man into the Divine Image, as it is said, by the power of the resurrection. Respecting the *verum aurum*, it is fire and life

conforms it to the likeness of the angels, for *Theosophia Fluddana* fell short of real mysticism and conceived the end of being in terms of the Blessed Vision, the Paradise of Thomist Theology and of Dante, not in the state of unity with God, though Fludd has been charged with pantheism by those who have failed in reading him to any serious purpose. But if he did not raise created human being over the threshold of Divine Identity, it was for him the Holy Place, and there was a Holy of Holies within it.[1]

" As for Man, there is such a supereminent and wonderful treasure hidden in him, that wise men have esteemed that the perfect wisdom of this world consisteth in the knowledge of a man's self, namely, to find out that secret mystery which doth lurk within him. For man is said to be the centre of every creature, and for that cause he is called *Microsmus*, or the little world, *centrum et miraculum mundi*, containing in himself the properties of all creatures, as well celestial as terrestrial. . . . Man is *Templum Dei, Corpus Christi, Habitaculum Spiritus Sancti*, as the Apostle hath taught us. Neither verily may it be imagined that God would make choice of an unworthy dwelling-place. . . . Seeing that Man is rightly reported by Hermes to be the son of the world, as the world is the Son of God—seeing that it is framed after the image of the archetype—for which cause he is termed the Little World, it will be requisite to understand that he is in like manner divided into a heaven and earth, as the great world was, and consequently containeth . . . his heavens, circles, poles and stars." [2]

In the light of his contemptuous references to the gold and silver of the common herd and to the vulgar fire of the false alchemists, it may be concluded that Fludd had no part in the dream of material transmutation by the power of spirit and proffered no such thesis as his contemporary Jacob Böhme. It must be said, however, that if we read between the lines it may be found that they were not far apart from

from Christ, in Whom all treasures of wisdom and science are hidden, according to Fludd's last work, entitled *Philosophia Moysaica*. The " Spiritual Christ " is the " true fountain of essential philosophy ".

[1] It should be added, however, that while affirming the creation of the soul, there is at least one place in which Fludd testifies that it is of the essence of Deity and is not divided from its source.—*Historia Microcosmi, Lib.* iii, *cap.* 9, Oppenheim, 1619.

[2] *Philosophia Moysaica*, Goudæ, 1638.

one another, though there are at best but vague intimations on the side of the English mystic, since desire of the spiritual gold had eaten him up. In the person of his anonymous defender, Joachim Fritz, he affirms that when the Divine Spirit covenants to teach all things there is no science excluded; and on his own authority [1] it is maintained (1) that Alchemy is part of natural philosophy, (2) that the work of the alchemist is analogous to that of the Divine Spirit, and (3) that the breath of the power of God is "the True Theophilosophical Stone, whereby all animal, vegetable and mineral things are blessed and multiplied." But he does not apparently suggest that those who, spiritually speaking, have become mystic alchemists and tingeing stones in and through Christ are for that reason empowered, actually and literally, to transmute material metals, or otherwise to produce physical gold by a super-physical act. We shall see when the time comes to what extent, if any, Paracelsus was the originator of this fantastic view and may be the source of Böhme's reveries, as well as of the undeveloped arrière pensée in the mind of Fludd and his apologist.

Two things remain to be said, as final considerations arising out of this chapter: (1) Had Jacob Böhme proceeded to what he calls the praxis, his deep consideration of powers and offices belonging to the regenerated would have brought him grievous disillusion when it was applied to the work on metals. If any one in the occult schools and their houses of supreme folly should challenge this statement, the matter must be left in his hands, not that he would be called upon to produce gold on his own part by arch-natural means, but as an irreducible minimum he should give evidence that it has

---

[1] It is quite certain and matters nothing to the present subject that Fludd would have accepted the historical claims and evidences in respect of metallic transmutation as they stand forth in the alchemical literature which preceded his own time. The evidences on the point of alleged fact would have satisfied him if they had been only half as strong as they are actually in appearance, for on such matters he was by temperament unduly credulous in an age which must be called credulous, within and without the circle of occult arts and philosophy. On the other hand, I do not think that he understood the jargon of alchemists or had much patience towards it, though he would not have challenged the duty of those who had performed the work to keep its secrets secretly. When he says that it belongs to natural philosophy he is recognizing its broad claim as a valid mental proposition, but he proceeds forthwith to that which for him is its only true and practical aspect, the Theosophical Stone—"Christ the power of God and the wisdom of God," by Whom the world was made and being made was blessed and set to grow and multiply in its own order and kingdom.

been performed, shewing when, by whom and where. We have seen radium transform into helium and matter changes daily in the hands of many chemists ; but it is a work of Nature in the one and of science in the other case : it takes place in laboratories, not in Sanctuaries of rebirth. We may yet arrive at a process for " building up heavy atoms of gold from lighter metals " ; but where shall search be followed in any lexicon of physicists or in sane psychology for terms to characterise the proposition that such upbuilding is reserved to those who have been " born again in the spirit " ? (2) In respect of Robert Fludd his Spiritual Alchemy is excellent and perfect, like the " new commandment " of a Prince Rose Croix, but unfortunately it leads nowhere. It signifies but little in the living sense if there is an Alchemy which tells us that the Stone is Christ, unless it can offer also a fuller light on the finding of this Stone within us than is taught in official houses of faith and doctrine. The Lost Word of Freemasonry is Christ in the High Degrees, and is said to be found therein ; but here is only an aid to reflection, and Masonry for this reason is a gift of remembrance and not a way of attainment. If such and such only is the story of Alchemy on its physical side, it profits nothing that it has been told. We might fare no worse in believing that there is something in the transmutation of metals on the faith of any single witness who seems to carry authentic seals.

CHAPTER II

MODERN VIEWS ON THE HERMETIC MYSTERY

WE have seen that Jacob Böhme, by his own account, had not gone on to the *praxis*. There is no evidence to shew that he had ever engaged personally in any experiments which would answer to the denomination of chemistry at that period, or even that he had witnessed any. On the other hand, there is every reason to suppose that he was fairly conversant with what was being said and done in a subject which was about him on every side, which was in all men's mouths, and on which almost every month brought forth some new venture in the form of tract or volume. In his own revelations he made use of the simple and more comprehensive alchemical terms, which were indeed of general acceptance. His extant correspondence tells us that he was at least occasionally appealed to by those on the quest in metals, and he is likely to have been visited by alchemists. In the booths and the market places, in his own stall or kitchen, the Great Work may have been debated often enough, he taking a part therein. His revelations, moreover, belong to the hectic epoch of Rosicrucian claims and clamour: they are never mentioned in his writings, but he could not fail to know concerning them, and it is even possible that some of the pamphlets put forth on behalf of the Brotherhood may have given him a first intimation that there was another ground of Alchemy than that which Thomas Vaughan called in his later day " the blind torturing of metals ". But whether he derived impressions in this manner and they were unfolded subsequently by the quick spirit within him, or whether they came independently, the point is that he had neither been taught a lesson by failure in laboratory gropings nor had he attempted to produce gold by the arch-natural process in the authenticity of which he believed, so that he was spared—as we have also seen—another and for him more serious failure. It follows that his contribution to the alchemical subject was one of wild speculation, reflected possibly—as I have intimated—among other sources from the obscure reveries of Paracelsus, on a kind of psycho-transmutation, which was simpler and much more efficient than anything accomplished in laboratories. With these I shall deal in their place, being concerned in this initial chapter with those only who have fashioned the spiritual hypothesis at their desks and familiarised it in the modern occult circles. It happens that, from first to last, they were not practitioners in chemistry.

Robert Fludd, of course, must have tried experiments in his day, for the paths of his quest were many, as his folios shew; [1] but the fact remains that he came out of the laboratory to write on *Alchemia*, as upon a Divine Art and Science, upon the Theosophical Stone of Scripture and the Mystic Body of adeptships in light derived from St. Paul. It cannot be said that he contributed anything substantial to the modern theme and view, for his works were in Latin, and they have never been easy of access in this country, because they were printed abroad and found a public there. He is at best a connecting link between Jacob Böhme, who had a considerable following in England, and the next stage of the subject, more than two hundred years after the Kentish Theosophist was laid in his grave at Bearstead. In the year 1850 there was published anonymously *A Suggestive Inquiry into the Hermetic Mystery*, written by Mary Anne South, afterwards Mrs. Atwood, at the age of thirty-three years : it was printed in large octavo and extended to nearly five hundred pages. [2] Written with extraordinary

[1] The most elaborate and ambitious of his works is *Utriusque Cosmi Majoris scilicet et Minoris Metaphysica, Physica atque Technica Historia*. It embodies distinct treatises on arithmetic, geometry, music, perspective, cosmography, astrology, and even the art of war, not to speak of music—including that of the spheres—geomantic and pythagorical numerology, and so forth. He wrote also on optics, physiognomy and the art of memory. It is more especially in *Summum Bonum, sub nomine* Joachim Fritz, that a specific and considerable section is devoted to Alchemy, but it is of the class that has been described in my text, a spiritual and mystical chemistry, contrasted with another which is spurious and goes in quest of vain tinctures. *Clavis Philosophiæ et Alchymiæ* includes a new exposition and defence of Divine Alchemy, as an answer in fine to his continental critics.

[2] *A Suggestive Inquiry into the Hermetic Mystery, with a Dissertation on the more celebrated Alchemical Philosophers, being an attempt towards the Recovery of the Ancient Experiment of Nature.* London : Trelawney Saunders, 1850. A posthumous second edition appeared at Belfast in 1918, based on two corrected copies—one being in the hand of the authoress—and a third, at the same place, in 1920. Always excessively rare in its original issue, the fashion which I have mentioned caused a demand to grow up during the intervening sixty-eight years.

elaboration and in terms as strange as its subject, there is no doubt that it set the fashion of occult thought for something like fifty years on the higher understanding of Alchemy. There is no doubt also that as the work of a young woman it was and will remain a notable and almost monumental performance. The fact of its authorship did not emerge clearly for many years after its appearance, but it happened that during the interim adventitious circumstances added an artificial mystery to that which inhered in the subject and—it may be said—in the peculiarity of its treatment.

The *Suggestive Inquiry* opens with a summary sketch of alchemical literature and its writers, nearly in chronological order and designed apparently to shew that there was not only a long line of claimants to success in metallic transmutation but a recurring testimony to the fact that metals were transmuted literally in the past. It begins in the twilight of myths, accepts all attributions of authorship, however questioned and questionable, and concludes its examination —not perhaps unwisely—with Eirenæus Philalethes. A Theory of Transmutation is presented in the next place, with special reference to the First Matter of Alchemy, concerning which it is affirmed, as an inference from many citations, (1) that it is " the homogeneity of the radical substance of things ", otherwise " the radical moisture of which they are uniformly composed " [1]; (2) that this is " a fluid or vitalising principle invisibly permeating all things ", a " distinct substance universally diffused "; (3) that it is " the simple generated substance of life and light, immanifestly flowing throughout Nature " ; [2] (4) that it is " a pure ethereality " [3] which can be separated by artificial means ; (5) that it reaches perfection " earliest and easiest " in the mineral kingdom and there produces gold ; (6) that in vegetable life it gives the Elixir of the Wise, " through superior skill and coction " [4]; and (7) that as regards the

---

[1] See part i, c. 2, original edition, pp. 68, 69, and reprint of 1920, pp. 72, 73. The whole Hermetic doctrine is said to hinge hereon.

[2] *Ibid.*, p. 74 and pp. 78, 79. Homberg, Boerhaave, and Boyle are cited in this connexion. Also pp. 85 and 90.

[3] *Ibid.*, p. 91 and p. 96. This definition is said to be founded on the concurrent sense of many alchemical philosophers. But the " pure ethereality " of Nature is an expression which belongs to Mrs. Atwood. and to her only ; it is not used by alchemists and no definite meaning can be attached to it.

[4] *Ibid.*, p. 91 and p. 97.

kingdom of animals it assumes in men " an Image that is Divine and more potent than all the rest ".[1]

This constitutes Mrs. Atwood's " exoteric view " of the subject, for we can pass over the fact that she adds thereto a translation of *Tractatus Aureus* under the name of Hermes Trismegistus, premising (1) that it has been " considered to be one of the most ancient and complete pieces of alchemical writing extant ", and (2) that " it wears the impress of very great antiquity." [2] The question of metallic transmutation is now suspended completely and in the bulk of the work which follows, after one initial statement, we have to glean as we can best her reasons for presenting it as a fact of science reposing on veridic testimony. And the attempt proves a failure.

The sole connection, according to Part II of the *Suggestive Inquiry,* which subsists between Alchemy and the modern science of chemistry is one of terms only.[3] Alchemy is not an art in metals, but it is the Art of Life; the chemical phraseology is a veil only. It was adopted, however, not with any arbitrary desire to conceal for the sake of concealment, or even to insure safety during ages of intolerance, but because the alchemical experiment is attended with real danger to man in his normal state. That which the adepts strove most strenuously to protect in their writings was the nature of the Hermetic vessel.[4] It was affirmed to be a Divine Secret, and yet no one can study the texts intelligently without being convinced that this Vessel is Man himself. The *Centrum Naturæ Concentratum,* for example, to quote only one among many texts, declares that the universal orb of the earth contains not so great mysteries and excellencies as Man re-formed by God into His image, and he that desires

---

[1] *Ibid.,* The " image " is said to remain an embryo " in this life ", but this is presumably under normal circumstances and for the rank and file of man. It is added immediately that " when unfolded through a new birth in universal intelligence " the Divine Image " transcends the limits of this nether sphere and passes into communion with the highest life ". The inspiration is Jacob Böhme.

[2] This is Mrs. Atwood's judgment, but it " wears " nothing of the kind ; there is no Greek original and even as a Latin forgery it must be called late. I shall mention it again at the end of my fourth chapter.

[3] See Mrs. Atwood's original edition, p. 135, and that of 1920, p. 143.

[4] *Mariæ Prophetissæ Practica* and other texts are quoted in this connection and will be considered on this subject in their several places. Meanwhile it must be said that there is nothing less concealed than the Vessel of Art in the general succession of texts on which Mrs. Atwood depends for her thesis that the alchemical subject is Man.

primacy among the students of Nature will nowhere find a greater or better subject wherein to obtain his desire than in himself.[1] For he is able to draw unto himself what alchemists call the Central Salt of Nature ; he possesses all things in his regenerated wisdom and can unlock the most hidden Mysteries. Man is for all adepts the one subject that contains all, and he only need be investigated for the discovery of all. Man is the true laboratory of Hermetic Art, his life is the subject, the grand distillery, the thing distilling and the thing distilled, and self-knowledge is at the root of all alchemical tradition. To discover then the secret of Alchemy the student must look within and investigate true psychical experience, having regard especially to the germ of a higher faculty which is not commonly exercised but of which he is possessed, and whereby the forms of things and the hidden springs of Nature become known intuitively. Concerning this faculty the alchemists speak magisterially, as if it had enlightened their understandings, so that they had entered into alliance with Omniscient Nature, and as if their individual consciousness had become one with Universal Consciousness. The first Key of the Hermetic Mystery is in Mesmerism, not working, however, in the therapeutic sphere but rather with a theurgic object, comparable to that after which the ancients aspired and the attainment of which is affirmed to have been conse- quent on initiation into the Greater Mysteries of ancient Greece. Between the process of these Mysteries and the process of Alchemy there is said to be a traceable corres- pondence, and it is submitted that the end was identical in both cases. The danger which demanded secrecy was the same also, being that of the Dweller on the Threshold, according to the goblin terminology which modern occultism has borrowed from *Zanoni*, otherwise, the distortions and deceptions of the astral world, which lead into irrational confusion.

Into this world the mesmeric trance commonly transfers its patients, while the endeavour of Hermetic Art was not only to liberate the subject from his material bonds but to guarantee the truth of his experiences in a higher order of

---

[1] There is something to be said of this tract which appeared under the name of Alipuli, for the first time, in a German edition of 1682, with a claim on an Arabic origin.

subsistence. It sought to supply a purely rational motive, which enabled the subject to withstand temptations of the astral sphere and follow the path upward to the discovery of wisdom and highest consciousness. There the soul knows herself as a whole, whereas now she is acquainted only with a part of her humanity : there also—by theurgic help—she attains her desired end and participates in Deity. The alchemical process is thus a secret method of self-knowledge which the soul follows far through its realm of being.[1] In contemplation of the Highest Unity, in desired conjunction with the Divine Nature and consummation in the Absolute, there is reached the final stage, wherein the soul attains " divine intuition of that High Exemplar Which is before all things and the final cause of all, Which seeing is seen and understanding is understood by him who, penetrating all centres, discovers himself in That finally Which is the Source of all, and passing from himself to That attains the end of his progression. This was the consummation of the Mysteries, the ground of Hermetic Philosophy, prolific in super-material increase, transmutations and magical effects."

In further development of these general heads of the subject it is advanced (1) that the true methods and conditions of self-knowledge are to be learned from the ancient writers —not otherwise particularised at the moment, and not apparently a reference to the body of alchemical literature ;[2] (2) that a discovery of the veritable Light of Alchemy is the reward of an adequate scrutiny of authentic psychical experience ;[3] (3) that Alchemy proposes " such a reduction of Nature as shall discover this later without destroying her vehicle but only the modal life ", and professes that this has not alone proved possible but that man by " rationally conditionating " has succeeded in developing into action

---

[1] It will be understood that the materials of this summary account are derived as a conspectus at large from all parts of the text, while in justice to the author it should be said (1) that they are expressed practically in her own terms, and (2) that they embody the main points which she has set out to prove and believes that she has so done. They remain, however, the questions left at issue, because in the method of her citations and amidst the wilderness of her words there is nowhere any ordered evidence, especially on the identity of alchemical and neoplatonic objects.

[2] *Loc. cit.*, pp. 170 and 180 in the respective editions. Compare pp. 153 and 162.

[3] *Ibid.*, pp. 166 and 176. The affirmation is that here is " no common trance or day-dream " and " no fanatical vision of celestials ".

the " Recreative Force " ; [1] (4) that the one thing needful, the sole act which must be accomplished perfectly for man to know himself, is exaltation, by an adequately purified spirit, of the cognising faculty [2] into intellectual reminiscence ; (5) that the transcendental philosophy of the Mysteries hinges entirely on the purification of the whole understanding, without which they promise nothing ; [3] (6) that the end in view is identical with Hermetists, Theurgists and with the Greek Mysteries alike ; [4] (7) that it is the conscious and hypostatic union of the soul with Deity and its participation in the life of God ; [5] but (8) that the Divine Name is to be understood here in an " infinitely transcendental " sense, for in Hermetic operations above all it must be remembered that God is within.

The purpose of this summary has been reached, but I will add one further citation because it seems to embrace every department of this assuredly " suggestive " Inquiry. The affirmation is that an " initiated person sees the Divine Light itself, without any form or figure—that Light which is the true *Astrum Solis*, the Mineral Spiritual Sun, which is the Perpetual Motion of the Wise and a certain Saturnian Salt which, developed to intellect and made erect, subdues all Nature to his will. It is the Midnight Sun of Apuleius, the Ignited Stone of Anaxagoras, the Triumphal Chariot of Antimony, the Armed Magnet of Helvetius, the Fiery Chariot of Mercaba, and the Stone with the new name written on it which is promised to him that overcometh by the initiating Saviour of mankind."[6]

---

[1] *Ibid.*

[2] See respective pages 170 and 180. Reminiscence is said to be " as of some long past life forgotten ", a recurrence to familiar scenes ; and this path of remembrance is compared to a journey towards one's native land.

[3] See respective pp. 188 and 199.

[4] *Ib.*, p. 248 and 263.

[5] O.e., p. 214 ; n.e., pp. 225, 226 ; also p. 224 and p. 237 : 241 and 255 ; 245 and 259, 260. Compare also o.e., pp. 511, 512, and n.e., pp. 539, 540, as follows : " Once delivered from the exterior bondages of sense and heterogeneous desire, from the passions and false affections of this transitory life, the final step is declared comparatively easy ; as transcending by the energy of faith, from the separable selfhood, the Identity passes into universal accord. . . . This is the work—this the Hermetic method and its end . . . , the true Christian Philosopher's Stone . . . , confirmed in operation, visibility and luminous increase, when rising in rational supremacy over sense and finite reflection, the Ethereal Hypostasis revolves in its First Cause."

[6] *Loc. cit.*, pp. 218, original edition, and p. 230 of reprint. It must be said that enumerations like this exhibit only the confused mind of the writer and its inextricable medley of images. A particular case in point is the institution of an

It is not to be supposed that this or any other presentation of Mrs. Atwood's thesis will convey a really intelligible impression to those who are unacquainted with her work. Notwithstanding a general division under certain heads,[1] which would connote a logical method in different hands, there is, at least within my knowledge, no book claiming to offer an interpretation of any subject which is so involved in its treatment, so utterly confused and confusing on all its issues. The affirmed purpose of Ancient Mysteries practised at Eleusis from time immemorial, of so-called Chaldaic Rites and late Mysteries of Isis, the intimations of Plato and the line of Platonic Successors, of Zoroastrian Oracles, of Jewish *Midrashim*—derived through uncertain channels—of late and early alchemists are combined in a chaos inextricable, so that a reader is now in " the foremost files " of Hermetic time, with Sendivogius, Thomas Vaughan or the later Philalethes; now dwelling on treatises falsely attributed to St. Thomas Aquinas, Albertus Magnus, and Synesius; now following obscure tracks with pseudo - Democritus and Psellus; now glancing from the *Sepher Yetzirah* to Book VI of the *Æneid*, or from Francis Bacon to the *Water-Stone of the Wise*. The confusion is worse confounded by what I have called Mrs. Atwood's fatal quarrel with quotation

---

analogy between the Zoharic Chariot of Mercaba—a *theosophia* developed from the Wheels and Living Creatures of Ezekiel's Vision—and the fantasy of Basil Valentine's title for a work on Antimony, that substance which he prescribed recurrently for its virtues in the scourge of *Lues Gallica*. Moreover, as he tells us : " if a man wishes to fatten a pig, let him give to the pig, two or three days before. he begins to fatten it, half a drachm of crude antimony. . . . The pig will then eat more freely, fatten more quickly and be freed from any bilious or leprous disease." The Kabalistic Mercaba—which does not symbolise a purgative—has, if possible, less connection with the Triumphal Chariot of Antimony than with a four-in-hand of the coaching days. As regards *Astrum Solis*, *astrum* is the *virtus et potentia rerum ex præparationibus acquisita*, and *Astrum Solis* is therefore *Virtus Solis*, acquired by the way of eduction ; we can judge in this manner the validity of its comparison with the Stone of the *Apocalypse*.

[1] The main sub-divisions are (1) an exoteric view of the progress and theory of Alchemy; (2) a more exoteric consideration of the Hermetic Art and its Mysteries; (3) concerning the laws and vital conditions of the Hermetic Experiment ; and (4) the Hermetic Practice. The first part includes—as we have seen—a translation of *Aureus Tractatus*, with references to the *Scholium* thereon which follows the text in Mangetus ; the second part is mainly devoted to a long excursus on Eleusis and later Mysteries ; the third part is by intention preparatory to the fourth ; and this is concerned *ex hypothesi* with things which lie behind the alleged symbolism of a gross and subtle work in the alchemical practice : it includes the *Six Keys of Eudoxus*, which claim to open the " most secret philosophy " of the Stone, its projection and multiplication. The reference is really to an *Epistle* which follows the *Ancient War of the Knights*, otherwise *Hermetical Triumph*.

commas, the consequence of which is recurring uncertainty as to where a given extract reaches its term and where her comments or another extract begin.[1] Of her stilted and undigested style, at once so vague and voluble, so full of what in olden days would have been called curious conceits, I forbear to speak.[2]

That which emerges in fine as the root-matter of her interpretation is a peculiar understanding of the experience presented to Candidates by the Greek Mysteries, especially those of Eleusis, and of spiritual states described and *ex hypothesi* attained by Plato, Plotinus, Proclus and so onward. With these are contrasted the teaching conveyed in ultra-cryptic language by alchemical literature, to establish an identity of subject in the three cases. If the author is in error about Greek Mysteries, if Plato and the successors did not pursue their search for the Good and True, the discovery and attainment of the " Causal Nature " after the method which she seeks to establish,[3] her scheme in

---

[1] The two reissues offer no improvement unfortunately in this respect, but it might demand a wide acquaintance with alchemical literature to produce a text of the *Inquiry* which would be " revised " in the sense of scholarship.

[2] There is another " curious conceit " which may as well be noted at this point as anywhere else in the criticism. As her long consideration is drawn to its term Mrs. Atwood takes courage to tell her readers what she should have certainly stated at the outset : she avows her " wilful reservation of an important link in the application of these principles to practice," her alleged reason being " lest any attempting to realise without a full investigation of the method, should fail utterly in the pursuit." It follows in the nonsense-writing that to omit an " important link " will make for success in attempting to recover " the ancient experiment of Nature". Moreover, the " principles " referred to are left for us to determine, as they are not specified in the context. It is difficult to believe that a lady with such gifts in the art of thought and its expression has anything hidden in her mind which is of the least real consequence. The bibliography of the *Six Keys* is another question which we are left to follow out if we can. There is no trace whatever of any alchemist under the name of Eudoxus at any period of the Art or of any tract so attributed, and I have expended a considerable time in looking round the literature before it was found that the Keys of Eudoxus are appended, as seen, to a tract entitled the *Ancient War of the Knights*.

[3] The experience is connected with what is called " a vital experiment", the same being followed according to the rule of " certain arts " and using certain " media ", the result of which is described as " producing the central efficient into conscious being and effect ". We shall come immediately in my text to the writer's notion concerning her vital experiment, the arts involved and the media, but I cite this passage to indicate the hopeless chaos of her wording and her persistent use of terms—e.g., " central efficient "—apart from all definition. There are real difficulties in Hegelian dialectic and they demand special study, but they are not wilful perversities, and they are not obscurities which arise from confusion of thought or the want of will to define. Mrs. Atwood, on the other hand, dwells in a cloud of mental images, where she loses herself and us, because in the metaphysical region she does not think clearly. References : *Inquiry*, o.e., p. 169, n.e., p. 179.

this case collapses. On the other hand, if she is borne out herein by evidence, it will still remain to be seen whether she has valid warrants for supposing that the quest followed and the term attained by expositors of Greek Mysticism were also those of Alchemy and its records of a thousand years.

In respect of the Mysteries it must be pointed out that Mrs. Atwood's hypothesis is her own and no other's; she did not borrow or develop it from anything to be found on the surface of Greek records, nor is there any seed or hint of it in works of scholarship—accepted as such at their period—antecedent to the *Suggestive Inquiry*.[1] In any case she cites none, and I am acquainted with none. We can suppose, if one cares to do so, that some French writer on the subject to which it belongs may have ventured on a bare allusion, some casual and highly speculative suggestion, put forward at a mere venture. But the question does not signify: whether born of an obscure hint found in her reading or an idea conceived in her mind, the development, if not the creation, was her own; and this is all that matters. The subject in question, and Mrs. Atwood's Key of the Mysteries, Key of Practice in Greek Mysticism and Key also of Alchemy was Animal Magnetism; but not that of Mesmer himself, of Puységur, Deleuze, Dupotet and so forth, the phenomena and experiences of which moved in a narrower groove and never exceeded their bounds. It is affirmed that the ancients in their investigations worked on the same " material "—meaning a human subject—with similar " instruments "—meaning the hands of an operator—but their practice was conducted upon " established principles " which were truly philosophic in their kind. These principles, according to Mrs. Atwood, are intimated under veils by the Greeks in their allusions to Theurgic Art.[2] In this manner " we are

---

[1] Mrs. Atwood sets out on her own part to offer a light at its value but after her peculiar method omits to make it available. She observes that " a few writers on Animal Magnetism " have " within these few years become enlightened by that singular discovery ", and " suggest their trance and its phenomena as a revelation of the temple mysteries and various religious rites ". She was in a position presumably to supply the essential references, but none are given, and it happens that by the year 1850 the literature of mesmerism was exceedingly large. The alleged suggestion would be, however, a leap into the dark of speculation apart from all warrant, because it happens that no writer on the subject was entitled to speak of what was done at Eleusis, at other Sanctuaries of initiation, or of classical religious rites anywhere.

[2] θεουργία was miracle, so-called Divine Art, but it was a denomination more especially of Magic on its practical side, evocation and sorcery.

led ", she affirms, " to infer that the Hermetic Purifications and Mysteries celebrated . . . by the priests at Eleusis were real and efficacious for the highest ends that philosophy can propose to itself, namely, the purification and perfection of human life ; and that inasmuch as the object was different and immeasurably superior to those (*sic*) proposed by modern Mesmerism . . ., so also were the means employed . . . and the administration in proportion purer, holier and entirely scientific." [1]

It is affirmed further (1) that modern Mesmerism gives proof of " the intrinsical intelligence and power of the Free Spirit, which can . . . reveal hidden things . . ., can philosophise also more or less well according to the direction, natural purity and relaxation of the sensual bond " ; [2] (2) that " there are many ways known and practised of entrancing the senses ", " dissolving the sensible medium " and converting it to " the experience of another life " ; [3] but (3) that the Keepers of the Mysteries were able to translate the consciousness of their subjects " towards the Central Source " [4] so that it could pursue " an inquiry of Intellect after its Paternal Source " ; [5] and finally (4) that so led, so assisted and so exalted, " the souls of the Initiated, being made perfect in every telestic accomplishment and virtue, and having passed orderly through the whole progression of Intelligible Causes . . ., were next promoted to a contemplation of their Highest Unity." [6]

Now, Mrs. Atwood's equipment—outside Latin classics and translations of Greek texts—consisted of expositors like Warburton, Sainte-Croix,[7] Court de Gebelin [8] and Thomas

---

[1] *Inquiry*, o.e., p. 188, n.e., p. 199.

[2] *Ib.*, p. 191 and p. 202.

[3] *Ib.*, p. 192 and p. 203.

[4] "To translate the consciousness . . . by obscuration " is the impossible terminology under which the supposed experiment is described, p. 193, ed. of 1850 and p. 204 of the 1920 reprint.

[5] *Ib.*, p. 197 and p. 208.

[6] *Ib.*, p. 241 and p. 255. The authority seems to be an Orphic Fragment quoted by Warburton, about which I will say only that it is a counsel of simple contemplation directed to the one God. See the *Divine Legation*, Mrs. Atwood's reference being to vol. i of an edition which she does not name. I will cite therefore the reprint of 1837, in 2 vols., vol. i, p. 232, for the Fragment in question.

[7] *Mémoires pour servir à l'Histoire de la Religion Secrète des Anciens Peuples*, 1784.

[8] Court de Gebelin : *Le Monde Primitif*.

Taylor,[1] excluding apparently the *Aglaophamus* of the
German scholar Lobeck, published in 1829.[2] All these works,
and the last perhaps most especially, represented real
research and scholarship at their periods, and they are now
exploded. They offered nothing in support of Mrs. Atwood's
hypothesis, and most certainly militated against it ; but the
question is not very material. In the light of modern knowledge
her speculation is impossible. The suggestion is that the priests
and hierophants of the Lesser and Greater Mysteries, as practised
at Eleusis, entranced Candidates by a super-mesmeric art,
and during their entranced condition promoted such inward
spiritual experiences that the soul of man was united with
the Spirit of God. As the results of cumulative research, it
is now certain : (1) that there was no personal, private
initiation into either class ; [3] (2) that to the Lesser Mysteries
the Candidates came in crowds and a law had to be enacted
as to the number of horses harnessed to the chariots of the
wealthy, when they drove on the way to Eleusis ; [4] (3) that
the Purificatory Rites, to which Mrs. Atwood attaches
such importance as a vital preparation for her supposed
deep experiences in trance, were purely material, being
sprinkling with salt water and pigs' blood, apart from
emblematic significance, though centuries after their institution Greek mystical philosophers represented them as
symbolising the purity of the soul ; (4) that what the Mystæ
beheld in the Hall or Temple of Initiation was a religious
drama belonging to the Eleusinian Myth ; (5) that they may
have joined in the search for Kore, " moving in rhythmic
measures, with torches waving " ; [5] (6) that the Greater
Mysteries represented the marriage of Zeus and Demeter
in the persons of the Hierophant and Priestess of the Rite ;

---

[1] She has used Taylor's translations of Iamblichus, Proclus, Porphyry,
Pausanias, etc.

[2] *Aglaophamus*, 1829.

[3] See Paul Foucart : *Recherches sur l'Origine et la Nature des Mystères d'Eleusis*
in *Mémoires de l'Académie des Inscriptions et Belles Lettres*, vol. xxxv, 1895, and
idem, 1896 ; *Les Mystères d'Eleusis*, 1912. Lewis Richard Farnell, D.Litt., *The
Cults of the Greek States*, vol. iii, 1907. See in particular, pp. 173–187.

[4] I have said elsewhere that initiation and advancement took place apparently
in droves, " the philosophers, poor students, and common people arriving on
foot, but the wealthy being driven in chariots." See *Encyclopædia of Freemasonry*,
vol. i, p. 246, *s.v. Eleusinian Mysteries*, pp. 233–252, containing a brief consideration of the subject, and also dealing with and discussing the speculations of the
Suggestive Inquiry.

[5] Farnell, v, p. 181.

(7) that it included a suggestion, simulation or fulfilment of the nuptial act, the tenor of the evidence being on the whole against the last view; [1] (8) that the recompense of initiation was felicity in the next life, but independently of conduct in this; [2] (9) that the profane or non-initiated had only suffering in prospect after death, also independently of conduct; [2] (10) that the qualifications of Candidates were not of a moral kind, at least originally; (11) that barbarians and homicides were excluded, as also persons of notorious guilt; (12) that in later ages there is a suggestion of something like " moral scrutiny ".[3]

In the year 1850 it was by no means possible, having in mind the researches of Lobeck,[4] to present Eleusis, as illustrating in any manner whatsoever the progression and culmination of inward experience according to Neo-platonic philosophy; it was never possible at any stage of scholarship to suggest and much less to affirm that Candidates were put into deep trance, the soul liberated from the body and led by Great Masters of Spiritual Life through the successive states and epochs of return to God. Not only were all available records against the proposition then as they are thrice over against it now; not only was it beneath serious criticism to suggest then, as it is deeper beneath it now, that the doctrine of the Mysteries in the sixth century B.C. was that of late Platonism belonging to the Christian era; but the whole period of the Mysteries, as even

---

[1] *Ibid.*, p. 176, quoting Asterius, a writer of the fourth century A.D., in his *Encomium Martyrum*, p. 194 of Combe's edition. Asterius speaks—" with unpleasant inuendo " it is said—of " the underground chamber and the meeting of the hierophant and the priestess, each with the other alone, when the torches are extinguished and the vast crowd "—so much for individual initiation when entranced in a pastos—" believes that its salvation depends on what goes on there."

[2] Foucart: *Les Mystères d'Eleusis*, pp. 82, 84, 85, 86.

[3] " By the time of Aristophanes the Mysteries had come to make for righteousness in some degree : probably not so much through direct precept or exhortation, but rather through their psychologic results." Farnell, v, p. 192.

[4] " The Eleusinian Mysteries were the paramount fact of the Attic state-religion, and their administration the most complex function of the Attic state-church. . . . To express any kind of opinion, with any contentment of conscience, on the Eleusinian problem is only possible after a long study of multifarious and dubious evidence ; and the result may seem very meagre and disappointing, unless one realises that there is often scientific advance in admitting and revealing ignorance . . . , in distinguishing between proved truth and hypotheses of varying degrees of probability. In regard to the whole inquiry we are at least in a better position than the scholars were in the generations before Lobeck's *Aglaophamus*; when to touch on the Mysteries at all was to plunge at once into a bottomless quagmire of fantastic speculation."—Farnell, v, p. 127.

Mrs. Atwood must have known, lay within measure of hours, while mystical experience is the work of life ; and therefore on the hypothesis that it is possible to liberate the soul in trance and pass it through successive seeming mystic states—for which there is no evidence—they could produce only shadows and substitutes, phantasmagoria of the great reality. But on other considerations than these we know now that in respect of the Mysteries at least the *Suggestive Inquiry* erected a house of cards and that house has fallen. We know now that the kind of communion which initiates attained at Eleusis was attributed, formal and *ex officio*,[1] that it came from participating as spectators and perhaps as supers in the ceremonial pageant, and that the bond so established was with Demeter and Kore in the Lesser Mysteries but presumably with Zeus and Demeter from what we can glean of the Greater. We know further that the completion of the Mysteries in both cases was not the suspension of distinction between subject and object by the identification of the soul and God, but an exhibition of mystic symbols— e.g., the ear of corn.[2]

It remains to say that Mrs. Atwood, who is out of court, and that utterly, regarding the purport, path and term of the Mysteries, is not less in a dream-state about the inward experiences to which the later Platonists bear their testimony. As there was no hetero-suggestion impressed at Eleusis on entranced subjects, so there was none at Alexandria. The late Greek theosophists did not practise mesmerism or super-mesmerism one upon another. The inward states of Plotinus and others of the school were attained in contemplation of the kind followed by Ruysbroeck, St. John of the Cross and the rest of the Christian mystics. There was no school of

---

[1] According to Farnell, the sacramental meals of which there is evidence in Greece, and which " implied some idea of communion with the divinity " are not characteristic of Eleusis. " We have no right to speak of a sacramental common meal . . . , to which, as around a communion-table, the worshippers gathered." And again : " There is no text or context which proves that the initiated at Eleusis was regarded as of one flesh with the deity." Once more : " Still less . . . is there any sign that the initiated believed they were partaking through food of the divine substance of their divinity."—*Loc. cit.*, pp. 195, 196.

[2] According to Hippolytus, the *epoptæ* were shewn " that great and marvellous mystery of perfect revelation, in solemn silence, a cut corn-stalk." It will be understood that this is said in scorn ; but Farnell and others regard it as "credible and even probable that a corn-token was among the precious things revealed ". *Loc. cit.*, p. 183.

philosophical initiates, who practised a science of entrancement handed down through the ages.[1] These things are
neither the gate nor way of the inward life, and their proper
exponent, had he happened to come across them, would have
been the magus Éliphas Lévi, who is our next witness
on the subject of Transcendental Alchemy. We have finished
with the *Suggestive Inquiry* for the time being, leaving
open till the end of our research—that is to say, until it
disproves itself—the main question of her thesis, whether
alchemical literature is or is not a record under veils of
spiritual experience, which carried on the inward work of
Plotinus, Porphyry, Proclus and others of the Greek line.
It may be said only in the sense of a general foreword that the
same indiscriminate treatment, the same dogmatic assumptions, apart from all evidence, obtain here, and that therefore
the method of alchemical interpretation set forth in the
Suggestive Inquiry recalls the shewing of a great vision, a
pageant of sounding words and mental pictures unlikely to
bear analysis. With no canon of distinction, it exalts all
claimants on the Philosopher's Stone into hierophants of the
Mystery of God. They had seen Diana unveiled ; they had
loosed the girdle of Isis ; they had crossed the threshold of
eternity. They did not—as their lives and works tell us—
grope after physical secrets ; they did not investigate the
properties of matter in putrefaction ; they did not work
with common quicksilver and sulphur ; they did not
distil urine ; they did not decoct egg-shells. They were soul-
seekers, and they had found the soul ; they were artificers,
and they adorned the soul ; they were true adepts, and they
transmuted it. But—for the rank and file at least—we may
find that they worked in metals ; that they ransacked
every kingdom of Nature for substances which—by a bare
possibility and following some happy guess—might transmute
the hypothetical base metals into gold. Self-educated
seekers at the dawn of physical science, they tried all things
that came their way and bought experience hardly, without
a hand to guide. Among martyrs of science, they may

---

[1] It may be noted that *Nature's Divine Revelations*, delivered in " the magnetic
state " by Andrew Jackson Davis, called " the Poughkeepsie Seer ", had appeared
concurrently in America and London in 1847, forming two considerable volumes,
and may have directed Mrs. Atwood's attention to alleged trance experiences.

deserve to bear their palms. Unenlightened and unequipped, they laid the foundations of a providential and life-saving knowledge. But we may find also that their furnaces were erected occasionally " on a peak in Darien ", and that through the smoke of their coals and their chemicals they beheld illimitable vistas, where the groaning totality of Nature advanced by degrees to perfection. "A depth beyond the depth and a height beyond the height " opened beneath and above them, and glimpses of glorious possibilities in all the kingdoms overlighted their barbarous language and transfigured their strange symbols. The explanation is not that they were spiritual masters, as Eckehart or greater than he ; not that they dwelt in a vision, as in a *Paradiso* of Dante, at the heart of the Mystical Rose ; though most of them were men of religion and hallowed in mind by faith. But in those days a world of wonder opened wherever any quest began, because it was ever pursued in a great unknown, the unmeasured cosmos of Nature, where never a plummet could sound the vast abysses and never a shaft of thought penetrate the starry height. The occasional greatness of alchemical literature is accounted for in this manner, while at the same time its intimations of spiritual realities are reduced within their proper limits. The work which they watched in alembics was for them like God's work in creation, when there was " darkness upon the face of the deep ", when the light was divided from the darkness, when waters were divided from waters and the dry land appeared. For them also, or many who ranked among them, it was like the work of redemption and the work of God in the soul ; but Alchemy was not for this reason a commentary on creation myths or an account of the Lord's dealings with " the holy spirit of man ". From the age of Byzantine records to the end of the sixteenth century, we shall find that it was investigating Mysteries of Nature and not Mysteries of Grace ; but it saw omens everywhere and strange high lights in analogies.

It remains to say that Mrs. Atwood makes no reference throughout the *Suggestive Inquiry* to the thesis of Jacob Böhme on the arch-natural transmutation of metals. She leaves her tales of veridic transmutation at a loose end, serving no manifest purpose, and shews to her own satisfaction in several centuries of pages so complete a dedication of her adepts to another and greater business that it is as if she had forgotten the concern with which her " dissertation " opened. It is otherwise as if an important section had been torn out of the work, or a final chapter omitted.[1] There is no question, however, that her opinion was precisely that of Böhme, as appears by one of the observations in certain *Table Talk* which has been appended by her recent editor to the third edition of the *Inquiry*. It is affirmed therein that " the Philosopher's Stone is a real entity produced by spiritual generation ; it is a real *ens* of light ; it is both objective and subjective—an actuality as well as a theory." [2] Though Böhme is not cited, this is definite on the point of view, and there can be no question as to whence it derives. For the rest, the statement in the note-book is a little like a spark hammered unawares out of an anvil ; there is nothing which leads up thereto and nothing follows therefrom. It is of moment only as indicating the kind of reveries which would have linked up the first part of her inquiry with all that enters into what is termed " the more esoteric view ", had some obvious omissions been supplied. But the inevitable result would have been to place Mrs. Atwood still more completely out of court.

---

[1] We may do well, however, to remember in this connection her affirmed reservation and that it belonged to her hypothetical application of assumed principles to practice. For all that we know to the contrary, it might have been about manufacturing the Stone psychically, so that it should transmute metals materially.

[2] *A Suggestive Inquiry*, etc. *Revised edition*. 1920, p. 576. The note is numbered 85 in the series. It is preceded and succeeded by oracular utterances on lives which do not " create " and on " living in the Second Principle ".

CHAPTER III

FURTHER SPECULATIONS ON PHILOSOPHICAL GOLD

THE *Suggestive Inquiry* was withdrawn from circulation a few weeks after its appearance, and some five years later the French occultist Éliphas Lévi began to issue his long course of pretended initiation into " absolute knowledge ". It included an understanding of Alchemy as part of the body-general of secret arts and sciences. A single citation will suffice, and it happens to be characteristic after its own manner, magisterial in language but reaching no term as usual. " Like all magical Mysteries, the secrets of the Great Work possess a threefold significance : they are religious, philosophical and natural. Philosophical Gold is in religion the Absolute and Supreme Reason ; in philosophy it is Truth ; in visible Nature it is the Sun ; in the subterranean and visible world it is most pure and perfect gold. For this cause the search after the Great Work is called the Search for the Absolute, while the Work itself passes as an Operation of the Sun. All masters of the science have recognised that material results are impossible till all analogies of the Universal Medicine and the Philosophical Stone have been found in the two superior degrees. Then is the labour simple, expeditious and inexpensive; otherwise it wastes to no purpose the life and fortune of the operator. For the soul the Universal Medicine is Supreme Reason and Absolute Justice ; for the mind it is mathematical and practical Truth ; for the body it is the Quintessence, which is a combination of gold and light." [1]

It will be seen that these dicta belong to the category of affirmation *ex cathedra* and that if for purposes of debate we admitted successively the truth of the major postulates we should be no nearer to the performance of what is called

---

[1] See *Transcendental Magic : Its Doctrine and Ritual*, translated by myself. New and revised edition, 1923, pp. 343, 344. Also the original *Dogme et Rituel de la Haute Magie*, vol. ii, c. 12, in any edition.

the Great Work, for a gulf remains between them. The Quintessence may be *ex hypothesi* a combination of gold and light; we may worship the Supreme Reason by—let us say—unreserved dedication to Intellectual Truth; but after what manner this desirable estate of mind will communicate *per se* the secret of combining that which is denominated light with the particular precious metal does not happen to emerge in the thesis. We are in the same position when it is explained a little later on that the First Matter of the Great Work is enthusiasm and activity in the superior world, intelligence and industry in that which is intermediate, labour in the inferior world, while in science it is Sulphur, Mercury, and Salt, " which—volatilised and fixed alternately —compose the *Azoth* of the Sages ". We are in the same position, because the alchemists themselves tell us that their Salt, Sulphur, and Mercury are not the substances which are commonly so denominated, and failing a Key to their meaning, zeal, intelligence and industry will be expended to no purpose.[1]

There would be no object in enumerating these items of a highly artificial occultism, depending from personal implicits, except for the extraordinary vogue that Éliphas Lévi obtained in France and elsewhere, the traces of which are with us even at this day in several of the occult circles. He is a witness, moreover, after his own manner, to the thesis that gold was manufactured by adepts not in accordance with any chemical process, but by psychic or spiritual power, or as he termed it, by Magic, which he understood as a traditional science of secret things transmitted from the magi. On the basis of occult and alchemical records, and—as he claimed—on that also of experience, he postulated the existence of a Great Magical Agent " which the old Hermetic Philosophers disguised under the name of the First Matter of the *Magnum Opus* ". He affirmed that it determined " the species of modifiable substance " and that metallic transmutation could be accomplished by its means.[2]

[1] Éliphas Lévi speculates in the same chapter that " Sulphur corresponds to the elementary form of fire, Mercury to air and water, Salt to earth." But in so far as these explanations are in harmony with the findings of alchemists, they are not less figurative than the denominations of the Three Principles.

[2] We may compare *La Synthèse de l'Or*, 1909, by F. Jollivet Castelot, President of the Alchemical Society of France. " Alchemical theories were based on the doctrine of the four elements—Earth, Air, Water and Fire—convertible one into

To summarise the method in a sentence, this great Universal Agent, *Azoth* or what not, is susceptible of adaptation by will; and alchemical gold, when it is not to be understood as an emblematic or figurative expression, is gold ultra-physically produced by the developed will of adeptship; and such will "employs chemistry only in a secondary sense", a qualification—however—to which no intelligible meaning can be attached. The reverie may be left at this point because Éliphas Lévi was in the position of Böhme before him and had not "proceeded to the *praxis*". This was also Mrs. Atwood's position, so that in respect of the thesis at large we shall find when the time comes that there remains Paracelsus, if indeed anyone, as the sole theorist who spoke from experience by his claim, at the claim's value. The Sage of Hohenheim has—and deserves— his not incautious admirers at this day, as he had many who were set free from caution in his own century and later, when he was "the beloved monarch Aureolus". But I question whether any one now living would be prepared to maintain that he produced gold—by psychic means or otherwise. We shall ascertain his views and their value at a later stage. As the author of the *Suggestive Inquiry* and the author of *Dogme et Rituel* stand in immediate succession one to another, so also a witness in America follows on Éliphas Lévi, but with a briefer intervening period : independently and unknown to each other, they were contemplating the same subject at the same time.

In the year 1857, General E. A. Hitchcock published anonymously a small volume of *Remarks on Alchemy and the Alchemists*, written—so far as can be seen—quite independently of Mrs. Atwood, as of Éliphas Lévi, who at that date was utterly unknown outside his own country. An original

another, since they are diverse manifestations of the First Matter. This First Matter is identified with the Mercury of Philosophers, which constitutes all bodies of the universe. To produce any given body—gold, for example—we must take analogous approximate bodies which differ therefrom only in particular qualities and eliminate that by which they are differentiated, thus reducing them to their First Matter, the said Philosophical Mercury. In other words, each metal must be stripped of its individual properties and thus reduced to the state of its First Matter, which must be tinged by Sulphur and Arsenic. The tincture of gold and silver, thus formed of fermented, sublimed Mercury and of amalgamated Sulphur, constituted the Philosophical Stone or, Powder of Projection, a powerful metallic ferment, capable of transforming lead and other imperfect metals into gold."— pp. 6, 7.

contemplation, it reached also a variant understanding of the Hermetic subject, mainly ethical in character, for Hitchcock attempted to shew that alchemical adepts were not in reality chemists but great masters in the conduct of life. The experiment fell dead from the press, but the author returned to his subject and extended some of its findings in a second volume entitled *Swedenborg, a Hermetic Philosopher,* which—so far as publicity is concerned—met apparently with no better reception. For the voice of special pleading on such a topic as Alchemy there were no listeners in America at that epoch of abysmal dullness, while the New Church, established in the name of Swedenborg, would inevitably turn a deaf ear to considerations of which it understood nothing, then as perhaps now. A similar fatality might well have been in store for the *Suggestive Inquiry,* had its circulation been permitted to continue. To this day the two publications of Hitchcock have not been reprinted, and like some other works which have been hawked for pence on barrows they have become as excessively rare as they are sought by those who know.

Producing a not inconsiderable series of verbatim citations from writers of successive centuries, Hitchcock undertook in the *Remarks* to establish that the concealed subject of all true Hermetic adepts is one only, namely, triune Man, and that their object also is one, in other words, his improvement, " while the method itself is no less one, to wit, Nature directed by Art in the School of Nature, and acting in conformity therewith ; for the Art is nothing but Nature acting through man." Again, " the genuine alchemists were not in pursuit of worldly wealth or honours. Their real object was the perfection or at least the improvement of man. According to this theory, such perfection lies in a certain unity, a living sense of the unity of the human with the Divine Nature, the attainment of which I can liken to nothing so well as to the experience known in religion as the New Birth.[1] The desired perfection or unity is a state of the soul,

---

[1] Compare the *Suggestive Inquiry* : " The Theurgic Art professed a power of purifying and informing the Mind . . ., approaching . . ., as it would seem, toward a fulfilment of the perfect doctrine of regeneration preached by Jesus Christ and His apostles. . . . For, by an effectual baptismal purification, they also prepared the way, and by a gradual subjugation of the passions and adaptation of the subordinate powers to reason, the whole hypostasis was converted finally through

a Condition of Being and not a Condition of Knowing. This Condition of Being is a development of the nature of man from within, the result of a process by which whatever is evil in our nature is cast out or suppressed, under the name of superfluities, and the good thereby allowed opportunities for free activity. As this result is scarcely accessible to the unassisted natural man and requires the concurrence of Divine Power, it is called *Donum Dei*." [1]

When the affirmed natural process, described in alchemical language as devoid of haste and violence, has brought individual man into unity with himself by a harmonious action of understanding and will, he is said to be on the threshold of comprehending that Transcendent Unity Which is the perfection of the totality of Nature, " for what is called the absolute, the absolute perfection and the perfection of Nature are one and the same." [2] Proceeding from these speculative considerations more especially to the subject in hand, Hitchcock explains that in the symbolism of alchemists, according to his own interpretation, the word Sulphur signifies Nature and Mercury the Supernatural, while the inseparable connection of the two in man is called *Sal*; [3] but " as these three are seen to be indissolubly one, the terms may be used interchangeably." [4] Hitchcock refers also to a mysterious instrument of preparation in the work of Alchemy, but he is intending to specify the so-called First Matter, by which he understands Conscience. It is designated in the records under a thousand misleading and confessedly incongruous names. By means of this instrument, quickened into vital activity under a sense of the presence of God, the Philosopher's Stone, namely, Man, is purged and purified,

faith into the identity of substant light within."—p. 262, and pp. 278, 279. " That which they "—namely the alchemical philosophers—" sought after . . . is this miraculous principle of regeneration, by which the relationships of the vital elements are exchanged, the sensible medium . . . made occult, and the occult supernatural reason of life, which is catholic, becoming manifest in self-evidence and power."—p. 287 and p. 305.

[1] *Remarks*, pp. 100 and 227.

[2] *Ibid.*, p. 194.

[3] The text says *sol*, but it seems an obvious error in printing. See p. 229.

[4] Hitchcock quotes Plato in this connection, as follows : " After long contemplation of the subject, and living with it, a light is kindled on a sudden, as if from a leaping fire, and —being engendered in the soul—feeds itself upon itself." There is no reference afforded.

to make possible the internal realisation of Truth.[1] " By a metonymy, the conscience itself is said to be purified, though in fact the conscience needs no purification, but only the man, to the end that the conscience may operate freely." [2] One of the names given by alchemists to conscience on this assumption is that of a middle substance which partakes of an azurine Sulphur—that is, of a Celestial Spirit, the Spirit of God. It is said further that " the still small voice is in Alchemy,[3] as in Scripture, compared to a Fire which prepares the way for what many of the writers speak of as a Light ". Having thus broadly explained the sense which he attaches to his citations and their imagery, Hitchcock reaffirms his position, namely, that there is but one subject within the wide circle of human interests that can give a Key to the cryptic literature and the Art for which it stands : it is that which is known in theology and in religious experience as Spiritual Regeneration.[4] It is this Gift of God which was investigated by the alchemists as a work of Nature within Nature. [5] " The repentance which in religion is said to begin conversion is the ' philosophical contrition ' of Hermetic allegory. It is the first step of man towards the discovery of his whole being.[6] They also called it the black state of the Matter, in which was carried on the work of dissolution, calcination, separation and so forth, after which results purification, the white state," and this " contains the red, as the black contained the white ". The eduction

---

[1] Hitchcock says also, speaking of the alchemists at large, that conscience " is the touchstone of all their writings " and that " the way to the Philosopher's Stone is through and by means of it." Generally on the subject of conscience see *Remarks*, pp. 44 *et seq.*

[2] *Ibid.*, p. 239.

[3] To illustrate further the " light " mentioned in this extract, Hitchcock cites the entire chapter on the *Regimen of Sol* in the *Introitus Apertus ad Occlusum Regis Palatium*, under the name of Eirenæus Philalethes, but it contains only one reference to light, howsoever understood : " At last, by the will of God, a Light shall be sent upon thy matter, which thou canst not imagine." I do not find that the context of this extract offers Hitchcock the least help.

[4] *Loc. cit.*, p. 251.

[5] *Ib.*, p. 254.

[6] *Ib.*, p. 255. The nature of this discovery is not unfolded by Hitchcock. Leibnitz has been quoted in immediately preceding lines : " The human soul is infinitely richer than it is itself aware of : its being is so broad and deep that it can never wholly develop and comprehend itself in the consciousness. Man is a mystery to himself, a riddle which will never be solved in the consciousness : for, should he ever attain to the internal intuition of his whole being, he would be swallowed up and consumed in himself."

of the glorious and radiant red state ultimated in the fixation or perfection of the Matter, and then the soul was supposed to have entered into its true repose in God.[1]

For the rest, when the alchemists speak of a long life as one of the endowments of the Philosopher's Stone, Hitchcock considers in his simplicity that they are referring to the immortality of souls; when they attribute thereunto the marvellous virtues of an Universal Medicine, it is simply their intention to deny any positive qualities to evil and, by inference, any perpetuity; when they testify that the possession of the Stone is the annihilation of covetousness and of every illicit desire, they mean that all evil affections disappear before the light of the Unveiled Truth. By the transmutation of metals they signified the conversion of man from a lower to a higher order of existence, from life natural to life spiritual, albeit these expressions are inadequate to convey the real meaning of the adepts. The powers of an ever active Nature must be understood by such expressions as Fires, Menstrua and so onward, all of which work in unison because they work in Nature, the alchemists denying unanimously the existence of any disorder in the creation of God. At the end, the *Remarks on Alchemy* returns to its point of departure, the author affirming that his purpose throughout has been to exhibit the Subject of Art, and this only.

Hitchcock was a man of some spiritual insight, and if this was rather primitive in kind it enabled him still to see that his explanatory method belongs to the mere beginning of inward experience: he speaks therefore of an end, the formless light of which was glimmering ever and continually before him, though something always intervened to hinder its presentation in more than a bare allusion. He says therefore

---

[1] Not only does Hitchcock agree with Swedenborg in affirming that the opening verses of *Genesis* are concerned with the regeneration of man, but he regards the prefatory remarks in an English translation of *Novum Lumen Chemicum* as concerned with the same subject, and so also the first paragraph in *cap* v. of *Introitus Apertus*. When Espagnet says in his *Arcanum* that " the generation of our Stone is made after the pattern of the creation of the world ", the real allusion is to " man passing through the process " of the second birth, to regeneration instead of generation. See *Swedenborg, a Hermetic Philosopher*, pp. 67, 73, 74, 75, 76. And on p. 81 he suggests that Swedenborg's teaching concerning *Genesis* violated the Hermetic Law of Secrecy. It happens, however, that if regeneration is the Secret of Alchemy, it had been betrayed previously by Böhme, with whom it was the working instrument.

that he does not attempt to make the " practical treatment " plain to the issue thereof, and it comes about in this manner that his thesis is in reality a fragment broken off at an early stage, the vital part missing, supposing that it was present to his mind.[1] It is obvious also, and for the same reason, that he makes out no colourable case, for so far as his hypothesis proceeds, respecting the nature of the work upon its postulated subject, it renders alchemical literature ridiculous by representing it as veiling in allegory and illustrating by symbols the most familiar principles of ethics, the ordinary laws of conduct and the counsels of thinking in the heart—in other words, the daily matters of public teaching, not only by schoolmen and theologians but by mendicant friars in the booths and market-places. It would have been possible for Mrs. Atwood to say of her own adepts, as she conceived them, and of their Art, as it was presented to her own reflections, that it was necessary to cloud their knowledge by the invention of an elaborate scheme of emblematic representation, because it was not only dangerous to unwary practitioners but because alchemists through many centuries had the rack and the faggot to fear. It was most certainly not possible for Hitchcock to put forward this plea, but it must be added that he made the attempt.[2] Either he failed to realise that inscrutable folly of rational position in which he placed the alchemists or for some obscure reason he ignored it.

I should add that as a plain man seeking to put forward what might pass as a plain manual of interpretation, Hitchcock was antecedently quite unlikely to imagine of his own accord that the super-physical production of precious metals was included among the gifts or powers of regenerated man, and he does not seem to have met with the obscure allusions of Jacob Böhme on this subject. He was likely to

[1] We may compare the wilful reservation of Mrs. Atwood.
[2] " The alchemists were reformers in their time, obliged indeed to work in secret. . . . They lived, for the most part, in an age when an open expression of their opinions would have brought them into conflict with the superstition of the time and thus exposed them to the stake."—Preface, p. viii. Speaking elsewhere of the " obscure mode of writing " adopted by alchemists, Hitchcock argues that it was inadvisable and unsafe " to shake the hold of tradition by proposing a new rule of conduct, not easily apprehended ". But the counsel to " know thyself ", quoted in this connection, was no new rule, nor is the result of self-knowledge, as developed by him, at issue with prevailing religious doctrine or practice in the middle ages or later.

have passed over them if he had : they would have seemed ridiculous in his eyes.   As regards experimental work performed in laboratories he presents his notions with characteristic clearness and simplicity.   " That chemistry is indebted for its introduction among the sciences indirectly to the alchemists is certainly true—at least I have no disposition to question it—but not to the immediate labours of the alchemists themselves, whose peculiar work was one of contemplation and not of the hands.   Their alembic, furnace, cucurbit, retort, philosophical egg, etc., in which the work of fermentation, distillation, extraction of essence and spirits, and the preparation of salts is said to have taken place, was man—yourself, friendly reader ; and if you will take yourself into your own study, and be candid and honest, acknowledging no other guide or authority but Truth, you may easily discover something of Hermetic Philosophy. And if at the beginning there should be ' fear and trembling ', the end may be a more than compensating peace.

" It is a plain case that, for the most part, the experiments which led the way to chemistry were made by men who were misled by the alchemists and sought gold instead of truth; but this class of men wrote no books upon Alchemy.   Many of them no doubt died over their furnaces, ' uttering no voice,' and none of them wrote books upon the Philosopher's Stone, for the simple reason that they never discovered anything to write about.   I know that some impostors purposely wrote of mysteries to play upon the credulity of the ignorant, but their works have nothing alchemical about them.[1]   It is true also that many books were written by men who really imagined that they had discovered the secret, and were nevertheless mistaken.   But this imaginary success could never have had place when gold was the object, because in the bald fact no man was ever deceived ; no man ever believed that he had discovered a method of making gold out of inferior metals.   The thing speaks for itself.   It is impossible that any man can ever be deluded upon this bare fact ; but it is quite otherwise with the real object of Alchemy, in which men have been deceived in all ages . . ., for the

[1] I have no notion what books are referred to in this qualifying sentence.   The disquisitions of quacks were couched in the terms of philosophers and would have missed their mark otherwise.   In appearance therefore they wore an alchemical guise.

Subject, is always in the world, and hence the antiquity claimed for the Art by the alchemists." [1]

The last question which arises out of the *Remarks* is the significance which Hitchcock attached to his affirmed " sense of unity " between the human and Divine Nature and to his comparison of the Stone " at the Red " with the soul's condition of being when it has attained " true rest in God ". So far as an answer is given, it is in halting accents. He indicates at the inception that he does not undertake to say " precisely what the alchemists sought," but revises this by affirming that " they sought the truth upon evidences drawn from the nature of things . . . and were influenced in its reception by neither traditionn or authority ". Later on he may have realised that there was no evidence for the independence thus postulated and that truth so derived was very much up in the clouds. He qualifies therefore his original point and observes that he has not been " disposed to say much of the end ", for which he gives the reason, namely, because it is easy to see that this must be " developed in the experience of those who put themselves in a condition for it." He must have felt, however, that this was mere

---

[1] It must be said that Hitchcock was neither acquainted with the history of chemistry nor with that of Alchemy, though he had collected many texts of the literature. It was the search after the Philosopher's Stone which led to chemical discoveries, and the adepts themselves were those who made some of them or are the first to record the fact that they had been made previously. It happens that many texts which claim to reveal the mysteries of transmutation succeed effectually in hiding them, but make known that the exploration of Nature was proceeding in laboratories—such as they were—and in cabinets where manual toil was not apart from prayer. There is no need for argument ; the facts speak sufficiently. Compare Louis Figuier in *L'Alchimie et les Alchimistes*, p. 93, and I cite him because of his proximity to the Hitchcock period and the fact that the American interpreter had the book mentioned before him. " It is impossible to disown that Alchemy has contributed most directly to the creation and progress of modern physical sciences. Alchemists were the first to put the experimental method in practice, that is, the faculty of observation and induction in its application to scientific researches. Moreover, by uniting a considerable number of facts and discoveries in the order of the molecular actions of bodies they have brought modern chemistry into being. This fact . . . is beyond all doubt. Prior to the eighth century Geber put in practice the rules of that experimental school, the practical code and general principles of which were merely developed later on by Galileo and Francis Bacon. The works of Geber—the *Sum of all Perfection* and the *Treatise on Furnaces* —contain an account of processes and operations conformed wholly to the methods made use of at this day in chemical investigations ; while Roger Bacon, applying the same order of ideas to the study of physics, was led in the thirteenth century to discoveries which were astounding for his time. It is impossible therefore to contest that the alchemists were the first to inaugurate the art of experience. They prepared the advent of the positive sciences by basing the interpretation of phenomena on the observation of facts and openly breaking with the barren metaphysical traditions which had checked so long the progress of the human mind."

floundering and that there was no *raison d'être* in a study which left its subject suspended in mid air. So he made one trial more, and after speaking of implicit obedience to " an experienced imperious sense of duty, leaving the results to God ", as the true way of the wise, he proceeds thus : " Now the end is perhaps the fruit of this obedience. The man, by steady preservation of the inward unity, being prepared alike for all outward events, may finally be the subject of some special experience by which a seal of confirmation is set upon what at first was a certain divine trust in the ultimate blessing of rectitude. I suppose it to involve a peculiar knowledge of the unity of God, with a sense of participation in it, for God being ' perfect truth and perfect love ', it follows . . . that if a man can enter into the life of truth and love, he really enters into the life of God, and must feel conversely that the life of God has entered into him." [1]

The second publication of Hitchcock seems to exhibit, though it is by intimations only, a certain stage of advance-

[1] With these distinctions and all of them we may compare one paragraph in the work on Swedenborg, and it is worth quoting at length. " As I desire to guard against being misunderstood on a subject which I am sure is important, and wish above all things not to mislead anyone, I must explain that by referring to the conscience as the natural instrument of the purification of man, I do not mean . . . that this is the peculiar Secret of Hermetic Philosophy, but that it is the way to it. The Secret itself, we are told, has never been discovered, and never will be discovered by any one until, by a suitable moral and spiritual discipline, the seeker shall feel in a condition to stand unabashed in the presence of God under the simple but momentous text of Scripture : ' Blessed are the pure in heart, for they shall see God '—not," it is added, "that the wicked do not see God also, but they see Him as another personage."—*Op. cit.*, pp. 18, 19. There are several points to be noted as regards these *dicta*. In the first place, Hitchcock is meaning to use the word " discovered " in the sense of disclosed on the first occasion, but not on the second, and this begets confusion for himself as well as others. It is correct, and he knew it, that his *Secretum Artis* has never been put into writing, according to all its masters, and it is open for any one to ascertain the fact for themselves at their proper toil and cost. But in the second place no alchemical writer has ever laid down the conditions of discovery alleged above : they are of Hitchcock's own intimations, as he would most certainly have made clear, had he felt that he was creating a false impression. Thirdly, his suggestion that the wicked may see God but only in a state of separation is exceedingly pregnant, and the intention is to unfold the last end of a predominate self-centre ; but on the other hand the kind of seeing promised in the Beatitude to the pure in heart belongs obviously to the state of the Blessed Vision, and is not an authentic or complete antithesis to that state which beholds its object as " another personage ". The truth is that purity of heart is like conversion, a *terminus a quo* and not a *terminus ad quem*, except in one case which belongs to the uttermost exotics of the world within and is so rare that it may be said to loom remotely on the gold horizon of things, rather than to offer examples which it is possible to cite. I shall recur to this : it would be like making material gold by means of the *Epiclesis* Clause.

ment in the deeper ground of his subject.[1] He has emerged, partially at least, from the ethical atmosphere of the previous work, and has begun to discern that the assumed object of Hermetic philosophers, being " the perfection of man ", is to be sought by those who would understand their records as it was found by them—in a peculiar knowledge of God.[2] The nature of this knowledge does not emerge, but the way thereto is described as purification of heart. When he says a little later that the true secret of Hermetic Art cannot be written because man must keep silence when God speaks within him, and that such silence is a necessary condition of Divine utterance,[3] we can see, I think, where he stands—in contemplation of occasional flashes passing through encompassing clouds. He discerns that there is " one subject which God . . . teaches only to a select few " and that it is of " the very mystery of godliness " ; but I cannot find that he has any real grasp of it, even when he testifies [4] to his own possession of " some idea " as to that which " lies at the root of the Hermetic Art ", though he does not " feel at liberty " to risk an attempt at stating it. For him it is a secret which has always " closed the lips of the adepts ".[5] It is in this connection that—amidst many other extracts which are little enough to the purpose—he cites the affirmation of Morien : [6] (1) " thou needest not many things, but one only thing," and (2) that the " one thing " is in man himself. With all his sincerity, his clean and beautiful mind, it is to be questioned whether he realized more than a mere fraction of that which his words imply when he describes—yet a little

[1] *Swedenborg, A Hermetic Philosopher, Being a Sequel to Remarks on Alchemy and the Alchemists . . . With a Chapter comparing Swedenborg and Spinoza.* New York, 1858.

[2] *Op. cit.*, p. 13. He had long seen, as he says on his own part, that the knowledge of God is essential to the peace of man ", and that such knowledge must be something more than " the mere recognition of an unknown and powerful Being presiding over Nature."

[3] P. 21. He regards this as " the true ground of the much talked of Pythagorean silence ".

[4] P. 39. The " one subject " is not referred to subsequently. His view is that " the Art will take care of itself without the help of man ", if he is right in his supposition about it. He adds that " it will remain in the world though all the books about it should be destroyed ".

[5] P. 40. It was apparently only at a far distance that Swedenborg descried or divined " the Hermetic Secret ".

[6] P. 45. I will not forestall the criticism of this extract at the present point. Hitchcock quotes also from *Zoroaster's Cave*, which bears witness to one thing needful, on which there is one operation in one vessel : but it is described as Water.

later on—the Stone of Philosophers as " the Mystic Stone, with a new name, written upon it, 'which no man knoweth saving he that receiveth it.' "[1] There is finally—since it does not prove that he develops his implicits more fully in any later pages—the sum total of his testimony in the following findings : [2] (1) that no genuine Hermetic writer has ever hoped to make plain that " express work of the Spirit of God upon the heart of man by which he becomes a ' new creature ' " ; (2) that in his own view conversion—in the sense of Hermetic Philosophy, is " a rare spectacle in the world " ; (3) that it is designated as *Secretum Artis* ; (4) that the process has three stages, in the first two of which man may have a hand by working co-ordinately with what the Hermetists call Nature, but " in the third God works alone ", man being a passive recipient of a power which is from above him ; (4) that the fact of such reception connotes antecedently a state proper thereto ; and (5) that this does not exist so long as man is " in love, not with God but with the created things of God ". It follows that the third state " cannot be taught, as ordinary knowledge is taught ", for it belongs to that realm which is called " true faith " by Eugenius Philalethes, a mode of being which consists in love and not in reason. The kind of love is explained by the same theosopher to be a mediatory principle " which unites the Lover to that which is beloved ". The mistake of Hitchcock was to comprehend this working under the narrow name of conversion, which is the beginning of a process, the entrance into new life and not the life itself, as Thomas Bromley shewed in his *Way to the Sabbath of Rest*, at the end of the seventeenth century.[3]

---

[1] P. 72. Sendivogius is cited as one of its seekers in the *New Light*, apparently on the basis of a preface which says that the " sum of all divinity and philosophy" is to be found in the first two chapters of *Genesis*. I fail to see how this statement can be held to prove the point.

[2] Pp. 96, 97. This is *theosophia*, with its eyes fixed on the highest, and I make no question that Hitchcock had the true matter of the true mystical work in sight, so far as mental disposition was concerned. Compare Saint-Martin on the picture of an absent beauty and the Hermetic book cited by Hitchcock, unfortunately with no more specific reference : " The world does not know me, because it loves not me but mine." It is really from the discourse of *Beata Pulchra* in the opening of Thomas Vaughan's *Lumen de Lumine*.

[3] " Regeneration . . . greatly concerns us . . . in its initiation, progress and consummation. As it is taken for the beginning of the work, it implies that first change of the soul when . . . the frame of the will is swayed God and Heavenward. In its progress 'tis the growth and motion of the soul from the image of the earthly

The spiritual interpretation of Alchemy as presented by writers in the past who had made a study of the records but who laid and could lay no special claims on practical experience along physical lines, is now before my readers, and they will see that it is weighted by a hypothesis extrinsic to itself, antecedently most incredible and preposterous to all appearance. I proceed now to such a survey of the records, the history of adepts included, as will determine in the one only evidential manner whether a spiritual understanding of the subject is possible under any circumstances, whatever its kind or degree. We have learned something so far which is negatively at least of value—that " modern views on the Hermetic Mystery " are not views for our guidance, unless as counsels of caution. Of their sincerity I am utterly certain, but that of itself cannot offer a test of value. The devisers of Baconian hypotheses on the authorship of the Shakespeare plays are sincere in their own way, but it does not make for righteousness or saving reason in their views. As I regret that Mrs. Atwood did not see fit to shew us how—in her opinion—it came about that the " exoteric " history of Alchemy is that of a search for a way to transmute metals, with a recurring claim on an overwhelming success in the experiment, when her whole object was to affirm and shew that there was nothing in common between chemistry and Alchemy except " the borrowed terms ", so I regret that Hitchcock should have put himself, like her, out of court by failing to carry his interpretation to its essential end. We should have been persuaded in neither case ; but we should have been confronted by finished performances, creating at least an issue. It is not less than singular that two independent works setting out to consider the same subject should fail in this manner—one over the relation between

toward the image of the Heavenly. In its end it is the bringing forth of the perfect and complete image of God in our humanity. When we attain this we are complete in Christ, wholly new-born, and made fit to see and enjoy that Eternal Kingdom which hath been prepared for us from the beginning of the world. Regeneration then in its full latitude . . . is that transforming quickening work of God's Spirit which begins, carries on and complete's God's image in us. . . . But in the ordinary acceptation . . . it is used . . . for the first change of the soul . . . toward God in Christ ; and . . . I find too much weight laid upon this first work, as though it were the complete new birth . . . Hence many rest upon . . . and have a continaul eye to it, though they feel their chariot-wheels stand still."—*The Way to the Sabbath of Rest*, or *The Soul's progress in the Work of the New Birth*. By Thomas Bromley, London, 1710.

affirmed external evidences and postulated inward reality, the other over term in view. Mrs. Atwood had of course an insuperable difficulty before her, to prove or even affirm the regeneration and supreme spiritual attainments of her Gebers, her Aristotles, her mythic Moriens, her Agrippas, not to speak of Paracelsus, on whose alleged intemperance and irregular living she dwells and does not challenge; while Hitchcock is confronted also with a barrier of another kind, for the reason which I have intimated, that he was far too uncertain on the higher aspects of his subject to attempt unfolding them.

CHAPTER IV

Ancient Hermetic Books and the Way of the Soul Therein

THE protagonist of Alchemy is thrice-great Hermes, the Egyptian Messenger of Gods, and if it had not happened that the earliest records of the subject and the first personalities who made their claim upon the Art belong to the fifth century of the present era, being also Christian instead of pagan writers—notwithstanding certain mythical allocations—there is no question that Hermes would have figured as the tutelary deity of the adepts. As it is, he sits enthroned in the seat of authority, the prototypical Master and prime source of knowledge, who is in like manner the ultimate court of appeal. An explanation is to be found in the fact of that considerable cryptic literature which passes under his name, part of it being referable to about the end of the first century, while the body-general is antecedent to any records of Alchemy. A position of some literary and textual difficulty arises in this manner, and has begotten not a little confusion for generations or even centuries. If Alchemy is to be understood as an actual or supposititious science of metallic transmutation, by what process soever— Magic at need included—then it is very certain that the Hermetic writings do not belong to Alchemy, my reference being of course to the Græco-Egyptian group and not to certain very late forgeries, of which a word will be said subsequently.

No person qualified to judge concerning them has ever supposed that these texts were concerned, remotely or approximately, with the transmutation of metals, till the day came for indescribable nonsense to be talked in occult schools of modern foundation, apart from all knowledge which deserves the name. This notwithstanding, and *ab origine symboli*, the appeal of the alchemists was to Hermes, and on account of the cryptic character which is common to the

Trismegistic literature proper and to that of Alchemy both have been called Hermetic in the sense of concealed or veiled, as well as by allusion to legendary derivation from Hermes. Moreover, the earliest group of alchemical texts, being the Greek collection of Byzantium, includes two or three short pieces in a purposed Trismegistic guise, over and above the citations of Zosimus and the Hermes-atmosphere of Crates. When the time arrived for Mrs. Atwood to produce her exegetical treatise she could do no otherwise than annex the entire Græco-Egyptian Hermes-literature, because if Alchemy was an experiment on the soul the writings attributed to its protagonist dealt with that subject, and in all its ramifications had practically no other concern. This being so, there must be added to my previous paragraph the counter-affirmation that the Hermetic writings at large, one and all, may be colourably termed alchemical if the literature of Alchemy is itself to be understood spiritually, and if Mrs. Atwood is correct in her exegesis.

It is reasonably safe to assume that those who are undertaking the present critical study will be acquainted with the general trend of Trismegistic literature, by means of translations or otherwise, and in any case there is no need that I should give account at length concerning it, or of the deific personalities which—according to some views—are embodied under the generic name of Hermes, the distinctions between Thoth, Tat and so forth. The extant literature itself may be divided roughly for my purpose into three groups, being (1) the *Corpus Hermeticum*, represented by a mutilated manuscript, which came into the possession of Michael Psellus at Byzantium in the eleventh century; (2) the *Asclepius* or *Perfect Sermon*, preserved in a pre-Augustine translation into African Latin, the Greek original being known only by quotations of Lactantius, early in the fourth century, Joannes Laurentius Lydus and Stobæus; (3) a considerable collection of fragments in Stobæus—to the number of twenty-seven; in Tertullian, Lactantius and Cyril of Alexandria, twenty-five excerpts in all; two in the Panopolite Zosimus, and one in Fulgentius, who was of the sixth century or earlier. It should be added that there are first-hand references to the Hermetic writings in St. Justin Martyr, Athenagoras, Clement of

E

Alexandria, St. Cyprian, Arnobius, Suidas and the Emperor Julian.[1]

In so far as it is possible to set forth quite briefly the doctrine of Hermetic literature, it is desirable in view of its connection with the texts of Greek Alchemy. According to the preaching of Hermes to Tat, under the designation of *The Cup or Monad*, the world was made with Reason, not with hands, and that of which it consists is the four elements, or Fire, Water, Earth and Air.[2] The world-maker is God, the Cause of all, Who is the Eternal Good;[3] "not Mind, but Cause that the Mind is"; "not Spirit, but Cause that Spirit is"; "not Light, but Cause that the Light is";[4] Himself unmanifest and "beyond all name",[5] the Glory of all things,[6] all-pure and Father of the soul in man.[7] The most important intimations are, however, on man himself, his origin and destination at the highest. He is divine in that part of him which is Soul, Sense, Spirit and Reason, whence he can ascend into Heaven. "But in his cosmic part . . . he stayeth mortal on the earth. . . . Thus human kind is made in one part deathless, and in the other subject to death while in the body."[8] That which is deathless, that which is man essential, is "the form of the Divine Similitude".[9] It is said also that the soul in its rational part is "set above the lordship of the daimons" and is designed to be a "receptacle of God". Moreover, man in virtue of Mind, which is "of God's very essence", is not only recipient of God but also is "co-essential with Him".[10] The soul's divinity is contingent, however, on that which is understood as piety;[11] but the sense attached to this term removes it far from the familiar conventional meaning. It is the kind

---

[1] For the purposes of this sketch I have used throughout and here acknowledge my obligations to Mr. G. R. S. Mead's *Thrice-Greatest Hermes : Studies in Hellenistic Theosophy and Gnosis*, 3 vols., 1906. His translations of "the extant Sermons and Fragments of the Trismegistic literature" are contained in the second and third volumes, with his commentaries thereupon. The prolegomena are in the first volume.

[2] *The Perfect Sermon*, iii, 1.

[3] *Corpus Hermeticum*, vi, 1.

[4] *Ibid.*, ii, 14.

[5] *Ib.*, v, 1.

[6] *Ib.*, iii, 1.

[7] *Ib.*, xviii, 12.

[8] *The Perfect Sermon*, x, 4.

[9] *Ibid.*, vii, 2.

[10] *Corpus Hermeticum*, xii, 1 and 19.

[11] *Ibid.*, x, 19.

of piety on which the mind ascends to the Gnosis and its Light,[1] for " the virtue of the soul is Gnosis ", and it is possible therein and thereby to be made like unto God while the soul is still in the body—that is to say, by knowledge in goodness and the contemplation of the Beauty of the Good,[2] the Vision of which is " instinct with all immortal life ".[3] The desirable lot is to " fall asleep " from out the body " into this fairest Spectacle ".[4] But the Gnosis of the Good and the Vision which it connotes are attained in " holy silence " and in a " holiday " of all the senses. He who perceives it, perceives, sees and hears nothing else, nor can he " stir his body in any way ". It is said then of the Vision that " it shines through his whole soul and draws it out of the body, transfering all of him to essence ".[5] The Gnosis of God is the only salvation for man, the only way of Olympus, for by God, and not otherwise, does the soul become good of necessity,[6] and is most blessed when it is most filled with Him.[7]

But it is said also that Knowledge of God is attained only by becoming like unto God,[8] and this becoming is attained in devotion, which itself is called " God-gnosis ".[9] The path of devotion is presumably that which is termed otherwise " the Way of Birth in God ", *palingenesia* and the state of being " born " in Mind,[10] which comes to pass in the pity of God and by His Mercy.[11] It is called otherwise Birth in Understanding, the state in which we look on things no longer from the point of view of the body.[12] This considera-tion, so rich in pregnant suggestions, is not extended further,

---

[1] *Ibid.*, x, 21.
[2] *Ib.*, x, 9 and 6.
[3] *Ib.*, x, 4.
[4] *Ib.*, x, 5.
[5] *Ib.*, x, 6. This is Mrs. Atwood's "entrancement", which in her reverie was a work of magnetic hands, but in Hermetic literature it was attained by love of the real Self within—*Ib.*, iv, 6—that is to say, of God dwelling in the Soul's inmost Sanctuary.
[6] *Ib.*, x, 15.
[7] *Ib.*, x, 23.
[8] *Ib.*, xi, 20.
[9] *Ib.*, ix, 4.
[10] *Ib.*, xiii, 1, 3, 6.
[11] *Ibid.*, xiii, 7, 10.
[12] *Ib.*, xiii, 12. It is from the Hermetic source rather than from Christian doctrine and experience that Mrs. Atwood drew in her references to regeneration. On the other hand, General Hitchcock was acquainted only with records on the Christian side : he would probably have been surprised to learn that there was any other.

and in so far as my summary can be taken as representing the thesis in chief of Hermetic literature, it must be said concerning it that the great intimations are everywhere but the great developments nowhere. There is strong witness borne to a science of the soul, rooted in first-hand experience and not in mere doctrine ; but we do not become acquainted with the science by a study of the Hermetic texts : they affirm and do not expound it. One explanation is that the extant literature is but the remanents of a vast body of writing which has perished utterly ; but it must be remembered also that the whole output belonged to a secret teaching, and it may be questioned whether, if it were placed suddenly before us, it would be found to contain the science : the teacher would still be wanting, he who had performed the work and knew the ways thereof, the *ens* and *essentia* which may not have found expression in words. So does the vast concatenation of texts comprised by the *Sepher Ha Zohar*, in every page and line, belong to the Secret Tradition of Israel ; but this Tradition is presupposed throughout and is not formulated therein as an ordered system. The motto concerning it remains : *Traditum est.*

Now, it is almost as something which *traditum est* that the whole of alchemical literature has come down to us through all its generations : when the fact does not emerge on the surface it is at least implied ; but it is plain enough in most cases. The line of successive adepts, the golden chain of Hermes, the links of their secret science go back through the ages. Alchemy is an Art transmitted from the past on the faith of testimony borne by its great masters ; and this affirmation does not obtain the less when it is declared also and frequently that the Secret is a Gift of God, becoming known mostly in virtue of Divine Illumination. Communication from master to pupil did not apparently abrogate the validity of this teaching : the pupil was prepared in the mind before he was taught by the mouth. There was something which he must do with his might, a work of quest and practice, with a heart disposed thereto by unreserved dedication. The doctrine of transmutation came out of experience and was to be acquired in its living sense on the part of every postulant. I am putting it thus broadly because the quest-object—the thing transmutable and thing transmuted—is an open question at the moment and is that which we have set out to determine. On the hypothesis that it was a work in the soul, it is of all that followed a " birth in understanding " according—let us say—to the Hermetic texts; but if it was a work on metals brought up from mines it was acquired in cabinets of Art, with furnace, athanor and *vas philosophorum*. In either case the records of this work are represented by the literature; the texts embody a practice as well as a theory, and are so far distinguished from earlier Hermetic books: they comprised also that which was transmitted from the past and from master to son, while they designed transmission to the future.

It must be added that there are certain texts which have been termed " deposits of the Literature " and are later than the *Corpus Hermeticum*. A primary example of these is called the *Virgin of the World*, a discourse which is fairly well known in modern esoteric circles because the seventeenth century translation into English was edited in the eighties by Dr. Anna Kingsford and introduced in her familiar manner. In respect of our own purpose it belongs to the category of the *Corpus*, and its form of presentation is not therefore alchemical, however the symbolism of Alchemy may call to be understood. On the other hand, there are still later texts, among which is the famous *Tabula Smaragdina*, the *Emerald Table* of Hermes, and this has been of highest and indeed supreme authority among alchemists from the time when it became known among them, somewhere in the thirteenth century.[1] It was first printed in 1541 at Nuremberg, with the Latin works of Geber; its authenticity was vindicated, *ex hypothesi*, by W. C. Kriegsmann, in or about 1657; it was translated into French in 1612 and into German in 1613. The text of 1541 was accompanied by a commentary under the name of Hortulanus, who has been referred to the thirteenth or fourteenth century.[2] The text is in Latin and if there was ever a Greek original no trace of it remains. The *Emerald Table* is contained within the measures of a few paragraphs and is so well known that there is no excuse for citing them. It opens with the proverbial words

---

[1] There seems no evidence for the speculation of Louis Figuier which refers it to the seventh century. The earliest reference that I have met with is in the *Secretum Secretorum*, ascribed to Aristotle, the date of which is undetermined: it is posterior to *Turba Philosophorum*.

[2] The tenth has been affirmed also, but against all likelihood.

which affirm the doctrine of correspondences : *Quod superius est sicut quod inferius et quod inferius est sicut quod superius ad perpetranda miracula rei unius.* The nature of the one thing does not appear in the succeeding sentences ; but if it was produced at or about the period when it is cited first by alchemists there seems no ground for challenging the assumption that the *Table* was concerned with their Great Work.

There is also *Aureus Tractatus*, which appeared at Leipsic in 1600 under the editorship of D. Guecias, and again in 1610 : in 1691 an English version was included by William Salmon in his *Medicina Practica*, together with the *Emerald Table*. It is concerned with " the Physical Secret of the Philosopher's Stone " and is addressed by Hermes to his Son, who makes answer on a few occasions. There is not only no Greek original but as a Latin text it is a late production, while in respect of allocation it betrays itself in every line. Mrs. Atwood's version, which has been mentioned in a previous chapter, differs from that of Salmon. The imaginary Hermes claims that he obtained his science and art " by the inspiration of the living God and is transmitting on his own part", from fear of the day of judgment and the perdition of his soul " in the event of his concealing it. It is to be accepted by those who receive and understand the instruction as a gift of God, to Whom thanks must be also returned. The Stone is hidden in " the caverns of the metals ". It is said to be extracted from many things and to be of various colours : it contains, moreover, the four elements and although " most dear " is " cast forth upon the dunghill " and made altogether vile. This notwithstanding, it is " the most precious gold without spots " and an universal ferment which rectifies all things. The *Tractatus Aureus* is sometimes printed with a commentary under the title of *Scholium*, and Mrs. Atwood accompanied her translation by annotations after her own manner, citing passages regarded as illustrative from other alchemical texts under well-known names, and quoting the *Scholium* itself with reverent commendatory words, but doing little to unfold the supposed connection of the tract with her particular thesis.

There is finally a *Liber de Compositione* under the name of Hermes, first printed in 1605. It is concerned with the subject of Alchemy but seems to have exercised little influence on the literature, comparatively speaking at least.

CHAPTER V

ALCHEMY IN CHINA

THE Abbé Pernety, at the close of the eighteenth century, demonstrated to his own satisfaction that all classical mythology was but a vesture or veil of the *Magnum Opus*,[1] and the fable of the Golden Fleece was regarded generally at that period—following some earlier alchemical memorials—as a vindication of the wisdom of Greece in the Great Art of *Chrysopœia*. Here is precisely one of those facile tricks of allegorical interpretation which—once admitted—might involve all mythologies and all the old literatures. Long before classical countries had been thought of in this connection, it was assumed more naturally that the traditional science of Hermes had its cradle in Ancient Egypt. As a matter of fact, neither in Egypt nor in Greece has any trace of Alchemy been discovered till after the Christian era. "Despite the universal tradition which assigns to Alchemy an Egyptian origin, no hieroglyphic document relative to the science of transmutation has yet been discovered. The Græco-Egyptian alchemists are our sole source of illumination upon the science of Hermes, and that source is open to suspicion because subject to the tampering of mystical imaginations during several generations of dreamers and scholiasts. In Egypt notwithstanding Alchemy first originated."[2] But this was during and not anterior to the first Christian centuries.

Until recent years the available beginnings of the subject were for most of us in the Latin tongue, because nothing earlier had been printed. It will be remembered, however, that the main appeal of Latin Alchemy is to Arabia, while that of Arabia is to Greece and that of Byzantium to Egypt. But upon the matter of the Great Work the Sphinx utters nothing, and in the absence of all evidence, beyond the voice of tradition, on the question of origins it is not

[1] *Les Fables Égyptiennes*, etc., 2 vols., 1786.
[2] Berthelot: *Collection des Anciens Alchimistes Grecs, Introduction*, p. 3.

unreasonable to look elsewhere. Now, the first centre of Greek Alchemy was Alexandria, and the period was in or about the third century of the Christian era. Is it possible to carry the investigation further back in any direction whatever? An answer was attempted many years since by Dr. William A. P. Martin, a missionary and an old resident of Pekin, writing in *The China Review* of Hong Kong. He affirmed (1) That the study of Alchemy " did not make its appearance in Europe until it had been in full vigour in China for at least six centuries," or from *circa* B.C. 300. (2) That it entered Europe by way of Byzantium and Alexandria, the chief points of intercourse between East and West. The mere fact that the Art was studied there and then is notable as a possible starting point and is not without interest otherwise; but of itself it might signify only the inherent tendency of human minds to conceive identical notions, experiments, quests and so forth independently one of another. But Dr. Martin exhibits an extraordinary similarity between the theorems and literature of the subject in the far East and in the West. Moreover, in the course of his citations there are many points which he himself has passed over, though they are significant for a Hermetic student. There is, first of all, the fundamental assumption that the genesis of metals is to be accounted for upon a seminal principle. Secondly, there is the hypothesis that all existing things may attain a condition of higher development and greater efficiency [1] "owing to one active principle which abides therein." There is, thirdly, the fact that Alchemy in China, as in the West, was an occult art or science, that it was perpetuated mainly by means of oral tradition, " and that in order to preserve its secrets a figurative terminology was adopted." In the fourth place, it was bound up closely with Astrology and Magic. Fifthly, the transmutation of metals was allied indissolubly to the idea of an Elixir of Life. Sixthly, the supposed secret of making gold was regarded as inferior to the Supreme Medicine of man. Seventhly, success in operation and research depended to a large extent on the self-culture and self-discipline of the alchemist. Eighthly,

---

[1] Gold was the perfect metallic substance for Chinese alchemists, as for those of Europe.

all metals indifferently were regarded as composite. Ninthly, the concealed matters of the work were indicated under names which were used also in the West: they included mercury, lead, sulphur and cinnabar. There are, tenthly, strong points of identity in the symbolical terminology common to both literatures—for example, " the Radical Principle," the " Green Dragon ", the " True Mercury ", the " True Lead ", and so on. Finally, but most important of all for our purpose, Dr. Martin tells us that there were two alchemical processes, the first inward and spiritual, the second outward and material. There were otherwise two elixirs, the greater and the lesser. The alchemist in China was, moreover, usually a religious ascetic. The successful operator of the spiritual process was apparently translated to the heaven of the higher genii.[1]

Now, it is obvious that in these summarised points of information we may be brought to the threshold of a most important region of research; but unless and until Chinese scholarship shall undertake to guide our path we can proceed no further. We have every reason to accept Dr. Martin's testimony on the simple matters of fact, respecting the texts and their content. We can believe that he examined the texts and did what in him lay to give an accurate account concerning them. We know otherwise, moreover, that Alchemy has flourished in China, but whether at the remote period which Dr. Martin was led to think is a different question, and we are not justified in accepting his assigned date, firstly, because we have no evidence as to the extent of his critical equipment and, secondly, because the grounds of his judgment do not emerge in his narrative. If Byzantium and Alexandria received from the far East it is not impossible that they also transmitted thereto.[2] It will be remembered that a new city was built at Byzantium by Constantine,

---

[1] See also *The Chinese* by Dr. W. A. P. Martin, New York, 1881, cited by H. Carrington Bolton in *A Select Bibliography of Chemistry*, Washington, Smithsonian Miscellaneous Collections, No. 850, 1893, p. 1182. There was an English edition with a reprinted title-page.

[2] Mr. H. Carrington Bolton, *loc. cit.*, catalogues two Chinese texts thus: (1) *Wu-chen-pien*, by Chang Pih Tuan, 2 vols., 8vo, "a reprint issued during the reign of the present Emperor of China "—that is, reigning in 1893. The work itself is said to have been written *circa* A.D. 1075. (2) *Ts'an T'ung Ch'i*, also a modern reprint, but represented as " the earliest Chinese work on Alchemy now extant ", no approximate date being, however, assigned.

that it was inaugurated as his capital, A.D. 330, and was destined for centuries to be that of the Roman Empire, as well as a chief port of communication between East and West.[1] But whether there is evidence of Chinese influence on Greek crafts and arts of that period, not to speak of Greek metaphysical speculation, I am unfortunately not qualified to say.[2] We need also to know much more than Dr. Martin has told us about spiritual processes in China which passed under the name of Alchemy before we can take them into consideration on the quest of their correspondences in the groups of western texts. The subject is left therefore in this state of suspension.[3] If there is something behind Byzantium in the unknown world of the East it belongs to the problem of origins and to that, I think, only. Whensoever elucidated it will throw a certain light upon the Greek texts of the Art and the migration of language-symbols; but the prime

[1] Dr. Martin tells us that " one of the most renowned seats of alchemic industry was Bagdad, while it was the seat of the Caliphate "; that an extensive commerce was " carried on between Arabia and China "; that " in the eighth century embassies were interchanged between the Caliphs and the Emperors "; and finally that " colonies of Arabs were established in the seaports of the Empire."

[2] Among possible channels of transmission it is noted that Avicenna was born at Bokhara on the borders of China, but if this was not at the end of the tenth century it was almost certainly later. As regards the tracts on Alchemy which pass under his name, they will be considered at a later stage. It may be added that the " fundamental notions " concerning transmutation in its generic sense are referred by Dr. Martin to the Chinese classic known as *I Ching*, otherwise *Yih King*, the Canon of Change, a work variously ascribed to one and two thousand years before Christ. It is not, of course, to be supposed that the famous classic deals with Alchemy itself, but is alchemical in the sense that it is a supposititious Key to all sciences.

[3] My acquaintance with Dr. Martin was made under circumstances which illustrate the difficulties that beset this kind of research. Writing long ago in *La Revue Théosophique* on *Alchemy in the Nineteenth Century*, the late Madame Blavatsky observed that " ancient China, no less than ancient Egypt, claims to be the land of the Alkahest and of Physical and Transcendental Alchemy. . . . A missionary, an old resident of Pekin, William A. P. Martin, calls it the ' cradle of Alchemy '. Cradle is hardly the right word, perhaps, but it is certain that the celestial empire has the right to class herself amongst the very oldest schools of occult science. In any case Alchemy has penetrated into Europe from China, as we shall prove." Madame Blavatsky proceeded at some length to " compare the Chinese system with that which is called Hermetic Science," her authority being Dr. Martin and her one reference being to *Studies of Alchemy in China* under his name. I went in search of those studies, but no bibliography and no catalogue enabled me to trace a work bearing that title. While I ascertained that Martin was not himself a myth, it began to seem that a mythical treatise had been attributed to him. But after a long time I discovered that the work quoted by Madame Blavatsky—as it would seem, at second hand—was not, as she evidently thought, a book separately published but an article in *The China Review*. From this article she borrowed her information almost verbatim, so that she must have seen full extracts, and where she varied from the original it was to introduce statements which are not in accordance with the article and would have been certainly rejected by the writer.

inspiration of Greek Alchemy is Hermetic, and no one will venture to say that the remanents of Hermetic literature, with an account of which I have occupied the previous chapter, owe or can owe anything to China in the fact and nature of things. As the literature developed in the West, assuming Latin, German, French and English among other vestures, it removed more and more from this original ground and source, drawing symbols and analogies from the Christian scheme of things. The Greek texts passed out of all knowledge; the appeal to Hermes remained, but it was a name only, connoting a great master hidden in the " dusk of time " : in so far as the Art of Alchemy was still a Hermetic Art, it was in view of secrecy alone, of something which came from the past in the veil of a hidden language and must be so transmitted to future generations. The circulation of *Corpus Hermeticorum* by and after Psellus, and its translation by Marsilius Ficinus into Latin in 1471, leaving out of consideration the subsequent renderings into Italian and French, had no consequence for alchemical literature : no one mentioned *Poimandres*, the *Secret Sermon* or *Asclepius* : if here and there they were known to two or three of the adept masters, it would seem that they were left over as not belonging to their concern— a fact which consorts badly with the thesis of the *Suggestive Inquiry*. And yet—as I have said—the protagonist was always Hermes, and he the court of appeal ; but it happens that his faithful witness was delivered to the alchemists of later generations only in *Tabula Smaragdina* and much more rarely in *Tractatus Aureus*. On the other hand, there could be nothing more ridiculous than to suggest that mediæval Alchemy or that which followed thereon exhibits one shadow of influence from Chinese sources. And yet if in the third century B.C., or at any time prior to the Byzantine group, there were texts in China which made use of such veiling terms as the Green Dragon and the True Mercury, they were also veils in the West and must have been imported surely from the East. This is how the case stands, and this is how it must be left, except in so far as we may glean some further light from later publications of the same missionary. I have mentioned his work on *The Chinese*, which appeared in New York, but it contributes nothing to our subject, as it contains only a reprint of the thesis published in *The China Review* for the year 1879, being the revision of a paper read before the American Oriental Society so far back as October, 1868. In 1896 Dr. Martin published *A Cycle of Cathay*, which suggests that the disciples of Laotse " deduced the twin doctrines of the transmutation of metals and the elixir of life " from the ancient *Book of Changes*, referred to B.C. 2800 [1] and comprising a system of divination which is said to be still in use among Chinese fortune-tellers. After what manner it implies the doctrines cannot be said to emerge ; [2] but it is reaffirmed that the practice of Alchemy originated in this manner " centuries before it found its way into Europe ". Dr. Martin has said previously that " Alchemy is indigenous to China and arose with the dawn of letters ".

In 1901 Dr. Martin [3] published a further volume entitled *The Lore of Cathay*, in which he recurs to the subject, but it is by reproducing again his text of many years since, with unimportant variations, which offer no further ground for supposing that Alchemy may have been transmitted from China to Europe. The question remains therefore *sub judice* for the reasons already mentioned, but more especially (1) because the critical faculty of the author inspires little confidence, and (2) because most texts and authorities quoted are of the Christian period, with a limit on the hither side of 1000 A.D. [4] The main points of fact have been cited already in my extracts from *The China Review*. As regards an Elixir of Life, the treatises on this subject are said to be far more numerous than those which deal with the transmutation of metals ; but it is not held to work after the manner of ordinary medicines—or automatically, so to speak—

[1] This is in respect of the diagrams, the text being said to date from B.C. 1150. See Thomas MacClatchie : *I Ching . . ., or the Classic of Change, with Notes and Appendix*, 1876.

[2] Dr. Martin remarks, in the first place, that the *Book of Changes* is suggestive as name or title, and, secondly, that " we find throughout its contents the vague idea of change replaced by the more definite one of ' transformation ', the key-word of Alchemy." I am afraid that this is childish, but it is the sole justification offered for regarding the *I Ching* as " the true source of those prolific ideas which prepared the way for our modern chemistry ".

[3] We learn from his title-pages that he was at one time President of the Imperial University at Peking.

[4] There is particular reference to the writings of Lieh Tzu, Lu Tsu, Chuang Tze, Kao Shang Tzu and Tan Tzu. The texts include a *Mirror of Scientific Discovery*, otherwise, *Ko Chih Ching Yüan*, the date of which is left over.

for psychological stimulus is postulated in order to make it effective. Among the arts of the alchemist, according to Tan Tsze, there is " that of preparing an Elixir, which may be used as a substitute for food. This is certainly true," says the commentator, " yet the ability to enjoy abundance or endure hunger comes not from the Elixir but from the fixed purpose of him who uses it. When a man has arrived at such a state of progress that to have and not to have are the same . . . , it will be of no consequence whether he eat a hundred times a day or once in a hundred days." It is difficult under these circumstances to see wherein resides the virtue of the Elixir, if indeed anywhere. We are told otherwise on the same authority (1) that the adept is warmed by the fire of his own soul and therefore cannot be cold ; (2) that he inhales " the fine essence of matter ", whence hunger is for him impossible ; while (3) in respect of sickness, he who is " fed on the essence of the five elements " is not a prey thereto. For the attainment of this desirable state a hint is possibly afforded by a counsel of Lu Tsu, who is referred to the eighth century of the present era. He directs those who are in search of long life " to kindle the fire that springs from water and evolve the *Yin* contained within the *Yang*—otherwise the active and passive principles. The alternative is " one word from a sapient master, and you possess a draught from the golden water "—a shorter path to knowledge than was offered by Alchemy in the West. Dr. Martin was acquainted with a compilation in twelve volumes devoted to the Quintessence of Philosophers.

CHAPTER VI

The Testimony of Byzantine Alchemy

IN considering the literature of Alchemy as a whole, and in the broad historical sense, it may be said to have four periods : (1) Byzantine Alchemy, (2) Arabian and Syrian Alchemy, (3) Latin Alchemy, and (4) a host of late texts, many of which are negligible, in the vernaculars of various countries. It should be added that the third section merges into the period of the fourth, as Latin continued to be used long after alchemical works began to appear in French, German, English and other living languages. As regards the Latin literature, very little—if anything—that is extant can be· placed prior to the twelfth century, most earlier attributions being mythical. The things, for the rest, which pass under the names of Rhasis, Alfarabi, Avicenna and Morien have some roots in preceding cycles. The *Turba Philosophorum* is earlier, let us say of the eleventh century, perhaps even of the tenth, meaning however in its Latin guise, as it is almost certainly translation from an unknown original which was probably in Arabic, as we shall see at a later stage.[1] The Latin Geber is ascribed to the twelfth or thirteenth century ; but the criticism of these important memorials has entered recently on a new and unexpected phase, which is also left over till we come to the consideration at large of the early Latin literature.

The line of transmission in Alchemy has been made perfectly clear by the French chemist Berthelot, through the publication of his *Collection des Anciens Alchimistes Grecs* [2] and subsequently of the Arabian and Syrian alchemists.[3]

---

[1] It is quoted by Vincent de Beauvais in his *Speculum Naturale,* which belongs to the thirteenth century.

[2] The collection was issued in several *livraisons,* publication beginning in 1887—which is the date on the general title-page—and being completed in the following year. The work is in three parts, the first of which contains a valuable body of criticism ; the second gives the Greek text, as established and printed by M. Ch. Em. Ruelle. The third is translation into French.

[3] *La Chimie au Moyen Age,* 3 vols., 1893. The first volume comprises Berthelot's *Essay on the Transmission of Antique Science to the Middle Ages ;* the second contains Syrian Alchemy, the text and translation being the work of Rubens Duval ; the third is devoted to Arabian Alchemy, the text and its rendering being by O. Houdas.

From this point onward to the end of the next chapter my source and authority on all matters of fact will be found in these epoch-marking works, which at present—and failing antecedent possibilities in China—are the *terminus a quo* for the critical consideration of alchemical literature under all its aspects.[1]

The earliest extant work which is known in the West as connecting, actually or by imputation, with the alchemical subject is a Greek Papyrus of Leyden, which was discovered at Thebes and is referable to the third century of the Christian era.[2] It contains seventy-five metallurgical formulæ for the composition of alloys, the surface colouration of metals, assaying and so forth. There are also fifteen processes for the production of gold and silver letters. The compilation, as Berthelot points out, is devoid of order and is like the note-book of an artisan. It is pervaded by a spirit of perfect sincerity, despite the professional improbity of the recipes. These appear to have been collected from several sources, written or traditional. The operations include tingeing to represent gold, superficial colouring of copper so that it may pass as gold, gilding of silver, tincture by a varnishing process, superficial aureation by the humid way, etc. There are many repetitions and trivial variations of the same processes. M. Berthelot and his collaborator regard this document as conclusive proof that when Alchemy originated in Egypt it was an art of the sophistication or adulteration of metals. The collection is absolutely authentic and " it bears witness to a science of alloys and metallic tinctures which was very skilful and very much advanced, a science which had for its object the fabrication and falsification of the matters of gold and silver ". It is held also that

---

[1] There are also two other works, being independent critical investigations : (1) *Les Origines de l'Alchimie*, 1885 ; (2) *Introduction à l'Étude de la Chimie des Anciens et du Moyen Age*, 1889. Both are studies of the first importance ; but the ground of the first is to some extent covered by the much larger introduction to the Byzantine Collection, and that of the second by the *Essay on Transmission* of 1893. They demand notwithstanding the close attention of those who seek to be acquainted with the beginnings and early developments of the alchemical subject.

[2] It was printed in *Papyri Græci musei antiquarii publici Lugduni Batavi . . . edidit, interpretationem latinam, adnotationem, indices et tabulas addidit* C. Leemans, *Tomus* II, 1885. The first volume appeared so far back as 1843. A French translation of the particular papyrus is given in Berthelot's introduction to the Byzantine Collection, pp. 28–50. He suggests that it is one of the old alchemical books, of the kind burnt by Diocletian, *circa* 290 A.D.

" in this respect it casts new light upon the genesis of the idea of metallic conversion ". The more notable affirmation follows that " not only is the notion analogous but the practices exposed in this papyrus are the same as those of the oldest Greek alchemists, such as pseudo-Democritus, Zosimus, Olympiodorus and pseudo-Moses ". This demonstration is of the highest importance for the study of the origin of Alchemy. It proves—in Berthelot's opinion—that Alchemy was founded on more than purely chimerical fancies, namely, on positive practices and actual experiments, by the help of which imitations of gold and silver were fabricated. Sometimes the craftsman confined himself to public deception, as with the author of Papyrus X—being the Theban Papyrus of Leyden—sometimes he added prayers and magical formulæ to his art, " becoming a dupe of his own industry ".[1] It is advanced further that " the real procedures and actual manipulations of the operators are made known to us by the Papyrus of Leyden under a transparent form and in accordance with the processes of pseudo-Democritus and Olympiodorus. It contains the first form of all these processes and their doctrines ".[2] But a curious and perhaps pregnant intimation follows, that in pseudo-Democritus and still more in Zosimus—earliest among the Greek alchemists—the recipes are complicated already by so-called mystical fancies. Then come the commentators, who are held to have extended still further the mystical portion, obscuring or eliminating what was practical, to the exact knowledge of which they were frequently strangers. " Thus, the most ancient texts are the clearest." [3]

It is to be assumed that no intelligent reader will fail to see what a strange if clouded horizon opens out from this statement of fact. There is no question that the Egyptian Papyrus answers exactly and throughout to its description as given above ; the text is before our eyes ; and it follows that the earliest work which is known to archæology—at least outside China—as dealing with supposed metallic

---

[1] See Berthelot's *Introduction*, p. 6, also p. 20, for magical formulæ in connection with fraudulent practices.

[2] The thesis is otherwise that the Leyden Papyrus X shews how the hopes and doctrines of later alchemists were born from the practices of Egyptian goldsmiths in imitating and falsifying the precious metals. *Ibid.*, p. 5.

[3] *Ibid.*, p. 21.

tinctures and conversions belongs to the art of fraud. But a time came when the chaos of sophisticating recipes fell into the hands, *ex hypothesi*, of early Greek alchemists and subsequently of their commentators, who knew so little of the trick-craft and its purpose that they misconstrued the artisan's documents—or other collections belonging to the same class—and regarded it in the light of whatever may call to be understood as " mystical fancies ". With the content of the Papyrus before us, this is not on the surface a very plausible proposition, in view of its " most clear form ". Is it certain after all that pseudo-Democritus and the rest of them had ever seen Papyrus X ? What of its alleged sources, " written or traditional " ? The debt of Greek Alchemy was doubtless general to all, and if this only takes back the question without reducing the fraudulent nature of the devices, is it really of vital consequence that the processes of early Greek alchemists, when they produce processes, are sometimes reminiscent of and perhaps even identical with those of the Theban artisan ? It happens that among mystical fancies the artisan's transparent indications had a new intention read into them which transformed the Art and its' purpose. The tricks of a thievish trade suggested other possibilities to a very different school, and it went to work accordingly. But before proceeding further the following preliminary points call for notice : (1) It is impossible to separate the Theban Papyrus from the context of other Papyri with which it is in close relation, as admitted by Berthelot, who says : " The history of Magic and of Gnosticism is bound up closely with that of the origin of Alchemy, and the alchemical Papyrus of Leyden connects in every respect with two in the same series which are solely Magical and Gnostic." The proposition sounds inscrutable, for how in the name of reason can it be affirmed that the note-book of an artisan, containing methods of gilding silver and so forth, stand in any relation to a doctrine of the æons, not to speak of the invocation of spirits ? But if a Sacred Art arose under the name of Alchemy then—whatever the quest and term—there might well be such a connection in that time and place of the world. (2) It follows from Berthelot's thesis that a so-called mystical element not only entered early into alchemical literature, but brought it into

F

being. It was conceived, moreover, and developed by
persons having no interest in Berthelot's " practical part ",[1]
and they made use, therefore, of early practical documents
for their own purposes, understanding them, or misunder-
standing. in their own sense. Now the nature of those
purposes is the question which arises here, and the answer
is that they were in search of valid transmutations, not of
surface tinctures.[2] (3) The Theban Papyrus is therefore
the antithesis of Alchemy in the sense that the Greek
Zosimus or the Latin Lully, Arnold, Sendivogius and
Eirenæus are alchemical writers. It neither is nor pretends to
be more than a thesaurus of processes for the falsification and
spurious imitation of precious metals ; it has no connection,
remote or approximate, with their transmutation, and it
is devoid of all alchemical terminology. In itself it neither
proves nor disproves anything outside its own measures—
not even an Alchemy theologised. If we meet with its recipes
in texts belonging to the Latin age of Alchemy, it seems to
follow that the authors, like their Greek predecessors,
misconstrued the processes. But in reality they came down
to them like a vague and remote echo from past centuries.
It is indubitable further, on the evidence of all their records,
that they could have had—like them—" no interest " in
Berthelot's " practical part "—meaning the simple sophistication of metals.

The collection of Greek alchemists, its accretions apart, was
formed during the eighth or ninth century of the Christian
era, and at Constantinople.[3] Its authors are cited, as we

---

[1] It should be understood that for M. Berthelot the qualification of mystical
is synonymous always and only with foolish reverie, the product of extravagant
minds, and that he is by no means therefore suggesting the evidence of any spiritual
intention in the glosses of commentators or in the texts, e.g., of Zosimus. If he
were, I am afraid that it would belong for him to that realm of " fancies ", the
presence of which he is prone to discern everywhere. It does not need to be added
that in so far as Greek alchemists substituted the idea of actual metallic conversions
for the impositions of the Theban Papyrus they were turning—so far as Berthelot
is concerned—from practical and realisable processes into a dream world of their
own. In the year 1888 the blessed life of scientific certitude was as yet unbroken
by the revolutionary discoveries which have characterized later decades, and
speculations on the obscure borderland of physics are now couched commonly
in far more tentative terms.

[2] I am using guarded terms, in view of the research before me : if Greek
alchemists followed a mystic quest recorded in chemical terms, they were so much
the further apart from Papyrus X, though they may have used it sometimes as
a veil.

[3] The oldest known manuscript is that of Venice, which belongs to the end of

shall see later on for ourselves, by subsequent Arabian writers as the source of their own science, and in this manner they became also the fountain-head of western Alchemy, because the latter derived from Arabia. The texts admit of being separated into two leading classes, of which one is —let us say—theoretical, the other—comparatively small— being technical and concerned with special fabrications, the manufacture—for example—of various kinds of glass and of artificial gems. The one is alchemical, the other belongs to the false arts and crafts. It is outside the purpose in view to enumerate the manuscript codices which were collated to establish the text, as it appears in the great publication of 1887. I need only point out that while it does not claim to include the whole of the Greek alchemists, it is said to omit no author who was judged to be of value for either science or official archæology, and for Berthelot's purposes at least it may be held practically exhaustive.

The ensuing tabulation will furnish an adequate account of the printed text in respect of content. (1) General Indications, including a *Lexicon* of the Art Chrysopœia, a variety of fragmentary treatises, an *Instruction* of Isis to Horus, etc. (2) Treatises attributed to Democritus or belonging to that school, including one addressed to Dioscorus under the name of Synesius and another, of considerable length, by Olympiodorus, an Alexandrian philosopher. (3) The works of Zosimus the Panopolite. (4) A collection of supposititious ancient authors, but the attributions are apocryphal or imaginary, while the writings are referable in some instances to so late a period as the fifteenth century : Pelagus, Ostanes, Iamblichus, Agathodaimon and Moses are included in this section. (5) Technical treatises on the goldsmith's art, for the most part fraudulent and including the tincture of copper by gold, the manufacture of various kinds of glass,[1] the sophistical colouring of precious stones, fabrication of

---

the tenth century. For the purposes of Berthelot's codex, what is wanting in the Venice collection has been supplied from No. 2,327 of the *Bibliothèque Nationale*, belonging to the end of the fifteenth century. These two have been collated with twelve other MSS. It should be understood that the writers of the collection are referred to the third and fourth century, the period of Diocletian, Constantine and Theodosius, with the exception of pseudo-Democritus, who belonged to the beginning of the Christian era.

[1] Certain recipes for colouring glass and the composition of alloys are said to go back to ancient Egypt.

silver, incombustible sulphur and so forth.[1] (6) Selections from technical and pseudo-mystical commentators on the Greek alchemists, including the Christian Philosopher, Cosmas and a certain Anonymous Philosopher. This section is exceedingly incomplete and may have omitted much which would be of value for our own purpose, since it belonged presumably to the realm of mystical fancies condemned by Berthelot.

It is to be understood that the Greek alchemists are by no means in the same category as the compiler of the Theban Papyrus, and that their memorials are not comparable to the note-books of artisans. With each and all the subject is a secret science, a sublime gnosis, the possessor of which is to be regarded as a sovereign master. With each and all it is a Divine and Sacred Art, which must be communicated only to those who deserve such knowledge, for it participates in Divine Power, succeeds only by Divine Aid, and involves a special triumph over matter.[2] The love of God and man, temperance, unselfishness, truthfulness, hatred of all imposture are also essential preliminary requisites ; but it must be added that they are imposed with equal force in texts which are concerned unquestionably with a physical work as in those that on their surface may possibly suggest for a moment the presence of some higher concern. By each indifferently a knowledge of the Art is ascribed to Hermes, Plato, Aristotle and other great names of antiquity, while Egypt is regarded as *par excellence* the country of the Great Work. To recite

---

[1] It will be seen that one of my suggestions is ratified in this manner by the content of the Collection itself, which in addition to the texts of Greek Alchemy proper embodies a variety of processes brought from far and near, outside those of Papyrus X, though often reminiscent thereof. When recipes comparable to these—and in the case, let us say, of Democritus more or less identical—are found in the Greek alchemists on rare occasions, there is no question that Berthelot is correct in affirming that they are understood in another than their original and real sense. Greek alchemists were in search of a tincture which would penetrate metals and not tinge them on the surface, like the processes of Papyrus X and the rest of the artisan note-books of which it is a surviving example.

[2] Intimations like these abound, but the real explanation is not that Greek Alchemy was a science of the soul—secret, veiled and symbolised—for on the contrary we shall see that it was a Royal and Sacred Art, in the sense that it was meant only for kings and priests, because it was the key of power, being the key of wealth. The royal and sacerdotal warrants came from God, and that which the hypothesis reserved to priests and kings was hallowed because it was theirs, and for what it could confer upon them. When the Greek alchemists passed from theory to practice the results obtained may well enough have deceived themselves, because they worked in great darkness as regards all physics and *chemia*.

these features is to exhibit out of hand the debt of mediæval and later western Alchemy to Greek originals. The similarity in both cases of the hypothetical true process is in ever-recurring evidence, and the same particular stress is laid upon a moderate and continuous heat, as opposed to a violent fire. The materials are also the same, or at least the same terms are used to describe them ; but for the moment it will be enough to cite the importance attributed to Mercury by Greek alchemists, as it will place a student of the later literature in possession of a key to the correspondences which exist under this head. Finally, as regards terminology, the Greek texts abound with references to the Egg of the Philosophers, the Philosophical Stone, the Stone which is not a stone, the Matter of the Work, the Body of Magnesia, the Blessed Water, and other symbolical and figurative names which belong to the cryptic language of later adepts. It seems to follow therefore that a common bond of knowledge—real or supposed—was transmitted through the centuries and that it interlinked the Greek Masters of the Art with Lully and Arnold, or the Cosmopolite and Philalethes with Zosimus, Olympidorus and Synesius. If Arnold and Lully were veiling a spiritual science in the broideries of an artificial tongue it would appear difficult to affirm that Zosimus was otherwise engaged ; but if Zosimus and the Byzantine School generally were on the quest of metallic transmutation—as we shall find that they were assuredly—it is mere logic to conclude that those of the long succession through later centuries were on the same search also—failing the clearest evidence in a contrary direction—while if attainment be ascribed to the one class it must not be denied to the other. I am contrasting at the moment a supposed alternative to create a clear issue, and it may be added with the same intention that if some of the Greek alchemists were set upon a physical work but others on one of the kind which is called mystical —though scarcely in the sense of M. Berthelot—we need not be surprised if in later generations we meet also with two schools.

In respect of Byzantine texts we have seen that Berthelot does in fact create a distinction which corresponds hereto, but it belongs to the surface only, because his mystic school is one of mere dreamers who do not count for him, and whose memorials can be struck out at need. So also his physical workers, so far as they accomplished anything, were like the Theban artisan, or fabricators of false, sophisticated gold and silver, and those who came after them pursued the same course. If this were true and not, as it is, a case misread throughout, the material Art of Greek Alchemy ended as it began, that is to say, in imposture, which at the same time may have been " tempered with superstition ", since those who exploit credulity tend often to become credulous themselves. On the point of fact Berthelot undertakes to shew that the fraudulent recipes contained in the Theban Papyrus are met with again in the Byzantine collection itself; but the force of this simple fact, and of his whole hypothesis, is nullified by his own decisions, being (1) that valid transmutations are mere mystical fancies and (2) that the Greek alchemists misconstrued the processes, which they did assuredly on the hypothesis that they regarded them as veiled instructions on the manner of accomplishing the Great Work of true metallic conversions, and not of mere surface tinctures and varnishes. My own view, based on the texts themselves, is that they realised the false pretence of their inherited processes, that they endeavoured to do better and believed that they succeeded.

When the mystical interpretation of alchemical literature was first propounded formally in the year 1850—as we have seen—the Leyden Papyrus had been not only unrolled but had been translated into Latin. The fact was unknown to Mrs. Atwood, as also to her American successor, and would have signified little to either, seeing that the Byzantine literature proper was available only to specialists who could read the Greek texts in manuscript. The origin of Alchemy was in clouds of speculation which supposed that ancient Greece and Egypt were sanctuaries of chemical as well as more exalted wisdom. The works attributed to Hermes Trismegistus offered, vaguely enough, a certain point of departure, the *Tractatus Aureus* included and the *Emerald Table*; but if it were possible to assume that the Latin literature of the subject, from the days of *Turba Philosophorum*, ought to be understood spiritually and not physically, it is obvious that all Greek theosophy, especially that of Neoplatonism, could be used to elucidate the body general of adept records and memorials. And, so far as arbitrary affirmation is concerned, fortified by citations from alchemical writers apart from context,[1] we have seen that this is what occurred. It follows that in the whole range of the literature, as it developed through long centuries, there can be nothing so important as the testimony of the Byzantine Collection, in view not only of its early date as a body of alchemical tracts but of its proximity to the Neoplatonic and Trismegistic period.

The texts may be taken, for the most part, as they stand in the publication of Berthelot. There is a dedication which exalts the Sovereign Matter, those who are acquainted with its mystery and those who established the science. It lays down also the qualifications essential for seekers who would graduate themselves therein and that with which they are concerned, being the exploration of concealed veins charged with gold. It is otherwise an exploration of Nature because it is she only who brings forth shining gold. We are presented therefore at the beginning with the view taken of its subject-matter by the unknown editor who formed the collection. Those, however, who alone are worthy and able to discover Nature are those who are inspired by the Muses, described otherwise as lovers of Divine Gnosis. An invocation of Christ follows, which commends the book to His care and commends also a certain Theodorus, to whom the dedication is addressed.

After this proemium there is placed the alphabetical *Lexicon of Chrysopœia* which has been named already; it explains the sense of the symbolical and technical terms made use of in the body of the collection. The explanations are chemical throughout. The Seed of Venus is verdigris; Dew —which is a favoured symbol with the whole choir of alchemists—is said to be mercury extracted from arsenic, i.e., sublimed arsenic. The Sacred Stone is chryoslite, though it is also the Hidden Mystery. Magnesia—that great arcanum of later Hermetic Philosophy—is identified indifferently with white lead, pyrites, crude vinegar and female antimony, i.e., native sulphur of antimony. The Stone which is not a

---

[1] Mrs. Atwood was acquainted at first hand and familiarly with all the texts that she quoted, but her admirers and occasional expositors do not seem to have examined them.

stone is lime and " vapour sublimate ", diluted with vinegar.[1] Regeneration is the process of calcining and washing. These selections might be extended indefinitely, but would only display further the crude physics of the *Lexicon*. It is followed by a number of brief and fragmentary treatises which enumerate a large variety of substances, well known to chemists and otherwise, as well as a few which cannot be identified certainly. There is a tract on the Philosophical Egg, which discusses at length the arbitrary denominations applied to its constituents, the Egg itself being called Stone of Copper, Armenian Stone, Etesian Stone, and so forth. The yolk is termed celandine, Attic ochre, Cilician saffron, etc. The white is known indifferently as gum, juice of the fig-tree, mulberry and tithymal juice ; but in place of these symbols borrowed from the vegetable world, those which apply to the shell are metallic only, including alloy of iron and copper, alloy of lead and copper, or copper simply. These are tiresome enumerations, but they serve to exhibit the ridiculous absurdity which would characterise any attempt to allegorise upon them in a moral, spiritual or mystical sense. At the end it is said that Nature fulfils that mystery which is sought in and extracted from one only body. Two must become one, three also one, and one the whole composition, in order to achieve the end. Because it is the image of the world, the Egg contains the four elements. In another fragment which enumerates certain cities of the Thebaid,[2] wherein the " metallic spangle ", otherwise Metallic Stone, is prepared, we are told (1) that the said Stone resembles marble and is hard ; (2) that it is ground and reduced to powder ; (3) that the lighter part is washed away but the heavier remains ; and (4) that this is placed in an earthen vessel, wherein it is heated over a furnace for five days and nights.

In an address of Isis to Horus, the Queen-Mother and Goddess relates that she was visited by an angel and desired to learn from him the preparation of gold and silver ; but he explained that he was not permitted to reveal it because

[1] In this connection Berthelot cites pseudo-Aristotle on the identity of the Philosophical Egg and the Philosopher's Stone. See *Liber Secretorum*, which is, however, quoted at second hand.

[2] They are five in number : Heracleopolis, Lycopolis, Aphrodite, Apollinopolis and Elephantis.

of the high importance attaching to such mysteries. However, on the day following he sent a greater angel, named Amnaël, who had power to inform her, but administered in the first place a pledge of silence.[1] An instruction follows on the doctrine of generation by seed, on fixing Mercury by means of Magnesia, Bole, or Sulphur, on the washing of metallic bodies, the combination of various substances and so onward, manifest chemical procedures of their sort and kind, which Berthelot is able to elucidate there and here, of course from the chemical standpoint. Of these lights there is obviously no opportunity to speak now, nor in most cases does any need arise. About disquisitions on the fabrication of asem, cinnabar and so forth there is and can be no question as to the material ends in view. In a fragment on the morals of philosophers it is said (1) that " he who would pursue the study of science must first love God and man, be temperate, disinterested, opposed to falsehood, fraud, evil actions and every feeling of envy " ; (2) that he must be " a sincere, faithful child of the Holy, Consubstantial and Coeternal

---

[1] The angel—whose Hebrew name suggests Gnostic influence—recites a string of adjurations on his own part as if to attest the truth of his revelations to come, but the oath of Isis does not appear in the text. The fact that Secrets of the Art were communicated under pledges of silence is indirectly illustrated, however, by two oaths which stand by themselves in the collection apart from any explanation, and they are worth appending as evidence of the mode of transmission. The first is in the following terms and is designed, it would seem to indicate that the initiator who confesses to reservations expects similar " piety and prudence " on the part of the recipient. " I swear unto thee, my honourable initiate, by the Blessed and Venerable Trinity, that I have revealed nothing of those Mysteries of Science which have been transmitted thereby to me, into the secret retreats of my soul." This is followed immediately by its express contradiction in stultifying terms. "Whatsoever knowledge I hold from the Divinity, relating to the Art, I have set down without reserve in my writings, unfolding the thought of the elders according to my own reflections." They are to be approached in a spirit of piety and prudence. If errors are discoverable here and there, but apart from bad intent, they are to be amended for the sake of readers who are faithful to God. The concluding invocation is *nihil ad rem* and is added matter. " Hail unto the Name of the Holy and Consubstantial Trinity, that is to say, the Father, Son and Holy Spirit. The Trinity in Unity is the Son, Who took flesh without sin among men for the glorification of the Duad, wherein He himself participates. He has put on human nature, remaining blameless : seeing that it was subject to weakness, He has restored it."

The second is termed the Oath of the Philosopher Pappus and testifies to the quality of his faith in God : " I swear unto thee by the Great Oath, whosoever thou art : I understand the one God according to species, not according to number. It is He Who made heaven and earth, the tetrad of elements which derive therefrom, as also rational and intelligent souls, harmonising the same with bodies." He is also that God " Who is borne on chariots of Cherubim and is celebrated by legions of angels ". A process follows which does not belong to the so-called pledge or confession and has been obviously added thereto.

Trinity"; (3) that otherwise he will deceive himself in seeking things unattainable. But nothing follows from this, except that He Who is the sole Source and Author of all good gifts will communicate them only to those who walk in His ways, whether the endowments belong to things of earth and its knowledge or to the Science of the Heavenly School. There is also the *Assembly of Philosophers*, which postulates a fictitious debate on the vital question whether the Mystery is accomplished by means of one species or many. It is resolved that the furnace is one, one the way and one also the work, which is described as tincture of gold. The end in view is granted by the Lord God gratuitously. A short process follows for obtaining Philosophical Vinegar, but it is regarded as a transcriber's addition. An alleged *Diplosis of Moses* gives directions for combining, grinding and heating certain substances, the result being their change into gold. According to Berthelot, it is a process for the fabrication of gold *à bas titre* and is comparable as such to another *Diplosis* which passes under the name of Eugenius.

I have now considered the collection so far as its first part is concerned, being that which comprises the shorter tracts and fragments. It will be seen that there is no question whatever as to the real concern of what is termed the Art; but there must be remembered always the fundamental point of view. If the friction of flint and steel produces sparks, that fire comes *Deo volante*. This is the position in a sentence. He therefore who would transmute metals, unless he is taught by a master, must look for knowledge of the work to God, and must remember that any process is valid only because of the Divine Will : it is not otherwise even in the devices of successful sophistication, because it is certain that God, did He so choose, could " confound their knavish tricks ". The second part includes the longer treatises belonging to the school of Democritus, beginning with one which is ascribed—falsely of course—to this philosopher and treats of natural and mysterious questions. There are processes for the fabrication of yellow gold and of asem, explained by Berthelot as signifying in this case a particular alloy, " intermediate between gold and silver, and analogous to electrum." In a word, it is not only unmistakably physical but deals largely with methods of surface colouration and not the inward tincture postulated by the hypothesis of authentic transmutation. It is needless therefore to say that there is no seal of spiritual things, though after citing the practical manner in which the Sons of the Doctrine proceed to the preparation of medicaments, the sub-section called *Chrysopœia* continues thus : " But those who propose preparing the cure of the soul and liberation from all suffering do not perceive that they are hindered by an enthusiasm devoid of discernment and reason." [1]   There is nothing in the context which leads up hereto, and it proceeds immediately after to discuss tinctures, things that resist fire, and so forth. A discourse addressed to Leucippus under the same mythical attribution is concerned mainly with methods of bleaching copper by means of arsenic.[2] The thesis of Synesius addressed to Dioscorus,[3] which is a commentary on pseudo-Democritus, or rather a preamble thereto, exalts that unknown personage and contains some points of importance. (1) It is explained that the pledge of silence, references to which are found throughout the Byzantine texts, though couched in unconditional terms,[4] is to be understood only as a barrier against the profane, and is not intended to hinder free communication among those who are inititated. (2) The veridic intent of Chrysopeia, on the authority of Democritus, is to discover secret things which transform matter and produce metals, including those also which resist the action of fire.[5] (3) Outside these nothing is to be called certain. (4) It is affirmed further that the transformation referred to is of metallic bodies.[6] (5) As the carpenter who makes a chair is at work upon matter and nothing else but matter, " so is it in this Art . . ., when it divides the bodies." (6) It operates on Mercury, which receives all kinds of forms, even as wood is made into tables, chairs and so forth.[7] (7) It is a question of the

---

[1] *Collections des Anciens Alchimistes Grecs, Traduction,* p. 50.

[2] *Loc. cit.,* pp. 57 *et seq.*

[3] *Ibid.,* pp. 60 *et seq.*

[4] An actual wording is quoted from Democritus as follows : " The pledge has been imposed upon us to expose nothing clearly to any one."—*Ibid.,* p. 62. It is like the stultifying form of some Masonic Obligations. But see my note *ante,* p. 73.

[5] *Ib.,* p. 64.

[6] *Ib.*

[7] *Ib.,* p. 67.

modification of forms and of this only. (8) As regards bleaching and yellowing, the one is calcination and the other a fiery regeneration; but certain substances calcine and others regenerate themselves.[1] These citations have been drawn together for the sole purpose of demonstrating the unchallengeable concern of Synesius. Moreover, he registers, always on the authority and using the words of Democritus, a method of projection which indicates, according to Berthelot, that "each metal is modified by another more precious." This is in analogy with processes in the Leyden Papyrus, and it shews that "the preparation of alloys" in this artisan's note-book "has become, by a mystical interpretation, the actual transmutation of metals."[2] The point is important for the sincerity of Byzantine Alchemy. There is, I presume, no need to add that we should be indeed unwary if we identified the Synesius of the collection with the Christian Bishop.

An extended tract on *The Sacred Art* by Olympiodorus, a philosopher of Alexandria, is included among works appertaining to the School of Democritus, but it is in the main a commentary on Zosimus. It embodies indications which, taken apart from their context, might be as valuable to a spiritual understanding of Alchemy as almost anything that has been cited—under similar circumstances—from mediaeval and even later writers. It is said, for example, (1) that Zosimus, the crown of philsophers, preaches union with the Divine and disdainful rejection of matter; (2) on the same authority, that the Art is one, like God; (3) that the body should be left to repose and the passions stilled[3]; (4) that the searcher of Art shall call the Divine Being within him; (5) that He Who is everywhere will then descend upon the suppliant; (6) that those who know themselves shall know also the only God within them, attaining Truth and Nature. It is affirmed otherwise that what is stated concerning *minera* is an allegory, for the philosophers are

---

[1] *Ib.*, p. 63.

[2] *Loc. cit.*, pp. 90, 91. Herein lies the generic distinction between Greek Alchemy and those artisans who preceded it, whose note-books also were rightly burned by Diocletian.

[3] "Rest, seated by thy hearth, acknowledging alone the one God and one Art only: do not go astray to find out another God."—*Ibid.*

concerned not with *minera* but with substance.[1] If, however, we proceed further it is to find as usual that the attainment of a spiritual mind is for its direction to things of material knowledge. The Secret of the Sacred Art, of the Regal Art, is called the King's Secret, being the command of material wealth, and this was reserved because it is unbecoming that any save monarchs and priests should be acquainted therewith.[2] There are speculations on the philosophy of the four official elements and on the question which is to be regarded as the first principle of things; but on the authority of Zosimus instruction must be sought from God, because men in no wise transmit science.[3] This notwithstanding, there are instructions on bleaching and yellowing, on different colours in the work, on the maceration of sulphurous substances, the soldering of gold, and so onward. It is said of the Philosophical Egg that it is even as a copy of the universe, but this is seemingly because the four elements abide therein.[4]

I do not see that the position of the subject offers any real difficulty. There seems no question that Berthelot is right in his root thesis that Byzantine alchemists were acquainted with processes for the colouration of base metals, and they conceived on their own part that real transmutations might be effected. Their commentators followed and multiplied the "mystical fancies". The French chemist ascribes this to ignorance of the sophisticating tricks and their consequent interpretation after another manner. It may be left at this, without implying agreement, as it signifies little how the notion arose: the latter alone is important, as the beginning of a dream which was to prevail through long centuries, accompanied by an unbroken claim on some kind of success. The problem of realisation at the beginning remained to the end, except in so far as there was transmission by word of mouth. There was hence always an appeal

---

[1] As if a reference to that which is noumenal abiding within the accidents of phenomena.

[2] *Loc. cit.*, p. 97.

[3] The explanation is that there was obviously no authentic canon of criticism to determine such a question, and the appeal was therefore to revelation. At the end of the nineteenth century we find a modern alchemist like Strindberg affirming that the basis of gold is water, against others who referred it to fire.

[4] This thesis was transmitted to the Latin alchemists and obtains practically throughout the literature.

for the help of God, always a sense of dependence on Divine Inspiration, always a hope that it would not be denied to the earnest seeker. We can imagine that it was strong at the beginning in the complete dark of things, and that those who were seeking an object in the physical order felt it needful in so doing to be lifted in the mind above material things, the better to secure their purpose. It was the mind of the age in the Easter light of Christian faith and doctrine, and so far as Alchemy is concerned we know that it continued without change or shadow of vicissitude till the records of adeptship ended on the threshold of that new age which brought in the French Revolution.

The commentary of Olympiodorus, by its place in the Greek collection, is like an undesigned preface to the works of Zosimus the Panopolite, which form an important part of the ingarnering. Moreover, there are no remains of any one Greek alchemist to compare with his in their extent. They constitute the third part of the collection. There are tracts bearing such titles as *Concerning Virtue*; on *Virtue and Interpretation*; *Divine Water*; on the *Substance of Art* and its antithesis, "the non-substance"; on the *Body of Magnesia*, the *Time of the Work*, the *Philosophical Stone* and an *Exposition of the Work in Detail*. The Panopolite is ever the divine Zosimus, a man of vision, a reciter of visions in sleep.[1] He abounds in bizarre images and insists on the symbolical language which has characterised all adepts. The Stone is encephalous, a Stone and not a stone: it is unknown and yet known by all, despised and most precious, given and not given by God. This is the uncommunicated mystery which none of the prophets has dared to divulge in speech, except to initiates alone. It is the Mithraic Mystery [2] and is said to govern matter. It is unique as to nature, and its name is also unique.[3] The soul is in the heart of the Stone.[4] But Divine Water is the Divine and Great Mystery, the object of research : it is indeed the object of research, for he who possesses this has also gold and silver. In a word, it is all in all. All comes forth therefrom and

---

[1] *Loc. cit.*, p. 117.
[2] *Ibid.*, p. 122.
[3] *Ib.*, p. 130.
[4] *Ib.*, p. 133. This is on the authority of Ostanes.

all exists thereby. The world does not know it, and contemplation with difficulty can comprehend its nature, because it is not a metal, is not moving water, and in fine is not a body.[1]

I have grouped these extracts together—a few out of many—to prove that Zosimus speaks frequently in mysterious and exalted language upon things which apart from their context might seem of spiritual application, and this only. So also Stephanus is quoted, affirming that "the end of philosophy is the dissolution of the body and the separation of soul therefrom."[2] Had it been possible for Mrs. Atwood or General E. A. Hitchcock to become acquainted with these citations there is no question that they would have served to vindicate their respective hypotheses. But the tract on the Philosophical Stone puts an end to all such dreams,[3] quoting Mary the prophetess for the work on metallic bodies ; the philosophers at large for the black, white, yellow and violet stages in the successive operations of the Stone ; Democritus on the two sulphurs and two mercuries ; while Zosimus on his own part specifies that there are two bleachings and two yellowings, two liquid compositions, a yellow and a white.[4] When the matter has been reduced to ash the work is good, but this scoria must be ground, deprived of its soluble part and washed six or seven times. As regards the Divine Water, the composition is heated and burnt thereby, fixed and made yellow, decomposed thereby and tinged. Thereby also it is said to suffer *Iosis*, to be refined and cocted.[5] When whitened by things that whiten, it makes white ; when yellowed by yellowing substances, it communicates yellow. If, on the other hand, it is made black by means of copperas and oak-gall, it will blacken silver.[6] Finally, it is said at its value, but obviously in a contradictory sense, that Divine Water is a composition of all liquids, and a name given to all.[7]

[1] *Ib.*, p. 146.
[2] *Loc. cit.*, p. 138.
[3] *Ibid.*, pp. 194 *et seq.*
[4] *Ib.*, p. 195.
[5] *Ib.*, p. 147. *Iosis* was the process of yellowing, or—as it is termed later—" colouration in gold ".
[6] *Ib.*, p. 157. This kind of tincture is said to be of no account by Zosimus, though he also terms it fixed.
[7] *Loc. cit.*, p. 181.

Having counterchecked in this manner the previous citations, it may be added in further elucidation of Zosimus and his obvious concern, (1) that on the authority of Democritus the Substance of the Art is lead, which is recognised by the Egyptians as producing iron, tin and copper[1]; (2) that Magnesia signifies all things fabricated with the true measure of maceration necessary; (3) that the Body of Magnesia is "the secret thing which comes from lead"[2]; (4) that there are two arts, those of tinctures and of ores, and they have been confided to guardians for their subsistence; but the latter do not fabricate for themselves, as their activities are for the service of Kings[3]; and lastly (5) that among the special revelations which God vouchsafed to Zosimus is the secret concerning copper, namely, that it is first burnt with sulphur.[4] Descriptions of apparatus and furnaces fill many pages[5]; there are enumerations of substances used in the Art, especially for the white and yellow tinctures, and in the refinement and bleaching of copper.[6]

The last statement which demands a word of notice shall be given almost in full because of its very curious suggestion and that which follows thereon. It is said that "there are two sciences and two wisdoms—one of the Egyptians and one of the Hebrews, the latter being rendered more solid by Divine Justice. Science and wisdom at their best rule over lower sciences and inferior wisdoms: they come down from remote ages. Their generation . . . seeks nothing from material and corruptible bodies: it operates, apart from foreign intervention, sustained by prayer and grace. The symbol of chemistry is drawn from creation (in the eyes of its adepts[7]) who save and purify the divine soul enchained by the elements, and who separate above all the divine spirit confounded with the flesh. Even as there exists a sun, the flower of fire, a celestial sun, the right eye

---

[1] *Ibid.*, p. 167.

[2] *Ib.*, p. 190, on the authority of Mary.

[3] *Ib.*, p. 231.

[4] *Ib.*, p. 150.

[5] *Ib.*, pp. 216–231.

[6] *Ib.*, pp. 159–163.

[7] It is to be understood that these words, placed within brackets, are a conjectural addition to make sense in the translation; but there is no justification in the Byzantine Collection for affirming that the adepts of *Chemia* were concerned with liberating the spirit of man from flesh and the bondage of elements.

of the world, so copper, if it become flower (that is to say, if it takes the colour of gold) by purification, is made a terrestrial sun, which is king on earth as the sun is king in heaven.[1] The text proceeds to speak of perfect tinctures which communicate the colour of silver ; concerning alloys of gold and silver ; of copper and its bleaching, the fabrication of gold and the blending of metals. There is a preamble on " the measure of Mercury ", which is a method for the conquest of poverty by operators who can surmount obstacles, presumably those of the text. At the most therefore it follows that there is a science of the soul, which is apparently the science of Christ, and it is in broad analogy with so-called Egyptian *Chemia*, which is concerned with the purification of copper till it assumes the colour of gold.

It is to be supposed that this other and higher science is again under consideration in a *Final Summary*,[2] which distinguishes between right Tinctures and certain others obtained by " the supernatural way ", devices apparently of pagan priests, that they might continue to live on sacrificial offerings. Their promises are described as mendacious. The thesis is addressed to a woman disciple, Theosebeia, and in terms borrowed from Olympiodorus she is directed to seek God in the stillness of all passions, invoking the Divine Being Who is at once everywhere and nowhere, making sacrifices like those prescribed by Solomon, King of Jerusalem. Appropriate, authentic and natural Tinctures will be obtained in this manner, presumably those which have been described in a previous paragraph as resulting from the combination of pure " tinctorial species ", a catalogue of which is cited from Democritus and includes Attic ochre, native sulphur, Phrygian stone, cinnabar and several others. When apparently, as the result of her devotions, she has obtained perfection of soul the disciple is to fear henceforward the " natural elements of matter " : she is to seek the Shepherd and immersing herself in meditation " reascend thus to her source ". After this manner does Zosimus, like the prophets of American " new thought ", enable his follower to make the best of both worlds. But

---

[1] *Op. cit.*, pp. 206, 207. The title of the section is *True Book of Sophe the Egyptian* and *of the Divine Master of the Hebrews and of the Powers Sabaoth.*
[2] *Loc. cit.*, pp. 231-237.

G

he himself affirms his intention of returning to the question
of Tinctures, resulting from the decomposition of products,
and he proceeds to say that they are fabricated in small
furnaces, using glass vessels.

The writers who follow Zosimus in the fourth part of
the collection are termed the old authors, beginning with
Pelagus on the *Divine and Sacred Art*.[1] As the discourse
cites Zosimus it will be understood that its antiquity is in
relation to later authorities who are not specified ; but a
note of Berthelot says that it contains more recent additions
and glosses. I shall have dealt with it sufficiently for my
purpose by stating that it depends from an axiom referred
to the far past and according to which " copper does not
tinge but is itself tinctured, and when it has been so tinged it
tinctures ". Ostanes, described as the philosopher, writing
on the same subject,[2] furnishes the quantities and names
the materials which enter into the composition of the all-
important Divine Water ; this is said to raise the dead and
destroy the living, to enlighten dark things and obscure
those which are luminous. A few drops will impart the
aspect of gold to lead, but postulating concurrence on the
part of God, Invisible and Almighty. Of the Archpriest
John, who follows, still on the same subject, or at least
under the same title,[3] it shall be sufficient to cite a single
dictum, which affirms that " he who produces gold, produces
Ios, and he who produces not Ios produces nothing ".

It will be understood that an adept under the denomination
of Agathodaimon would naturally address Osiris and offer
him a commentary on the oracle of Apollo ; but when a
hope is added that the god will interpret intelligently, and
when he is required to quit some unspecified town of folly
and proceed to Memphis, we must conclude that a mundane
personality has adopted the divine name.[4] It appears that
Apollo or his oracle is making proclamation on the mysteries
of silvering and gilding, the methods of which are delineated
and are rendered at least tentatively and partially intelligible
by acute conjectural annotations of M. Berthelot. An
anonymous article affirms that the species, otherwise matter

---

[1] *Loc. cit.*, pp. 243–250.   [2] *Ibid.*, pp. 250–252.
[3] *Ib.*, pp. 252–256.   [4] *Ib.*, pp. 257–261.

of the work, is composite and not simple,[1] because things natural and also things artificial contribute their quota towards the completion of the whole. Gold is said to be produced by the operation of Iosis or yellowing. We may pass over some technical recipes which stand by themselves in the text : on the fabrication of " the all " which is performed in apparatuses for digestion ; on calx and its treatment.[2] There are processes under the name of Iamblichus for the fabrication and duplication of gold.[3] There is also the tract of Comarius, described as High Priest, instructing Cleopatra on " the Divine and Sacred Art of the Philosophical Stone," otherwise " mystical philosophy " and " mystic science ", couched sometimes in terms suggestive of spiritual intimations. But the work is accomplished by separating the fixed from the volatile ; by maceration ; by decomposition of species, which are burnt in an " Ascalon jar " ; by the process of yellowing ; and in fine by fusion, which advances the yellowed substances to " colouration in gold ".[4]

A chemical tract which, by an unusual perversity of attribution, is referred to Moses [5] contains nothing but processes, as for example, on mercury, arsenic, pyrites, sulphur, sandarac and so forth ; while, its allegorical title notwithstanding, another on *The Eight Tombs* [6] is a complicated method of calcination ; and it is followed by a final prescription for bleaching copper.[7] Here ends the fourth part, and the fifth comprises technical treatises—already characterised—on the goldsmith's work, the work of the four elements, the metallurgy of gold, the tincture of copper, the colouring of precious stones, etc.[8] There is finally a sixth part, which contains a selection from commentators belonging to various dates. The Christian Philosopher [9] is probably of the sixth century or even a little earlier ; the Anonymous Philosopher [10] is later ; the monk Cosmas [11] is very much later still ; the so-called Hierotheus [12] may belong to the ninth century and is in any case to be distinguished utterly from the master of pseudo-Dionysius, who is called

---

[1] *Loc. cit.*, pp. 261–264.   [2] *Ibid.*, pp. 264–273.   [3] *Ib.*, pp. 274–278.
[4] See *ante*, p. 79. The suggestion is seemingly that what had been tinctured previously on the surface was now tinctured within.   [5] *Loc. cit.*, pp. 287–302.
[6] *Ibid.*, pp. 302–304.   [7] *Ib.*, pp. 304–305.   [8] *Ib.,*, pp. 307–375.
[9] *Ib.*, pp. 382–403.   [10] *Ib.*, pp. 403–415.   [11] *Ib.*, pp. 416–419.
[12] *Ib.*, pp. 422–423.

the Areopagite ; Nicephoros[1] has been identified with a personage of the thirteenth century.

The Christian Philosopher is represented by studies on the *Constitution of Gold*, on *Divine Water*—this in detached articles, under several headings—on the *Division of the Matter*, the *Varieties of Fabrication*, and on *Secret Writings of the Ancients*. The Anonymous Philosopher has tracts on the modes of maceration—under the title of *Divine Water of the Bleaching*—on the *Practice of Chrysopœia* and on *Music and Chemistry*. The monk Cosmas is represented by a single article, which is called the *Science of Chrysopeia* ; Hierotheos by a very brief disquisition on the *Sacred Art* ; and Nicephoros by a few pages on the *Chrysopeia of the Egg*. Among all these writers the references to matters of religion or intimations of a spiritual kind are few and far between. Of Nicephoros it is said that he attained the end with the concurrence of Christ, " Who leads all things from non-being into being ". Hierotheos affirms that the gift is received from God, and that he who so obtains it becomes an executive agent of Emmanuel, because he allocates a tithe of that which the Art brings him to the building of churches and relief of the poor.[2] The Anonymous Philosopher says in his sub-title that the practice of *Chrysopeia* is developed by the aid of God, and this is his sole allusion, though it might be thought that the fantastic analogy instituted between music and chemistry would have given him an opportunity for what Berthelot calls " mystical fancies ". We come therefore to the Christian Philosopher, for whom Alchemy is a Divine Science. No explanation is offered, but it has been said in a previous discourse that appeal must be made to God with a pure conscience, according to a pure mode and practice. The counsel illogically enough arises from questions appertaining to arbitrary difficulties which encompass the Art and its records.

---

[1] *Ib.*, pp. 423–429.

[2] The importance of this intimation cannot be exaggerated, for it has a bearing on our whole subject and should be taken in connection with the testimony borne by Zosimus, according to whom—as we have seen—Alchemy was a Royal Art, since its secret of material wealth must and was to be reserved for the advantage of kings and priests. This was the mundane side of the subject : on the other it was *Donum Dei*, in the sense, according to Hierotheos, that it was communicated by revelation to some who would devote part of the proceeds to the glory of God and works of charity.

There remains to be said in conclusion that it is an essential part and more than the main intent of Berthelot's expert study to trace certain typical phrases and—as we have seen —certain fraudulent tingeing processes from their source in the Leyden Papyrus through the records of Byzantine alchemists and even to later texts. The recurrence of the phrases at least in Latin and French records is more frequent than his knowledge of the literature enabled him to realise. If a catch utterance like " Nature rejoices in Nature " occurs in the notes on processes of a Theban artisan it may seem very significant on the surface to find it in—shall I say on a chance ?—Arnoldus de Villanova or Raymund Lully, but in reality it is a fact without consequence. It does not mean that mediæval adepts were familiar with the Theban Papyrus and their writings concerned like that with common alloys and gilding. The explanation is that they borrowed from people like the Latin Geber, the Latin Rhasis, and so forth, who borrowed in turn from Byzantine writers ; but this was at second hand only, through Syriac sources. And as regards processes, according to Berthelot's own shewing the Greek Alchemists proper were on the quest of real trans-mutations, not of goldsmith's tricks. Such is his theme, however, and on the other hand it is my own design (1) to trace —if possible—spiritual doctrine, intimations and counsels from the earliest Byzantine sources, through successive texts of the literature, and estimate them at their proper value ; (2) to ascertain whether any texts call to be regarded as of mystical intent and that only, apart from physics ; (3) to determine in this case whether their number and importance are such as to suggest the presence through centuries—or through a certain definite period—of a secret and hidden school which used the language and emblems of one subject to veil the purpose of another. We may find that the texts do not decode easily and that we cannot dogmatise as to their message and its consequence ; we may find that the texts are few ; and finally it is more than possible that, notwithstanding the assured depositions of writers like Mrs. Atwood and E. A. Hitchcock, notwith-standing what must be termed the revelations of Böhme and Fludd as to the true understanding of the Art, an examina-tion of the *Corpus Hermeticum* will exhibit that there are no texts which are to be understood solely and only in a spiritual and high mystical sense, that the symbolical language of physical Alchemy was never transferred to veil a science of the soul. This at least is the one conclusion imposed upon us by the study, here completed, of the Greek alchemists, but of course so far only as their records are concerned.

CHAPTER VII

ARABIAN AND SYRIAC ALCHEMY

WE have now ascertained with all necessary fullness that which was Alchemy at its first beginning in the West, amidst the expanding light of the early Christian centuries. It was not a spiritual experiment and much less an attainment of the soul in God, illustrated by symbolism and veiled by a strange language : it was not on any quest of the spirit, and there is not one single word which betokens its connection with any form of Instituted Mysteries. Its highest aspiration was to accomplish such a tingeing of metallic substances that they would become penetrated with the essential principle of gold and not merely coloured on the surface, as in the processes which had been inherited from the practical metallurgists of Egypt, Greece and Rome. The Byzantine alchemists may or may not have understood these artifices in the plenary trade sense ; but in either case it is certain that as to the higher and imagined Art they had no key of procedure. In dream and in thought therefore they looked upon it as a possible gift of God, remembering the inspired teaching that *omne datum optimum et omne donum perfectum, desursum est*.[1] Hence their invocations of the Holy Trinity, their allusions to the saving work of Christ and their occasional counsels of perfection as practical aids in the work which they desired to perform. The next point in our inquiry takes us, still under the auspices of Berthelot, to a very different collection of texts, being those of the early Syriac and early Arabian alchemists. As the French chemist collaborated with a textual scholar for the production of the Byzantine collection, so in these later undertakings he had the assistance of Rubens Duval and of O. Houdas. The Byzantine tradition of Alchemy came down, as it has been seen, to the Latin writers of the middle ages through the mediation of Arabian successors; but Arabia, according to Berthelot, was not the sole channel. " Latin

---

[1] *Epistola Catholica Beati Jacobi Apostoli, cap.* I, 17.

Alchemy has other foundations even more direct, though till now unappreciated. . . . The processes and even the notions of ancient alchemists passed from Greeks to Latins before the time of the Roman Empire and, up to a certain point, were preserved through the barbarism of the first mediæval centuries by means of technical traditions of the arts and crafts." The keepers and transmitters of this old tradition were glass-makers, metallurgists, potters, dyers, painters, jewellers and goldsmiths, from the days of the Empire to and throughout the Carlovingian period, and so forward. The evidences are found in various old technical Latin treatises, such as *Compositiones ad Tingenda, Mappæ Clavicula, De Artibus Romanorum, Schedula Diversarum Artium, Liber Diversarum Artium*, and some others. It is to be noted, however, that these are anything but alchemical treatises in the sense of pseudo-Democritus and Zosimus, or any other sense ; they connect with the Theban Papyrus rather than with the Byzantine Collection : in a word, they were the craft-manuals of their period. Some of them deal largely in the falsification of precious metals. It will be seen that the distinction is valuable : on the one hand, mediæval craftsmen in metals derived from Greeks through Latins, while mediæval alchemists proper derived through Arabia from the Byzantine fountain-head. Arabia, however, did not mediate directly, for it was indebted on its own part to Syriac alchemists : it was these only who drew at first hand from the source in Greek.

The Syriac records comprise ten books translated from pseudo-Democritus and another treatise of later date but belonging to the same school, the text being accompanied by rude figures of vessels used in the processes. As regards the ten, they are devoted to practical recipes and include copious extracts of the same kind from Zosimus, together with a few semi-mystical and magical fragments, in a condition too mutilated for serious criticism. There is, moreover, an Arabic treatise written in Syriac characters and forming a connecting link with Arabian Alchemy. It is an ill-digested compilation from a variety of sources and is also essentially practical—in the sense of Berthelot. In other words, the " mystical fancies " of the French chemist are met with few and far between, while there is nothing whatever which

answers to that spiritual atmosphere of the later literature
which has begotten ethical and mystical hypotheses to
explain its concealed purpose.

The Arabic treatises include the *Book of Crates, Book of
El-Habib, Book of Ostanes* and the works of the true Geber;
for it happens that those which have been attributed for
so many centuries to the last named philosopher, which
have been quoted by western alchemists throughout as
of highest authority, with no appeal therefrom, are regarded
by Berthelot as ascribed falsely. It remained for him, as he
thought, in the late nineteenth century to present the original
and only Geber for the first time in an European tongue.
Now, the chief Arabic treatises are in marked contrast to
those of the Syriac cycle: they are prolix, while these are
terse; they are grandiose, these are simple; they are
romantic and visionary, these are unadorned recipes. The
Book of El-Habib is to some extent an exception, but the
Arabian Geber is more cryptic by far than his supposed
Latin namesake. El-Habib quotes largely from Greek
sources, Geber on occasion only, his chief references being
to other tracts of his own. It is significant that in his case
M. Berthelot offers no annotations to explain, tentatively
or otherwise, the chemical meaning of the texts. As a fact,
the Arabian Djarber, otherwise Geber, might be thought to
offer a tolerable point of departure for any spiritual hypothesis,
supposing one to be really tenable in the case of Latin
adepts. We shall find, however, in the sequel that problems
emerging from a literature which developed through long
centuries are not to be resolved in this manner, and that
salient spiritual aspects are found towards the end of things
rather than in their early stages.

Now, we know after what manner the real and imputed
science of Araby the Blessed passed into Europe, and we
can understand that Spain—under Moslem domination—
was destined to be a meeting-point for Alchemy, as for so
much else that came from the East westward. It was in
Arabian schools of the prophet that the Sheik Abou Moussa
Djaber ben Hayyân Es-Soufy, like Rhasis, Morien and other
later successors of so-called Hermetic Tradition, became
known to zealous students, who believed that there was a
Mystery of Nature concerning the transmutation of metals

and that it was not beyond attainment primarily by Divine help but also thereunder by the guidance of a master and by familiarity with the findings of past research. Not in Spain of necessity but because of that fountain-source—which overflowed, moreover, into the South of France—the books of adepts like these assumed a Latin vesture, in which it happened that they were transformed rather than rendered. We can understand further how it might come about that the most literal of all texts and the most physical side of the concern would increase rather than diminish the occasional religious vestiges which we have found to characterise Olympiodorus and Zosimus the Panopolite, with the feigned Cleopatra, Queen of Egypt, with most of the artists and all the Art of Chrysopœia, when it flourished at Byzantium several centuries previously.

Having summarised the general position in this manner, we may look a little more closely at the texts themselves, remembering once more that Berthelot's allusions to mystical elements are not concerned with Divine Invocations, religious counsels or postulated qualifications for the work in detachment from things of earth, and are much less significant of spiritual intent. When a Greek, Arabian or Syriac writer produces a recipe for the surface aureation of copper, that is a practical process, a thing belonging to " science " ; when he is at large among notions concerning veridic transmutations, an elixir of life and the quintessence, he is then among mystic dreams. Hereof is Mysticism as it was understood among French scientists in the last decades of the nineteenth century.

The Syriac text begins in the name of the Lord Almighty and imposes spiritual and physical purity as well as a vow of goodwill. These assumed, it is possible to proceed with the work and attain an end therein. The preliminaries being finished,[1] that which follows is the doctrine of the philosopher Democritus, and firstly on the preparation of gold, beginning by an instruction to fix Mercury in one or other of several ways enumerated, for example, with the body of Magnesia, alum or arsenic. The next book is concerned with the Philosophical Stone, about which it is premised as usual that

---

[1] The preliminaries comprise (1) a list of substances and terms, with the signs belonging to these ; (2) the seven kinds of earth ; (3) the twelve varieties of stones, extended to fifteen by later additions ; (4) the nineteen tinctorial Stones, including those of Magnesia and Mercury.

it is no stone and is worthless but very precious.[1] However,
it fades out of view and is replaced by a chaos of processes
for the purification of Mercury, gilding iron, etc. The preparation of sulphur, preparation of vinegar and so forth,
lead up in the third division to a practice of blending colours
and a method of gilding lead, so that it cannot be distinguished
after due treatment. A fourth section opens with the " rule
of silver " and includes the preparation of Magnesia among
other processes ; but there is an account also of the grand
dissolution, beyond which there is nothing, " and so is the
Concealed Mystery in fine revealed." [2] The Elixir of Eggs is
a main subject of the fifth series,[3] but we learn also of an
Elixir which converts silver into gold. Elixir of Diplosis,
Elixir of Magnesia, Elixir of Arsenic and many others are
comprised by the sixth division, after which there is an
Appendix entitled *Sayings* of Democritus ; but they are
processes and more processes. The seventh book or division
belongs to the work of silver, but this is by the hypothesis
of its title, for it is yet another medley, as if *de omnibus
rebus*. The eighth is on the work of gold [4] and the ninth on
Mercury, which again is about many things, including
a certain " secret power ", that is, a composite substance,
the constituents of which are enumerated at some length.
Thereafter follows a direction to add those things that
are wanting and then set to work. It is in the ninth book
that Berthelot perceives indications of mystical doctrines
for the first time—by example, on the Quintessential Mercury
of Philosophers. There is a tenth book, termed *Preparations*,
which is thought to be later than the others and external to
the Doctrine of Democritus. It contains thirty-three processes,
plus one Appendix on the treatment and fusion of lead, the
purification of copper, etc.

[1] I am citing really an appendix which follows Book II, the latter dealing
with Tinctures which produce silver : Sandarac, Saffron, Arsenic and White
Magnesia are specified.

[2] It is to be understood throughout the present summary that Berthelot
provides references to the Byzantine texts wherever possible, as these are the
Syriac sources.

[3] This is a process for gilding coins, and the operator is instructed to take
fifty chicken or goose eggs, the yolks of which are to be mixed with saffron, white
vinegar, orpiment and celandine. These ingredients are to be understood apparently
in a literal sense. Other Elixirs of Eggs will be found in Book VI.

[4] Dragon's Blood is one of the substances which enter into the gilding of lead,
while copperas assists the conversion of silver into gold, apparently more than a
simple surface colouration—by the hypothesis, of course.

The collection is completed by that Syriac treatise described already as written in Arabic characters and belonging also to a later period : it may be summarised briefly, following an editorial division into sections, though it is not found in the original (1) Processes for the fusion of lead, the preparation of gold ink, the sublimation of mercury and so forth. (2) A tract on natural and artificial vitriols, alums and the kinds of salts. (3) A description of various utensils. (4) A miscellany on the aureation of silver, on glass, cinnabar, etc., and on spontaneous generation.[1] (5) A treatise on the nomenclature of metals, on sal ammoniac, sulphur, the seven species of stones and on substances used in the fabrication of gold and silver. (6) Procedure in the liquefaction of pearls, the operation continuing for twenty days, but the purpose—which does not emerge—was presumably other than that of Cleopatra ; procedure also in the liquefaction of seed pearls for the production of a single large one. (7) Further formularies for the aureation of silver, with notes on the calcination of copper and distillation of marcasite, etc. (8) Notes on various calcinations and a complicated method of changing tin into silver. (9) A chapter on the fabrication of gold, specified as the chief and best of all chapters : it is once again a process on silver, but silver itself is obtained by projecting the Elixir on copper. (10) A chapter on perfect silver, on the fixation of mercury and various other processes. (11) Memoranda on the purification of tin, the whitening of copper and so forth. (12) More on the aureation of silver and surface colouration by varnishing. (13) On the art of the glass-founder. (14) On fuses and Greek fire. (15) Experiments with mercury in combination with antimony, lead, sal ammoniac and other substances.

The purpose of this arid tabulation is to present a bird's-eye view and so determine broadly the horizon covered by Syriac Alchemy. It remains to say that the translations so far dealt with have been based on two MSS. in the British Museum. There is, however, a third at Cambridge, of which

---

[1] The thesis is that a vegetable can become an animal and that one animal can produce another of a different kind, examples being given, but they are fabulous stories of matter in putrefaction. Decayed human hair generates a living serpent, beef produces bees, the raven gives birth to flies, and the basilisk to poisonous scorpions.

analyses and extracts are given by M. Rubens Duval, and they are annotated by Berthelot.   The sources are in Zosimus, Democritus and other Greek writers, the places in which the texts correspond to those of the British Museum being duly noted.   Under the general denomination of " other writers " are included certain fragments specified as mystical by the editors, and distinguished from alchemical remains—actual or imputed.   Among their many subjects of allusion may be mentioned (1) the unicorn found in India, (2) the Book of Hippocrates concerning the Stone which is not a stone, (3) the perverse testimony of Homer on the subject of Divine Art,[1] (4) the Synod of gold and silver, (5) a Magical Conjuration, (6) Thrice-Great Hermes as the beginning and end of the Art. Of such is Mystical Alchemy in the mind of French chemical science and oriental scholarship.   But those who understand it otherwise will conclude that Syriac Alchemy represents the transition from surface colouration in practice to hypothetical tincture within ; that it is like that of Byzantium, from which it derived; while as regards mystical elements it is a contradiction of their hypothesis *in toto*.   Thus passes the second epoch of the literature into what may be termed figuratively the limbus of the first.

The texts of Arabian Alchemy have been enumerated already, so far as titles are concerned, and the question remaining is that of their content within the limits of our purpose, as exhibited by the works themselves and not in the summaries of Berthelot, though they are excellent from another standpoint.   The *Book of Crates*, according to its own story, was discovered at Alexandria in a Temple of Serapis and was called the *Treasure of Treasures*, a literal and descriptive denomination, because nothing so clear had ever been penned previously, while nothing comparable thereto will pass into writing subsequently.   The Stone is not a stone, nor is it of the nature of stone, being engendered annually on the summits of all mountains, amidst the sand and rocks. The alchemical work has been called Magnesia, Electrum,

---

[1] The subject of this extraordinary fragment is the Greek poet and not an alchemist masquerading under his name. The charges are, among others, (1) that Homer concealed the Divine Gift under the words " Son of Peleus " and (2) that by " the wrath " of the Son of Peleus he is really meaning "the divinity ". It is suggested by Berthelot that the fragment is connected with the struggle of Christians against Hellenism, complicated by the hostility of physicians towards men of letters.

Water of Iron or of Sulphur and Divine Water; but there are other titles beyond number, according to the will of philosophers. The one and only Matter which they have refused to designate by a particular name is here denominated Lead, obviously in a figurative sense, and it becomes Water. In reality it is *Molybdochalcum*, understood as a tincturing agent which comprises the whole practice and is that also which is termed Elixir, wherein is all secret virtue. As such, it is spirit and not body, for spirit alone tinges and in so doing does not increase the weight of the substance tinged. It is symbolised otherwise by Crates as a symbolical animal which from a worm becomes a serpent and from a serpent a dragon, the destruction of which is termed the Secret of Hermes.

Such being the intimations on the First Matter, we may pass now to the process, and of this there are several versions: more correctly perhaps several operations are delineated. It is affirmed that all of them can be reduced to one, being that which " retains Sulphur and reddens ". The mode of procedure, however, is not indicated. Another direction is to operate on the composition by applying degrees of fire analogous to the heat of the four seasons, from winter to autumn. But that which apparently appertains to the whole subject is delivered as follows: " Take the required weight of ores; combine them with Mercury [1] and operate till the product becomes an igneous poison "[2]: you will then have that which is called *Molybdochalcum*.[3] When the bodies shall have been burned and are fixed, the product is denominated Incombustible Sulphur.[4] It will bring forth pure gold [5] and will tinge silver into gold. But this silver is not of the vulgar kind: it is silver " combined " philosophically. When the rest of the poison is added, it will tincture gold: again, however, this is no common metal but a combination which " tinges red and is called gold." The terms of the statement are stultifying: we have been

---

[1] La Chimie au Moyen Age, Tome III, p. 54.

[2] Compare my note *ante* on *Ios*, p. 79. Berthelot identifies it with the " igneous preparation " of Mary the Prophetess and with the Medicine of mediæval Latin alchemists, saying that " it was the tinctorial agent *par excellence*."

[3] An alloy of copper and lead.

[4] Otherwise, dry Sulphur.

[5] That is, " the combination which dyes red and which we call gold."—*Loc. cit.*, p. 55.

told of something which tinges and of something tinged thereby, namely, gold, but the qualification affirms subsequently that the so-called gold is itself a tingeing agent. The presumable intention, however, is to claim that when the figurative metal has been tinctured it tinges on its own part, producing either gold or something that will pass as such.

I have given this account at length (1) as a specimen of Alchemy according to a particular theory and practice of the work ; (2) to make it evident that Crates and his *Treasure of Treasures* are concerned with metallic transmutation and nothing else ; (3) on account of a very curious distinction with which the text opens. There are those, it is said, who dream of nothing but this world and its joys, while others are dedicated to virtue, wisdom, peace and goodness. The godly are capable of knowing the soul completely and that also which can improve it. Moreover, they are " qualified to recognise that the names which have been given to the latter by philosophers are not true names." As the text proceeds almost at once to enumerate various denominations by which the First Matter is symbolised it seems inevitable that this universal substance betters the soul of man. But it happens that Crates returns presently to his two categories of human beings and explains that devotion to wisdom signifies search after science, or that which is taught by natural laws, the interrelation of these, their advantages and hindrances. " He who belongs to this category is eager to acquire books and study them," as also to diffuse the knowledge contained therein. " When he finds something clear and precise, he offers thanks to God ; but if brought up against an obscure point he uses every effort to ascertain its exact meaning, so that he may reach his proposed end and proceed accordingly." It follows that he is a person disposed to natural philosophy, who is ambitious to graduate therein, and on the hypothesis that the First Matter of Alchemy is a fact and not a dream he is obviously one who may get to know concerning it. Obviously also such knowledge will improve his mind and the mind, so ameliorated, may improve the soul.

The *Book of El-Habib* has also its two categories of men, being those who attain the end and those who miss it.

According to a Mohammedan transcriber—who adds a note at the end—he has copied as best he could a manuscript in a bad state and otherwise full of errors. The question does not signify except from a textual standpoint, as the work of El-Habib does not compare with Crates, being one of citations instead of an original and highly individual thesis, even while permeated with the spirit of Greek Alchemy. El-Habib opens by affirming that all creation is constituted of agent and patient, otherwise male and female. In the Philosophical Work a mortar, boiler, flagon, receiver and crucible have been specified among the required vessels ; but it is accomplished in the last only. The point is important because Mrs. Atwood has postulated a Great Mystery attaching to the vessel,[1] as if it were a typical *Secretum Artis* : she terms it indeed a Divine Secret, apart from which " no one can attain to the Magistery ". Having ruled unawares on this question, the Arabian proceeds to the Tincture itself and says that it is a brilliant liquid of beautiful colour and comparable in its nature to a soul which animates a body ", meaning presumably in projection on the matter of the work. Sulphur is the part of fire, Cinnabar the part of air, Magnesia that of earth and Mercury the part of water. The Tincture, moreover, is that which is called Divine Water, the soul that moves all things capable of development, the principle—for example—of growth in plants. These four natures must be so combined and interblended that they shall form a single substance, the earth transforming into water, water into air and air into fire. " So is the Work accomplished, God willing," as a marriage of male and female, moist and dry, hot and cold : it is like the gestation of a child in the womb. The operator must remember always that no body can be fixed except by fire, and that in Alchemy this fire must be moderate and equal. I do not propose to present the process at length and indeed it would be almost impossible, the intimations of El-Habib being complicated by incessant extracts from Zosimus, Mary the Prophetess, Plato, Pythagoras and a score of mythical adepts, while—so far as I can judge—they do not seem to be given in an ordered sequence answering to the stages of the work.[2] They

[1] *Suggestive Inquiry,* 1920, p. 146.

[2] El-Habib is valuable for purposes of comparison between his long quotations from Mary and the Latin tract which passes under her name.

are thrown scattermeal together and the tract ends suddenly
with an affirmation of Zosimus that Salt, Vitriol and Ochre
are constituents of all substances.   The Secret of philosophers is said to be contained in a direction of the Panopolite
to combine moist with dry continually and maintain coction
until the composite becomes a Tingeing Spirit.

The Book of Ostanes the Wise on the Science of the Illustrious
Stone was originally in twelve chapters, but there are two
extracts only extant in a Paris manuscript, the first being
drawn from a work entitled *Kitab-al-Fihirst* by Ibn Khaldoun.
It is concerned with the qualities of the Stone, described as
the object of aspiration among the ancients, who have
defended its secret at the sword's point and concealed its
true name under the veil of enigmas.   Their work has been
performed so well that the secret has been known only to
those whose understanding is opened by God.   There is
nothing so hostile to fire, for it must be understood that it
is a black water, a white water and a red water, while it
answers also to other contradictory designations.   It is
found on earth and in the sea, in houses, shops, bazaars,
in mosques and baths, in cities and by the wayside.   It is a
Stone hidden in a stone, and one of the adepts has testified
that he has seen it, morning and evening, for forty years, so
that it has seemed unlikely to escape observation by all and
any.   In the second extract—which is fairly complete in
itself—Ostanes relates how the desire of the Great Work had
so possessed him that he could neither eat nor sleep : but he
was at length rewarded by a vision which opened his eyes.
A stranger appeared and led him to seven doors of wisdom,
the keys of which were in the keeping of a monster with a
vulture's wings, the head of an elephant and a dragon's tail.
It is said that the different parts of this incredible beast
devoured one another, but when called upon in the Name of
God Almighty the Keys were delivered and Ostanes opened
the doors, behind the last of which he came upon a dazzling
plate, having inscriptions in seven languages.   Four of these
were defaced, but he was able to read those in Egyptian,
Persian and Indian.   The first compared the body to a
lamp, the soul to an oil therein and the spirit to its wick.
This allegory is said to be important in the hidden science,
apparently because the wick of a lamp can give no light unless

H

there is oil within. A certain combination of fire and water will not only prevent their mutual destruction but will cause both to give forth greater radiance. These were the primitive elements at the beginning of things, and from their pairing resulted the animal, vegetable and mineral kingdoms. A process analogous hereto is followed in the secret science. The Persian inscription affirmed that the Work can only be performed by help extended from Persia, while the Indian claimed a superior intelligence for Hindus, though they could not accomplish the whole Mystery without Persian help. Having read the inscriptions, Ostanes was warned to come forth as the doors were about to close, and he encountered an aged man, who assured him that all knowledge was now in his hands, while the monster cried with a loud voice that the complete science was impossible apart from him. Thereupon the old man instructed Ostanes to find this animal—apparently in his waking state—give it an intelligence in place of his own intelligence—meaning that of Ostanes—a vital spirit in place of his, and a life in like manner. The beast would then become subject to him and insure him all that he needed. While he puzzled over this dark counsel, it was added : " Take a body like your own ; remove from it what I have said and then restore it." The tract affirms that this was done by the alchemist ; but his procedure is not imparted.

The voice of tradition ascribes five hundred treatises to the Arabian Geber and even so it is but half the output that is credited to Lully in mythical enumerations of the past. It happens, however, that six only were extant within the knowledge of scholarship at the period of Berthelot's publication, since when—as we shall see in the next chapter— there is something to add, and that of an unexpected kind, in connection with Latin texts under the same attribution. I will begin by enumerating those translated by Professor Houdas and edited by Berthelot, namely, (1) *The Book of Royalty*, (2) *The Little Book of Clemency*, (3) *The Book of Balances*, (4) *The Book of Mercy*, (5) *The Book of Concentration*, (6) *The Book of Eastern and Western Mercury, which is also concerning the Fire and Earth of the Stone*, being a work in four parts, loosely linked together. It has been possible to summarise the content of other Arabian texts, but those of Geber baffle all analysis : the brave attempt in Berthelot's Table of Contents indicates subject-matters but can give no impression of their connection, of what is being said about them, or why that and this are included.   It is evident also that the illustrious French chemist was in the dark on the drift of the tracts, for—as I have said—he does not annotate, except when it is possible, for example, to shew a source in Greek Alchemy.   Geber, moreover, is discoursing continually on things so remote from his business that—as also indicated—unwary persons might be tempted to regard the transmutation of metals as only incidentally in his mind.   Under these circumstances I must be content to offer a brief general review of his contribution to the alchemical subject, it being understood that what remains over is expatiation on, e.g., the logic of Aristotle, the views of Socrates on the seat of intelligence in the human body, the influence of stars on names, essence and accident, conditions of existence and so forth. It may be added that of all alchemists, early or late, he is perhaps the least tinctured by consciousness of spiritual things.

The Matter of the Work is the Elixir of all elixirs, the Ferment of all ferments ; [1] but it is termed also a subtle, nimble, spiritual and physical poison, presumably by way of contradiction and as an analogue of the term *Iosis*.[2]   It is specified as Elixir because a small quantity is of more worth than much vulgar gold and silver.[3]   We should understand, however, that there are in reality two Elixirs, distinguished by two colours, corresponding to silver and gold respectively.[4] It is perhaps in this sense that there are said to be two Stones which constitute the bases of the work,[5] each of them being composed of two things, namely, earth and water, the one being an Animal and the other a Mineral Stone ; [6] but I do not find that this last distinction is justified anywhere in the texts.[7]   The constituent forces of the Elixir are harmonised and united, so that they overcome divided substances,

---

[1] *Book of Royalty* : see *La Chimie au Moyen Âge*, Tome III, p. 129.
[2] *Book of Mercy* : *Ibid.*, p. 174.
[3] *Ibid.*, p. 181.
[4] *Book of Clemency* : *Ibid.*, p. 137, *Book of Mercy*, pp. 180, 181.
[5] *Book of Balances* : *Ibid.*, p. 161.
[6] *Ibid.*, p. 162.
[7] The meaning is that nothing follows therefrom : there are two kinds of Animal Stone and they must be joined to the Mineral, whence it follows that there is only one in the end.

compelling them to assume its own nature and relinquish that which was theirs.[1] If the Elixir is red it will convert its object into gold, while the white changes into silver.[2] It follows that the Art of Djaber is metallic transmutation, like that of his precursors in Greece and Syria, though he affirms in one of his operations that it is performed without distillation, purification, dissolution or coagulation ;[3] that even the word operation is in a certain sense evasive, a concession to the general and vulgar mode ;[4] and that no importance should be attached to the old statement which testifies that the world would be corrupted if the work were divulged, because gold would be fabricated then as glass is now made in the bazaars.[5]

All this notwithstanding, the fundamental principle of the Stone is the thorough purification of its elements, including their liberation from those oils by which they are corrupted and its full effect hindered.[6] We are led in this manner to the ever recurring problem of constituents. It is said in one place that the work is on fixed Mercury by means of one fire, no other agent being introduced from first to last.[7] It is said also that there is a sole and only thing, combined by one operation in a single vessel,[8] an unique nature which can dispense with all other substance [9] and is at once potent and consecrated. It is comparable to the microcosm, to man and analogous beings, is male and female, and is therefore capable of marriage.[10] The Mercury of the Stone is described otherwise as the object of operations, and it is distinguished from mineral quicksilver—" which has been subject to treatment "—solely by its congruity with the

---

[1] *Book of Mercy : Ibid*, p. 189.   [2] *Ibid.*

[3] *Book of Royalty*, p. 129. Compare *Book of Concentration*, p. 199.

[4] *Ibid.*, p. 128.   [5] *Ibid.*, p. 127.

[6] *Ibid.*, p. 132.   [7] *Book of Clemency*, p. 135.

[8] *Book of Mercy : Ibid.*, p. 169. But as regards the " sole and only thing " compare the same treatise, p. 174, where it is said that this unique nature was sought by philosophers " endowed with perfect intelligence ", but they found nothing of the kind in all the world. Alternatively therefore they combined spirits with bodies thereunto approximate, to obtain a homogeneous product and bring to light that which corresponded with gold and silver therein, as well as that which was opposed to these metals. " The latter they subtracted and co-opted all that was concordant, ameliorating natures, uniting male and female elements, equilibrating also heat and cold, moisture and dryness, according to determined and proportioned weights."

[9] *Ibid.*, p. 171.   [10] *Ibid.*, p. 179.

other principles.[1]   Of such is Philosophical Mercury and it is
divided into two kinds, which constitute together the
essential principles of the Work, the one corresponding to
soul, the other to spirit, their respective distinguishing names
being Eastern and Western Mercury.   The second of these is
termed also Tincture ; its office is to effect transformation
in the first,[2] understood as the more important principle,
that which is termed Tincture being fixed strongly to the
very substance of the Stone, but it is not itself the Stone.[3]
It must be added that on this subject, as on others, the texts
swarm with contradictions : for example, the tingeing Mercury
is called Water,[4] but in the tract which follows the substance
of the Tincture is the Fire of the Stone.[5]

We must be content therefore to note as regards the process
(1) that the object is to unite spirit with body and dissolve
them together ; (2) that the body answers to earth in the
Stone ; (3) that its air softens and refines ; (4) that its water
whitens ; (5) that its fire makes white red ; [6] (6) that when
the operation is completed the Stone is of purple colour ;
(7) that it is scintillating, pearly and dazzling to the eyes.[7]
As regards the principle of transmutation, it is to be understood that lead is gold and tin silver on their inward side.
Those in fine who attain the Elixir will prove in operation
that " one part will suffice for a million ". [8] They shall give
thereof to the poor and unfortunate for the sake of him who
has communicated these Mysteries of his own free will and
accord, the Sheik Abou Moussa Djàber ben Hayyân Eç-
Çoufy.[9]

It remains only to indicate the unchallengeable conclusion
which is imposed by the research of this chapter, and it can
be put in a few words.   In so far as Syriac and Arabian
Alchemy is a mirror which reflects the Byzantine texts,
it is rooted in the time-old craft of producing surface tinctures
which imparted to inferior metals an appearance of gold
and silver ; but—as in Greece—there arose out of these
practices an hypothesis that it was possible to penetrate

---

[1] *Book of Oriental Mercury*, p. 207. The explanation is that it does not act by
itself, but the other principles or matters penetrate and fix it.

[2] *Loc. cit.* pp. 208, 209.   [3] *Tract on Occidental Mercury*, p. 213.   [4] *Ibid.*

[5] *Book of the Fire of the Stone*, p. 216.   [6] *Book of Mercy*, pp. 186, 187.

[7] *Book of Balances*, p. 145. It is said to be soft as wax and yet it resists fire,
suffering no alteration.

[8] *Book of Clemency*, p. 137.   [9] *Ibid.*, p. 138.

beneath the surface by the aid of more powerful Elixirs and thus transmute metals. The claim in both cases was that such Elixirs were known to Masters of the Art. Most obscure of all but also the most convinced and dealing therefore in uttermost terms of certitude, the Arabian Geber stands forth as one who is his own and no other's, owing little comparatively to those who had preceded, speaking with the authority of assumed first-hand knowledge and quoting chiefly from himself. But I have given already in a sentence the message of his extant records by derivation from the *Book of Mercy* : " If the Elixir is red it will convert its object into gold, while the white changes into silver." It is literal, not symbolical, and we know exactly from whence the terms derive, from the old arts of surface colouration, but here transformed by the dream of authentic *Alchemia*. Syriac and Arabian Alchemy is not therefore a science of the soul in veils. If ever a change came over the spirit of its dream, so that the doctrine of metallic transmutation became itself transmuted, it was neither at Byzantium nor Bagdad but at a later day and in another place of the literature.

CHAPTER VIII

The Early Latin Literature

THE records of Alchemy are a long-drawn chain of testimony in the Latin tongue, for it continued till the last days of the seventeenth century, and even for a few years subsequently an occasional text appeared, though the day of Latin was over and the vernaculars prevailed everywhere. All that is great in the Secret Art, all that belongs essentially to the Great Work and constitutes its canon, was written in that language, some tracts of Paracelsus excepted, soon to be enshrined therein. At the end of the sixteenth century and thence onward there was a large output in German, but it belongs to another category, with a seal of suspicion set upon the major part, because—as I have shewn elsewhere—a thriving trade was driven at that time in the putative occult sciences from A to Z, but in this one most of all. When the Latin canon originated it was reflected so directly from Greek sources through Arabian channels that the early texts—which, moreover, are few enough—usually pass as translations from the second of these tongues : it is probable enough but cannot be termed certain. The chief memorials are those which survive under the dubious names of Morien, Artephius, Rhasis, the anonymous *Turba*—connected, however, with Arisleus—standing at the head and front and recalling irresistibly that *Assembly of Philosophers* which I have cited already among the Byzantine fragments.

The *Turba Philosophorum* is regarded as the oldest treatise on Alchemy in the Latin tongue, and about this there is no question, but—so far as can be ascertained, it was not originally written in Latin : the compiler or editor—for in several respects it seems to be a harmony of extracts presented in the manner of a symposium—wrote most probably in Arabic. There has been a suggestion of a Hebrew source, but this, in my own view, must be decisively set aside. It has been cited as an authority from which no appeal is possible by the Masters of Alchemy for some six or seven centuries, during which period it was known only in the Latin garb, though it is by no means certain that the original has been lost irretrievably, seeing that Arabic and Syriac manuscripts treating of early chemistry are to be found in considerable numbers up and down the libraries of Europe and have been only imperfectly explored. There are two known codices or recensions of the *Turba*, and they differ considerably from one another, that which is appreciably shorter being also clearer and on the whole the less corrupt of the two, though both are in a bad state.[1] The fact is scarcely important for my purpose, which is not a textual consideration, but it may be added that some alchemists of the seventeenth century, especially in Germany, seem to have been acquainted with at least one further version, as it is certain that citations exhibited by writers like Figulus belong to neither extant codex.

The researches of Berthelot have established, as we have seen, (1) that Latin Alchemy, which has been referred almost always to an Arabian source, connects with the Greek Alchemy which preceded Arabian " science ", because the latter was itself derived from Greece ; and (2) that the *Turba Philosophorum* in particular offers striking analogies with texts of the Byzantine School. The Greek influence was not, however, direct but derived mediately through channels that are now unknown.[2] We are acquainted sufficiently in this manner with the bibliographical history of the work, and it remains only to note that the great alchemical collections, that of *Theatrum Chemicum* and that of Mangetus, contain commentaries, colloquies and enigmas which claim

---

[1] Those who are concerned may consult my English rendering of 1896, entitled *The Turba Philosophorum, or Assembly of the Sages, called also the Book of Truth in the Art and the Third Pythagorical Synod, an Ancient Alchemical Treatise, with the chief readings of the Shorter Codex, Parallels from Greek Alchemists and Explanations of Obscure Terms.*

[2] This is the opinion of Berthelot and may reflect also that of his collaborator Professor M. O. Houdas, but it must be confessed that a Greek original does not seem intolerable as a tentative hypothesis, and it must be remembered that the imaginary *interlocutores* in the grand debate of the *Turba* are usually in the masques of Greek names, including the most illustrious—Pythagoras, Socrates, Plato, Parmenides and Anaxagoras. A few, however, are in Latin, *e.g.* Mundus, and Moses also takes part, in which connection we may remember his *Diplosis* in the records of Greek Alchemy. It should be added that there are certain names of substances which—like many of the proper names—are in a corrupt state, but they suggest an eastern derivation. Berthelot lays stress, however, on the debased proper names as evidence of passage through the channel of an eastern language.

to elucidate the *Turba*, or are at least attached thereto : they are of various speculative dates, though taken altogether they belong to a comparatively early period of Latin Alchemy.[1]

There are some translations of the colloquy extant in German and some also in French : those in the latter language are notable for the very slender way in which they represent the printed Latin codices, but it is of course possible that they are based on manuscripts with which alchemical bibliography is unacquainted. The versions contained in Salmon's *Bibliothèque des Philosophes Alchimiques*[2] and in the *Trois Traités*[3] are instances in point. There is also an English rendering in manuscript among the treasures of the Sloane Collection in the British Museum : it is made, however, from the French and proved useless for my purpose when I was translating the *Turba*, many years ago.

Berthelot has dedicated an entire chapter of his *Essay on the Transmission of Antique Science* to a study of the *Turba Philosophorum*,[4] shewing (1) that many of its phrases and even pages of discourse are almost translations of Greek alchemists ; (2) that its original text—in whatever language— was one of the most ancient on Alchemy ; (3) that its doctrine is in close correspondence with that of Byzantine texts ; (4) that processes which are clear in the Greek and are concerned with the surface colouration of metals have either become processes of pretended transmutation or otherwise unintelligible. The conclusion reached is that in its Latin guise the far-famed *Book of Truth in the Art* is " a broth of

---

[1] *Theatrum Chemicum* has (1) *In Turbam Anonymi Sermo* and (2) *Allegoriæ Sapientum et Distinctiones* 129 *in Turbam*. These reappear in the *Bibliotheca Chemica Curiosa* of Mangetus, together with (1) Further *Allegoriæ super Librum Turbæ* ; (2) *Ænygma ex Visione Arislei Philosophi et Allegoriis Sapientum* ; (3) *Exercitationes in Turbam Philosophorum*.

[2] The Sieur Salmon published his collection at Paris in two volumes, dated 1672 and 1678. Lenglet du Fresnoy describes his translation of Geber as exceedingly bad. The sub-title of *Turba* is given as *Code of Truth*. A corrected and extended edition which was to occupy six volumes began publication at Paris in 1741 under the auspices of Jean Maugin de Richebourg, a reputed adept, but was suspended at the third volume.

[3] The title in full is *Trois Traités* : *sçavoir, La Turbe des Philosophes* ; *La Parole Délaissée du Trévisan* ; *et les XII Portes d'Alchimie, autres que celles de Ripleus.* This appeared at Paris in 1618 and again in 1672. The collection is to be distinguished from *Trois Anciens Traictez de la Philosophie Naturelle* of 1626 and this in turn from *Trois Traictez de la Philosophie Naturelle*, belonging to the year 1659. The *Turba* is found in neither.

[4] See Part II, c. 2, pp. 253–268.

undigested fact and theory ", complicated further by commentary " after the manner of a theologian "—a comparison, however, the force of which has escaped me. He says also that " the theoretical tradition has lost nearly all contact with the practical tradition " ; but in the sense of terms this can signify only that it is not in relation to the knavish devices of surface tinctures, which in all probability have reached it at third or fourth hand. By intention at least *Turba Philosophorum*, like the Greek alchemists—let us say, after pseudo-Democritus—and like the Arabian Geber, was about the business of Alchemy, meaning veridic transmutation of metals. Whether or not it was and remained dream, it was " glorious great intent " compared with goldsmith's tricks, though it connotes for the French chemist an unfortunate divagation from the broad path of science.

We have ascertained in this manner not only the documentary position of the *Turba* from the standpoint of the sole expert criticism by which it has been approached but are also in possession of its established subject-matter. In its own evasive words this is (1) the extraction of " our Secret Ethelia, through which bodies are coloured " ; (2) that is, " tinged with an invariable Tincture ; (3) namely, a soul which penetrates the body " ; it being understaood (4) that " the beginning of the operation is the whitening, to which succeeds the redness and finally the perfection of the Work ".[1] Of such is " the revelation of our Stone ", and it is affirmed in concluding [2]—according to one of the recensions—that it is " enough for the sons of the Doctrine ". As regards the Stone itself : " the strength thereof shall never become corrupted, but the same—when it is placed in the fire— shall be increased. If you seek to dissolve, it shall be dissolved ; but if you would coagulate, it shall be coagulated. Behold, no one is without it, and yet all do need it. There are many names given to it, and yet it is called by one only, while—if need be—it is concealed. It is also a Stone and not a stone, Spirit, Soul and Body. It is white, volatile, concave, hairless, cold ; and yet no one can apply the tongue with impunity to its surface. If you wish that it should fly, it

---

[1] These citations are drawn respectively from the 25th, 26th, 67th and 15th *Dictum*.

[2] I have followed my English version of 1896.

flies ; if you say that it is water, you speak the truth ; if you say that it is not water, you speak falsely. Do not then be deceived by the multiplicity of names, but rest assured that it is one thing, unto which nothing alien is added. Investigate the place thereof. . . . Unless the names were multiplied, so that the vulgar might be deceived, many would deride our wisdom."

It will signify little in what order we take the early memorials of Latin Alchemy which pass under eastern names : they are sometimes reflected, sometimes possibly translated from Arabian sources, and in other cases are of the usual fictitious attribution. Were it possible to proceed on the basis of historical names, the earliest in respect of time —outside the forged Aristotle—would be " Khalid ", King and alchemist, the accredited author of *Liber Secretorum Artis* [1] and *Liber Trium Verborum*,[2] as he appears to be an historical person—Khâled ben Yezid Ibn Moaoriia—though he is described apocryphally as King of Egypt. His death is referred to A.D. 708. The postulated Arabic originals of the tracts mentioned have been referred to the ninth century or later, while the thirteenth is the probable period of their translation into Latin.[3] The preface to *Liber Secretorum* affirms that unless the Lord guards and leads our human minds [4] we can know nothing of this world, for He is the beginning and He the science of all. It is said thereafter that the Magistery of the Secret Stone is a secret of the secrets of God, the reason not emerging at any point of the text, which proceeds to enumerate four Masteries in the Art, namely, Solution, Congelation, Albification and Rubification, the object in view being *facere aurum ex Azoth vivo*. The instruments needed in the work are an aludel and cucurbite, having its proper alembic, while the four kinds of material are specified as bodies, souls, spirits and water. The operations performed upon them are described in successive chapters as operations on the Stone : when it has

---

[1] It was published originally at Frankfurt in 1615. It is said in the preface : *Edidi hunc meum librum in obitu meæ mortis.*

[2] The text will be found in *Theatrum Chemicum*, Vol. V, and in Mangetus, ii, 183 *et seq.*

[3] Berthelot : *La Chimie au Moyen Age, Tome* I, p. 246.

[4] My references are to the text in Mangetus, which is followed by *Liber Trium Verborum . . .*, *ex Manuscripto, longe aliis præcellentiore.* I am unacquainted with any other edition.

attained the white stage it is projected upon copper, and this is converted into silver, better than that of the mines. The Mastery at the White is also convertible into gold according to a prescribed method given at the end of the tract, the valedictory affirmation being : *Et erit aurum, et operabitur aurum*, on the recurring condition of Alchemy : *si Deus voluerit*.

The *Book of the Three Words* defines Alchemy as the Art of Arts and Science of Sciences, and is that by which imperfect metals are led into the perfect state, from corruption into incorruption, the design of Nature being always to make *Sol et Luna*, otherwise, gold and silver. As regards the Three Words, they are Water, Air and Fire : the Water conserves, the Air cherishes, the Fire guards. The final end and crown of all attainment is a fixed oil which rubefies corrupt metals. It is suggested, however, that there was another and distinct Arabic text, in which the Three Words are three letters, otherwise written communications, being firstly a relation of what passed between Khalid and an adept known as Morien—Morienus Romanus—and secondly a record in two parts of the circumstances under which the King attained his knowledge and came therefore to understand " the enigmatic utterances of his master ".[1]

There arises in this manner the legend of Khalid and Morien,[2] whose title *Romanus* arises from a story that he was born at Rome but left it at an early age in quest of Adfar Alexandrinus, an Arabian philosopher and adept of that city, whose writings he had seen and was eager to understand their meaning. He reached Alexandria and fared so well that in fine he discovered the philosopher, to whom he made known his name, country, but above all that he was of the Christian religion. He was welcomed by Adfar more especially on the last account, and was promised the inheritance *totius suæ disciplinæ*. Morien took up his abode with him who had become in this manner his father in secret science and pursued his studies so long, and with such success,

---

[1] Berthelot : *La Chimie au Moyen Age*, I, 246.

[2] Morienus : *Liber de Compositione Alchimiæ*. It is claimed to have been translated from the Arabic by Robertus Castrensis, who completed his task on Feb. 11th, 1182—old style—and in the opinion of Berthelot there was an original in that language. It is not easy to share this view because the text is militantly Christian and the chief concern of Morien is represented as the conversion of Khalid.

that *totius divinitatis secreta* were at length confided to his care. The mission of Adfar being thus, as it might seem, fulfilled, he departed this life, after which Morien quitted Alexandria, and went to Jerusalem, where he became a hermit. Now, the science of Adfar was transmitted to him through the earnest study of a book ascribed to Hermes, and under circumstances which remain in obscurity this work fell into the hands of Khalid, who ascended the throne of Egypt many years after Morien had left that country. He is described as *Rex sapiens et prudens vir, in omni scientia perspicuus* and eager to attain an understanding of the precious text. He sought therefore for wise men who might be qualified to interpret its mysteries, but the result was that he was surrounded speedily by false claimants, attracted by his promised rewards.

The report of these things reached the eremite in his solitude; he repaired to Egypt, with the idea of directing the King into a better path, and there he was provided with a house as well as all his requirements in order to produce the Mastery. He remained therein until the work was finished, when he wrote these words about the vessel which contained the Elixir: *Omnes qui secum omnia habent, alieno auxilio nullatenus indigent*, and leaving the Mastery behind him he returned to his hermitage. When the King entered the deserted house and found the vessel therein he did not doubt that he had come into possession of the great treasure, but realised bitterly that he could put it to no use in the absence of the artist who prepared it. Having beheaded the false alchemists who had promised him all things but performed nothing, he took counsel with his confidential servant Galip as to what he should do next. The answer was that God would provide and lead; but some years passed away, during which Khalid sought in vain for tidings of Morien, who had apparently not even disclosed his name. At length one day, during a hunting expedition, with Galip in attendance on the King, the servant discovered an aged man at his prayers in a solitary place. He questioned him and learned that the stranger came from Jerusalem, where he was acquainted with a holy hermit who was learned in the Mystery of Hermes. Being aware also of the King's frustrated desire he had left Palestine to inform Khalid that there was a way in which he might even now attain it.

Galip sought to dissuade him on the ground of the fate which had befallen false claimants ; but the stranger feared nothing and asked only to be brought into the presence of the King, which was therefore done. The traveller told his story and the result was (1) that Khalid sent his servant Galip, with a suitable escort, to Jerusalem ; (2) that Morien was found, now of great age, but under his hair-shirt he preserved a youthful frame ; (3) that Galip recognised him as the gifted artist who had performed the Mastery and left the Elixir behind him ; (4) that Morien consented to return with them into Egypt ; (5) that his subsurface desire was really the King's conversion to Christianity, but it does not seem to have been pressed ; (6) that Khalid and Morien had long discussions between them, in the course of which the adept revealed to him the Matter and Process of the Great Work, but using the cryptic language of Alchemy ; (7) that the King understood, a hypothetical proof being that he himself wrote upon the subject ; (8) that the favourite servant also entered into the freedom of the adepts and left his record behind him.[1]

We have seen that the sage Adfar communicated to Morien " the secrets of all divinity "—*totius divinitatis secreta*— but this extreme statement is without prejudice to the fact that the end of all their efforts was the composition of an Elixir which would transmute metals, and the last instruction—in the last lines of the treatise—directs the operator to project one part of it on nine parts of silver, when they will be changed into pure gold, " for which may God be blessed through all the ages." When it is said elsewhere in respect of the First Matter that *hæc res a te extrahitur*— that it is " found by thee " and " received by thee " and

---

[1] The *Liber de Compositione Alchimiæ* is divided as follows : (1) *Morieni Romani Sermo*, in which the adept tells his own story to the point when Galip is instructed to go in search of him ; (2) *Sermo Galip*, in which the servant recounts his journey to Jerusalem, his return to Egypt with Morien and gives a first discourse of the latter, addressed to the King ; (3) *Interrogationes Regis Khaled et Responsiones Morieni*, the later part of which is subdivided, giving prominence to the practical side of the adept's instructions. It is a highly artificial arrangement and betrays itself. For example, in a *viva voce* discourse *ex hypothesi*, Morien mentions that a specific point will be unfolded later in the book : it recalls *Turba Philosophorum*, that pretended report of a debate which makes the same slip.

" thou dost exist " therein—we can rest assured that the apostles of spiritual interpretation would lay great stress thereupon ; but unfortunately this kind of text cannot be cited safely apart from context, and it happens that Morien is exhibiting to his royal pupil the universal diffusion of the four elements, that their existence is postulated in the Stone and so also in man.[1] For the rest, the Matter is one and nothing that God has created can subsist without it : it is to be understood therefore as a substance behind the elements and that these are modes of its development.[2]

Among early names in Latin alchemical literature there is that of Artephius, who is mentioned by Roger Bacon, but nothing is known concerning him and even the voice of legend has scarcely uttered a rumour, possibly because he has provided something on his own part—sufficient to quench invention—in the sub-title of *De Vita Proroganda*, which affirms that the tract in question was written *anno* 1025 *ætatis suæ*. He is referred to the twelfth century, *Clavis Majoris Sapientiæ* having been first printed at Paris in 1609 and *Liber Secretus* in 1785 at Frankfurt. Berthelot declines to consider him because of his uncertain date, indicating only that his definition of the Stone as consisting of body, soul and spirit is applied generally to metals by Greek alchemists and exhibits their direct influence.[3] He has been identified with Al Toghrâi, described as an Arabic poet and alchemist, and is said to have died between 1119 and 1122. The evidence is not forthcoming. In the opinion of Hitchcock " it seems impossible not to perceive that Artephius is writing of man and is endeavouring to indicate some process by which man may be said to pass, under the discipline of God and Nature, from a chaotic state of ignorance

---

[1] *O filii sapientiæ, scitote quod Deus Creator Altissimus Benedictus, mundus ex quatuor elementis dissimilibus creavit, posuitque hominem inter ipsa elementa majus ornamentum.—Interrogationes* in Mangetus, ii, 515, col. 2.

[2] The bibliography of Morien is confusing : it should be understood that *Liber de Compositione* is the sole tract which passes under his name, but it has been printed also as *De Re Metallica, de Metallorum Transmutatione atque de occulta Summaque Antiquorum Medicina Libellus*. The original edition of Paris, 1559, appears under this title, which is reproduced in the text of *Artis Auriferæ Volumina Duo*, 1599, together with its alternative. It is translated into French as *Entretien du Roi Calid et du Philosophe Morien* in *Bibliothèque des Philosophes Chimiques*, 1741, tome ii.

[3] *Essai sur la Transmission de la Science Antique au Moyen Age*, in Vol. I of *La Chimie au Moyen Age*, p. 252. But in the twelfth century it may well have been derived at second hand.

and passion to a certain unity ".[1]   But the valediction of
Liber Secretus directs those who have attained the Great
Secret to praise God, Who imparts wisdom and consequently
riches to whomsoever He pleases, while denying them for
ever to the wicked.   The nature of this wealth and wisdom
emerges in the text with at least comparative clearness.

We may allegorise, if we please, on the central doctrine
of all, that " there is but one Stone, one Medicine, one Vessel,
one Regimen and one only disposition or method of making
the White and Red successively " ; but if words mean anything that can be identified—and they do from time to
time, even with alchemists—the Work remains physical
and is concerned with a certain substance which is " put
once for all in the Vessel ", while the latter is then sealed
until the completion of the process thereupon.   Artephius
calls this speaking clearly, as one who has been cured of
envy and has learned charity in the course of a thousand
years.   At the same time he confesses to a single reservation
on a subject concerning which no one is permitted to write,
because its communication belongs to God or a friend : it
will be found, however, in his text, unless one is utterly
stupid.   The reference is of course to the name and real
nature of the First Matter.   It is to be understood that the
Work itself is not long : the heat of the sun may take one
hundred years to produce a metal in the mines, but the
Secret Fire of Alchemy can perform the task quickly.   It is,
moreover, inexpensive and easy, so only that the artist
employs no substance which evaporates in the fire.   The fire
itself is mineral, equal and continuous ; it is, moreover, humid,
unconsuming and does not burn.   It is in fact a simple fire :
(1) fire of the lamp, which is vaporous and airy ; (2) fire of
ashes, in which the Vessel is placed after it has been sealed
hermetically ; and (3) the natural fire of " our Water ",
which is the mineral fire already mentioned and is needed
throughout the work, whereas the others are in use at certain
times only : it is that which makes gold a spirit.   The
colours appearing successively in the course of a successful
process are (1) black, which is the sign of mortification and
putrefaction ; (2) white, which marks the resurrection of the
body, transparent and immortal ; (3) orange, which deepens

---

[1] *Remarks on Alchemy*, pp. 79 *et seq.*

into red and bears witness to the Perfect Mastery in fine accomplished. As to this it is said in the crude and stultifying symbolism : " That which has its head red and then white, the feet white and red thereafter, and which previously had black eyes : such alone is the Mastery." Whosoever affirms that there is a great mystery of the soul behind veils of this kind is raving.

Recurring to the First Matter of the Secret Art, it is said that Antimony is of the same nature as Saturn=lead and that Saturnial Antimony contains a quicksilver. The antimonial quicksilver is termed mercurical water, heavy, viscous and glutinous. It is called by many names : Spirit and Soul of the Sun and Moon, Dissolvent Oil and Water, Fountain, Mary Bath, Contra-Natural Fire, Moist Fire, Secret Fire, Piercing Vinegar, Middle Substance, Vegetable, Animal and Mineral Fire, Living Water, White Smoke and May Dew.[1] The whole secret of the Work is by means of this Water to reduce the perfect bodies of gold and silver into a precious oil. When so dissolved the bodies of these metals are called Quicksilver, and this Quicksilver is not without its sulphur, nor is the Sulphur without " the nature of luminaries ", otherwise of Sun and Moon. The bodies of gold and silver become in this manner a true tincture for the transmutation of the bodies of imperfect metals. I am not presenting the complete process so far as it can be disentangled, but am sketching it sufficiently to exhibit that it is a work on metals by means of metals and a secret dissolvent, about the nature of which there is no real indication given. These points are illustrated further in the concluding words : " He who makes the Red Earth black and then white has found the Mastery, being that also which kills the living and raises the dead. Whiten therefore the black and make the white red. . . . When you see the true whiteness shining like a drawn sword, know that the redness is concealed therein. . . . Continue the coction . . ., when the orange colour will appear and finally the resplendent red."

[1] The list is useful for those of a curious mind, as they can compare it with other enumerations in later alchemical lexicons—for example, Pernety's *Dictionnaire Mytho-Hermétique*—and they will find that by the end of the eighteenth century the veiling names of the Great Mystery had attained vast proportions. It seems obvious that if the First Matter is everywhere and hence in all things it can be called by the names of all. But in reality its manifold denominations arise from the fact that the First Matter is hypothetical and is hence without a name.

I will take in the next place three names in succession and connect them in summary form because things that are little to our purpose must be treated shortly. They are Rhasis, Alfarabi and Avicenna, it being understood that the last is illustrious in medicine, outside his repute in Alchemy. Rhasis is said to have been born *circa* A.D. 850 on the frontiers of Khorassan. However this may be, his fame is that of a physician, his knowledge and skill surpassing the attainments of all other medical doctors belonging to that time. His repute was destined also to be lasting, for his influence extended to Europe, where his writings on medicine are said to have been the basis of university teaching till the seventeenth century. He wrote, moreòver, on chemistry, and a tract on the preparation of sal ammoniac under his name is printed in the third volume of *Theatrum Chemicum*. He is ignored by Mangetus and all other makers of collections, great and small alike. The explanation is perhaps to be sought in a story which comes from I know not what source but was abroad presumably on the Continent in the sixteenth and seventeenth centuries.[1] It represents Rhasis as writing a treatise on the transmutation of metals and presenting it to the Prince of Khorassan, who rewarded him with one thousand pieces of gold. When he asked also to see the work performed the alchemist was willing to comply on being provided with the necessary instruments and materials. The story says that they were furnished on a liberal scale, but the subsequent experiments proved a total failure, and the enraged potentate belaboured the head of his adept with the unprofitable alchemical book. The writings of Rhasis are said to enlarge on the importance of planetary correspondences, being the influence of stars on the formation of metallic substances beneath the surface of the earth. It may be only a scoffer who adds that *Recipe aliquid ignotum quantum volueris* is a direction in one of those twelve tracts on the Art which tradition has placed to his credit.[2] According to Louis Figuier, he was a zealous promoter of

---

[1] See *Lives of Alchemysticall Philosophers*, 1815.

[2] A tract under the name of Rhasis is found in two MSS of the *Bibliothèque Nationale*, Nos. 6514 and 7156. It is entitled *Lumen Luminum* and treats of alums, salts and *vina falsa ex saccaro, melle et riço*. *De Perfecto Magisterio* is the same text under another title, but it appears as the work of Aristotle in *Theatrum Chemicum*, Vol. III. Rhasis is quoted in *Rosarium*, in *Consilcium Conjugii*, and by

experimental methods, but this title of excellence may appertain to his writings on medicine.

Alfarabi needs only to be mentioned in passing as a man accredited with universal genius and therefore as one who could not be unacquainted with the Science of Hermes in his day and generation. He is supposed to have died A.D. 954. According to one of the legends, he was still in search of the Stone towards the end of his life. In any case he wrote upon Alchemy, but all that remains is an *Assertio Artis Alchemiæ*, translated into Latin. It has not been printed or even adequately described, within my knowledge.[1]

Avicenna, on the contrary, would demand considerable space in a methodical account of Alchemy from the historical point of view. He is said to have been born A.D. 980 and to have died *circa* 1036, at a comparatively early age, as the result of an irregular life. The question does not concern us, and we may pass over in like manner the proofs of his skill in medicine and the political eminence which it secured to him for a period. The question before us is the witness which he bore to Alchemy and the authenticity of the treatises which are extant under his name. We may set aside in the first place the interpretation of an epistle addressed to Alexander the Great, while in all probability the Arabic original—if any—is represented but thinly in *De Mineralibus*, which was printed for the first time in 1682.[2]

The treatise *De Anima* affirms (1) that Philosophical gold is the best, meaning better than that of the mines ; (2) that

Vincent de Beauvais in *Speculum Naturale*, where he is reported as stating that copper is essentially silver and becomes such when its redness is extracted. See Berthelot : *La Chimie au Moyen Age*, t. I, pp. 68, 139, 145, 234, 249, 278.

[1] See, however, a brief reference in Berthelot, *loc. cit.*, p. 19.

[2] The *Artis Chemicæ Principes*, first published at Dantzic in 1572, contains Avicenna's treatise entitled *De Anima, in arte Alchemiæ*, which was quoted by Vincent de Beauvais in the mid-thirteenth century. *De Mineralibus*, mentioned in my text, was added in the later edition of 1682. The first volume of *Artis Auriferæ . . . Volumina Duo* contains *De Conglutinatione Lapidis* and *Tractatulus de Alchimia*, as well as *Expositio Epistolæ* which I have sought to set aside. A *Tractatulus de Tinctura Metallorum* appeared in the collection of Frankfort, 1550, entitled *De Alchimia Opuscula Complura Veterum Philosophorum*, 2 vols. *Theatrum Chemicum*, Vol. IV. has Epistola *de Re Recta* and *Declaratio Lapidis Filio Suo*, which is substantially the same as *De Anima*. Finally, Mangetus: *Bibliotheca Chemica Curiosa*, Vol I, 1702, prints apparently for the first time an opuscule entitled *Tractatus de Alchemia*, but it calls for careful collation with *De Anima* and *Declaratio Lapidis*. The statement applies to all the printed works, in the critical consideration of which it would be necessary to determine how far they repeat one another and are referable ultimately to two or three sources at most ; but it is obvious that an analysis of this kind lies far beyond my present scope and term.

whatsoever exists in the world is formed from the four elements ; (3) that these elements are constituted by the First Matter ; (4) that they change one into another ; (5) that they can be converted therefore by the power of man, who brings into activity the hidden nature of things ; and (6) that every metal consists of Sulphur and Mercury. We may compare *Tractatulus Alchimiæ*, according to which every mineral substance was created by God from Mercury, which Mercury contains Sulphur within it. It is the universal living spirit, which penetrates, exalts and develops everything. It acts, moreover, as a ferment on every body with which it is united chemically and is the Great Elixir of metals, accordingly as it is developed—under the action of fire— to the white or the red state. The potency of the Perfect Magisterium is one upon a thousand.

A word must be said upon two tracts which pass under the name of Aristotle, being (1) *De Perfecto Magisterio*, the authenticity of which is illustrated by the fact that it cites the Christian eremite and alchemist named Morien: we have seen that it is identical with *Lumen Luminum*, ascribed to Rhasis. (2) *De Practica Lapidis Philosophici*, which in another collection reappears substantially, though under another title, namely, as *De Lapide Philosophorum*.[1] *De Perfecto Magisterio*, said to be of Syriac origin,[2] describes gold as generated from a clear quicksilver, combined with clear red sulphur, the close cohesion of its parts being due to long decoction by a moderate heat in the bosom of the earth. Silver, on the other hand, is generated from quicksilver of similar quality but in combination with clear sulphur, namely white, though there is also a certain redness which passes off in the generating process, for which reason silver does not mature as gold. There are recipes for the composition of the Stone, and according to one of them it is obtained by combining a most clear coagulated water with a fixed philosophical oil, which is red for the work of gold and white for that of silver. The Red Elixir produced in

[1] *De Perfecto Magisterio* will be found in the following collections: (1) *Vera Alchimiæ Artisque Metallicæ Doctrina*, Basle, 1561 ; (2) *Theatrum Chemicum*, Vol. III ; (3) *Bibliotheca Chemica Curiosa*, Vol. I. *De Practica* was first printed at Frankfurt, 1550, in *De Alchimia Opuscula Complura*, Vol. I, and again in Mangetus, Vol. I. For *De Lapide* see *Artis Auriferæ . . . Volumina Duo*, 1572, Vol. I.

[2] Berthelot, *loc. cit.*, I, 275.

the one case is projected on silver, when it is converted into good gold : in the other the White Elixir is projected on brass, and this becomes silver. The *Tractatulus* quotes Avicenna, Rhasis and other adepts, not excepting Aristotle, its supposed author. Its fundamental dictum is familiar otherwise in Alchemy : *Converte ergo elementa, et quod quæris invenies.* Two of these elements are petrine, namely, fire and earth—presumably because sparks can be obtained from a flint—and two are aqueous, namely, air and water. To attain the Mastery, peace must be made between them, and this is accomplished by converting one into another.

There remains for our consideration the Latin Geber, described by Lenglot du Fresnoy as the chief and master of all who have toiled over Hermetic Philosophy. Berthelot has expended great pains to prove that the texts extant under this name and in this language are not only distinct as texts from the writings of Djaber in Arabic, and as at the poles asunder in respect of manner and method, but that they are also opposed thereto. The Latin compositions are for these reasons described continually as the fraudulent work of a *faussaire.* There is almost a trace of animus against Geber in one who is otherwise the most unprejudiced and impartial of critics. Now, it is of no consequence to my subject whether the *Sum of Perfection,* the *Invention of the Mastery* and a certain testamentary tract which are claimed for the Arabian alchemist have or have not been ascribed mythically. Experience teaches that most people have written the books which appear under their names, but in Alchemy the case is otherwise : we are concerned, however, with content, not with authenticity in attribution and not with text-source—as, for example, whether it is in East or West. This notwithstanding, and prior to passing on, it may be well to register the fact that since Berthelot presented his results in 1887 other Arabian Djaber texts have come to light and may help to retrieve the position of the Latin Geber.[1]   So far as alchemical literature is concerned, he stands above impeachment, being of absolute authority for all *adepti* and holding a higher rank—if possible

---

[1] This is as much as need be said in the present place, and it should be added that having no call at present in such a direction I have not examined the subject. My authority on the point of fact is Mr. H. Stanley Redgrove in *The Occult Review,* Vol. XL, 1924. He refers to researches of Mr. E. J. Holmyard.

—than the immortal debate of the *Turba*. The explanation is that his writings mark a new epoch in Alchemy, are methodised in form, logical in procedure, or—as M. Berthelot intimates—like a product of the Schools over which St. Thomas Aquinas reigned in his day supreme. It is affirmed in the *Sum of Perfection* that philosophers are only ministers of Nature and do not transmute metals : that office belongs to her ; but they prepare the way, because they prepare the Matter. There are Three Principles—Sulphur, Arsenic and Mercury. Sulphur perfects metals, because it is Light and Tincture ; but it cannot operate by itself in the Work of philosophers. This is true also of Arsenic, which is a subtle matter of like nature with Sulphur. Mercury unites easily with metals, being of their own nature, but it is not the Matter of the Work, nor yet the Work itself. The Three Principles are imperfect as such, and there is in each of them a certain middle substance, which can become Tincture for the Red in Sulphur, for the White in Arsenic, while it provides in Mercury the principle of perfection for metals, fixing that which is volatile and causing metallic bodies to resist the fire. The Universal Medicine of metals is to be sought in Mercury, but it cannot change those which are imperfect until it has been changed itself. Of all imperfect metals Jupiter-Tin is that which has most disposition to acquire perfection by the help of the Great Work.

After such manner does the Latin Geber bear his faithful witness to the Work and Term of the Art in metals, protesting before God that whosoever will follow his teaching and its method will attain therein, it being understood only that he has been grounded already in the natural principles of philosophy—not in the Mysteries of Religion and not in the Grace of God, to Whom I think indeed that there is no reference outside that which I have quoted. There are no important texts of alchemical literature which can compare with the *Summa* for the complete absence of any spiritual motive or recognition of things divine, save only the other tracts of the Latin Geber [1] and of his Arabian *alter ego*. The conclusion of this chapter follows from its entire content :

[1] The best edition of Geber is that which appeared at Gedani in 1682, based upon a Vatican manuscript. It was reprinted by Mangetus in his great collection,

the early Latin literature is that of pure physicists, expounding
the principles and practice of a purely physical work.

and the contents are (1) *Summa Perfectionis Magisterii, Libri* IV ; (2) *De Investi-
gatione Magisterii* ; (3) *Testamentum.* The last two are little more than short
collections of processes. The *Investigation* testifies to things that have been seen
with the eyes and touched by the hands of the witness. The *Testament* ends by
saying that the Salt of Metals dissolves Mercury into water, and when this Mercury
and that Salt have been coagulated together there is produced the Perfect Medicine.

CHAPTER IX

THE LATER CHAIN OF HERMES

THE Greek and Arabian tradition, represented by probable translations and commemorating eastern Masters of the Art who were in the main matters of legend, began to be replaced in the West by records of research on the spot, though put forward too often under the disguise of false names. To the extent that this rule obtains, we have finished with one class of pseudonyms but open another series, in which great doctors of the Church like Albertus Magnus and St. Thomas Aquinas, not to speak of a Sovereign Pontiff, are brought into that which I have denominated the later Chain of Hermes. But we meet also with personalities who are responsible under their proper designations for that which they affirm and claim. At the head of the list there stands the illustrious name of Roger Bacon, of whom it may be true to say that his real greatness has only emerged recently from the penumbra of the middle ages. From Bacon to Arnoldus de Villanova and the mysterious Raymond Lully —another unknown master assuming the vestures of him who was *doctor illuminatus* and apostle to the Moors of North Africa—from Lully to the two Isaacs of Holland the story moves, to be followed by Basil Valentine and Paracelsus, after the account of a famous invention which stands apart from all others in the romance-annals of Alchemy. We shall hear also in passing some of a few lesser voices which bore their witness through the centuries in the choir of adeptship.

" Take Salt, and rub it diligently with water, and purify it in other waters. Afterwards, by divers contritions, rub it with salts and burn it with sundry assations, that it may be made a pure earth, separate from the other elements. . . . Understand me, if thou art able : for it shall be composed undoubtedly of the elements, and therefore it shall be a part of the Stone which is no stone, and is in every man ; which thou shalt find at all times of the year in its own place."

This is a specimen instruction of Roger Bacon taken from *De Potestate Mirabili Artis et Naturæ*,[1] and it has been used as a self-evident instance of the alleged fact that the subject of Alchemy was man and not the metals ; [2] but I have shewn already that the reference is to the four elements of which the Stone was composed in common with all things else, including human beings.   It happens, however, that in the same tract Bacon defines Alchemy as the science of a certain Medicine or Elixir by which metals are transformed into other metals and those which are imperfect are raised into a perfect state.   The secrets of philosophy are said elsewhere [3] to be hidden in the four elements, Mercury and Sulphur being the principles of all metals.[4]   In common with other alchemists it is affirmed that the intention of Nature is always to produce gold, but " many accidents intervene " and the resulting metals are pure or impure, base or perfect, according to the local condition of the constituent principles.   It is these and no others which are to be used in the work of Alchemy, and as against the nonsense which has been written on the basis of a casual statement by the so-called Mary the Prophetess,[5] Bacon devotes a chapter to his description of vessel and furnace.[6]   Such are the materials, with no suggestion that Philosophical Mercury is other than the quicksilver which is known to all the world or that common Sulphur is not Sulphur of the Wise.   But these things being in the vessel and the vessel set upon the furnace, it is affirmed that the God of Nature has indicated the lineal way of procedure, namely, by a continuous decoction over a continuous and moderate fire.[7]   So shall those colours appear to which the whole literature testifies—the black of

---

[1] That is, *Speculum Alchemiæ*.   There are various editions, but it will be sufficient to cite Mangetus : *Bibliotheca Chemica Curiosa*, Vol. I.

[2] Hitchcock, in *Swedenborg, a Hermetic Philosopher*, pp. 202, 203.

[3] See *Radix Mundi*, but the authenticity of this treatise is doubtful.   However, the hypothesis recurs everywhere.

[4] *Speculum Alchemiæ*.

[5] See the *Dialogue of Mary and Aros*.   The question of Aros is : " What is that vessel without which the work cannot be performed ? "   And Mary answers that it is " the Vessel of Hermes which Philosophers have concealed and the ignorant cannot understand " ; but as if to stultify beforehand the notion that it is the body of man, she adds immediately : " It is the measure of the Philosophical Fire."

[6] *Speculum Alchemiæ*, cap. v.

[7] *Fiat ignis vester blandus et mitis, qui per singulos dies semper æqualis ardendo perduret, nec invalescat, sin aliter, sequetur maximum damnum.—Ibid.*, cap. IV.

putrefaction, and the white is contained therein, but there is a rainbow succession of ever changing hues before the operator obtains what is called *albedo vera*. And this perfect whiteness contains the red, the manifestation of which is preceded by a certain ashen grey : thereafter, NUTU DEI, the King is crowned with his ruby diadem. The Red or Ruby Elixir transmutes all metals into purest gold, while the White Elixir whitens and leads every metal to the grade of perfect whiteness. *Et rubeum quidem Elixir citrinat in infinitum . . ., album vero dealbat usque in infinitum,* the capacity of the Tinctures at their highest being as one upon a thousand, for which cause it is added in the last lines : *Semper mirabilis est laudandus Deus noster in æternum.*

The application of Alchemy to the extension of human life was another subject of study with Roger Bacon.[1] It is said that the Great Secret—meaning that of Alchemy—not only insures the welfare of individuals and the commonwealth—i.e., by providing the precious metals—but contributes to length of days and years of life ; for the Medicine of Metals eliminates the virus of corruption from the human body, so that the life of mortality can be extended to several centuries. The aspiration of the alchemist is not therefore that of Senancour : " Eternity, be thou my refuge " ; but always and only : Give me " the glory of going on and still to be ", in the world that is here and now. Those who are curious in such matters may find also that Bacon has processes of Alchemy on pearls and other precious stones [2] so that at need the adept may be not only " brow-bound with burning gold " but adorned with rings of profession for the greater glory of the Art.

Magnus in Magia, major in Philosophia, maximus in Theologia is the encomium *in crescendo* pronounced by a Belgian Chronicle of 1484 on him who is known to us always and only as Albertus Magnus. The quality of discernment which found that he was great in things called magical might have added with as much and as little authenticity that he was *ter-maximus in Alchemia.* His title of distinction is sufficient

---

[1] *De Secretis Operibus Artis et Naturæ et de Nullitate Magiæ,* in which the seventh chapter considers the retardation of the accidents which are the cause of old age. It is, however, " about it and about," with the object of shewing *quod autem hoc sit possibile,* and it presents some quaint stories but no " process ".

[2] *Ibid., in capitibus* ix, x, xi.

as an illustrious Doctor of the Church, and even the term
Magnus—much as it belongs to him and fully on this account
—was not at the beginning a consequence of his reputation,
but the Latin equivalent of his family name, by which he
was Albert de Groot.   Theology and Philosophy walked
hand in hand through the pageant of the thirteenth century,
and for the most part, if not always, those who were expert
in the one had earned their titles in the other : there was
at least no tolerated wisdom of man apart from that wisdom
which belongs to the doctrine of God. *Maximus* therefore
in Theologia, but *Alchemia* and *Magia* are matter of romance,
fortified by legend on the one hand and on the other by
fraudulent texts.   We may look at a legend for one moment
through the seering glass of a poet.

> Folk say, a wizard to a northern king
> At Christmas-tide such wondrous things did show,
> That through one window men beheld the spring,
> And through another saw the summer glow,
> And through a third the fruited vines a-row,
> While still, unheard, but in its wonted way,
> Piped the drear wind of that December day.[1]

The wizard was Albertus Magnus, while the royal personage
was William II, Count of Holland and King of the Romans,
whom the former had invited to supper in his monastic house
at Cologne.   The tables were found prepared in the garden
of the convent, although it was mid-winter and the ground
was covered with snow.   The astonishment was great and
great also the complaint of courtiers in the suite of William
when they saw their prince—and presumably also themselves
—exposed to such severity on the pretence of hospitality
and festival.   They sat down, however, to be amazed yet
further, if we can credit sober history, which is that of the
University of Paris—a mammoth in-folio—for the snow
melted suddenly and not only did the guests experience all
the softness of spring but there was the scent of flowers in
the garden, birds were singing in the trees, and these were
in leaf or blossom.   It is known that suppers were early in
those good days, though under such circumstances the

---

[1] William Morris in his Proem to *The Earthly Paradise*; any edition : I have
used that of 1890, in one volume.

sun might have shone at midnight. When the particular feast was over its magic ended also : there was winter again in a moment and its bitter cold about them.

This is a specimen of legend and among things that belong to myth is the android or automaton constructed by Albertus and endowed with the power of speech. According to Michael Maier, it took thirty years in the making, but in the end it proved an infallible oracle which answered patiently and accurately every question put to it. The gift, however, led to its destruction by St. Thomas Aquinas, according to one account, because it was unquestionably a diabolical contrivance; but there is another and more ingenious which says that he was confused by its intelligence and presumably put to the blush. Now, a myth is like a challenge offered to the faculty of interpretation, and Éliphas Lévi, who exercised this gift so that at times it looks like genius, came forward with a taking explanation and said : " This story is an allegory : the android was primitive scholasticism, which was broken by the *Summa* of St. Thomas, that daring innovator who first substituted the absolute law of reason for arbitrary divinity, by formulating an axiom which we cannot repeat too often, since it comes from such a master : ' A thing is not just because God wills it, but God wills it because it is just ' ".[1]

In the literal fact of things it happens that Albertus Magnus had as little to do with magian arts as he had with the invention of cannons and pistols, which has been attributed to him by Matthias de Luna. His position on occult subjects may be gathered from one observation, in which he affirms that " all those stories of demons prowling in the regions of the air, from whom the secrets of futurity may be ascertained, are absurdities which can never be admitted by sober reason ".[2] His alleged works on " incredible secrets " are here pilloried as spurious before the event of their appearance. The first of these I suppose to be *Secretum Secretorum*, said

---

[1] See my translation of Éliphas Lévi : *History of Magic*, Book IV, cap. 5, pp. 258–262. Also *Transcendental Magic*, similarly translated, second edition, pp. 206, 406.

[2] It follows that Albertus was on the whole what is called enlightened for the period in which he lived, as there is no question that such beliefs were prevalent, and I am not at all sure that some exponents of orthodox teaching would have been prepared to deny that the devil and his ministers could and did occasionally exhibit foresight of coming events.

to have been published at Venice in 1508, but I know not who has seen it except an anonymous believer in Albertus as alchemist and erudite on that subject.[1] Out of it may have come *Les Admirable Secrets d'Albert le Grand*,[2] a storehouse of curious superstitions with a strong astrological bias; *De Secretis Mulierum*;[3] and *Alberti Parvi Lucii Libellus*,[4] the last being a grimoire pure and simple. The name of Albertus Magnus was a name with which to conjure when the time came—in the sixteenth and seventeenth centuries— to produce occult chapbooks and colportage tracts dealing with decried arts.

As regards Alchemy and its connections, there is *Albertus de Rebus Metallicis et Mineralibus Libri Quinque*, first published in 1519 and accepted as genuine.[5] The author says that he tested personally some gold and silver manu- factured by an alchemist; that it resisted six or seven searching fusions; but the pretended metal was reduced to *scoriæ* by an eighth.[6] So much for gold of philosophy, reputed incessantly as better than that in the mines. It remains no less that the famous Provincial of the Dominicans and Bishop of Ratisbon [7] is classed by "lovers of the Art" as a true adept and master, in view of *Libellus de Alchymia*, printed at the end of his works [8] among supposititious tracts, and of *Concordantia Philosophorum*, in the fourth volume of

---

[1] It is mentioned in the *Lives of Alchemysticall Philosophers*, edition of 1815, *s.v.*, Albertus Magnus.

[2] The editions are too numerous to mention, nor is there any call in the present place.

[3] Another spurious attribution which is perhaps the earliest of all, first published in 1498. It is concerned also with the virtues of herbs and stones.

[4] There are modern reprints of this French chapbook—which does not seem to have any Latin original—and sometimes the date on their titles is put back through the centuries. References to the *Albertus Parvus* and certain citations therefrom will be found in my *Book of Ceremonial Magic*, 1910. The *Little Albert* deals with the composition of philtres, the interpretation of dreams, the manu- facture of "the hand of glory", the ring of invisibility, the sympathetic powder, and so forth. There are processes also for the sophistication of gold.

[5] The fact is noted by Berthelot, but I am not aware that there is any authentic canon of criticism on the subject.

[6] At the same time the transmutation of metals is regarded as hypothetically possible.

[7] He is said to have resigned the latter dignity to pursue his studies in con- ventual retirement at Cologne. It is said also (1) that he was very dull in his youth; (2) that his devotion to the Blessed Virgin was rewarded by a vision and a sudden intellectual illumination; (3) that this remained with him till his old age, when he relapsed into original mediocrity; (4) that an ass was thus trans- formed into a philosopher and the philosopher again into an ass.

[8] The *Libellus* will be found also in *Theatrum Chemicum*, Vol. II.

Theatrum Chemicum.[1] As regards the first its attribution is determined in a hostile sense by Berthelot, who says that it is the translation of a fifteenth century Greek text, under the name of Theoctonicos, extant in a manuscript of the Bibliothèque Nationale.[2] The second does not happen to be disposed of in this summary manner by the fatal discovery of its source, and there is, moreover, a *Compendium de Ortu Metallorum* in the second volume of the collection mentioned above, but it is *nihil ad rem alchemicam*, being drawn from *De Rebus Metallicis* and belonging therefore to metallurgical speculation, not to the conversion of metals. It is obvious that in the last resource there can be no consequence attaching for myself to the question whether the Great Albert did or did not write on Alchemy, or even on Magic Garters in *Le Petit Albert*; but the literature of transmutation has been propagated so extensively under false ascriptions that it is well to know where we stand. I will end therefore by citing the considered and competent opinion of Professor Ferguson,[3] according to whom most if not all the alchemical tracts passing under the name of Albertus Magnus " are probably spurious ". Those who think otherwise—if any—can take refuge in another *legenda aurea*, the discovery of that great alchemist of romance and the Rosy Cross, Michael Maier, who testifies that Albertus received from the disciples of St. Dominic and that he communicated in turn to St. Thomas Aquinas the Secret of the Philosopher's Stone. Here is a story from the " land of heart's desire ", in which Éliphas Lévi—who knew of it—might have found a greater allegory than he did actually.[4] For myself I can discern only its spiritual consanguinity with a traditional tale of older Templar Masonry, which was told to Knights of God gathered in the Chapter of Clermont.[5] They heard that the Templar Secret was also that of the Stone, for when Hugh de Payens and his companion explored the foundations of a House assigned for their habitation by

---

[1] It is followed by *Compositum de Compositis* and *De Philosophorum Lapide*, under the same ascription.

[2] Berthelot, *op. cit.*, pp. 71, 155, 290.

[3] *Bibliography*, as cited previously, Vol. I, *s.v.*, Albertus Magnus.

[4] " As for the Philosophical Stone bequeathed by St. Dominic to Albert and by the latter to St. Thomas Aquinas, we must understand it as the philosophical and religious basis of ideas prevalent at the period."—*History of Magic*, as cited, p. 262.

[5] It was called the Fifth and last Grade of Freemasonry. See my *Emblematic Freemasonry*, 1925, pp. 290, 291.

Baldwin II, King of Jerusalem, they discovered a sealed
vessel containing not only the Powder of Projection but a
true way of its making. Now, the House in question was
over against the site of the First Temple, and the truth of
the matter was that the Great Mystery of Alchemy had been
revealed to Solomon by his Master Builder, Hiram Abiff.
Were it otherwise, the Temple could never have been covered
so lavishly with treasures of gold.

These things are faithful and true after their own manner,
which is the manner of tales of faërie, and most tracts on
transmutation come out of the same wallet, with the names
of their reputed authors. In this sense—and this only—
let us look at Albertus Magnus as the author of *Libellus
de Alchymia* and see how the matter of the work stands in
his view.[1] The thesis is that all metals are "composed of an
unctuous and subtle humidity, incorporated intimately with
a subtle and perfect matter." The degeneration of metals
is not therefore the consequence of essential impurities but
of local conditions in the bowels of the earth, and they are
capable of redemption, otherwise of transmutation, given
only a skilled artist who adheres strictly to the principles of
Nature.

Supposing that Albertus Magnus had inherited or discovered
the Philosopher's Stone it is of all likelihood that he would
have imparted *Secretum Artis* to his pupil St. Thomas Aquinas,
and in such case assuredly we should regard with an indulgent
eye those little alchemical books which are ascribed to the
Angel of the Schools, whether or not we could rank them
side by side with the *Summa*. But as it is certain that St.
Thomas never demolished, even allegorically, a talking
image constructed by Albertus, so it is beyond all question
that he was neither taught nor did he write upon the transmutation of metals, any more than on judicial astrology,
as proposed by one father of lies who reigns over false ascriptions. When it is said that *Thesaurus Alchimiæ*[2] is his

---

[1] It is to be noted that Mangetus, as the latest collector of tracts on Alchemy
into great volumes, seems to have had some notion on the probability of false
ascriptions, and in his vast *Bibliotheca* he took care to exclude the alleged works
of Albertus Magnus as he did those under the name of St. Thomas Aquinas, the
tract attributed to Pope John XXII, and several others.

[2] *Thesaurus Alchemiæ Secretissimus*, in *Theatrum Chemicum*, Vol. III. The other
ascribed works are *Secreta Alchemiæ Magnalia, ibid.*; *Lilium Benedictum, ib.*,

genuine work, it is to be understood that there is no better reason than is offered by the thoughtful forger, who cites Albert as his master in all things, but especially in Hermetic Philosophy. St. Thomas wrote with a pen of man and of angels on the Blessed Vision and of the soul's state in transcension, beyond the Rose and the Vision, which is called " one with One " : had he been admitted therefore into the chain of Hermes we should have looked for great things in Spiritual Alchemy ; and it is true that *Thesaurus Alchemiæ* testifies to children of light, who live in the presence of God, as those who alone are fit to know and to guard the Great Secret of adepts. But again and for ever it is concerned with (1) that sole substance of which all alchemical students are in search ; (2) which resists the action of fire ; (3) which penetrates everything, but above all (4) which tinges Mercury. There is one vase, one substance, one way and one only operation, *ad perpetranda miracula rei unius.* And this last does not mean the recovery of an " ancient experiment of Nature " performed in the soul of man, but the secret method by which imperfect metal is changed into that which is perfect.

There is a considerable and not altogether barren opportunity of research offered any leisured student who feels called to enlighten the world—unfortunately none too anxious —on several obscure questions which I will ask on my own part but do not propose to answer respecting the life and writings of Arnold de Villanova. (1) Was he born in Catalonia, Milan or Montpellier, and was A.D. 1245 the actual or probable date ? (2) What is the value, if any, of his works on medicine for the history of that science at this day of the world ? (3) What is the content broadly of his *Commentary* on the School of Salerno, and why precisely was that School entitled to such consideration ? (4) Was Peter of Apono his friend, and when this alleged sorcerer—presumably on account of his *Heptameron*—fell into the hands of the Inquisition, is it true that Arnold " withdrew prudently " from whatever was the danger zone and abode under the patronage of Frederic, King of Naples and Sicily ? (5) When—if ever—

Vol. IV ; *De Essentia Mineralium, ib.,* Vol. V : *Aurora. sive Aurea Hora,* in Joann. Rhenani *Harmoniæ Imperscrutabilis Chimico-Philosophicæ Decades Duæ,* 1625 ; and *In Turbam Commentarius Brevis, ibid.*

did he write the alchemical books which have placed him on
a high throne of adeptship by the verdict of all who love the
Hermetic Art ? (6) Is it true that he perished in a storm,
anno 1314—locality and circumstances to be ascertained, if
possible—and supposing that he did, why does a certain
alleged " circular letter " of Pope Clement V—dated 1311—
inquire for a copy of Arnold's *Treatise on Medicine*—which
out of many treatises ?—affirming that he was the Pope's
physician, and that it was promised to the Holy Father, but
the author died before he could present it ? (7) If Arnold
was body-physician to the murderous Avignon pontiff, was
he not better protected by that fact than by the power of
the King of Naples, and how could he be the Pope's physician
in exile from the Papal Court ?

To these interrogatories which concern the outward life
of Arnold there may be added (1) that he was accused of
magical practices ; (2) that his alchemical knowledge was
due to commerce with the devil, in the opinion of a certain
François Pegna ; (3) that Mariana tells a fantastic story of
the alchemist placing strange drugs in a pumpkin, in the hope
of creating a man, presumably a Paracelsian homunculus,
long prior to Paracelsus ; (4) that he is justified by the
demonologist Delrio from these imputations ; but there
remains the charge of heresy, as to which it is affirmed (5) that
the Inquisition of Tarragona condemned his books to be
burned for their strictures on the monastic state ; and also
because they maintained (6) that works of divine faith and
charity were more acceptable to God than the Holy Sacrifice
of the Mass. It is presumably on this account that Arnold
is said to have written the *Three Impostors*, of which we have
heard so much and seen so little, except the attributions of
its authorship, and these have been distributed over three
centuries, pending the discovery of the text.

The whole works of Arnold appeared at Leyden in 1520 and
in 1532, being reprinted also at other places in 1585 and 1613.
A collected edition of his alchemical writings is mentioned
as published in folio under date of 1509, but I have not been
able to trace it : there was a selection at Vienna in German,
anno 1742, containing eleven tracts. The entire output,
actual and mythical, is exceedingly large, but has been
expanded by variant titles representing the same texts and

K

by things unheard of prior to their first publication in the seventeenth century.[1]   Mangetus made an independent selection of nine tracts, which may be regarded as representative for those who would know Arnold's record,[2] there being nothing in English or French.[3]   We are concerned, however, solely with the kind of work which he claims to have performed in Alchemy,—as it might be said, with his own hands, under his own eyes;[4] and amidst the cloud of his testimonies it will be sufficient to cite as follows from *Liber Novi Testamenti*: (1) The Lord God Almighty has given us two Stones, one for the White and the other for the Red, by means of which two base and infirm metals are transmuted, namely, (2) Saturn into Sol and Jove into Luna.   On the theme of attainment there are various changes rung throughout the texts, but here is the term in view.   The foundation of the Art is solution, according to *Semita Semitæ*, being the reduction of the particular body—whether copper or some other metal —into Mercury.   This is the reduction into water of which all philosophers treat.   But the second secret of Art is the manifestation of earth out of water, while the third—under the name of purification—is performed by way of putrefaction for the combination of the moist and the dry.   The fourth is ascension, which aerifies the part of earth, after which there is sublimation by fire; and thus are the four elements represented and manifested in the Work.   The sublimation brings forth a spirit, which is said to be Mercury, and the calcined earth sinks to the bottom of the vessel; but this earth contains the seed and the seed is crown of all.   A ferment is added to earth and thereby it receives a soul for the perfection of the Mastery: the spirit is joined to these, and they are fixed and rejoice together.   Of such conjunction it is said that it is the beginning of marvels, a rainbow succession of colours, and the imperfect body is tinged according to

[1] *Theatrum Chemicum* is rich in Villanova texts : Vol. I, *Testamentum* ; Vol. II, *Perfectum Magisterium, Lumen Luminum, Flos Florum* and *Practica* ; Vol. IV, *Speculum Alchemiæ, Carmen* and *Quæstiones ad Bonifacium* VIII ; Vol. V, *Testamentum (aliud)*.

[2] The titles are (1) *Thesaurus Thesaurorum*, called also *Rosarium* : (2) *Novum Lumen* : (3) *Perfectum Magisterium et Gaudium*—otherwise *Flos Florum* ; (4) *Epistola ad Regem Neopolitanum* ; (5) *Speculum Alchemiæ* ; (6) *Carmen* ; (7) *Quæstiones* ; (8) *Semita Semitæ* ; (9) *Testamentum*.

[3] Lenglet du Fresnoy mentions a French MS., *Clef de la Grande Science de l'Œuvre Philosophique d'Arnaud de Villeneure*, but does not give any particulars ; it would seem to be the work of a commentator.

[4] See *Novum Lumen*, cap. I.

the quality of the ferment, becoming gold or silver.[1] As regards Philosophical Mercury, it is held to be the medicine and perfection of all metals, their degeneration being due to vulgar Sulphur. Hereof is the Great Work of Alchemy, according to Arnold.

According to Raymond Lully, metals cannot be transmuted unless they are reduced into their First Matter, being a fixed Mercury, otherwise Mercury of the Philosophers, and this is to be distinguished as such from common quicksilver, which no art can alter into that substance which is known and handled by the wise. But when the latter is mixed with the former they become united in a bond of love and never part. The phlegmatic humidity of common or running Mercury is dried up ; that which remains becomes black as coal and is afterwards turned into powder. The Mercury of Philosophers possesses the heat of Nature and imparts its temperate quality to the vulgar kind, transmuting it into pure metal, being Sol or Luna—one or other, accordingly as it is extended. It changes also the volatile Mercury into Medicine, and this Medicine can transmute imperfect metals into perfect. The Sophic Mercury is said to be a secret of the philosophers. I have drawn this summary statement from a memorial which claims (1) to elucidate the other writings of its author and (2) to declare the whole Art without any fiction. That it does nothing of the kind in either case there may be probably no need to register ; but it is late, on the hypothesis, in a long series and travels the same ground by a shorter method, so that in any case it brings the theme at large into a kind of focus,[2] while it is declaratory and clear enough as to the scope of alchemical Art. In the visions of Éliphas Lévi Raymond Lully appears as " a grand and sublime adept of Hermetic Science ", and since I have cited on a previous occasion this dictum of him who is still an occult *magnus Apollo* for Parisian circles, it is desirable to know where we are and to define the real limits

---

[1] When Arnold de Villanova utters aphoristic sentences reflected from Greek alchemists through Arabian and *Turba* sources, such as *vita vitam concipit* and *natura naturam vincit ac superat*, the *Suggestive Inquiry* regards them as referring to mesmeric operations : see 3rd ed., p. 273. The suggestion looks weird in the light of the analysis given in my text.

[2] The title in full is *Raymundi Lullii Clavicula, quæ et Apertorium in qua omnia quæ in Opere Alchimiæ requiruntur, aperte declarantur.* There is no need to cite the editions, but there is one in Mangetus.

of such an unqualified panegyric. Lully is great in certitude, without hesitation and without compromise ; it is difficult to read his *opera omnia chemica* and not to feel that he was talking of things that he knew, or that there must be something in his great claims, ever and again reiterated. But the measures within which they lie are indicated yet more briefly in one of his recurring Testaments,[1] where it is said (1) that Alchemy is part of natural philosophy ; (2) that it teaches the way of restoration for human bodies to the enjoyment of perfect health ; (3) that it communicates the secret of transmuting every metallic body into true silver and thereafter into true gold ; (4) that this is accomplished by one medicinal body and one manual regimen revealed to the Sons of Philosophy.

Having established in this manner the particular field of adeptship, it is to be held that my task is done, for I do not propose to summarise the monograph which I wrote recently on the subject and to which I refer those who are concerned.[2] For the rest, it must be understood that the purpose of this chapter is to give salient examples rather than to exhaust a list, as if I had taken all alchemists for my province ; and in the few pages that follow there will be found short notices only of well-known names and texts, it being understood that I have omitted no one and nothing that can be conceived as bearing another kind of testimony on the subject-matter of Alchemy.

There are at least two features of interest attaching to *Pretiosa Margarita Novella*, referred to Pietro Bono of Ferrara by his editor Janus Lacinius. In the first place, it ranks among the earliest works printed on Alchemy, and the original is a beautiful specimen of typography, being issued from the press of Aldus in 1546, with the privilege of Pope Paul III and the Senate of Venice for the space of ten years. The edition is exceedingly rare and is prized, I believe, by collectors. In the second place, it is a methodical and reasoned treatise which compares favourably in these respects with too much of alchemical literature. Concerning the author himself there are no particulars forthcoming, nor is there even any legend extant. It has been said only that he was a native

---

[1] *Testamentum Raymundi Lullii, Doctissimi et Celeberrimi Philosophi*, Liber II, cap. I.

[2] *Raymund Lully : Illuminated Doctor, Alchemist and Christian Mystic*, 1922.

of Lombardy and that he performed his alchemical experiments at Pola, a maritime town of Istria, about 1330. He is described sometimes as Bonus of Ferraria,[1] and on this and other grounds Tiraboschi[2] identifies him with the monk Eferarius, who flourished about the same period and produced two treatises, namely, *De Lapide Philosophorum* and *Thesaurus Philosophiæ*, which are printed in *Theatrum Chemicum*.[3] A survey of these works, which—unlike *Pretiosa Margarita*— are exceedingly obscure, and do not appear to have been esteemed when alchemical texts had readers, does not justify the attribution.[4]

The original manuscript upon which the monk of Calabria laboured, collecting, elucidating and expurgating, according to his own statement, has not only remained unpublished but is utterly unknown. The abridgement made by Lacinius has earned the reputation of fidelity on the faith of its editor's claim, but is still of unmanageable length and abounds after the fashion of its period in prolix disquisitions upon side issues. When therefore the time came, now many years since, for me to present it in English form, it was found necessary to abridge the abridgement by a reasonable pruning of mere repetitions and irrelevances, which notwithstanding the text and preliminaries are considerably over four hundred pages.[5] But the subject-matter and end of the Art in the

---

[1] Also of Traguria in Dalmatia, Mantua and other places.

[2] *Storia della Lettatura Italiana*, T.V., part i. The author—whose work is well known—characterises Lenglet du Fresnoy, the historian of Alchemy, as an inexact writer, which is not only true but almost inevitable at his period. Tiraboschi himself had, however, no acquaintance with Alchemy at large and little enough with the Masters whom he seeks to identify.

[3] See the Argentorati edition which began publication in 1613. Vol. III, *s.v.*, Monachus Efferarius.

[4] One is perhaps more inclined to question the Calabrian Minorite Friar on the not wholly improbable ground that his Master Bonus may have been his *alter ego*. As regards Ferarius, compare Lenglet du Fresnoy : *Nous avons le Traité du Moine Efferari ou Ferrari, mais ce dernier est peu lû par les connoisseurs, quoiqu'au milieu de beaucoup d'obscurité on y trouve quelques rayons de lumière, mais qu'il faut y savoir découvrir. On le croit de la fin du treizième siècle, ou du moins du commencement du quatorzième, parcequ'en citant Geber, la Tourbe et le solitaire Morien, il ne dit pas un mot d'Arnaud de Villeneuve, ni de Raymond Lulle ; c'etoient cependant deux grand maîtres, qui meritoient bien d'être citées, s'il avoit vécu après eux.*—Histoire de la Philosophie Hermétique. It may be noted also that these authors are not cited by Bonus, who quotes incessantly but only from old writers, thus suggesting that 1330 is a possible date for his records. On the other hand, Lacinius makes much of Arnold and Lully, thus justifying himself unconsciously by shewing that he was not the concealed author of *Pretiosa Margarita*. What, however, was the date of Lacinius ? The only possible answer is late in the fourteenth century.

[5] *The New Pearl of Great Price . . . The original Aldine edition, Translated into English*, 1894.

mind of Bonus, as in that of his editor, happen to lie within
an unexpectedly small compass, and there is no doubt concerning them from beginning to end. (1) That which Alchemy
undertakes is to transmute base metals into gold and silver.
(2) In so doing it follows the method of Nature and thus
produces natural and true gold, true and natural silver.
(3) Mercury is understood as the substance and Sulphur as
the active principle of all metals. (4) There is one substance
and from it is evolved the White Tincture and thereafter
the Red. (5) The Philosopher's Stone is the form of gold in
metals. Hereof is the testimony of Bonus, but like those who
preceded and those who came after him *Secretum Artis* is
the Gift of God, and the Stone of Alchemy would be made
in vain without the Hidden Stone, the life, the heart, the
Tincture, which come from Him.

About the beginning of the fourteenth century an Italian
Artist known as the monk Efferarius—often identified
with Ferarius—produced or is accredited with producing
those two treatises already mentioned, entitled *De Lapide
Philosophorum* and *Thesaurus Philosophiæ*. The first affirms
that it is essential before all things to know what is
signified by the myrionimous *argentum vivum sapientum*,
but there is offered on its own part no light on the subject.
The second cautions the amateur that the philosophers must
be regarded as most illusory, when they profess to be speaking
plainly. It is testified that Alchemy is a science of the four
elements, which are to be found in all creative substances
but are not of the vulgar kind. The practice of the Art
is the conversion of these elements one into another. The
seed and matter of every metal is Mercury, as it is decocted
and prepared in the bowels of the earth. Each of them can
be reduced into this *prima materia*, by the help of which
they are also, one and all, susceptible of augmentation and
multiplication, even to infinity. It will be seen that these
doctrinal affirmations are the common property of alchemists,
and there is very little to detain us in the texts when we
have once ascertained their purport.[1] With the testimony
of Ferarius I am acquainted by report only, as I have failed
to find his memorial. Efferarius was sufficiently recom-

[1] There seems little doubt that Efferarius wrote the tracts mentioned in my
text or that Ferarius is connected with a work described as *Tractatus Integer*.

mended to the editors of *Theatrum Chemicum* for his inclusion in the third volume of that historical collection.

The attribution of a tract on Alchemy to Pope John XXII, who was raised to the pontificate at Lyons and reigned at Avignon till his death in 1334, may be explained on two counts : (1) that he left vast sums in money and jewels, but this is according to legend, and (2) that he issued a Bull condemning traders in Alchemy as impostors who promised that which they were not able to perform : it is probable enough, but I have not met with it in the records. The first story suggested to the occult mind of his own and later days that he was really an adept of that Art which, according to the second, he denounced as trickery. For the same occult mind it was in any case a pious act and a just judgment to father an alchemical text upon a pope who had thus pronounced against the followers of Hermes. There appeared accordingly under his name a treatise on *L'Art Transmutatoire* in a collection entitled *Divers Traités d'Alchimie*, which was issued at Lyons in 1557. By the hypothesis, it was translated from the Latin, but there is no trace of the alleged original, nor do I find an earlier edition of the French form, though another of the same year and the same place appeared by itself, according to Lenglet du Fresnoy. The constituents of the Perfect Medicine are said to be vinegar, salt, urine and sal ammoniac, with the addition of sulphur vive, which is not defined to be that of the philosophers and is not otherwise described. The attribution is completely fraudulent and reads like an excerpt from *The Magus* of Francis Barrett. As regards the " vast sums ", an accuser has said that they were made by the sale of indulgences. In those days it might be credibly a more easy task than to make them by Alchemy.

The testimony of Picus de Mirandula—though he had no claim on adeptship—is worth quoting from his treatise *De Auro* : it is contained in two narratives, the first of which is as follows. " I come now to declare that which I have beheld of this prodigy, without veil or obscurity. One of my friends who is still living has made gold and silver over sixty times in my presence. I have seen it performed in various manners, but the cost of producing the silver with a metallic water exceeded the value of the produce." What happened in the experiments for gold does not appear in the account. The other story tells of a good man who had not enough for the support of his family and fell into extreme distress. " With a disturbed mind he passed one night into sleep and beheld an angel, who instructed him by means of enigmas in the art of making gold, including the water which must be used to insure success. He went to work on awaking and produced the precious metal, truly in small quantities and yet sufficient for his needs." Mirandula says that he made gold twice of iron and four times of orpiment, apparently in his own presence, for he adds that the operator " convinced me by the evidence of my own eyes that the art of transmutation is no fiction " I have introduced these stories partly because a natural affection for the illustrious Picus does not permit their omission but also to relieve a considerable chain of professional deposition by the production of an independent witness. And the last voice to which we shall listen in this chapter shall also connote relief, for it is that of a poet, though he calls for a word only.

The life of Jean Fontaine is hidden behind the door of his laboratory, and I know not what credit should be given to a report that he was sojourning at Valenciennes in 1413. In reality he is known only by the fact of his Hermetic poem *Aux Amoureux de Science*, which has been printed several times. He lays claim on adeptship therein and describes in an allegorical manner, after the fashion of the *Romance of the Rose*, but in a later form of its quaint and beautiful tongue, the different processes which enter into the art of transmutation. It is like a paradise in its dainty devices of old-world Nature-pictures, but I can conceive no amateur of practical alchemy deriving anything from its couplets. There is, however, no other intent but to shew that metals may suffer conversion and that they do in fact.

The provisional survey of Latin alchemical literature has now reached a stage when certain individual personalities not only stand forth from the general cloud of witnesses—as indeed has been the case previously with Arnold and the pseudo-Raymund Lully—but we know more fully concerning them : they will be studied therefore successively in particular monographs.

CHAPTER X

THE MYTH OF FLAMEL

THE alchemical quest and attainment of Nicholas Flamel are first in the time-order of three remarkable narratives which may claim to count, at the value of their proper warrants, among romances of real life in Alchemy, though how far their historical position can be sustained is another and—as we shall find in the present instance—something more than a debateable question. The second is well known under the name of Bernard Trévisan, who is of venerable memory among all later Hermetists. The third is scarcely less celebrated under that of Denis Zachaire, though he is cited comparatively seldom by those who came after : he was even the subject of an indifferent but not unreadable novel towards the close of the nineteenth century.[1] All the original narratives are characterised by an air of veracity, but in respect of matter and manner the story of Flamel seems to stand forth from the others. The *Book of Abraham the Jew* is at least a notable invention, while its story is told with such seeming transparent sincerity that it is not altogether easy to regard it as a mere myth. The history of Nicholas Flamel shall be given in the first place and in what purports to be his own words.

Be praise for ever to the Lord my God, Who exalts the humble out of mire and dust; Who rejoices the hearts of those who hope in Him ; Who opens of his own grace the springs of bounty unto believing souls and sets their feet upon the crowns of earthly felicity. Let our trust be always in Him, our joy in His fear, our confidence in His mercy, looking for a glorious restoration of our nature, and in prayer be our impregnable safeguard. And Thou, O God Almighty, as Thy bounty has deigned to open the earth before me—Thine unworthy servant—and to reveal the treasures of its riches, may it please Thy mercy, when I shall

---

[1] *A Professor of Alchemy*, by Percy Ross (the pseudonym of a woman writer, otherwise—I believe—unknown). It appeared in 1887.

be counted no more among those who abide in this world, to unveil for me the Treasures of Heaven, vouchsafing that even I may look upon Thy Divine Countenance, the ineffable delight of Thy majesty, which it hath not entered into the heart of mortal man to conceive. This I beseech in the Name of the Lord Jesus Christ, Thy beloved Son, Who in the unity of the Holy Spirit abides with Thee, world without end for ever.

I, Nicholas Flamel, Scrivener, living at Paris, this year of our Lord 1399,[1] in Notary Street, over against the Church of St. James of the Boucherie, do hereby and herein testify that I learned not much Latin because of the poverty of my parents, notwithstanding which they were accounted good and honest by those who envy me most. It befell, however, by the great grace of God, the intercession of His saints in Paradise and of St. James chiefly, that I have not lacked understanding in books written by philosophers or failed to learn the secrets concealed therein. For which reason there shall pass no moment of my life wherein, remembering this so high a good, I will not on my bare knees, if the place permit, or otherwise in my heart, with all my love, give thanks unto my good and gracious God, Who never suffers the children of the just to beg their bread and never deceives those who place their firm trust in His blessing.

After the death of my parents I, Nicholas Flamel, earned my living by the art of writing, engrossing inventories, making up accounts and checking the expenses of tutors and scholars. In the course of these avocations there came into my hands for the sum of two florins a gilded book which was very old and large. The leaves were neither paper nor parchment like those of other books but—as it seemed to me—of the rinds of young trees. The cover was of brass, well bound and covered with a strange kind of letters, which I took to be Greek characters or those of some other ancient tongue.[2] Whatever they were, I was not able to read them, from which it follows that they were neither Latin nor French, seeing that I know something of these. As to that which was written within, on the leaves of bark, there were

---

[1] Flamel is supposed to have been born in 1330.
[2] It is obvious, by the hypothesis concerning the book and its origin, that the characters would have been Hebrew, and the intention is to suggest this.

fair Latin letters curiously coloured and inscribed very skilfully with an iron graver. The book contained thrice seven leaves, so numbered at the top of each folio, every seventh leaf having painted images and figures instead of writing. On the first of these seven leaves there was depicted a virgin who was being swallowed by serpents; on the second a Cross upon which a serpent was crucified; on the last a wilderness watered by many fair fountains, out of which came a number of serpents, running here and there. On the first written leaf the following words were inscribed in great characters of gold: "Abraham the Jew, Prince, Priest, Levite, Astrologer and Philosopher, unto the Jewish nation scattered through France by the wrath of God, wishing health in the name of the Lord of Israel." Thereafter followed great execrations and maledictions, with the word *Maranatha* repeated over and over, poured forth against anyone who should glance within, unless he were priest or scribe.

The person who sold me this book must have known its value as much and as little as I who bought it. My suspicion is that it was either stolen from the miserable Jews or found hidden somewhere in the old place of their abode. On the second leaf the said Abraham consoled his people, praying them to avoid vices and idolatry more than all and await with patience the Messiah to come, who would vanquish all kings of the earth and thereafter reign, with those who were his own, in eternal glory. Without doubt this Abraham was a man of great understanding. On the third and rest of the written leaves he taught them the transmutation of metals in plain words, to help his captive nation in paying tribute to Roman emperors and for other objects which I shall not disclose. He painted the vessels on the margin, discovered the colours, with all the rest of the work, but concerning the Prime Agent he uttered no word, advising them only that he had figured and emblazoned it with great care in the fourth and fifth leaves. But all his skill notwithstanding, no one could interpret the designs unless he was far advanced in Jewish Kabalah and well studied in the books of the Philosophers. It follows that the fourth and fifth leaves were also without writing but full of illuminated figures exquisitely designed.

On the obverse of the fourth leaf there was shewn a young

man with winged feet, having in his hand a caducean rod, encompassed by two serpents, and with this he stroke upon a helmet which covered his head. I took him to represent the heathen God Mercury. Unto him came running and flying with open wings a very old man, having an hour glass set upon his head and a scythe in his hands, like the figure of death, with which scythe he would have struck off the feet of Mercury. On the reverse of the fourth leaf a fair flower was depicted on the summit of a very high mountain, round which the North wind blustered. The plant had a blue stem, white and red flowers, leaves shining like fine gold, while about it the dragons and griffins of the North made their nests and their dwelling. On the obverse side of the fifth leaf there was a rose bush in flower, in the midst of a fair garden, and growing hard by a hollow oak tree. At the foot bubbled forth a spring of very white water, which ran headlong into the depths below, passing first through the hands of a great concourse of people who were digging up the ground in search of it. But they were blind and therefore failed to recognise it, save one person only, who paid attention to its weight. On the reverse side appeared a king carrying a great faulchion who caused his soldiers to destroy in his presence a multitude of little children, the mothers weeping at the feet of the murderers. The streams of blood were gathered by other soldiers into a great vessel, wherein the sun and moon came to bathe. Now, seeing that this history appeared to depict the slaughter of the innocents by Herod, and that I learned the main part of the Art in this book, it came about that I placed in their Cemetery these hieroglyphic symbols of the Secret Science.

I have now described the content of the first five leaves, but I shall say nothing of all that was written in fair and intelligible Latin on the other pages, lest God should visit me for greater wickedness than that of him who wished that all mankind had but one head, so that he could cut it off at a blow.[1]

---

[1] The story betrays itself at this point, for it is obvious that what had been written in Latin could be written also in French and that if the Prince, Priest, Astrologer and Philosopher was not in danger of the judgment for teaching " the transmutation of metals in plain words ", concealing only the First Matter, the scrivener would not be more criminal than Nero if he reproduced the Jewish testimony. The Paris cemetery named in the text was that of the Innocents.

The precious book being in my possession I did little but study it night and day, till I attained a fair understanding of all its processes, knowing nothing, however, respecting the Matter of the Work. I could therefore make no beginning, and the result was that I became very sad and depressed. My wife Perrenelle, whom I had married recently and loved as much as myself, was astonished and concerned greatly, endeavouring to comfort me and desiring earnestly to know whether she could not help me in my distress. I was never one who could hold his tongue and not only told her everything but shewed her the book itself, for which she conceived the same affection as my own, taking great delight in the beautiful cover, the pictures and inscriptions, all of which she understood as little as I did. There was no small consolation, however, in talking with her about them and in wondering what could be done to discover their meaning. At length I caused the figures on the fourth and fifth leaves to be painted as well as I could and had them put up in my workroom, where I shewed them to many scholars of Paris; but these also could throw no light upon them. I went so far as to tell them that they had been found in a book about the Philosopher's Stone, but most of them made a mock of it and also of me. An exception however was one named Anselm, a licentiate in medicine and a deep student of the Art. He desired earnestly to see my book and would have done anything to have his way in the matter, but I persisted in saying that it was not in my possession, though I gave him a full account of the process described therein.

He declared that the first figure represented Time, which devours all things, while the six written leaves shewed that a space of six years was required to perfect the Stone, after which there must be no further coction. When I pointed out that according to the book the figures were designed to teach the First Matter he answered that the six years' coction was like a second agent; that as regards the first it was certainly shewn forth as a white and heavy water, which was doubtless quicksilver. The feet of this substance could not be cut off, meaning that it could not be fixed and so deprived of volatility except by such long decoction in the pure blood of young children. The quicksilver uniting with gold and silver in this blood would change with them, firstly into a herb like that of the fair flower on the reverse of the fourth leaf, secondly by corruption into serpents, which serpents, being perfectly dried and digested by fire, would become Powder of Gold, and of such in truth is the Stone.

This explanation sent me astray through a labyrinth of innumerable false processes for a period of one and twenty years, it being always understood that I made no experiments with the blood of children, for that I accounted villainous. Moreover, I found in my book that what the philosophers called blood is the mineral spirit in metals, more especially in gold, silver and quicksilver, to the admixture of which I tended always. The licentiate's interpretations being more subtle than true, my processes never exhibited the proper signs at the times given in the book, so I was ever to begin again. At last, having lost all hope of understanding the figures, I made a vow to God and St. James that I would seek their key of some Jewish priest belonging to one of the Spanish Synagogues. Thereupon, with the consent of Perrenelle and carrying a copy of the figures, I assumed a pilgrim's weeds and staff, in the same manner as you see me depicted outside the said arch in the said churchyard where I put up the hieroglyphic figures, as also a procession representing on both sides of the wall the successive colours of the Stone which arise and pass off in the work, and the following inscription in French : " A procession is pleasing to God when it is done in devotion." These are the first words, or their equivalent, of a tract on the colours of the Stone by the King Hercules, entitled *Iris*, which opens thus : *Operis Processio Multum Naturæ Placet.*[1] I quote them for the benefit of scholars, who will understand the allusion.

Having donned my pilgrim's weeds, I began to fare on the road, reaching Mountjoy and finally my destination at St. James, where I fulfilled my vow with great devotion. On the return journey I met with a merchant of Boulogne in Leon, and to him I was indebted for acquaintance with

[1] The French text reads in crude verse :

> Moult plaist à Dieu Procession
> S'elle est faite en devotion,

and it is obvious that it bears no relation to the Latin text. King Hercules means the Emperor Heraclius, who had Hermetic tracts fathered on him by the tradition of Greek Alchemy.

Master Canches, a doctor of great learning, who was Jewish by nation but now a Christian. When I shewed him my copy of the figures he was ravished with wonder and joy, and asked with great earnestness whether I could give him news of the book from which they were taken. He spoke in Latin, and I answered in the same language that if anyone could decipher the enigmas there was good hope of learning its whereabouts. He began at once to decipher the beginning. To shorten this part of my story, he had heard much talk of the work but as of a thing that was utterly lost. I resumed my journey in his company, proceeding from Leon to Oviedo and thence to Sareson, at which port we set sail for France and arrived in due time, after a prosperous voyage. On our way to Paris my companion most truly interpreted the major part of my figures, in which he found great mysteries, even to the points and pricks. But unhappily when we reached Orleans this learned man fell sick and was afflicted with extreme vomitings, a recurrence of those from which he had suffered at sea. He was continually in fear of my leaving him, and though I was ever at his side he would still be calling me. To my great sorrow he died on the seventh day, and to the best of my ability I saw that he was buried in the Church of Holy Cross at Orleans. There he still lies, and may God keep his soul, seeing that he made a good Christian end.

He who would see the manner of my arrival home and the satisfaction of Perrenelle may look on us both as we are painted on the door of the Chapel of St. James of the Boucherie, hard by my house. We are shewn on our knees, myself at the feet of St. James of Spain and she at those of St. John, to whom she prayed so often. By the grace of God and the intercession of the Holy and Blessed Virgin, as also of the Saints just mentioned, I had gained that which I desired, being a knowledge of the First Matter,[1] but not as yet of its initial preparation, a thing of all else most difficult in the world. In the end, however, I attained this also, after errors innumerable through the space of some three years, during which I did nothing but study and work, as you will see me depicted outside the arch at the feet of St. James and St. John, ever praying to God, rosary in hand, engrossed in a

[1] The intimation is that the converted Jew had explained the meaning of the symbolical figures and in so doing had revealed the First Matter.

book, pondering the words of the philosophers and proving various operations suggested by their study. The fact of my success was revealed to me by the strong odour, and thereafter I accomplished the Mastery with ease : indeed I could scarcely miss the work had I wished, given a knowledge of the prime agents, their preparation and following my book to the letter. On the first occasion projection was made upon Mercury, of which I transmuted a half pound or thereabouts into pure silver, better than that of the mine, as I and others proved by assaying several times. This was done on a certain Monday, the seventeenth day of January, 1392, Perrenelle only being present. Thereafter, still following—word for word—the directions of my book, about five o'clock in the evening of the twenty-fifth day of the following April, I made projection of the Red Stone on the same amount of Mercury, still at my own house, Perrenelle and no other with me, and it was truly transmuted into the same quantity of pure gold, much better than that of the ordinary metal, softer and more pliable. I speak in all truth : I have made it three times with the aid of Perrenelle, for she helped me in all my operations and understood the subject as well as myself. She could have done it alone without doubt, had she desired, and would have brought it to the same term. The first occasion gave me all that I needed, but I took great delight in contemplating the wonderful works of Nature within the vessels, and to signify that I made three transmutations you have only to look at the arch and the three furnaces depicted thereupon, answering to those which served in our operations.

For a considerable time I was in no little anxiety lest Perrenelle should prove unable to conceal her happiness and should let fall some words among her kinsfolk concerning our great treasure. I judged of her joy by my own, and great joy—like great sorrow—is apt to diminish caution. But the Most High God in His goodness had not only granted me the blessing of the Stone : He had given me a chaste and prudent wife, herself endowed with reason, qualified to act reasonably, and more discreet and secret than other women are for the most part. Above all she was very devout and having no expectation of children, for we were now advanced in years, she began—like myself—to think of God and to occupy herself with works of mercy. Before I wrote this commentary, which was towards the end of the year 1413, after the passing of my faithful companion whom I shall lament all the days of my life, she and I had already founded and endowed fourteen hospitals, had built three Chapels and provided seven Churches with substantial gifts and revenues, as well as restoring their cemeteries. These things were done in Paris, besides which there was all that we did at Boulogne, to about the same extent. Of our work among poor people, principally widows and orphans, I shall say nothing, that my reward may not be in this world and because it might pain those whose names I mentioned.

Building therefore these Churches, cemeteries and hospitals in this city of Paris, I caused to be depicted in the fourth arch of the same Cemetery of the Innocents the most true and essential signs of the Art but under hieroglyphic veils and coverings, in imitation of those in the gilded book of Abraham the Jew. According to the capacity and knowledge, of those who saw them, they could stand for two things, being (1) the mysteries of our future and indubitable resurrection at the day of judgment and the advent of the good Jesus, a story most appropriate for a graveyard ; but (2) all the principles and necessary operations of the Mastery for the expert in natural philosophy. It may be said therefore of these hieroglyphical figures that they are like two paths leading to celestial life, the first and more open sense teaching the sacred mysteries of our salvation and the second instructing all, however, little they may be versed in the matter of the Stone, concerning the true way of that Work which, if perfected by anyone, changes him from bad to good, takes away avarice which is the root of all sin, makes him liberal, mild, religious and Godfearing. For thenceforward he remains continually ravished by the great grace and mercy which he has obtained from God and by His divine and admirable works.[1] These are the reasons which led me to put up the

---

[1] The suggestion is that the admirable work of composing the Philosopher's Stone is in analogy with the work of God in creation, and it is set out at length in some later texts of Alchemy, though the root-matter of the correspondence is found even in *Turba Philosophorum*. As regards the alleged change from bad to good, on the hypothesis that "the love of money is the root of all evil", it is obvious that the possession *per se* of great riches by no means connotes in fact the turning of the heart to God, but the text is seeking to shew in exaggerated language that a successful alchemist has all the opportunities for good which unlimited

figures as aforesaid in the Cemetery so that if anyone attains the inestimable blessing of the Golden Fleece he may be led like me not to hide the gift of God under a bushel, purchasing earthly possessions, which are mundane vanities, but may rather give charitable help to his brethren, remembering how he learned the secret amidst the bones of the dead, amidst which also he will presently find himself, and that after this transitory life he will be called to account in the presence of a just and terrible Judge, by Whom even the idle word will be found deserving blame.

Let him therefore who has weighed seriously these my words, who has come to understand my figures and is acquainted otherwise with the First Matter and the Prime Agents, concerning which he will find no hint either in the present treatise or in the figures themselves, accomplish the Mastery of Hermes and be mindful thereafter of the Catholic, Apostolic and Roman Church, of all other Churches, Cemeteries and Hospitals, but most of all the Church of the Holy Innocents and the Cemetery in which he has contemplated my true demonstrations, opening his purse generously to the poor and sick, to widows and unhappy orphans. So be it.

The story of Nicholas Flamel has two sequels at their value. The gift which proved fortunate to himself became a curse to one at least of his descendants. It is affirmed that he gave some transmuting powder to a nephew of Perrenelle, named Perrier, from whom it passed down to an alleged Dr. Perrier, after whose death it was found among his effects by Dubois, described as his grandson. The prudence and moderation which safeguarded the gift to the Perriers was not found in their heir, who exhibited the Great Secret to improper persons and was brought before Louis XIII, in whose presence he produced gold out of base metal, and this gold augmented its weight in the cupel. Moreover, in his vanity Dubois imagined that he could make or at least augment the powder and promised so to do, but his experiments proved a failure. He was then suspected of withholding

wealth can give. Now, the best commentary on this is the story of Lascaris, whose mission it was to distribute the powder of projection and who brought misery on those who received it.

the Art from the King and is said to have been hanged.[1] According to the other story, after the death of Flamel, we hear of persons turning their curious eyes on the house which he had so long inhabited and in which his transmutations had been accomplished. It was likely and more than likely to contain buried treasures. Such at least was the opinion of one individual so late as the year 1576, when a stranger applied to the Provost of Paris, pretending that a deceased friend had entrusted him with certain sums for the restoration of Flamel's house. The building was exceedingly dilapidated and the official fell into the trap ; but the true object in view became evident when the stranger began to lay bare the whole foundation and ransacked from top to bottom. He found nothing, however, and suddenly vanished without paying for the operations which he had caused to be set on foot.[2]

According to Lenglet du Fresnoy,[3] the evidences of Flamel's claims were extant in the year 1742 : in the Cemetery of the Holy Innocents there stood the arch built by him, having the hieroglyphic figures upon it. In two niches without the arch, being on the further side, were statues of St. James and St. John : below the latter was the figure of Flamel himself, reading a book, a Gothic N. F. representing his initials. The progression of colours which marked the

---

[1] It is obviously impossible to investigate the evidence—if any—for this tale of an inheritance in which the heirloom itself is mythical for most persons in the world. Louis XIII ascended the throne of France in 1610, when innumerable alchemists were putting their claims forward and their voices were " in all men's ears ". There were those, moreover, who " travelled " in the Red and White Powders, sometimes for no apparent purpose except to demonstrate the truth of the Art, as in the case of Alexander Seton—which will be reached shortly—but more often as rogues and hucksters. There was nothing more simple at the period than to deceive the rank and file of those who saw, including kings and princes. It is by no means unlikely that a Dubois, among others, was flaunting alchemical wares at some time or another—no date is cited—between the accession and death of the particular French King ; and as the autobiography of Flamel was then recently in evidence and probably attracting great attention, not alone in alchemical circles, there is nothing unlikely also in the hypothesis of a cheating alchemist accounting for his pretended treasures by an alleged inheritance from a great French adept. It is hypothesis only, but it follows the line of least resistance, supposing that there was a Dubois carrying the alleged Tinctures, supposing that he was summoned by Louis XIII and was hanged or not ultimately for making a false claim. But the story as told offers no warrants and gives no references whatever : its historical value is therefore *nil*, awaiting the highly unlikely time of its investigation by a competent hand in France.

[2] The curious pretender, according to Figuier—*op. cit.*, p. 199—affirmed that he was an old friend of Flamel himself, who had deposited money for the purpose, thus rendering the credulity of the city authorities still more ridiculous.

[3] *Histoire de la Philosophie Hermétique*, Vol. I.

progress of the work was, however, effaced. The same Cemetery contained a charnel-house or depository for skulls and bones distinterred by the digging of new graves, and on the entrance pillars the initials N. F. were graven in the same way, with the following further inscription :

> Ce charnier fut fait et donné à l'Eglise,
> pour l'amour de Dieu, l'an 1399.

The second of these evidences was on the Marivaux door of the Church of St. Jacques-la-Boucherie, namely, a figure of Flamel kneeling at the feet of St. James, with a Gothic N. on the pedestal. This was on the left side of the entrance, and on the right was a figure of Perrenelle at the feet of St. John, the pedestal in this case bearing a Gothic P. The third evidence was in the Rue Notre Dame, at the portal of Geneviève of Arden, where Flamel's statue was to be seen in a niche, kneeling with a desk at his side and looking towards St. James. There was a Gothic N. F. below and the inscription : " This portal was built in 1402 by the alms of many." Flamel, it is suggested, concealed in this manner the fact that he was donor-in-chief; but nothing attaches to the notion. The fourth and final evidence was in the street of the Cemetery of St. Nicholas in the Fields, where the wall of an unfinished hospital has figures inscribed on a stone and the Flamel initials.

After the death of Perrenelle the bereaved adept is supposed to have prepared for posterity several works on the science which had enriched him : *Le Livre de Nicolas Flamel* :[1] *Le Sommaire Philosophique*,[2] in rhymed verse ; *Trois Traités de la Transformation Metallique*,[3] also in verse ; *Le Désir Désiré, ou Trésor de Philosophie* ;[4] *Le Grand Eclaircissement* ;[5] *La Musique Chimique* ;[6] and at least one other to which I

[1] *Le Livre de Nicolas Flamel* is an alternative title of *Les Figures Hiéroglyphiques,* containing the autobiographical narrative, which I have translated practically in full, followed by a Theological and Hermetic Interpretation of the Abraham pictures and those erected by Flamel in the Cemetery of the Innocents. 1612 and several later editions.

[2] Otherwise *Le Roman de Flamel,* which does not mean that it reproduces his story but that it is written in romance form, namely, rhymed measures, like the *Roman de la Rose.* Paris, 1561.

[3] Unknown to Lenglet du Fresnoy.

[4] Alternatively *Le Livre des Six Paroles*, 1629.

[5] Concerning the Philosophical Stone for the transmutation of all Metals, 1628.

[6] Cited by Lenglet du Fresnoy without place, date or particulars of any kind. He had evidently never seen it.

shall refer later. Approaching the end of his life, he is said
to have chosen his place of burial before the crucifix in the
Church of St. Jacques-la-Boucherie, and to this end he
contracted with its wardens, as specified in his will,[1] which
is said to be in the Church archives, is dated November 22nd,
1416, and begins thus : " To all those unto whom these
presents shall come, I, Anneguy du Castel, Chevalier.
Councillor, Chamberlain of the King our Sire, Keeper of the
Provost of Paris (*sic*), Greeting : Know ye that before Hugues
de la Barre and Jean de la Noe, Notary clerks of the King at
the Chatelet, was established personally, Nicholas Flamel,
Scrivener, sound in body and mind, speaking clearly, with
good and true understanding," *etc.* It fills four sheets of
parchment stitched endwise together, thus forming a roll.
The thirty-four clauses bequeath his possessions to the Church
and poor, subject to legacies amounting to forty livres, which
went to relatives. He is supposed to have lived for two
years after executing this will, dying at an uncertain date
in or about 1418.

Hostile criticism went to work early on the story of
Nicholas Flamel and its testimony to the fact of transmutation, adopting various means. It has sought to minimise
his wealth by reducing his munificence, representing him as
an honest burgess, who, thanks to economy and assiduity,
acquired a competence, and having no children he devoted
it to works of benevolence, including the erection of public
buildings on a moderate scale. An early expositor of this
view is the Abbé Villain,[2] and there is something to be said
in its favour, but having regard to the testament of Perrenelle,
dated 1399 and apparently genuine,[3] and to the endowment
of Hospitals and Churches, which were on quite a considerable
scale, it seems unquestionable that he was a person of

---

[1] The authority is Lenglet du Fresnoy, and as he quotes the preamble to the
document it is to be presumed that he had seen it and so also the Last Testament
of Perrenelle. As nothing attaches to either from the standpoint of Alchemy,
it will serve no purpose to discuss them.

[2] That is, Étienne François Villain, who wrote *Essai d'une Histoire de la Paroisse
de Saint Jacques de la Boucherie*, Paris, 1758, and *Histoire Critique de Nicholas
Flamel*, 1761. The Abbé Pernety intervened to prove that Flamel was an alchemist,
in view of a manuscript Breviary which he had examined and which was in the
scrivener's autograph : it had an " allegorical treatise on Alchemy " written upon
the margins. Villain replied in the *Année Littéraire* of 1762.

[3] See Louis Figuier : *L'Alchimie et les Alchimistes*, p. 191.

substantial means. Gabriel Naudé,[1] who detested Magic and seems to have despised Alchemy, does not challenge the wealth of Flamel but accounts for it on the hypothesis that he managed affairs for the Jews. When they were banished from the Kingdom of France and their property confiscated by or on behalf of the King, " he—knowing the sums due by several individuals—made a compromise with them, they paying over and he receiving a part, to prevent him giving information which would have involved the surrender of all." There is not only no particle of evidence for transactions of this kind, but the gratuitous slander is at issue with facts of the time. There were three expulsions of the Jews from France between 1300 and 1420. They were banished in 1308, were allowed to return soon after and then again banished in 1320. These persecutions occurred before the birth of Flamel. The Jews were reinstated by Charles V in 1364 and remained undisturbed till certain riots of Paris in 1380, at the beginning of the reign of Charles VI, when the people rose up against them, committing great outrages and demanding their expulsion. The sedition was quelled and protection extended to the Jews until 1393, when several charges were preferred against them and they were enjoined to quit France or else become Christians. The historian Mezeray says that some of them chose to forsake their religion rather than the kingdom, but others sold their goods and retired.[2] It appears therefore that the only enforced exodus of Israel which might agree with the charge of Naudé was without confiscation of property and could not have given Flamel the opportunity alleged.[3] However he made his riches it was not in this manner. They are admitted by other writers, including Louis Figuier,[4] but they enlarge—like Abbé Villain—upon the remunerative nature of a scrivener's occupation before the invention of printing and upon the

---

[1] *Apologie pour tous les Grands Personnages qui ont été faussement accusés de Magie.* Paris, 1625. See also Figuier, *op. cit.*, pp. 191–195, and compare Théophile Halley : *Les Juifs en France*, 1847.

[2] I am unable to verify this statement at its source, so it must be left to stand at its value : there is no work of Mezeray, historical or otherwise, to be found in English libraries, so far as I have ascertained.

[3] It is of course pure speculation to suggest that the Jews of Paris entrusted their affairs to Flamel or that he had any dealings with them in the course of his business.

[4] He mentions two minor persecutions of Jews, one in 1346, when Flamel was a boy, and another in 1354, when he was scarcely established in business.

frugality of the supposed alchemist : it is needless to say that there is no evidence before us in respect of the second point.

The first real question which arises in the criticism of the Flamel legend is the authenticity of the writings which pass under his name. Of his personal existence there is of course full evidence in view of the inscribed monuments, an account of which has been given, and I do not find that his will or that of his wife has been subjected to serious challenge. But these documents contain of course no reference to his alchemical pursuits, while it happens that the famous allegorical pictures are open to no such interpretation as that which appears in the legend—a point to which I shall recur. The legend itself come before us solely in the autobiographical record contained in *Les Figures Hiéroglyphiques*, a work that first saw the light of printing in 1612, when it appeared at Paris, together with the tracts ascribed to Artephius and Synesius, and is described like those as translated from the Latin by " a gentleman of Poitou " who was also a *sieur de la chevallerie* and was named P. Arnaud.[1] It follows that this publication took place almost two centuries after Flamel's death, with a claim in respect of its original language which is almost certainly false. A Latin version has never been seen or indeed heard of otherwise, and other writings attributed to Flamel are invariably in French, save only the blatant forgery of *Theatrum Chemicum*, Vol. I, 1613, being certain *Annotationes* of a supposed Nicholas Flamel on the *Opusculum* of Denys Zachaire, who happens to have been born about one hundred years after the death of his ascribed commentator. The metrical *Sommaire Philosophique* appeared in 1561 and *Le Grand Eclaircissement* in 1628, when the editor, who apparently abounded in Flamel MSS., promised also the publication of *La Joie Parfaite de Moi, Nicolas Flamel, et de Pernelle, ma Femme*, of which nothing further has been heard. *Le Désir Desiré ou Trésor de Philosophie* belongs to

---

[1] Figuier suggests idly that Arnaud paraphrased a lost manuscript of Flamel. On the other hand the *Biographie Universelle* has an article signed by Delaulnaye, who proposes that the Flamel legend is symbolical of the Hermetic work itself and that it was put in circulation, if not invented, by Jacques Gohorry, in a preface to *Sommaire Philosophique*, mentioned in my text, the reference offered being *Transmutation Métallique*, 1561. An edition of the *Sommaire*, otherwise *Le Roman de Flamel*, is cited under this date by Lenglet, but not under this title. I have failed to trace a copy. If the particulars given are correct it would mean only that the Flamel myth was in course of manufacture prior to 1612.

1629 and is the only tract which has been defended on the score of antiquity. I cite as follows under the name of Auguste Vallet : " There exists in the *Bibliothèque du Roi* a small manuscript book, *grossement relié*, according to all appearance belonging to the end of the fourteenth century and treating of alchemical operations. It opens with these words : ' *Incipit* the True Practice of the Noble Science of Alchemy, the Desired Desire and unappraisable prize, compiled from all the philosophers and drawn out of ancient writings.' It teaches the manner of accomplishing the Great Work by means of successive operations which are termed *lavures* in the treatise. On the last leaf of the manuscript is the following inscription, written by the same hand as the rest of the text : ' The present book is of and belonging to Nicholas Flamel, of the Parish Saint-Jacques de la Boucherie, who has written and illuminated it with his own hand ' ".[1]

Here is a bibliographical item of very considerable interest ; but (1) the romantic Flamel memoir gives no indication that he wrote anything except that monograph—otherwise *Les Figures Hieroglyphiques*—and its garrulous narrative suggests that there was nothing omitted ; (2) if there is anything in the statement, already cited, that his contributions to Hermetic literature were made subsequently to the death of Perrenelle, they belong to the early fifteenth century ; (3) no printed edition of the *Trésor* opens in the way quoted, nor does such a passage occur anywhere in the text ; (4) the operations are not termed *lavures*, a fact that suggests grave and perhaps essential difference between the two recensions, which may correspond only in title. Finally, the statement that the MS. is " of and belonging to " Flamel, by whom it has been written and illuminated, in no sense involves his authorship, but rather that he transcribed and he also adorned it. It happens that he was a scrivener. It serves, however, to shew that he was so far concerned with Alchemy that—if not indeed the author—he was at the pains of making a copy with his own hands for himself.

---

[1] The source from which I have drawn this citation gives no reference, and the only work which I have been able to examine *sub nomine* Auguste Vallet is *Saint-Germain l'Auxerrois*, Paris, 1837 : it has naturally no reference to Flamel. Figuier was acquainted with the fact of the manuscript and gives the opening words, following Vallet, who is cited as stating that there is usually some history behind a legend ; but the irresponsible French littérateur omits to give any reference.

It is understood of course that I assign the full measure of
its importance to the bibliographical fact, but am indisposed
to overestimate the judgment of M. Vallet on the antiquity
of a manuscript which he has described so badly in respect
of its whereabouts. The least that could be expected of one
who made the discovery would be to give references to
facilitate its identification, a very reasonable *désir desiré*,
having regard to the chaos of French collections and to the
fact that they were probably greater when the *Bibliothèque
National* was a *Bibliothèque du Roi* or *Bibliothèque Impérial*.

The most childish invention of all is that which attempted
to place an alchemical construction on a miscellaneous
collection of designs with which the historical Flamel is
supposed to have adorned an arch of a certain cemetery,
being the site of one of his charities, actual or alleged. We
have seen a bare recitation of the fact in his memoir, but the
French text has a supplement giving details in full, and it is
usually accompanied by a diagram, containing (1) the symbols
presented in the Book of Abraham the Jew; (2) portraits
of Christ, St. Peter and St. Paul, representing statues erected
by Flamel; (3) those of himself and Perrenelle; (4) the imputed
alchemical designs on the arch, already mentioned. Among
these last are depicted the slaughter commanded by Herod,
as commemorated by the name of the graveyard, which
was called that of the Holy Innocents; and the traditional
emblem of our Saviour, being a serpent entwined about a
cross, the recognised correspondence of which was the
serpent uplifted in the wilderness for the healing of rebellious
Israel. There were others of sufficiently dubious significance
to bear almost any construction that might be placed upon
them, that of Alchemy being the least reasonable of all.
The meanings of those described spoke so plainly of themselves and on their own behalf that whosoever made up the
Hermetic interpretations saw to it, before he put them in
the mouth of his imaginary Flamel, that there should be a
preamble summarising their obvious messages, as if to disarm
criticism. It was disarmed accordingly for the credulous
and for those especially who were prepared to recognise everywhere the symbols and teaching of Alchemy, from *Genesis*
to *Revelations*, from the Pantheons of Pagan Mythology to
the cobble stones on the streets of Paris.

As an example of a late stage in the manufacture of Flamel mythology it seems worth while to cite Paul Lucas, testifying in his *Journey Through Asia Minor* : [1] it is to be recommended in respect of mendacity above many travellers' tales. " I was at Bronosa in Natolia and going to take the air with a person of distinction I came to a little mosque, adorned with gardens and fountains for a public walk. We were shewn quickly into a cloister, where we found four dervishes, who received us with all imaginable civility and desired us to partake of their meal. We were told, and it was presently verified, that they were persons of notable worth and learning. One of them, who said that he was of Usbec Tartary, appeared more accomplished than the rest, and I believe indeed that he spoke the chief languages of the world. Having conversed in Turkish, he asked whether I was familiar with Latin, Spanish or Italian. I requested him, if he pleased to speak with me in Italian, but he discovered by my accent that it was not my mother-tongue. When he heard that I was a native of France, he addressed me in the French of one who might have been brought up in Paris. " How long, sir," I asked, " did you stay in France ? " But he replied that he had never been there, though he had a great inclination to undertake the journey. I did all in my power to strengthen this disposition, to convince him that France was the nursery of learning and its King a patron of the sciences who had defrayed the expenses of my travels for the collection of antiquities—to all of which he deferred with becoming civility. Our conversation being ended, the dervishes brought us to their house, where we drank coffee and then took our leave, but with a promise, however, on my part that I would return shortly to see them.

" Some days later the dervish whom I took for an Usbec came to pay me a visit. I shewed him the MSS. which I had bought, and he assured me of their value, as written by great authors. I found him a man of extraordinary learning, who might have been a century old from his discourse —though he seemed externally no more than thirty years. I ascertained that he was one of seven friends who travelled to complete their studies and were accustomed to meet once

[1] There is also *Voyage du Sieur Paul Lucas au Levant*, 2 vols., 1705. Both works went through several editions.

in every twenty years at some appointed place. It was Bronosa on the present occasion and four of them so far had arrived. Religion and natural philosophy engaged our thoughts in turn, after which we passed to Chemistry, Alchemy and the Kabalah, when I told him that these subjects—especially the Philosopher's Stone—were regarded as fictitious by most sensible men. ' That,' said the dervish, ' should cause you no surprise : the sage suffers the ignorant but does not sink his understanding to their level. When I speak of a sage it is of one who sees all things die and revive without concern : he has more wealth at his command than the greatest king, but as one above the circle of events he is content to live temperately.' Intervening at this point, I observed that, all these maxims notwithstanding, the wise man dies like the rest. ' I perceive that you are unacquainted with sublime science,' he replied with compassion. ' Such an one as I speak of does indeed die, since this is inevitable, but only at the uttermost term of the mortal span. Hereditary disease and debility reduce the life of most, but the use of the True Medicine enables a sage to ward off whatever may hinder or impair the animal functions for a thousand years.' In great astonishment I asked if he sought to persuade me that all who possessed the Philosopher's Stone had lived to this incredible age, and his answer was that it rested solely with themselves, as there was no question that they might. At last I cited the famous Flamel, who was said to possess the Stone and was yet assuredly dead. . But he smiled at my simplicity and demanded with an air of raillery : ' Do you really believe this ? No, no, my friend : Flamel is still alive ; neither he nor his wife have died. It is not above three years since I left them both in the Indies : he is one of my best friends.' Thereupon he related the history of Flamel, as he had learned it from himself, much as I had read it in his book up to a certain point, but with this notable variant. A certain magistrate, by name Cramoisi, was sent by Charles VI, then upon the throne of France, to ascertain from Flamel the origin of his riches, and the latter realised at once the extent of his danger. Having sent Perrenelle into Switzerland, there to await his coming, he spread a report of her death, had her funeral obsequies performed and in a few years arranged for his own coffin to be interred.

Since that time they have both lived a philosophical life, sometimes in one country, sometimes in another. Such is their true history, not that which is believed in Paris, where few have had even a glimpse of true wisdom.' " [1]

In appending to the transparent myth of Flamel the story of le Bon Trévisan I am not proposing to contrast a true history with fable, but a narrative of extreme and direct simplicity with one of a decorative kind. An account which revolves about such a pivot as the *Book of Abraham the Jew* belongs to romantic invention and to nothing else, but that which here follows does outrage only to one probability, being the circumstances under which it is pretended that the goal of a quest in Alchemy was reached after long toils.

The autobiographical memorial of Bernard, Comte de la Marche Trévisan, is found in an *Opus de Chemia* which was printed for the first time in 1567,[2] outside which he is the reputed author of several esteemed tracts, one of which has been translated into English.[3] His father was a physician of Padua, the descendant of a distinguished family, and as he is said to have been born in 1406 he is described as a contemporary of the two Dutch Isaacs, who were prosecuting their labours with supposed success, while he was toiling vainly till the close of his long life.[4] The account of his quest in Alchemy is the second of those three most curious recitals in the annals of occult chemistry to which I have referred. At the age of fourteen years, under the auspices of a grandfather and with the consent in full of his family, he made his beginning in the subject which was to become the absorbing occupation of his days. His first authoritative sources were Geber and Rhasis, the inspiring motive being

---

[1] A variant of the Cramoisi visitation is given by Figuier, on I know not what authority. It represents the King's messenger returning with a report that Flamel was living poorly in a humble abode : the philosopher was allowed therefore to remain in peace.

[2] This is on the authority at its value of Lenglet du Fresnoy and must pass at that, but there is some ground for believing that Bernard's memoir was written originally in French and is more likely to have been printed in that form before it was put into Latin. However, this is a bibliographical question and nothing attaches to it otherwise.

[3] This was the *Epistle to Thomas of Bononia*, London, 1680 ; but I have been reminded since writing as above that the so-called *Fountain of Trévisan* appeared also in English—I think, in *Collectanea Chymica*.

[4] See Joann. Isaaci Hollandi : *Opera Mineralia, sive de Lapide Philosophico*, in *Theatrum Chemicum*, Vol. III.

no higher hope than that of multiplying his patrimony an hundred-fold. The experiments which he undertook during his tuition by those oracular masters resulted only in the dissipation of eight hundred crowns, or alternatively of three thousand—according to another recension. He was surrounded by pretended philosophers who, finding him rich and zealous, proffered the secrets which they neither understood nor possessed, earning subsistence for themselves at the expense of the young alchemist.

Disappointed but not discouraged, he dismissed these impostors at length, transferring his attention to the works of Rupecissa and Sacrobosco, whom he followed for a time in all his operations.[1] At the next stage he experimented in concert with one who is described as " a good monk ", hoping to profit by the help of a prudent companion, his family mentor having been presumably removed " to where beyond " alembics " there is peace ". They rectified spirits of wine more than thirty times, or " till they could not find glasses strong enough to hold it ". These operations cost nearly three hundred crowns and produced nothing.

For fifteen years he continued his preliminary research into " the first principles of Art ", and at the end of this time he had purchased an extensive first-hand familiarity with the highways and byways of alchemical roguery,[2] as well as an acquaintance with a great variety of substances —mineral, metallic and otherwise—which did not enter apparently into the composition of the Philosopher's Stone or belong to the Great Work. He had laboured in vain to congeal, dissolve and sublime common salt, sal ammoniac,

[1] According to Johannes de Rupecissa, the matter of the Philosophical Stone is a viscous water which is to be found everywhere ; but the world would be revolutionised if the Stone itself were named. For the possessors it is a Divine Science, an incomparable treasure ; they are enriched with wealth beyond all kings of earth, are just before God and men, and they enjoy the special favour of heaven. As regards Sacrobosco, he is practically unknown, is in none of the collections—great or small—and is neglected by alchemical bibliographers. His prename Archelaus suggests a certain Greek *Carmen Iambicum Archelai Philosophi* in a fifteenth century MS. of the *Bibliothèque National*, No. 2327, treating *De Sacra Arte*, that is to say, the transmutation of metals. It consists of 322 verses and is found in several codices. Berthelot has a bare reference to two in the Library of St. Mark at Venice and the Escurial at Madrid ; but my reference otherwise is to Lenglet du Fresnoy, Vol. III. pp. 16, 18, 23, 25, 28.

[2] It appears to have been scarcely less extensive in the days of Bernard than at the beginning of the seventeenth and end of the sixteenth century, unless we elect to conclude that the Trévisan memorial was written about the period when it began to be known in print.

every variety of alum, and copperas. He proceeded also upon ordure, both of man and beast, by distillation, circulation and sublimation. These experiments, based on a literal understanding of antecedent alchemical symbolism, cost him roughly six thousand crowns ; and at last—discouraged beyond words at such waste of time and fortune—he gave himself up to prayer, hoping to discover the real aim of the Art by the grace and favour of God.[1] In conjunction with a magistrate of his district, he attempted subsequently to prepare sea-salt as the chief ingredient of the Stone. It was rectified fifteen times during the space of a year and a half, without finding any change in its nature. Thereupon he abandoned the process for another proposed by the magistrate, being the dissolution of silver and mercury by means of aquafortis. These dissolutions—performed separately—were left to themselves for a year, when they were combined and concentrated over hot ashes, to reduce their original volume. The residuum of this operation, placed in a narrow crucible, was exposed to the action of solar rays and afterwards to the air, in the hope that it would crystallise. The mixture filled twenty-two vials and five years were devoted to the whole operaton : but at the end of that period no crystallisation had taken place, so this experiment was abandoned, like the rest, as a failure.

Bernard Trévisan was now forty-six years old, and at the end of his experimental if not his financial resources he decided to go on his travels in search of true alchemists. In this manner he met with Maître Geoffroi de Lemorier, a monk of Citeaux, who was in possession of a hitherto unheard of process. They purchased two thousand hens' eggs, hardened them in boiling water and removed the shells, which were calcined in a fire. The whites were separated from the yolks and both were putrefied in horse-manure, the results being distilled thirty several times for the extraction of a white and red water. These and other operations occupied to no purpose eight further years of the toil-worn seeker's life. Dejected but not disheartened, and still adhering pertinaciously to his quest of the Grand Secret, Bernard

---

[1] It was his practice apparently in the midst of all his work, for the text says : *Verum enimvero semper interea meas preces ad Deum fundere non sum oblitus, ut subvenire meis conatibus dignaretur.*

now set to work with a protonotary of Bruges, whom he describes as a great theologian and who pretended to extract the Stone from sulphate of iron, by distillation with vinegar. They began by calcining the sulphate for three months, after which it was steeped in the vinegar, which had been distilled eight times. The admixture was placed in an alembic and distillation was repeated fifteen times daily for a whole year, at the end of which Trévisan was rewarded by a quartan fever which consumed him for fourteen months and almost cost him his life.

He was scarcely restored to health when he heard from a clerk that Meister Heinrich, confessor of the German Emperor Frederick III, was in possession of the Philosopher's Stone.[1] He set out at once for Germany, accompanied by some baffled Sons of Hermes like himself. They contrived—*par grands moyens et grands amis*—to become acquainted with the priest, and with him they set to work. Bernard contributed ten marks of silver and his associates thirty-two for the cost of the proposed process, which began by combining mercury, silver, oil of olives and sulphur. The admixture was dissolved over a moderate fire and stirred continually. After two months it was placed in a glass vial, which was covered with clay and heaped over with hot ashes. Lead, dissolved in a crucible, was added at the end of three weeks, and the product of this fusion was subjected to refinement. As a result of these operations the imperial confessor expected that the silver which had entered into the combination would be augmented by at least one third, but on the contrary it was reduced to a fourth.

Bernard Trévisan determined in his utter despair to abandon all further experiments, and the resolution was applauded by his family : but in two months the Circean spells of occult chemistry had asserted their former dominion over the whole being of their victim, who recommenced his travels in a fever of eagerness, visiting Spain, Italy, England, Scotland, Holland, Germany and otherwhere. Then, anxious to drink at eastern fountains of Alchemy, he spent several years in Egypt, Persia and Palestine, after which he passed

[1] The German Emperor in question reigned for fifty-three years, and the alleged visit to his confessor does not help us therefore in determining the dates of Trévisan's memorial.

into southern Greece, visiting remote convents and experimenting in conjunction with monks of repute in the science.[1] In every country he found that there were alchemists at work but of those—if any—who were successful his journeys told him nothing. Impostors in search of the credulous were, however, on all sides. In these travels and in false operations which they brought to his knowledge Bernard expended a further sum of over ten thousand crowns, one result of which was the sale of an estate yielding an annual income of eight thousand German florins. He was now sixty-two years of age and, having been deaf to the advice of his family, he found himself forsaken and on the threshold of want and misery. With the design of concealing his poverty he sought refuge in the Isle of Rhodes, where he planned to live unknown. But the old fatality pursued him and inflamed once again the old passion. He became acquainted with *un grand clerc et religieux*,[2] who was devoted to philosophy and enjoying, by common report, the gift of the Philosopher's Stone. He managed to borrow eight thousand florins and laboured with this monk in the dissolution of gold, silver and corrosive sublimate : once more he accomplished so much that within the space of three years he had exhausted these funds and was again at the end of his resources. Being thus effectually prevented from pursuing experiments, he returned to the study of text-books, and after eight years, or at the age of seventy-three, he professes to have discovered their secret. By comparing the adepts with one another, by collating their points of agreement and points of difference, he came to see that the truth must lie within the limits of those issues about which they were practically unanimous.[3] We are told that two years were permitted to elapse before his supposed discovery was put to the test, when, however, it was crowned with success and—infirmities of age notwith-

[1] It is at this point that the story assumes for the time being a mythical aspect. There was much travelling in those days, though it was hard and long faring, but in the impoverished condition of the alchemist the distances covered are incredible.

[2] The Latin text says : *Una dierum de quodam audiveram viro valde religioso magni nominis, etc.*

[3] This is a tenable proposition, but it is such on the surface only, for the real problem belongs to the deep root of the subject and is no question of finding a mean or harmony between contradictory statements. As I have indicated already, the essential secret, being that of the First Matter, is found nowhere in the texts, according to their own statements, and is not to be discovered therefrom by any work of comparison.

standing—he lived for some time in the enjoyment of his belated reward.

It follows that Bernard Trévisan owed nothing to initiation, save that of unwearied toil, that he was instructed by no master and bound by no vow. He had lived in a very hard school and had bought his experience bitterly by an apprenticeship of nearly sixty years. One might think that in common charity he would bequeathe to those who came after the benefit of a plain path. There was everything by presumption to warrant him and on the surface nothing to hinder. When therefore we find that his presumably authentic tracts are written in the same dark tongue adopted by his peers and co-heirs who confess that they were bound by a pledge, we seem to be in the presence of an alternative over which we may exercise whatever choice we please. The long quest of Trévisan is either a romantic story which introduces another contribution to a thousand rules of practice in the supposed transmutation of metals or one who has been taught by experience recounts at full length the age-long error of his ways while he tortured metals and also the way of escape which he found in fine when he had made for the time being at least an end of crucibles and Mary-baths. What in this case is that which lies behind his alleged study of texts ? What opened before him in a solitude with a few books in his hands ? Let us examine on our own part and carefully the *terminus ad quem* of his autobiographical narrative, being his delineation—in so far as it transpires—of that which he claims to have found.

The *Opus de Chemia* is called otherwise *Natural Philosophy of Metals* and is divided into four parts : (1) Concerning the founders of the sacred science ; (2) concerning himself, and this is the story which I have told ; (3) concerning the roots and principles of metals ; (4) concerning the Practical Work of Alchemy. The sole concern of the Art is to find a way of escape from " accursed poverty ", and it is to be loved for this reason. Moreover, those who attain it can give unstinted alms, and thus save their souls. It was founded by Hermes, was delivered to the elders of Israel and spread into various countries. It was perpetuated from age to age and among recent custodians of the Secret were Arnold de Villanova and Raymond Lully. The Metallic

M

Form is a pure Mercurial Substance, with an innate Sulphur abiding therein ; but these terms are to be understood philosophically. The practice is hidden in an allegorical fiction, but the *Parole Delaissée*—another tract by or ascribed to Bernard—affirms that the Stone in the red stage tinctures common quicksilver and all imperfect metals, so that they are converted into most true and excellent gold, better than that of the mines. It follows that we have questioned " the good Trévisan ", and he has answered by shewing that he has nothing else to veil in cryptic language-symbolism and illustrate by allegory to which he offers no key except that which has been veiled and hidden by those who were pledged to masters or perhaps to a circle of adepts. He tells us indeed that he had made a promise to God and had assured persons whom he met—and who shewed or said that they also possessed the Art—of his intention to reserve the secret. But the reason does not emerge, except that it is the Divine Will, the evidence of which is wanting. At the same time, as others have said before him, and yet others after, no one has written so plainly, no one has extended greater compassion towards " poor toilers in this Art ". We are travelling therefore in the old vicious circle, with less excuse than usual for being immured therein. My personal conclusion is that if the Great Secret of transmuting metals was ever attained by Bernard Trévisan, it was not as he tells us, namely, by reading books. Moreover, I am almost persuaded personally that his narrative is graphic fiction.

CHAPTER XI

The Chariot of Basil Valentine

SHOULD any uninstructed person who might chance upon
the *Triumphal Chariot of Antimony*, under the name of
Basil Valentine, undertake to read that work, he would be
mystified by much of its contents, by its references to a
Spagyric Art, to the Grand Magisterium, the Universal
Medicine, the Tinctures which transmute metals and other
mysteries which constitute the alchemical *Sacramentum
Regis*. But if he were asked what he thought of Basil Valentine
in his historical and personal character, it is unlikely that
he would prove conscious of a certain romantic veil encompassing the life of the man. He would take him on the faith
of his own record and would answer that he was a pious
monk, uncommonly well versed for his period in several
departments of experimental and medical chemistry, but
otherwise a bizarre speculator in the cloudy borderland
of physical science, when all science was in its cradle. Now,
it happens that there are those still among us—whether they
count or not—who would maintain that such a person
was mistaken in his estimate of Valentine the alchemist,
not to speak of Valentine the investigator of antimonial
therapeutics ; and to this it must be added on my own part
that he is in no better position as regards the man, for it is
not possible to determine what personality was concealed
under the pretence of a monastic garb and under the *bene
sonans* but assuredly fictitious name.

"When I had emptied to the dregs the cup of human
suffering," says Basil Valentine in a preface concerning the
Great Stone of the Sages, prefixed to his *Practica*, "I was led
to consider the wretchedness of this world and the fearful
consequences of our first parents' disobedience. Then I saw
that there was no hope of repentance for mankind, that they
were growing worse day by day, and that for their impenitence
God's everlasting punishment was hanging over them ; so
I made haste to withdraw myself from the evil world . . .

and devote myself to the service of God." After the manner of his age, as he goes on to inform us, he took refuge in a monastery, where the time that he could spare from his devotions was made use of for " the study and investigation of those natural secrets by which God has shadowed forth eternal things ".[1] In this dedicated retirement there was revealed to him ultimately " that great arcanum which God hides for ever from those who are wise in their own conceits ".[2]

As appears from the *Currus Triumphalis Antimonii* and other of his works, he belonged to the Order of St. Benedict, and he is said to have been canon of the Priory of St. Peter at Erfurt. It is affirmed further that his *Last Testament* remained concealed for a number of years within the High Altar of the Church belonging to the Priory. There seems no reason at first sight to challenge the fact of these matters. The conventional institutions of the middle ages were frequently centres of learning and of natural research; innumerable monks have practised Alchemy; and works which their authors or literary executors deemed unsuited for the time when they were written have been entombed for the benefit of a more enlightened epoch to come : things of this kind have happened both before and after the age of Basil Valentine. There is good occasion notwithstanding for thinking that here, as in so much that is connected with alchemists and with Alchemy, the most simple things are liable to be most deceptive. " Even to the points and pricks here are to be found great Mysteries," and what is asserted to be true of the literature is true of the personalities also. To put it more roughly, those who have not lied about themselves have been lied about by others who came after them ; and those who did not produce fraudulent treatises on their own part have had them fathered upon them subsequently.

[1] This is to be understood as a general expression of the current doctrine that things invisible are shewn forth by those that are visible, and is at the moment rather a simple reflection of Pauline teaching than a variant enunciation—let us say—of the *quod superius* dogma with which the *Tabula Smaragdina* opens.

[2] See *Practica cum XII Clavibus et appendice de Magno Lapide Antiquorum Sapientum, scripta et relicta a Basilio Valentino, Benedictini Ordinis Monacho.* Outside the edition to which I shall refer later, there is that of Mangetus in *Bibliotheca Chemica Curiosa,* vol. ii, pp. 409 *et seq.* There is also an English version in *The Hermetic Museum,* 1893, edited by myself, vol. i, pp. 313 *et seq.*

The suspicion that there is something amiss with the autobiographical allusions in books by or attributed to Basil Valentine is not, as it happens, either an arbitrary inference of my own hardened unbelief about things occult and their history or a personal discovery following original research. It was far back, or early in the seventeenth century, that a doubt was first raised, and subsequent investigations have tended to confirm rather than dispose of it. It is advanced that the monastic character assumed by Basil Valentine was a veil and an evasion to conceal his real identity and further that the pseudonym under which he is known was itself of Hermetic significance. Maximilian Stoel,[1] the author of a handbook of practical medicine which even now is not inaccessible in its fourth edition, adopted this view. So also did Boerhaave, the celebrated physician of Leyden, whose proposed chronological history of alchemists is a loss yet to be repaired.[2] Jacobus Tollius contrived to resolve the enigma of the supposed assumed name by a consideration of the philological significance attaching to its two terms in Greek and Latin respectively.[3] According to this interpretation, Basil signifies royal in Greek, while Valentine comes from the Latin *valendo*. In their union the terms formulate the symbol of power " which gives the regulus for the penetration of bodies." It is obvious that this is puerility, but in another aspect Basil Valentine is said to mean Mighty King, presumably him who rules in virtue of adeptship what Éliphas Lévi terms " the three analogical worlds of occult philosophy ". But again all this is fantasy. It remains, however, that so early as the year 1515 the identity of Basil Valentine was involved in such uncertainty that the Emperor Maximilian I, in his zeal for the supposed sciences, is said to have searched the Benedictine archives at Rome and made also many inquiries in different monasteries for particulars of the

---

[1] See *La Médecine Pratique*, being the seventh division of *Encyclopédie des Sciences Médicales*, Paris, 1834.

[2] On this, and other points consult Dallowe's translation of Boerhaave's *Elements of Chemistry*, 2 vols., London, 1735. Also Herman Boerhaave : *His Academical Lectures on Lues Venerea* (translated), London, 1763.

[3] *Fortuita* : *in quibus præter critica nonulla, tota fabularis historia Græca Phœnicia Ægyptiaca Chemicum pertinere asseritur*, Amsterdam, 1687. This work calls to be examined more closely than has been required for my present purpose, as its alchemical interpretation of Mythologies forms a link between certain beginnings of this pretence in the writings of Michael Maier and the elaborate volumes of Abbé Pernety to which I have referred already under the title of *Fables Égyptiennes*.

Benedictine Basil and his remains in writing. But he met with no success.

Vincent Placcius,[1] one of the earliest bibliographers and investigators of the secret history of anonymous and pseudonymous authors, states that the real name of Valentine was Tholden : others affirm that it was John Estchenreuter. But as Prosper Marchand [2] calls the compilation of Placcius *mare magnum erratorum* it is difficult to take him as a guide in the present case, while the alternative statement appears in biographical dictionaries which supply no reference and betray little acquaintance with the writings of the German adept. To place its proper value on the identification offered by Vincent Placcius we must realise that it was owing to the solicitude of John Tholden Hessius, otherwise Johann Thoelde, that the works of Basil Valentine began to be issued from the press. Under his editorial auspices the *Tract of the Great Stone* appeared in 1602, that *Concerning Natural and Supernatural Things* in 1603 and the *Triumphal Chariot of Antimony* in 1604. It would look therefore as if Placcius had either confused editor and author or had purposely identified one with the other for reasons which do not emerge. As regards Thoelde he appeared himself as an author in 1599, when he issued a medical pamphlet at Erfurt,[3] and in 1603 he published *Haligraphia* at Eissleben, in which he himself figures as a person of authority on things alchemical.[4] The bibliographical history of this work may account for the identification by Placcius of Basil Valentine and his editor. In 1644 Thoelde fell himself into editorial hands and part of his *Haligraphia* was translated into Latin, not however under his own name but under that of Basil, from whose manuscripts and not from the printed text it was said to be produced.[5] Placcius would have seen this

[1] *Theatrum Anonymorum et Pseudonymorum*, Hamburg, 1708.
[2] *Dictionnarium Historicum*, 4 vols., 1758, 59.
[3] It was a memorial of twenty-two pages, entitled *Information concerning the Revolting Malady of Red Dysentery, Diarrhea, and the extremely swift and dangerous sickness of the Pestilence.*
[4] *Haligraphia : That is, a Complete and Exhaustive Description of all the Mineral Salts, describing effectively the Salt of the First Matter, the Tests for Salt Waters, the means of obtaining the Salt of the Sun through Fire, according to various methods, and the improvement of the same. By Johann Thoëlde Hesse.* At the cost of Jacob Apel, bookseller, Eissleben, 1603.
[5] See my subsequent bibliographical note. The new text represents less than half of the original, namely, from p. 168 onward, as far as p. 310, omitting the *Conclusio Authoris* and other matter at the end.

edition and in this case accepted the fraudulent statement as matter of fact.   Had he read the Latin verses prefixed to the original German he would presumably have been undeceived.[1]   There is nothing in the content of *Haligraphia* to suggest that it is by the same author as the Valentine texts, and if the story of Maximilian is true some at least of them are a century older.

The claim of John Estchenreuter to have worn the mask of Valentine is negatively more difficult to dispose of because nothing is known about him, nor indeed has it been possible to ascertain by whom his claim was advanced in the first instance.   At the period of Thoelde's activity, we find Johannes Tanckius editing a collection of alchemical tracts, among which there is a brief epistle by Gallus Escherventer or Schonreuter, but there is nothing extant concerning him.[2]

Boerhaave denies that there was a Monastery of St. Peter at Erfurt, but there is no reasonable doubt that he was mistaken on the point of fact.   A certain Mollenbæck— whose identity is not easy to determine, while his record is not to be found, so far at least as libraries in England are concerned—is said to have visited it personally and to have ascertained from the Prior that the name of Basil Valentine did not appear in the records.   What is more to the purpose is the testimony of Joannes Mauritius Gudenus, the historian

---

[1]   *Sic tu Mater es autorum, quos, Tholde, sophorum,*
            Eruis e tenebris, dasque videre diem.
          Per te Basilius lucem squallore remoto
          Cernit, Basilii mater es alma tui.

They were the production of Hermannus Kircnerus. But M. Johannes also contributed his quota in the following terms :

          Depromis Sal, Tholde, penu mortalibus ; ergo
            Condimenta coquus, tumque Hygeia paret
          Non condus sis, Basilii monumenta recondens,
            Sed promus, poteat Basiliique penu.
          Quo mage Basilii a doctis nunc scripta leguntur,
            Tanto major erit gloria, Tholde, tua.

Was the editor of the decapitated *Haligraphia* suggesting covertly that Thoelde had invented Basil Valentine and all his texts ? In view of these extracts it seems impossible that he could have blundered.

[2] See the *Epistle* of Gallus Schonreuter, doctor of Medicine, etc., addressed to Gulielmus Gratalorum : it is the third tract in a collection entitled *Opuscula Chemica*, 1605, and the editor, as will be observed, is one of the two persons whose metrical panegyrics of Thoelde have been cited in the previous note. He is to be distinguished presumably from Joachim Tanckius, another alchemical editor, who printed the *Clavis Philosophiæ* of Paul Eck with an anonymous tract *De Lapide Philosophico*, Frankfurt, 1604, and subsequently *Promptuarium Alchemiæ*, Leipsic, 1610.

of Erfurt, which is conclusive as to the existence of the Convent and testifies at its value to the connection of the alchemist therewith ; but the latter point may be presented on the authority of Basil Valentine and not on that of records belonging to the place.[1] It is obvious, however, that on the hypothesis of this being only an assumed name he who is concealed thereby may well have been a monk of St. Peter's and may have his record in its archives, but of course under his real designation.

Despite the doubts that have been raised, the preponderating sense of criticism inclines to the belief that a person so named really existed and did fill that position in devout life which is described in *Currus Triumphalis*. This, however, is the uttermost extent of unanimity, for it is asserted on the one hand that he was born at Alsace, on the borders of the Rhine, and otherwise that he was a native of Erfurt. By some again he is referred to the twelfth century and to the fourteenth by others, the year 1394 being specified as the date of his birth, while in 1415 he is supposed to have begun his practical and literary labours in Alchemy and Hermetic Medicine. But these dates are unable to withstand any test of examination. A passage in *Currus Triumphalis* is conclusive as to the mythos of the earlier period. " You should know that Antimony is used for a number of purposes besides those of the typographer." While it is difficult to assign an exact date to the first use of Antimony as an alloy in the founding of metal types, the fifteenth century is likely to have been the earliest period. But there is another and more important point. A reader of *Currus Triumphalis* will find numerous references therein to the recent appearance in Germany of a certain venereal scourge, which Basil Valentine calls " the French disease ", *Morbus Gallicus* and *Lues Gallica*. Now, it appears to be certain that this denomination was given to the complaint after the expedition of the French to Naples, under Charles VIII, which took

---

[1] *Dicitur fuisse adeptus*, says Gudenus, and again : *Eadem ætate (scilicet, anno 1413) Basilius Valentinus in divi Petri monasterio vixit, arte medico et naturalium indagine mirabilis. Insuper iis accensetur quos in augmentum spei nominant aurum confecisse, sic aliena dementia post secula fallit, ideo minima culpabilis, quod non nisi decipi amantes facultatibus exuat. Rerum Moguntiacarum Volumen primum*, 1722. The history was published at Erfurt.

place in 1495.[1] It is to be concluded therefore that this particular work is not earlier than the beginning of the sixteenth century, and I am moderately certain that texts other than the *Chariot*, in so far as they are attributable to the same writer, are later than is that.

In the works which there is colourable reason for accepting in this tentative sense—such as *Currus Triumphalis*, *Practica* and the *Twelve Keys*—Basil Valentine is one of those alchemical authors who does not help us to the approximate date of a given treatise by citations from slightly anterior adepts ; but if we allocate his output to the first decades of the sixteenth century, it is possible and likely that he had passed the prime of life when he entered on his experiments in Hermetic literature, and almost a century was destined to elapse before any of his memorials found their way into the hands of a printer.[2]

[1] A synopsis of the testimony is as follows : In 1497 Nicolaus Leonicenus of Vicentia calls it by this name, though he denies the novelty of the disease, saying : " I can by no means imagine with some that this complaint never appeared till now." In 1498 Natalis Montesaurus of Verona remarks upon " those dispositions commonly called *Mal Franzozo* ". In 1499 the Spaniard Gaspar Torella narrates that it broke out in Alvernia in the year 1493, thence making its way into Spain, afterwards into Italy, and from Italy into all Europe. Joannes de Vigo of Genoa, writing in 1503, says that it appeared almost all over Italy in the month of December 1494, and he adds : " The French disease when once it comes to be confirmed, seldom admits of any other than a palliative cure." Leonardus Schmai of Salzburg, in 1518, bears witness to the same date and makes use of the same name. In the year following, 1519, Ulrichus de Hutten, a German, discoursed upon a " method of curing the French disease by Guaiacum ", fixing 1493 for the date and Naples for the place of its appearance. Joannes Baptista Montanus, 1550, affirms on the other hand that it was the soldiers of Columbus who imported the disease from Antigua and the West India Islands to the Siege of Naples, in 1496. In 1554 Joannes Langius of Limburg speaks of the French disease, maintaining that, " although some would have it to be a new one," it is " no other than a farrago of diseases known to the ancients ". Compare Bernardinus Tomitanrus of Padua, 1566 ; Joannes Astruc : *De Morbis Veneris* ; Adrianus Tollius ; Herman Boerhaave, etc. See also John Armstrong : *Synopsis of the History and Cure of Venereal Diseases*, 1737.

[2] The following bibliographical list includes all *opera*—authentic and attributed—which have appeared under the name of Basil Valentine and is arranged chronologically. (1) *A Treatise concerning the Great Stone of the Ancients, at which so many thousands of Masters have worked since the beginning of the World. . . . Wherein the True Light of the Wise is exhibited philosophically. I. An Account of the Chief Metals and their Properties. II. Of the Microcosm, or the Little World of Man. III. The Great Secret of the World and of the Medicine pertaining to Man. IV. Of the Knowledge and Hidden Secrets of the Planets.* . . . Published for Sons of the Doctrine by John Tholden of Hessius, at the cost of Jacob Apel, bookseller, in the year 1602. (2) *Concerning Natural and Supernatural Things : also concerning the First Tincture, Root and Spirit of Metals : how they are generated, brought forth, smelted, changed and augmented. A True Account, by Frater Basil Valentine, of the Benedictine Order.* Printed from his own Manuscript by John Tholden Hessius, *cum privilegio.* Leipzig, at the cost of Jacob Apel, bookseller, in the year 1603.

The *Triumphal Chariot of Antimony* is by far the most important work which bears the name of Basil Valentine and has done more than any other to establish his reputation as a chemist on the basis of practical experiment. It has passed through several editions, has been translated into German, French and English, and is still a subject of reference for the archæology of chemistry. Even the biographical dictionaries of the early nineteenth century did honour to the traditional philosopher of Erfurt.[1] Later on Louis Figuier

(3) *Triumphal Chariot of Antimony*, said to have been first published in 1604 under the same editorship, but I have traced it by rumour only. In 1646 it was edited with Notes by Peter Faber, with other tracts ascribed to the same authorship. The best edition is that of Amsterdam, 1671, with a Commentary by Theodorus Kerckringius. (4) *Twelve Keys of Frater Basilius Valentinus, whereby the Doors are Opened to the Ancient Stone of our Forefathers and wherein Inexhaustible Fountains of all health are found.* Frankfurt, 1611. It was translated into Latin by Michael Maier and formed the first tract in his *Tripus Aureus*, 1617. There is no call to speak of the alchemical collections in which it was included. (5) *The Revelation of Frater Basil Valentine, of the Benedictine Order, concerning Hidden Operations directed towards the Universal Subject, also conclusions and arguments from all his Writings on Sulphur, Vitriol, the Magnet Stone—id est, Philosophical, from which the Universal originates, and Ordinary, which originates the Particular.* Printed at the expense of John Birkner, bookseller of Erfurt, 1624. The first treatise in this collection is better known under the Latin title of *Apocalypsis Chemica*. (6) *Azoth, or the Secret Aurelia of the Philosophers, faithfully and clearly explaining the First Matter and the Famous Stone . . . unto the Sons of Hermes, by way of a Philosophical Enigma, a Parabolic Colloquy, the Smaragdine Tablet of Hermes and the Saturnian Parables and Figures of Frater Basil Valentine.* Interpreted by M. Georgius Beatus, Frankfurt, 1613. It is difficult to say whether any part of this work can be attributed to the author of *Currus Triumphalis*. There was a French translation in 1624. (7) *Haliographia (sic), concerning the Preparation, Use, and Virtues of Salts Mineral, Animal, and Vegetable, from the MSS. of Basilius Valentinus, collected by* And. Salminicius. Bononia, 1644. As explained in my text, this is spuriously attributed. (8) *Secret Books, or Last Testament of Basil Valentine, of the Benedictine Order. Copied from the original which was discovered in the High Altar of the Church at Erfurt, under a marble tablet. Now printed in accordance with numerous requests on the part of Sons of the Doctrine.* Strasburg, at the cost of Caspar Dietzel, 1645. It contains long treatises on mines and the generation of metals, a Commentary on the *Twelve Keys*, and other matters, and is almost certainly of spurious attribution. Lenglet du Fresnoy mentions an edition at the same place in 1651. (9) *The Fifth Part of the Last Testament of that estimable Hermetic Philosopher, Frater Basil Valentine, part of which has never been printed previously, part of which is now reissued in a new order, differing from former exemplars. All translated literally from a secret manuscript and printed for the public good by Johann Hiskias Cardilucius, Com. Pal., Phil. et Medicus.* ? Strasburg, 1651. I should class this as spurious in a critical codification of the texts. (10) There is also *Manifestatio Artificiorum*, said to have been published at Erfurt in 1624, but I have not been able to trace it. It is reported further to have been translated into French as *Révélation des Mystères des Teintures Essentielles des Sept Métaux et de leurs Vertus Médicinales*, described as translated from the German by Israel, a German physician. It appeared at Paris in 1646. But as Lenglet du Fresnoy points out it is really a rendering of *De Rebus Naturalibus et Supernaturalibus*, omitting the first two chapters. Finally, Boerhaave mentions a *Manuductio Medicinæ*, which has been cited by no other writer.

[1] " Among his discoveries and still medical preparations in constant use, though

also bore his testimony, and though he is not to be trusted as a historian he seems to have been on ground that he knew when he spoke of matters belonging to chemistry. " Every one is acquainted with the remarkable discoveries relative to Antimony which are contained in the celebrated work of Basil Valentine, *Currus Triumphalis Antimonii.* The German alchemist had investigated so thoroughly the properties of this metal—scarcely indicated before him—that we find many facts stated in his treatise which have been brought forward as modern discoveries in our own day. In the same work Basil Valentine specifies many other chemical preparations of the first importance, such as spirit of salt, otherwise hydrochloric acid, extracted in our own manner from marine salt, and oil of vitriol, i.e., sulphuric acid. He gives the method of obtaining brandy by distillation of wine and beer, rectifying the product of distillation on calcined tartar, i.e., carbonate of potassium. He even teaches the extraction of copper from its pyrites, or sulphur, by transforming it first of all into vitriol of copper—i.e., sulphate of copper—with the help of moist air and afterwards plunging a bar of iron into the aqueous dissolution of this product. The said operation—which Basil Valentine was the first to describe—proved profitable to alchemists at a later date, but—the fact notwithstanding of the precipitation of metallic copper—they mistook it for a transmutation of iron into copper, or at least as the beginning of a conversion which could be perfected by art. . . . One may regard this alchemist as having been the first to obtain sulphuric ether, which he prepared by distilling a mixture of spirit of wine and oil of vitriol. In a word, there are few chemical preparations known at his period concerning which Basil Valentine has not registered some valuable facts." [1]

Such being the judgment of a chemist on the attainments of an early investigator of things that belong to chemistry, and noting as we pass that it concurs with that of others

now improved upon, are sulphuric ether, vinegar from honey-water, sugar of lead, litharge, fulminating gold, many mercurial preparations, empyreumatic carbonate of ammonia, claimed as his own by Sylvius Deleboe," etc.—*Biographie Universalle.* Professor Ferguson says that the writings of Basil " contain apparently first notices of a good many chemical reactions and products."—*Bibliography of Alchemy,* i, 81.

[1] *L'Alchimie et les Alchimistes.*

who have titles to speak,[1] let us see how Basil Valentine approaches his reader, on the assumption that he is about to undertake an experimental study of that metallic substance which is termed Antimony.

The preparations for his laboratory practice unfold as follows : [2] (1) " Invocation of God, with a certain heavenly intention, drawn from the depths of a sincere heart and conscience, liberated from ambition, hypocrisy and all other vices which are in affinity with these, including arrogance, boldness, luxury, petulancy, oppression of the poor and similar evils. All these are to be eradicated from the heart, that when a man desires to prostrate himself before the Throne of Grace, in order to obtain health, he may do so with a conscience free from unprofitable weeds, that his body may be transmuted into a holy temple of God and purged from all uncleanness." It will be seen that Basil Valentine does not address an amateur of science pursuing it for the sake of science but for ministration to his personal needs. The counsel proceeds to admonish each and all that " God will not be mocked, as worldly men, pleasing and flattering themselves with their own wisdom, are disposed to think. On the contrary, the Creator of all is to be invoked with reverential fear and confessed with due obedience. . . . So true is this that I rest assured and certain that no impious man shall ever be partaker of the True Medicine and much less of the Eternal Heavenly Bread. Place therefore your whole intention and all your trust in God ; call upon Him, pray that His blessing may descend upon you. The fear of the Lord is the beginning of wisdom ; be such the beginning of your work, that by the same you

---

[1] There is no call to enumerate. Hoefer credits him with the discovery of oxygen, and Mr. M. Pattison Muir, in his *Story of Alchemy*—a popular handbook—mentions his eminence as a chemist, while recording his high repute in Alchemy.

[2] We may compare the notable account of his own motives in communicating to others that which he had learned himself. " That which I have done has not been taken in hand from a desire of vain and transitory glory, but I have been induced thereunto by command of Christ the Lord, that His glory and goodness in eternal and temporal matters should not be concealed from any man but—to the praise and honour of His holy, everlasting Name—that it might be exalted, acknowledged and revealed in its majesty by reason of His highness and almightiness, through the confirmation of His wonderful deeds. And secondly I have been led thereunto by love and charity towards my neighbour, for his good as for my own . . ., that the Most Supreme Mystery may not be quite suffocated in darkness nor drowned in overflowing waters, but delivered out of the deep and filthy mire of the foolish crowd by a right appearance of the true light."

may attain your desired end." An inward disposition of this kind constitutes the first qualification of those who would know Antimony, its uses and its virtues.

(2) But the second is called contemplation, by which, says Basil, " I understand an accurate attention to the work itself in hand, and it falls under these heads : what are the circumstances of any given thing ; what is the matter and what the form ; whence its operations proceed, whence it is infused, implanted and how generated ; how also the body of the thing may be . . . resolved into its first essence. Contemplation of this kind is celestial and to be understood by spiritual reason, for the circumstances and deeps of things can be conceived in no other way than by thought in the spirit of man. It is, moreover, twofold, otherwise, possible and impossible. The latter consists of abundant cogitations which never proceed to effects, nor ever exhibit any form of matter which falls under the touch. An example is if any one should attempt to comprehend the eternity of the Most High, which exceeds human capacity. It is a sin against the Holy Ghost to pry arrogantly into Infinite Divinity and subject to human inquisition the incomprehensible counsel of the secrets of God. Contemplation in its possible aspect is called theory : it has regard to things which are perceived by sight and touch, which have a nature formed in time. Such contemplation is set to consider how the given nature may be helped and perfected by resolution of itself; how each body may be caused to put forth from within the good or evil, venom or medicine which is latent in it ; how destruction and confection may be handled, so that the pure may be separated from the impure by a right procedure, apart from sophistical deceits. Separation of this kind is performed by divers manual operations . . ., some of which are familiar in vulgar experience while others are remote therefrom." The instruction proceeds to enumerate various chemical workings, and ends by saying that " hereof is the second foundation of philosophy, being that which follows on prayer, wherein lies the root of the whole matter, and it is summarised in these words : " Seek first the Kingdom of God and His righteousness by prayer, and all other things shall be added unto you."

This citation is felicitous for my purpose in more than a

single way. The expositors of Spiritual Alchemy, and those more especially who are to be met with in occult circles and heard in their official organs, are not unlike the Baconians, or uncritically eager to bring anything into their castingnets. They have shewn themselves quite willing to include the Antimony of Basil Valentine among the veils of the Great Work, spiritually understood. It is not to be assumed that they have read *Currus Triumphalis*, but they have met with certain extracts. They would be greatly surprised to learn on his own authority that the Antimony of his treatise was used in casting types and utterly scandalised if they found him commending its virtues as a specific in " the French disease " ; but this—as we have seen—is one of the considerations which brought the *Triumphal Chariot* into being. These things apart, my citations are of moment because they exhibit unawares, in his distinctions on contemplation, how utterly apart was Basil from that thinking in the heart on Divine things which belongs to the mystic state. He is concerned solely with the elements, largely external, of commonly devout life, and we can picture him offering counsels of the same kind if he preached from a pulpit in Erfurt as when he issued instructions on how to proceed so that Antimony may be truly enthroned in a Triumphal Chariot.

Here is the first point, but the second is more to my purpose, as it is also more in value. The enchanting citations shew how a chemist of the sixteenth century—or whenever Basil may have lived—instructed his pupil to proceed in a particular work. They would be comic reading enough for a student in laboratory classes at this day ; but if he had enough humour in his composition, one can imagine him directing his instructor, if he met him out of the classes, to their high purport and demanding whether it would profit him to proceed in the same manner, for the rapid acquisition of technique. In reality, however, they are of great importance for their point of view at their period. The investigations of chemistry, as of all things else in physics, were untutored delving into a great mystery, and poor was the chance of those who could not get help from God. If any one cares to hear it, I believe that they were wise in their darkness who took the only way and approached the mysteries of material things in the same spirit as they approached those of religion ; and I am prepared also to think that they did not go unaided : " the spark from heaven " may fall to give light on physics, as it does certainly —and within my own knowledge—on those of soul and mind.

If such were the spirit, the intention and point of departure for the monk of Erfurt, it is reasonable to assume that the counsels imparted and conditions established by other Masters of Art must be understood in the same manner. We have Basil's own testimony that God opened his eyes in answer to earnest prayer, which means that God permitted him to make " many experiments " on the " powers and virtues " laid up in metals and minerals, and that " one discovery led to another ". This is also the sense in which he affirms that the Stone is reserved to a " favoured few ", being those " who study our Art earnestly by day and by night ". It signifies that, given the right spirit—that of the love of truth—prayer is work and work is also prayer, a duality in unity which does not fail of its reward. This in his particular terminology—which has its correspondences and connotations throughout the literature—leads on to a knowledge of that great Stone " which has power to cure leprous and imperfect metallic bodies and to regenerate them ", as well as "to preserve men in health and procure for them a long life." There is no question therefore as to what we must understand literally when he speaks mystically of a thing which is " All in all ". It is not the state of God in the transcendence, when Christ delivers up the Kingdom, but that which contains " the attracting force of all metals and minerals derived from Salt, Sulphur and twice-born Mercury ". It is (1) the matter and (2) the life within it, these always and only ; and the work is one of generation from seed contained in the body, which seed is also life. I could multiply citations from all the works which pass under the name of Basil Valentine : they are about me as these lines are written ; and did it serve a purpose I should not consider the space. But it would respond to no object which is here in view. Like that of his peers and co-heirs, the monk's works are written in a cryptic symbolism as regards essential materials but not as to intent and end : the end is perfect health in human and metallic bodies.[1] I speak of the hypothesis only and am not concerned with its validity. As to what must be done with metals, the last of the *Claves Duodecim* is plain enough in its way. " When the Medicine . . . has been prepared perfectly . . . , take one part of it to three parts of the best gold, purged and refined with antimony, the gold being previously beaten into plates of the greatest possible thinness. Put the whole into a smelting pot and subject it to the action of a gentle fire for twelve hours : let it be melted then for three days and three nights more." The ferment of gold is prepared in this manner. The next operation is to take " one part of this prepared ferment for the tingeing of a thousand parts of molten metal, and then you will learn in all faith and truth that it shall be changed into the only good and fixed gold ". Here, in the words of Basil, is " the end of the final end ". But his prototypical adept in an earlier part of the thesis affirms that the prime connotation of this all-gracious gift is the rendering of thanks to God " now and evermore ". So also Basil in his devotional manner praises the Creator of all in his last words for the Secret of the Art and its Practice. It provides whatever is needed in soul and body— *mens sana*, that is to say, *in corpore sano*, and the soul turned to God by a contemplation of his wonderful works.

---

[1] It is idle, therefore, to cite *Currus Triumphalis Antimonii*, when it affirms that *Lapis noster inter duos monticulos nascitur*, adding that *in te et in me et in nostri similibus latet*, as if the work were therefore spiritual. Alchemy is a doctrine of life, life in metals and minerals, life in all vegetable things, life in beast and man. So far as man is concerned, it may be said of it that *inter duos monticulos nascitur*, though it is rather a flimsy symbolism : it is obvious also that *in te et in me latet*, though it is of course manifested also. But the alchemical " object " for Mrs. Atwood was " to improve, perfect, and bring the Causal Light to manifestation " in man by a super-mesmeric work of the hands, and when she quotes *in me et in te*—3rd edition, p. 159—she forgets to tell us what is meant by *inter duos monticulos*.

CHAPTER XII

Paracelsus

QUI suus esse potest non sit alterius is a motto ascribed to Aureolus Phillippus Theophrastus Bombastus of Hohenheim, immortalized in occult annals as Paracelsus; and it is at least characteristic of one who, amidst all his cloud of fantasies and his terminology from a world of nightmare, was a new spirit in the age to which he belonged, a dauntless seeker in the heart of things, untrammeled by authority or tradition. But we are concerned with him only in Alchemy, and among his predecessors there were two at least whom he seems to have held in esteem and from whom he derived something. These were the Dutch Isaac, who is called the Hollander, and his son, followers in the path of Geber and of whom it has been said that their alchemical experiments are among the most explicit in the whole range of Hermetic literature. It is said also that their lives are almost unknown, for, " buried in the obscurity necessary to adepts . . ., their study or laboratory was the daily scene of their industrious existence ".[1] They are said in fine to have been placed by conjecture in the fifteenth century, because they cite no authorities later than Arnold, while they were acquainted with aqua fortis and aqua regia, discovered in the previous century.

For the facile interpretations of writers like Éliphas Lévi, it is obvious that Isaac of Holland and his son were workers in a figurative Alchemy, since they affirmed that the Grand Magisterium would convert a million times its own weight into gold [2] and that those who took weekly a small portion of the Philosophical Stone would be preserved in perfect health to the last hour assigned to each by God. But the *Opera Mineralia* of Isaac, otherwise *De Lapide Philosophico*, is an elaborate treatise on the Art of exalting dead and impure

---

[1] *Lives of Alchemysticall Philosophers*, 1815.

[2] We have seen, however, that this was precisely the testimony at its value of the Arabian Geber. No other alchemists, to the best of my recollection and belief, have established the transmuting capacities of the Stone on such a scale of vastness.

metals into true Sol and Luna. The First Matter is said to be Saturn, and though the *Vas Philosophorum* has been always hidden by adepts—according to a recurring myth—the vessels used in the art of the Dutch alchemists are engraved with all plainness in the illustrations which accompany the text. For this and for other reasons the father and son are cited once only by Mrs. Atwood as Dutch adepts who "are said to have worked successfully and are much lauded by Boerhaave"; but their alleged skill in the "manufacture of enamels and artificial gem-stones", on other authorities than hers, might have commended them to the attention of Berthelot. Their accredited explicit disposition makes it abundantly plain that they worked in metals, but it must not be supposed that their Saturn as the First Matter is other than a Philosophical Lead or that their *De Triplici Ordine Elixiris et Lapidis Theoria*, their *vera operatio manualis* and *libelli secretissimi* are more intelligible than other contributions to the Great Work.

Paracelsus was born on 26th November, 1493, and his strange, stormy career closed at the early age of forty-eight years, or in 1541. Among his notable contemporaries was Cornelius Agrippa, whom I mention because the instructor of both was Johannes Trithemius, of Spanheim and Würzburg, an occult philosopher, who is cited as of great importance at his epoch, as alchemist, magus and authority on secret writing, though he seems unread for the most part—even by those who praise him. There is a sense in which both pupils outgrew their master, for Agrippa lived to discover the vanity of most arts—at least as then practised—which passed for occult sciences, while Paracelsus travelled remote, untrodden ground in Medicine, Alchemy and Philosophy, leaving Trithemius far behind him—if we can judge by the remains of the latter.

There is a story that the German Hermes and beloved Trismegistus—as his ardent disciples called Paracelsus—had another and much more obscure teacher, in the person of a certain Solomon Trismosin, of whom very little is known, apart from his pretended autobiographical account of adventurous wanderings in search of the Philosopher's Stone. The authority for this fable is a German alchemical tract by or ascribed to Trismosin under the title of the *Golden*

Fleece, first printed in 1598. It is comparable to that other myth reported by J. B. Van Helmont, according to which the Philosopher's Stone was given to Paracelsus—or its secret communicated—by an unknown adept at Constantinople in 1521. Trismosin himself, by tradition as well as by claim, is accredited with possession of the Catholic Tincture and Medicine. It is said also (1) that his true name was Pfeiffer and (2) that he was still alive at the end of the seventeenth century—or so testified a French traveller, who affirmed that he saw him.

So far as Alchemy is concerned Paracelsus served his apprenticeship at Schwatz, in the laboratory of Sigismund Fugger : on the other hand, Trismosin avoided individual practitioners and went direct to the mines. At one of these he encountered Flocker, who was alchemist as well as miner, and in Trismosin's opinion he had attained the Secret of the Art. The evidence was that—apparently in his presence—Flocker took prepared lead and unalloyed silver, put them in flux together and then extracted the silver, half of which proved to be gold " when cast in an ingot ". The miner, however, refused to disclose his secret, and therefore in 1473 Trismosin went further, still seeking an artist in Alchemy. But he encountered sophisticators only till he entered the service of a Venetian noble, where he saw all kinds of operations and was intrusted with a translation of some Greek MS., on which he was set to work at experiment. By closely following its instructions he affirms that he " tinged three metals into fine gold ". Later on he quitted Venice, proceeding to a place which served his purpose better—but it is not named in the story. By means of Kabalistic books and books on Magic, which he caused to be translated from Egyptian into Greek and thence into Latin, he says that he " captured the treasure ", learning the Subject of the Art—otherwise the First Matter—with the mode of extracting the Tincture, one part of which transmuted fifteen hundred parts of silver into gold.

Such in brief summary was the adventurous quest of Trismosin in search of the Art and its Masters; but his testimony, such as it is, shews that he learned nothing in the mines and nothing also from living instructors : the real teachers were in books. It happens, however, that at the end of the fifteenth century, there was no scholar in Europe or the wide world who could render " the Egyptian language " into Greek or any other tongue, if there was anything in Alchemy which could be translated therefrom. The claim of Trismosin falls to pieces for this and other transparent reasons and it is to be concluded that the fiction of his attainment is like the instruction which he gave to Paracelsus or like the testimony of that unspecified Frenchman who saw him two hundred years later, possibly " somewhere in France ", more probably at a Castle in Spain. We may suppose in reality that he was gathered into the Paradise of Hermetists at the more ordinary allotted time and that as nothing was heard of him in his life so also there was silence concerning him for almost the space of a century, when the publication of his *Golden Fleece* revealed him and his pretensions to eager German students, pursuing the quest of Alchemy at fever-heat.

The autobiographical fragment is found in this tract, but whether the rest of it is referable to the same hand is a question which Hermetic bibliographers are not likely to determine. I register in my own part a note of interrogation. In 1602 a portion of the German work was translated into French, and was reprinted or reissued in 1612. Partial versions of the French text in an English vesture are available at the British Museum in the Sloane collection, and there is also a priceless volume in the Harleian called *Splendor Solis*, with very beautiful painted pictures. Notwithstanding the distinctive title, it should be understood that this text forms part of the original German and is therefore extant in three languages, several printed editions and three manuscripts, not to speak of what Oxford possesses. Finally, a modern English version appeared in 1921, with black and white plates reproducing the illuminations of Harl. 3469. It may be added on the bibliographical side, that *Splendor Solis* forms Part III of the original *Aureum Vellus* of 1598. Kopp, whose authority is considerable, regards the whole collection as spurious and Trismosin as a fictitious personality, in which case the adventures related in the prefatory part of *Aureum Vellus* were a publisher's device to introduce the tracts that follow. The question does not signity, as the narrative betrays itself. I note in conclusion that the hand-coloured designs of the

German and French printed editions are exceedingly crude and rough ; the artist of the Harleian MS. performed upon them a veritable work of transmutation, adding also elaborate borders.

Such were the precursors and such the traditional instructors of him who was Paracelsus the Great and Thrice Greatest German Hermes. I have included Trismosin because according to the testimony of *Aureum Vellus* he was not only the teacher but the giver of the Philosopher's Stone to the Sage of Hohenheim. It happens, for the rest, that in the year 1894 there were published under my auspices the whole works of Paracelsus on the subject-matter of Alchemy in an English version,[1] and I do not propose therefore to present his claims and hypotheses at any length in the present place. In fulfilment of that which is outlined in my first chapter, we have indeed only to consider the sense in which—following some vague affirmations met with there and here—Paracelsus calls to be regarded as the first witness of an Alchemy which was not that merely of metallic transmutation or a supposed Elixir of Life—as when he says that it is " the method of preparing medicaments ".[2] He is a witness after various manners, including unprofitable and frivolous distinctions, e.g. (1) " that which the fire operates is Alchemy, whether in the kitchen or in the furnace " ; (2) the work of the artificer is Alchemy when he forges a sickle or a sword from the iron created by God ; and (3) it is an alchemist in the stomach who digests the food consumed by the mouth of man and other animals.[3]

But he is a witness also to a cosmic aspect of the subject in his thesis on the First Matter, and though it is not to be affirmed that he created a new departure, since the old cosmologies and the old Hermetic dreams announce an universal substance, it is put forward by Paracelsus after at least a new manner and in terms of unusual clearness. It came about also that, owing to his great vogue in Germany, he influenced those who succeeded him. It may be said that

---

[1] *The Hermetic and Alchemical Writings of Aureolus Phillipus Theophrastus Bombast of Hohenheim, called Paracelsus the Great. Now for the first time faithfully translated into English.* Quarto, 2 vols, 1894.

[2] See *ibid., s.v. Alchemy the Third Column of Medicine*, vol. ii, p. 163.

[3] *Ibid., s.v. The Book of Alchemy*, ii, p. 166.

there was a school of Paracelsus in the sense of an ever widening circle of admirers, followers and interpreters for considerably more than a century after his death. He was the inspiration in chief of Jacob Böhme, and the later alchemists also derived from him, Thomas Vaughan included, as the chief exponent in England of an " ancient and universal " science under the name of *Alchemia*.

In his commentary on an alleged *Revelation* of Hermes[1] Paracelsus affirms an " indestructable essence ", an *una res* which is " a perfect equation of the elements ", the Subject of Art and that which is brought forth thereby. It was revealed from above to Adam, is " the Secret of all Secrets ", and " the last and highest thing to be sought under the heavens ". It is, moreover, " the Spirit of Truth which the world cannot comprehend without the interposition of the Holy Ghost, or without the instruction of those who know it." From the beginning of the world the Saints, it is said, have desired to behold its face, and Avicenna is cited as denominating this spirit " the Soul of the World ". In language recalling that of several preceding and above all of many later alchemists, we are told (1) that " it is sought by many and found by few " ; (2) that it is beheld from afar but is also near at hand ; (3) that it exists in all things, in every place and at all times ; (4) that it has the powers of all creatures ; (5) that it operates in all elements ; and (6) that " by virtue of this essence did Adam and the Patriarchs preserve their health and lives to an extreme age, some of them also flourishing in great riches ". It was thus for Paracelsus at once the substance of the Transmuting Stone and of the Life-Elixir.

It is this essence or spirit the nature of which has been hidden in strange parables and in cryptic language, lest that should become known to the unworthy concerning which it is affirmed further that " eye hath not seen, nor ear heard, nor hath the heart of man understood what Heaven hath naturally incorporated " therewith and therein. " It heals all dead and living bodies without other medicine." It " reveals all treasures of earth and sea, and converts

---

[1] The text is cited by Paracelsus in his *Tincture of the Philosophers, cap.* 3, but was first published under the auspices of Benedictus Figulus in his *Golden and Blessed Casket of Nature's Marvels*, 1608, a translation of which was edited and introduced by myself in 1893.

all metallic bodies into gold ". It is "the secret hidden
from the beginning, yet granted by God to a few holy men
for the revealing of these riches to His glory ". In fine,
"it is the last, greatest and highest secret of Nature " because
" it is the Spirit of God which in the beginning filled the
earth and brooded over the waters ". It is, in a word, " the
Stone and Spirit of Truth," the Water of Life, the Oil and
Honey of Eternal Healing.[1]

There are pages in Thomas Vaughan and in Rosicrucian
pamphleteers who preceded him which are like a paraphrase
of this " revelation ", but Paracelsus stands alone when he
proceeds as follows. " Through this spirit have the
philosophers invented the Seven Liberal Arts and thereby
gained their riches. Through the same Moses made the
golden vessels in the Ark and King Solomon achieved many
beautiful works to the honour of God. Therewith Moses
built the Tabernacle, Noah the Ark, Solomon the Temple."
But more unthinkable still, " by this Ezra restored the Law
and Miriam—Moses' sister—was hospitable." It sounds like
records of dreamland, though I suspect that it might have
served Mrs. Atwood had she happened to be acquainted with
the text ; but Benedictus Figulus and his ingarnerings are
nowhere quoted in her book, while Paracelsus himself—his
vast output notwithstanding—is mentioned some four
times only and then in rather casual connections.[2]

When he descends from universals to particulars he
becomes like a prototype of Böhme, discoursing of a dark,
small, disesteemed Stone of grey colour, and this is important,
for we see again whence Böhme derived. The universal
essence has five states or natures : (1) " as an impure earthly
body, full of imperfections," yet it heals the sickness and

---

[1] " Christ is my witness that I lie not," Paracelsus testifies, " for all heavenly
influences are united and combined therein," adding subsequently, " though it
may appear impossible to fools that no one has hitherto explored Nature so
deeply." He confesses, however, to a hidden sense which requires to be understood
properly and appeals therefore to initiates.

[2] See the edition of 1920. It is said : (1) that he proposed to discover the hidden
secret of philosophy, but the world laughed at his pretensions, and that most of
his writings are " filled with subtle malice "—p. 50 ; (2) that an English translation
of De Natura Rerum appeared in 1650—p. 59 ; (3) that in his Philosophy to the
Athenians separation is declared to be the greatest miracle, " the principle and
beginning of all generation "—p. 84 ; and (4) that in the same work the free will
is said to give form and essence to everything—p. 286. What Paracelsus says,
however—Book I, text 10—is that separation, the great divider, performs this
office. Mrs. Atwood has misread her authority.

wounds of man, inwardly and outwardly; (2) as a watery substance of much greater virtue, curing cold and hot fevers, acting as a specific against poisons and of great comfort in all diseases; (3) as an aërial body of an oily nature, which is almost freed from imperfections and of manifold medical virtues that need not be recited here; (4) as a substance of fiery nature, in which it makes the old young, revives those at the point of death, and is called the Elixir of Life; (5) as " a glorified and illuminated form, without defects, shining like gold and silver ": in this form it makes dead trees live and converts crystals into the most precious stones of all colours. If combined with the oil in a lamp, it will burn without diminution for ever. It is this also which converts all metals into gold.

Such is the "revelation" of Paracelsus—*sub nomine Hermetis*—concerning the First Matter; but it does not appear in what sense it has been desired by saints from the beginning. In itself it is evidently neither good nor evil and is turned that way or this at the will of the user. "If every one knew it all work and industry would cease; man would desire nothing but this one thing, people would live wickedly and the world would be ruined, seeing that they would provoke God by reason of their avarice and superfluity." It follows that "the discoverers of the mystery of this thing to the unworthy are breakers of the seal of heavenly revelation, thereby offending God's Majesty, bringing upon themselves many misfortunes and the punishments of God".

It is to be observed that the five states of the indestructible essence, for all that is said on the subject, might be found as such in Nature, but ordinary considerations would lead us to infer that, the first perhaps excepted, they were prepared by the artist according to the rules of chemistry and not the laws of magic; with still, retort and crucible, not by the exercise of peculiar virtues acquired in the second birth. But when we are assured that the "perfect equation of the elements" is that Spirit of Truth which the world as such does not know and is otherwise the Soul of the World, it looks likely enough that ordinary considerations must be suspended, that *Aurum Potabile* and *Aurum Philosophorum* may have been produced by the psychic power of the adept, as Paracelsus is reported to have affirmed, or that the Great

Mystery which comes only by illumination of the Holy Spirit of God—or otherwise from a master presumably illuminated by that Divine Font and Source—is reserved for those who have been converted in regeneration, as inferior metals are transmuted in the alchemist's crucibles. But appearances notwithstanding, the Helvetian Monarch of Arcana was acquainted indisputably with the Christ-doctrine of a second birth and, with every opportunity before him, he makes no such suggestion.

I have no doubt, on the other hand, that there was a certain authentic sense in which the Sovereign Creator and Sustainer was both Magus and Alchemist, so far as Paracelsus was concerned. A platitudinarian symbolism of this kind is to be found with its connotations and equivalents in all his memorials which deal with the Hermetic subject, as well as in the *physica et metaphysica inaudita* of *Philosophia Sagax*. But I do not find that he had a shorter path to metallic transmutation in the work of magic, rather than in that of the crucible.[1] On the contrary, that tract upon Tinctures which appeals to his *Revelation* of an imaginary Hermes is full and definite on the chemical path that he followed in practice, and so are its connections throughout his *corpus generale* of Alchemy. There are also definitions which remove all doubt as to the end of the Art in their respective cases. According to *Cælum Philosophorum*, "Alchemy is nothing else but the set purpose, intention and subtle endeavour to transmute the kinds of the metals from one to another." This is in respect however, of the mineral kingdom; but when the Art is considered as one of the Pillars of Medicine

---

[1] That there may have been something, so to speak, at the back of his mind is another question, though it would be pressing the point of logic too far in a case like this to affirm the unescapable inference from one of his texts, namely, that the Magus—as defined by him—should be able to produce gold magically as do others *ex hypothesi* by chemistry. My reference is again to *Philosophia Sagax, Lib.* i, cap. 6 : *In Probationem Artis Magicæ*. The thesis is : *Quicquid natura in corpore alieno perficere potest, idem etiam potest homo.*—*Opera Omnia*, Geneva edition, vol. ii, p. 557. And again, p. 559 : *Quicquid natura habet ac potest, homini subjectum esse oportet*, the reason being that *homini enim natura subjecta est*, apparently without qualification of any kind. But there is no mention of *Alchemia* in all this chapter. At a much later stage—*Lib.* ii, *cap.* 4, p. 615—it is affirmed, however, that in one of its divisions *Magia naturalis . . . ita se habet, ut unum mutare possit in aliud, ferrum in cuprum, etc.*—not, unfortunately, into gold. See also *De Colica* in *Priores Quinque Tractatus*, vol. i, p. 634, where it is said in the editorial marginalia that *Magia Alchimiæ Philosophia est*, because the text identifies *Nigromantia et Alchimia*, on the ground that *Nigromantici enim omnes sunt qui Vulcano deserviunt.*

we have seen in the tract under this title that Alchemy is
the method of preparing medicaments, while in *De Colica* its
office is described as the separation of medicine from poison
and of that which is useful from refuse. In *De Tinctura
Philosophorum* the successive colours assumed by the matter
of the work in the Philosophical Egg are enumerated in the
usual order : (1) blacker than the crow, (2) whiter than the
swan, (3) yellow, and (4) " more red than any blood ". When
the Tincture has been prepared " a pound of it must be
projected upon a thousand pounds of melted Sol ", if it is
to be used for transmutation ; but as an Universal Medicine
" the dose is very small ", though its effect is of great potency.

The process is worthless as it stands (1) because the matter
of the work is veiled under the name of *Lili*, (2) because the
quantities are ridiculous, and (3) because we are told nothing
as to the use of Sol, if and when it has been tinged as directed.
It is cited here solely to exhibit the alchemical concerns of
Paracelsus : there is no purpose in multiplying instances,
or others could be produced which leave things unfinished
and obviously at a loose end, or alternatively are manifestly
false.[1]

In the tract which expands by supposition a text that no
one has seen and no one has heard of otherwise, which
proceeds on its course, moreover, without citing a line or
word of the imagined original, it is to be observed and is
notable that the Universal Essence of Alchemy is a single
substance and that there is no mention of Mercury, Sulphur
and Salt, those three primal elements which prevail everywhere in the literature. They appear, however, as the
Universal Matter of the Philosopher's Stone in that tract
entitled *Aurora* which passes under the name of Paracelsus
but is certainly not his work and reflects him at a far distance
only, if indeed at all. On the other hand, the *Economy of
Minerals*, which is not less certainly genuine, has a thesis
concerning the Ultimate and Primal Matter, according to
which " the element of water is the mother, seed and root

---

[1] There is, e.g. the following recipe, taken from the *Gradations of Metals* : see
Hermetical and Alchemical Writings, i, pp. 32, 33 : " Take of Antimony one pound
and of sublimated Mercury half-a-pound. Let them both be distilled together
over a powerful fire by means of an alembic, and the redness will ascend as thick
as blood. This tinges and graduates all Luna into Sol, and brings the latter when
pale to the highest degree of permanent colour."

of all minerals ". It is defined otherwise as the First Matter of Nature, in itself weak and soft, yet the most solid metals issue forth therefrom." We may compare the " impure earthly body " which is the first state or nature of the essence described in the *Revelation* and shall conclude that if Paracelsus had a definite hypothetical notion of the prime substance which he discussed so frequently, he did not intend that his readers should derive on their part any benefit from the fact.

The conclusion of this investigation is that his physico-metaphysical First Matter which, in his most remarkable description, was also the Spirit of Truth made known by revelation of the Holy Spirit, was that which prompted Jacob Böhme to conceive the work of Alchemy as a work of the Second Birth. From Böhme it was transmitted to Mrs. Atwood, perhaps also to Hitchcock. But revelations of Hermetic knowledge exhibited in the magnetic trance were unknown to the Sage of Hohenheim, although he was Monarch of Arcana, as they were like wise to the Teutonic Theosopher, and it was a journey in the blue distance of dream which had not been attempted by the plain thinking American citizen who wrote his remarks on Alchemy and on Swedenborg as a Hermetic Philosopher.

CHAPTER XIII

DENYS ZACHAIRE AND OTHERS

THERE is something which much too often has to be taken
perforce on trust, tentatively or otherwise, in the examination of alchemical texts. I have tested there and here the
validity of attributions to great names of the past and
have found them worthless. But there is also the question
of antiquity in respect of various tracts which either lay
claim on the far past or have had the benefit of such claim
preferred in their favour. On this subject we shall be read
an instructive lesson in the case of a supposititious eastern
text and have learned something already in that of Nicholas
Flamel. The question thus intervenes as to where we stand
in reality respecting several others, and we can find nothing
reassuring by way of answer. When Michael Maier printed
the *Claves Duodecim* under the name of Basil Valentine it is
certain that he used a manuscript which had come into his
hands—as he did in the case of Norton's *Ordinal*. On the
other hand, whence came the Valentine text, its real age and
the authenticity of its supposed authorship are mysteries
which no one can solve, for Maier tells us nothing himself.
What also was the antiquity of that notable document which
was first printed in 1567, while it is held that its author,
under the name of Bernard Trévisan, was born in 1406?
What library possesses a codex in MS. which is prior to the
date of publication? With all his seeming sincerity he may
have wished, for purposes of concealment, to put himself
back in the centuries, while it is even possible that his
story is pure invention. It happens fortunately, however,
as regards Denys Zachaire—another writer of memoirs—
that he is sufficiently late, and that his romantic story
was printed sufficiently near to his own affirmed time,
for it to be idle to ask whether he was really in evidence
during the first half of the sixteenth century. He may be
presented like Trévisan, less or more at full length and mainly
in his own words.

" Having arrived at the age of 20 years or thereabouts and having received the rudiments of education at home, I was sent by my parents to Bordeaux, to undertake the college curriculum, and I was there for four years, chiefly studying philosophy. I made such progress—by the grace of God and the pains of a certain master—that it was decided for me to proceed to Toulouse, in the charge of the same instructor, for a course of law. There I made acquaintance, however, with other students who had numbers of Alchemical books, my preceptor himself having meddled in these workings. In fact when I went to Toulouse I carried with me a thick volume of processes, collected from all the texts which I had been able to discover. . . . It seemed to me—being thus fortified—if I could undertake the practice, perhaps even with the least of the processes, I should prove the most fortunate of beings. . . ." At Toulouse the ostensible study of law was abandoned for that of Alchemy, and the money supplied for their maintenance during the next two years was expended in the purchase of furnaces, vessels and other necessities for experiments. " Before the end of the first year," as he goes on to tell us, "my two hundred crowns were gone in smoke, while my tutor died of a fever which he contracted in the course of the summer through unremitting attention to the furnace. His death afflicted me much, and the more as I was refused further supplies beyond bare necessities in connection with my proper studies." Denys Zachaire was therefore unable to prosecute further the Great Work. His parents died, however, and he returned home, being now of age, to put himself out of guardianship and take over the charge of his possessions. He appears to have let an estate or family house for a certain period of years, obtaining four hundred crowns, required for the execution of a process communicated to him in Toulouse by an Italian, who claimed to have seen it proved.

" I retained him near my person," says Denis Zachaire, " to see the end of the business." They dissolved gold and silver in aqua fortis, calcined them by evaporation, performed other dissolutions with other waters and repeated distillations, so that two months passed before any powder was ready to make projection. This was done at last in accordance with the said recipe but proved all in vain, for two ounces of gold and one mark of silver had shrunk to the value of half a mark, not to speak of connected expenses. The four hundred crowns of capital were reduced also to two hundred and thirty, of which the Italian received twenty that he might proceed to Milan where, according to his testimony, the author of the process lived and whence he would return with explanations. " I was at Toulouse all the winter awaiting him and might have tarried there still, as I saw nothing of him after."

The story goes on thus. " In the following summer the city was visited by plague and that I might keep in touch with acquaintances I went to Cahors and continued for six months, during which I did not lose sight of my work but frequented the society of a good old man, commonly called the Philosopher. To him I communicated my uncertainties and asked his advice. . . . He mentioned ten or twelve processes which he thought better than others, and I put them in practice on my return to Toulouse when the plague had ceased. The winter passed in this way, and I did so well that my four hundred crowns were now reduced to one hundred and seventy. The enterprise was not for such reason abandoned, and the better to continue operation I made acquaintance with an Abbé, who informed me that one of his friends, in the suite of Cardinal d'Armagnac, had sent him a process from Rome which he believed to be genuine, but it would cost two hundred crowns. We found this sum between us, and the work began with the erection of new furnaces of various kinds. Our process required very strong spirits of wine for the dissolution of a mark of gold. We purchased for this purpose an excellent puncheon of wine of Gaillac, from which we drew the spirit with a great pelican, distilling it many times over, and more if anything than was needed. We then employed various glass vessels to purify and refine it further. We calcined our gold for a month with great heat in two retorts, adding subsequently the spirits of wine to the amount of two poonds' weight, hermetically sealed the retorts, which were placed in the pelican and the pelican itself in the furnace, this being maintained for a whole year. During the interval we tried some minor processes, from which we were destined to derive as much profit as from the Great Work itself. We might have gone on to this day so far as the major process is concerned, . . ., for spirit of wine does not dissolve our gold. We found it in powder, much as we had placed it in the vessels, save only that it was a little more unfixed. We made projection with it on heated quicksilver, following our process; but again all was vain. You may judge of our dismay, especially as the Abbé had warned all his monks that they might be melting the lead cistern of their cloister, to convert it into gold as soon as our experiment was finished. But it was for another purpose that he caused it to be melted subsequently, being to furnish material for the vain experiments of a certain German, who came to his Abbey when I was at Paris. He was not less eager to continue and urged me to raise three or four hundred crowns, he doing likewise, that I might proceed to the capital, a city containing more alchemists than any other in the world. . . . I resolved to remain there as long as the eight hundred crowns lasted, or until I succeeded in my object. This determination drew down on me the displeasure of relations and friends alike, who had imagined that I was a hard working lawyer. I was reduced in fact to making them believe that I had a plan for purchasing an appointment in the Courts. I reached Paris soon after Christmas and was for a month almost unknown; but as soon as I began calling on goldsmiths, smelters, glass-blowers, makers of furnaces and so forth, I became acquainted in the second month with more than a hundred operators. Some were working at the tincture of metals by projection, some by cementation, others by dissolution and yet others by long decoctions. Some sought to extract the mercury of metals and others their fixation : in short no day passed, including festivals and Sundays, that we did not meet together to discuss the position of affairs. . . . But I was deaf to all their arguments, recalling my costly experience as the dupe of similar expectations.

" In the course of the summer I was tempted all the same by a Greek who had a process with Cinnabar, but it failed ; and about the same time I became acquainted with a stranger who sold the fruit of operations to goldsmiths, often enough in my presence. I kept up our relations for the better part of a year before he was willing to confide anything to my knowledge ; but in fine he uncovered his secret, which he appeared to esteem highly, though it was anything rather than perfect." The sequel in fact shews that it was a sophistication more ingenious than most. Zachaire notwithstanding duly sent it on to the Abbé, who seemed to think better of the business and recommended him to continue at Paris for another year, saying that the means should not fail. The story continues :

" I had been three years at Paris and had spent most of my money when I received news from my Abbé, who had something to communicate and desired that I should join him at once. On my arrival at Toulouse it proved that he had received a letter from the King of Navarre, who was a lover of Art and desired that I should proceed at once to Peau in Bearn and teach him the secret which I had learned from the stranger at Paris, as well as others which he understood me to have acquired. Compensation was promised up to three or four thousand crowns. The possibility of this sum tickled the ears of the Abbé and there was no rest till I complied. . . . I found the prince goodwilled and went to work as commanded when materials were available. I succeeded in accordance with the process and obtained the expected recompense. . . . In the end I was dismissed with great acknowledgements and desired to report whether there was anything in his estates which would gratify me, such as confiscations or the like, as he would divert them with pleasure to myself. I was not misled by these empty promises and returned to the Abbé at Toulouse.

" On my road I heard of a man of religion who was wise in natural philosophy and went therefore to visit him, but only to be diverted by his earnest counsel from all modes of sophistication, over which I had wasted my time. . . . I was rather to study henceforward the books of ancient philosophers, that I might become acquainted with their True Matter, wherein was the perfection of the science. I went therefore to my friend at Toulouse, that I might give him an account of the eight hundred crowns which we had put in common and divide with him the reward from the King of Navarre. It must be said that my story dismayed him and more especially my decision to abandon the enterprise which we had begun in common. I remained firm, however, and the next morning we parted one from another, dividing what remained of my proceeds, being ninety crowns each. I returned to my house to collect certain rents, and in 1546 I proceeded to Paris, where I decided to remain until I was fixed in my theory by reading the works of the adepts. I bought some printed books and manuscripts, including *Turba Philosophorum*, the good Trévisan, the *Remonstrance of Nature* and so forth. Having hired a small lodging in the Faubourg St. Marceau and a lad for my servant, I devoted day and night for the space of a year, without seeing anyone. In this manner I fared so well that I chopped and changed my schemes continually, but could reach no fixed point.

" In this perplexity I began again to frequent those who were pursuing the Divine Work, not, however, my old acquaintances or others of the same category, who were dabbling in sophistications. This notwithstanding I came upon a cloud of experiments, some of them on gold only, others on gold and mercury, some on fulminating lead : in a word, blind workings without end. The multiplicity of such operations, combined with the contradictions in books, reduced me to the verge of despair, when the Holy Spirit of God prompted me to recommence the earnest study of Raymond Lully, his *Testament, Codicil* and *Epistle* addressed to King Robert. At length I formed a plan and one entirely different from all operations which I had seen previously. It was one, moreover, which I did not find in books, save only in the *Grand Rosary* of Arnold de Villa Nova, where it is buried somewhat deeply. Another year passed in this manner, studying and developing my scheme, while awaiting the expiration of the period for which my house was leased. I returned there at the beginning of the following Lent, made all necessary arrangements, the erection of a furnace included, and with such expedition that I set to work on the morrow of Easter. I was destined, however, to experience certain difficulties and hindrances on the part of near neighbours, relatives and friends. What, it was asked me, was I now preparing to do ? Have you not lost enough by this delusion ? Another assured me that if I bought such quantities of coal I should be suspected of counterfeiting coin, about which rumours already were abroad. It was also held very strange that I did not follow my profession of a lawyer, and so obtain some honourable office in my own town. As to my relatives,

o

they not only reproached me bitterly but threatened to bring
officers of justice into my house, with instructions to destroy
my furnace. I was still only thirty years old but I looked
fifty and was grey already through the toils which my craze
involved. I leave you to judge of my weariness, but there
was consolation at least in my work, to which I was ever
attentive and watched its favourable progress from day to
day. The summer brought plague in the town, business and
traffic were suspended, but for my part I beheld with trans-
port the evolution of the three successive colours which testify
to the True Work. It came about finally that at next Easter-
tide I made a projection of my Divine Powder on quicksilver,
and in less than an hour it was converted into fine gold.
God knows how joyful I was, how I thanked Him for this
great grace and favour, and prayed for His Holy Spirit to
pour yet more light upon me, that I might use what I had
attained only to His praise and honour. For the rest I took
heed not to boast of my discovery and started the next day
in search of my friend in his Abbey, to fulfil that bond between
us by which each was pledged to communicate his successes
to the other. It was only to find that he had been dead some
six months, and so also it proved with that other man of
religion who gave me his wise counsel. I did not go back to
my house but sought another place and awaited the coming
of a relative whom I had instructed to sell all that I possessed,
discharge my debts and distribute the remainder among
those of my kindred who were in want. It was my design in
this manner that they should profit by the great gift vouchsafed me. All the same I was destined to learn, when the
relative in questive joined me, that in their opinion I had sold
up ashamed of my extravagances and in search of a hidden
refuge. He joined me in the month of July; we set out for
Lausanne, my intention being subsequently to end my days
in a famous German city."

In his unknown retreat Denys Zachaire recorded his
adventures and experience, that he might lead pious seekers
from the realm of sophistications to the straight path of
perfection in what he calls this Divine Work. His one
memorial is entitled *Opusculum Chemicum*, and it opens
with the narrative which I have thus summarised crudely.
It calls Hermes *magnus propheta noster*, insists that the Art is

the Gift of God alone, on the authority of all the adepts, and quotes so largely from previous writers that it can be scarcely considered an original work. The methods of projection upon metals, the composition of precious stones and the Tincture as a Medicine are considered successively. A single grain of the *divinum opus*, dissolved in white wine, imparts to it a rich citron colour and has innumerable healthful uses. It follows that the *Donum Dei* gives gold to those who receive it, that they may possess the wealth of this world, and a physic which is not of the soul but for the removal of infirmities belonging to the body of flesh. In other words, that which Denys Zachaire attained in fine was that which he had sought in toil, with the sweat of his brow, through all the days of life. For this he counsels his readers to implore God that He would vouchsafe His grace and wisdom : for this he affirms that prayer is the chief means to attainment. When he mentions therefore that some operators use ten and more furnaces, we know exactly what he means, and so also when he describes his own practice we are in no doubt whatever : *Unicus operandi modus in unico vase, in unica fornacaula, præter a motione, donec decoctio compleatur.*[1] The probable commentary on this is : *De qustibus non est disputandum.*

The alchemists are many in the sixteenth century, and their records also are many : as it drew to a close they grow from more to more, but names without number are negligible. I need not dwell upon Leonardi Fiorovanti, who has been called an alchemist on the faith of his own *Summa*, which claims to comprise the arcana of that Art, as well as of Medicine and Surgery. The two latter were his province, and the work in question—one of many, as it happens— went through several editions, besides that which appeared originally at Venice in 1571. He is supposed to have applied Hermetic principles and methods to medical science, but *vita brevissima nostra* has not permitted me to search his pages seriously and thus earn a title to pronounce on the

---

[1] The original *Opusculum* seems to have been written in French and appeared at Antwerp in 1567. The editions are numerous and a Latin version—from which I have quoted—will be found in *Theatrum Chemicum*, vol. i. It must be added that Lenglet du Fresnoy terms the fascinating memoir *ouvrage supposé*—I know not on what ground, as he happens to accept and reproduce the memoir contained therein.

success of his device. I know only that on the alchemical side he discourses of *Petra Philosophorum*, but this designation is frivolous, since it proves to be a compound of mercury, nitre and so forth, designed to act on the stomach, as it would assuredly and probably with such results that the formula is not to be looked for at this day in the pharmacopœia or its supplements.

There is also Giovanni Braccesco, who wrote a commentary on Geber which Mangetus deemed worthy of a place in *Bibliotheca Chemica Curiosa*. He followed also the editor of *Vera Alchemiæ Artisque Metallicæ Doctrina*, a collection of 1561, and included in like manner the same author's *Lignum Vitæ*, written originally in Italian and published at Rome in 1542. The Latin version says in its sub-title that it is a discourse on the Matter of the Stone, but that of *Ligno della Vita* tells the whole truth by adding: " wherein is revealed the Medicine by means of which our Primeval Ancestors lived for nine hundred years." This notable performance is cast in the form of a dialogue between Gulielmus Gratarolus, who edited the *Doctrina* collection, and Raymund Lully, who must have been present at the debate in the spirit body or must have communicated his part of it in automatic script. In either case he is instructing a zealous disciple who is seeking a safeguard against the infirmities of " the humid radical ". It is affirmed that such a medicine is extracted from a single substance, which is the sophic *Aqua Metallorum*.[1] It would have been counted therefore by Thomas Vaughan as another contribution to the " blind torturing of metals ". So also he is likely to have judged that Latin poem called the *Zodiac of Life* about which something must be said because of its high authority among presumed experts in the Art.

Pietro Angelo Manzolli, called Palingenius, was a personage of the sixteenth century. According to Facciolati, he was born at Stellata in Ferrara, and some say that he was " body-physician " to Hercules of Este. But this must have been subsequent to the appearance of his poem, its dedication exhibiting him as a stranger to the person of that noble.

---

[1] I must add that Wood of Life appears in the cloud of names applied by alchemists to the matured and perfected Stone. Another title is Universal Panacea or Balsam.

Another account represents him as a Lutheran courtier in the train of the duke's wife, but this seems contradicted by the poem, and by its dedication above all. Few particulars and none of sufficient moment to demand enumeration here have survived concerning him. The *Zodiac of Life* is a part of the Italian Renaissance, a part of that period when high ecclesiastical dignitaries of the Latin Church " imitated the roll of Ciceronian periods " in their episcopal charges, when also the only sin of a classical forgery was some vulnerable point which discovered it. The *Zodiac of Life* was, however, no forged document : it made great claim on originality, acknowledging Lucretius alone as pioneer in the path that it travelled. There is thus and of course a valiant and sustained effort at classical excellence, whether or not the encomium which it obtained from Scaliger would be endorsed fully at the present day.[1] The poem passed through numberless editions and has been translated into several languages, occasionally in metrical versions which by no means do credit to the original.

Now, the poem of Marcellus Palingenius Stellatus may be regarded from two points of view : (1) As a picture of the manners of its period, and it may be not without value as such for historians who deal in the subject ; (2) as the work of an alleged adept in the Art of Alchemy, in which case it is presumable that there is some concealed sense beneath the letter of the twelve books which seem otherwise referred arbitrarily to the twelve Signs of the Zodiac. It has been understood in this alternative manner by precisely those persons who—outside the actual author—might be supposed to know best about it, namely, practical alchemists themselves. An inward meaning is by no means suggested on the surface, nor do I know that Hermetic criticism has done more than suggest or affirm it. On that surface it is didactic, weary, commonplace, tautological beyond toleration, a labour to read and a misery to remember afterwards. The suggestion of a high concealed sense which does not emerge will be left under these circumstances for those, if any, who can find it. But how it came to be attributed is a question

[1] " The poem of Palingenius is wholly satirical, but sober at the same time—not erratic and not horrible. Its diction is pure, while its versification and style are such that—to say the least—we should despair of attaining them."—*Poetics, Lib. x.*

which can be answered readily. The poem contains a single passage which refers to the Great Work of Alchemy; and while it is comprised within a moderate compass, those who thought they knew have found it so pregnant in meaning that it has been accepted as proof positive of the writer's practical acquaintance with their Great Mystery and of his high skill therein. That which remains is inference : why should an Adept and Perfect Master, who could summarise the whole Art in the course of a few hexameters, be at the pains of writing a long *Zodiac of Life*, if it were not to unfold secretly the whole principles and practice of their *philosophia realis* ? So stands the hypothesis and so also may be left to those whom it concerns.

Among ten thousand banalities in a setting of Pagan mythology one might have thought that the one pearl of great price would have escaped detection, and lost no doubt it was except for the eyes of initiates. They did not fail to discover it, and Marcellus Palingenius Stellatus, who dedicates his poem to Hercules, Duke of Ferrara, in a tuft-hunting preface, every line of which touts for patronage, is included with Hermes and Paracelsus, with Geber and Arnold, among " the true sages who really knew this Art ". He is described further as a " distinguished man " and as " evidently a possessor of the Stone ". Panegyrics of this kind will be found among other places in the *Sophic Hydrolith* or *Water-Stone of the Wise*. The contempt for riches which is preached —somewhat artificially, as it might be thought—by the author of the *Zodiac*, has also elicited high praise, on the ground that it indicates the proper attitude of " a lover of learning " who has boundless command of wealth. Was ever a great reputation earned as cheaply, or did his peers and co-heirs possess a canon of criticism which enabled them to recognise at once those who belonged to them ? Did Marcellus in reality produce thus briefly his undeniable titles and warrants ?

We must be content on our part to say only that the passage by which he has been thus immortalised [1] in Hermetic memory

[1] It opens with these lines :

Proinde sophi veteres subtili indagine quendam
Commenti lapidem, sibi fida viatica cunctis
Permansura locis nunquam interitura pararunt,
Quo auxilio varias terras, diversaque regna
Cernere, et a multis quamplurima discere possent, etc.

Lib. x, v. 180 *et seq.*

will be found in the tenth book, entitled *Capricornus*, and that it contains a process on Mercury. But if *est in Mercurio quicquid quærunt sapientes* is an honoured alchemical maxim, it has to be remembered also that as " not all men who say unto me, Lord, Lord, shall enter into the Kingdom of Heaven ", so it is not every one who, in the course of Hermetic ages, has exclaimed *est in Mercurio* that is entitled to be called an Adept.

The thesis on the Great Work is preceded by some platitudes on the lot of the destitute and the need of riches to insure a life of happiness, it being understood that true wealth is a patrimony of the mind, while that which is desirable for the rest is like " the elegant sufficiency " of Thomson. There is the difficulty, however, that those who possess or can acquire this golden mean must dwell in their own houses, encompassed by their own estates, within the measures of which they are bounded and cannot survey the vast world, to behold its varied productions. It is for this reason, we are told, that ancient philosophers devised a certain Stone, which furnished them with sure resources, available in all places, so that they could pass through many states and kingdoms, acquiring knowledge in all. In other words, they carried an inexhaustible purse. But their discovery of the Stone came about as a consequence of the prayers which they put up to Mercury, Sol and Luna,[1] explaining that they were persons of exalted intellect, who cherished wisdom in their hearts, were searchers of causes and strove to penetrate the secrets of Nature. Notwithstanding these titles to consideration, they were oppressed by poverty, endured manifold other evils and almost perished of hunger, while the senseless crowd piled up wealth for its own use. They were compelled to dig the ground, bait horses, cleanse stables and could still barely obtain a livelihood. The plea and purpose of their invocation was that they might be shewn a ready way by which they might be enabled to live honestly and pursue their investigations of the truth.

This prayer was heard by Phœbus, who communicated the following instructions on the understanding that his

---

[1] The appeal opened as follows : " O glory of the universe, O Titan, fairest of the gods, O Latona, who scatterest the shades of night, O inconstant and fugitive offspring of Jove and Maia, O thou of many shapes and gifted with endless mutations : be present with favour amongst us and incline to our complaint."—*Zodiacus Vitæ, Lib.* x.

hearers would hide them in their hearts. " Take you the young Arcadius, inconstant and too volatile ; drown him in the waters of Styx. Then shall God receive him on the breast of Hyales, nymph of Diana, worshipped in the land of Lemnia. He shall uplift and fix him on a cross. Thereafter he must be buried in a warm womb and dissolved by putrefaction. A spirit proceeding from one body shall penetrate his melting members and recall from the black shades that which has been gradually destroyed. When he has put on a golden cloak and when he shines with silver, he must be cast finally upon coals. So shall he be renewed like the Phœnix and will make perfect those bodies which he touches, overcoming the order of Nature. He will change species and put poverty to flight." It is affirmed that Mercury assented and Diana approved the words. The dark oracles were pondered by those who heard ; and after a long time and great labours they discovered the Art, being the composition of the Ethereal Stone. It is added that the possessor can live decently, wherever he pleases, but that the gods vouchsafe such a gift to few.[1]

Whether Palingenius had " proceeded to the *praxis* " himself in the opinion of those who succeeded him and acclaimed his work must be left an open question : it will be sufficient for my purpose and my readers that he was confessedly in search of a patron, which does not happen in the case of persons who have found the key of wealth. But it was this and no higher secret which is represented as desired and attained by those who received from Phœbus a method of operating with profit to themselves on the inconstant and volatile Arcadius. It seems to me in conclusion that the doctrine of Alchemy in the *Zodiac* is like its doctrine of White Magic, as unfolded in the twelfth book,[2] and that

[1] I observe that Mrs. Atwood is able to quote these lines—p. 537 of her last edition—including

Quem qui habet, ille potest, ubi vult habitare decenter,

as referring to the kind of people for whom her *Inquiry* is written, being those " who may be able amidst so many heterogeneous elements of Nature, to discern the rational possibility by the infallible touchstone of her Original Light."

[2]   *Forte aliqui ex his, qui credunt intra œthera et extra*
        Esse Deos, vellent artem quoque discere (si qua est)
        Per quam illos possint affari, illosque videre.
        O quam sublime hoc, et quam mirabile donum est !
        Quo nihil in terris homini contingere majus
        Posse puto, at pauci tanto dignantur honore, etc.
                              Lib. xii, v. 329 et seq.

the claim of Palingenius to be regarded as a Hermetic adept is like his claim to pass as a magus : his Latin hexameters are " about it and about " in each case, but he did not transmute metals, either in a chemical laboratory or in a dark room set apart to psychical research, and he did not evoke the gods, using occult formulæ and hoping *videre illos*. Though held for some obscure reason in far higher estimation he is very much less to the purpose of Alchemy than the unreadable Johannes Aurelius Augurellus, his predecessor, whose *Vellus Aureum et Chrysopœia*, another hexameter poem, is inspired by the *Magnum Opus* and is concerned with nothing else. It was presented to the magnificent pontiff and potentate Leo X, who—according to one account—rewarded the author with a green mantle, the colour of hope, or—according to another—with an empty purse, that it might be filled for ever by his science.

One of these alternatives in the other's absence might pass as history, but in the presence of both we cannot doubt that they are Rabelaisian inventions which illustrate the feeling of the period on the quest and claim of Alchemy, alike in palace and schools. But the Art never lacked a witness or the search for the Great Secret a cloud of eager followers, while school and palace alike—amidst their ribaldry and persiflage—were eager as any to lend an ear when a new voice was speaking on the old, old subject, delivering dark counsels on " reversions of gold *in futuro* ". But it was always and only gold, save and except only when the ravages of the last plague brought them back to the dreamstory which testified that the medicine of metals was that also of men. These and no other were the treasures desired in the sixteenth century—as before and after—by those who listened ; and these and no other were the *dona Dei*, the *Secreta et Mysteria Artis* which the adepts offered.

CHAPTER XIV

Famous English Philosophers

MY title is borrowed from him to whom we owe the one and only collection, and there is a sense in which it is true, for some of the *Adepti Anglici* with whom I am concerned here appeared in Latin translations abroad before their original remains were printed in English. For example, the *Ordinal* of Norton was published—by Michael Maier—in 1618,[1] the tract of Dastin in 1625 [2] and practically the whole works of Ripley in 1649,[3] whereas the general ingarnering produced under the auspices of Elias Ashmole and based upon old manuscripts belongs to the year 1652.[4]

The School of English Alchemy is a curious and not uninteresting product of its time and place. We know that there were memorials of the literature which were written in Latin verse, having glanced in the last chapter at Marcellus Palingenius and Augurellus, one of whom is regarded as an adept, while it would appear that the other is not classed generally as more than an amateur or aspirant, though Mangetus must have thought otherwise, seeing—as we have found—that he assigned him a place in his great collection of presumably authoritative writers. We know also that among French alchemical memorials a position of some importance is assigned to that portion of the *Roman de la Rose* which is concerned with the Great Work—at least on the side of its follies—and there are other contributions to the

---

[1] That is to say, in *Tripus Aureus*, issued in quarto at Frankfurt and containing : (1) the *Practica* and *Claves* of Basil Valentine, (2) Norton's *Crede Mihi, seu Ordinale, ex Anglicano MS. in Latinum translatum*, and (3) the *Testamentum* of so-called Abbot Cremer, not included by Ashmole.

[2] *Joh. Dastin vel Daustenii Visio, seu de Lapide Philosophico*, in the *Decades Duo* of Johannes Rhenanus.

[3] *Georgii Riplei, Canonici Angli nempe Bridlingtoniæ, Opera Omnia Chimica, quotquot hactenus visa sunt, ex MS. curis Ludovici Combachii Medici Hassi.* Published at Cassell.

[4] *Theatrum Chemicum Britannicum, containing several Poetical Pieces of our Famous English Philosophers, who have written the Hermetique Mysteries in their own Ancient Language. Faithfully collected into one volume, with Annotations thereon, by Elias Ashmole Esquire, Qui est Mercuriophilus Anglicus, 1652.*

subject in French verse. The archaic remains of English Alchemy collected by Ashmole are all in doggerel measures, and, if it be possible to distinguish a deep below the deep in irredeemable badness, then it should be said that they are worse than the metrical translation by Henry Lovelich of the *Grand Saint Graal*: it will be decisive for those who know. On their own authority or by inference on the part of their editor, those with which I shall be concerned belong to the fourteenth and fifteenth centuries, though they seem rather curiously modern in language for these periods.

The place of prime importance must be assigned to George Ripley on the evidence of Eirenæus Philalethes, whose commentaries on the Canon of Bridlington form a substantial volume, in the preface to which it is affirmed of Ripley that " a true artist he was, as every one who hath attained the knowledge in this Mastery can testify ". [1] It is said also that " for his experience herein he was eminent, yea, his writings indeed are in my opinion, for the fullness of them and eminent descriptions of things, to be preferred before any that I have read or seen : yet I have seen many ", adding subsequently : " Ripley to me seems to carry the garland ".[2] Now, the testimony of Eirenæus is of the highest authority among later Sons of Hermes. The consideration of his own contributions to the literature of the Great Work belongs to a later chapter, but in order to determine the position of commentator and original alike as to the concern and end of Alchemy it should be understood that the substance of Ripley's philosophy is summarized by Eirenæus under the five following " conclusions " or heads.[3] (1) " That as all things are multiplied in their kind, so may be metals ", the same having in themselves a capacity of transmutation from an imperfect to a perfect state; (2) that " the main ground for the possibility of transmutation " resides in the antecedent possibility of all metals being reduced to " their first mercurial matter "; (3) that two Sulphurs only are related

[1] *Ripley Revived, or an Exposition upon Sir George Ripley's Hermetico-Poetical Works. Containing the plainest and most excellent Discoveries of the Most Hidden Secrets of the Ancient Philosophers that were ever yet published. Written by Eirenæus Philalethes, an Englishman, styling himself Citizen of the World,* 1678.

[2] The Commentary of Eirenæus was based on the text of Ashmole, compared in respect of Ripley's *Epistle to King Edward IV* with Ralph Rabbard's edition of 1591.

[3] It is the " philosophy " as embodied in the *Epistle* mentioned in the previous note.

to the Work and that their Mercuries are united to them essentially; (4) that he who understands rightly the two Sulphurs and Mercuries " shall find that the one is most pure Red Sulphur of Gold—which is *Sulphur in manifesto and Mercurius in occulto* "—while the other is " most pure White Mercury "—which is " true Quicksilver *in manifesto* and Sulphur *in occulto* "—these being " our two Principles "; (5) that if " a man's principles be true and his operations regular, his Event will be certain, which Event is no other than the True Mystery ". If any one proposes that these *conclusiones alchemicæ* belong to any other subject than the work of the Art in metals there is no memorial, ancient or modern, on metallurgy that would not suffer a construction along the same lines.[1]

In addition to the material which enters into these Conclusions, Ripley's dedicatory *Epistle*, prefixed to his *Compound of Alchemy*, affirms that the philosophers speak of many things, though of a truth there is one thing only, being that from which White and Red spring naturally and in succession. Proportion is the chief secret. It is said also that Ripley will never write the secret, even for the king; but the latter shall see it " when he lists ", though he may gain knowledge concerning it from his instructor's other writings. In a *Prologue* which follows it is laid down that God will infuse wisdom only into the humble who are clean of soul and offer no offence to Him. The counsel is therefore to begin with God, that He may abide with the seeker by grace: so shall the latter win knowledge of " our great privity ". The explanation is that those only who attain the science of things Divine are worthy of the science of this world; or, as expressed by Eirenæus, God is " the only

[1] There is a certain highly unconscious humour about Mrs. Atwood's judgment on Ripley, whom she found little to her purpose, though he is cited several times. He is said—p. 47 of the last edition—to have been made " envious " by private misfortunes. Moreover, his composition is disorderly and his *Twelve Gates* " have, we conceive, little edified any without the Lodge "—meaning his fellow-adepts, regarded as an incorporated body. Respecting his commentator Eirenæus, whose title-page is misquoted as to content he " will appear infamously sophistical and inevitably disgust a beginner ". The explanation is that both were physical alchemists and offered testimony to nothing but Alchemy on the physical side, so that it was difficult to drag them into a metaphysical net. It is attempted, however, and they bear bad witness. To a critical mind which happens to know the literature, it is at once instruction and delight to contrast her thesis with the citations on which it pretends to be grounded.

Giver of Wisdom ", whether of things above or things below :
therefore the student must " address himself to the Author
and Fountain of goodness " for His help and for grace to
honour Him " in the use of so great a talent ".[1]

After the *Prologue* comes a *Preface* which was so important
in the opinion of Eirenæus that he devotes over ninety pages
to an exposition of its meaning. When Ripley affirms that
the Stone is " one and three " and is called " the Lesser
World ", it is said in *Ripley Revived* that " our Stone is likened
to man, who although he have a wife different from him in
sex, yet she is one with him in nature ; and in this sense man
is called the microcosm or less world : for indeed, next to man
—who is the image of God—the Stone is the true little system
of the great world ". It is impossible for words to enunciate
more clearly than these a distinction and yet an analogy
between the alchemist and his work in Alchemy. Compare
also as follows, on the oneness and triplicity of the Stone.
" This Stone is also called Trine or Trinity in unity, from
the homogeneity of the matter. As Trévisan saith : ' Our Stone
is made of one root—that is, of two mercurial substances ',
etc. This Trinity is discerned in the components : for first
there is the body, which is Sol, and the water of Mercury,
in which—besides its mercuriality—there is a spiritual seed

---

[1] "It is to be understood that the Most Wise God hath a ruling hand herein, and
all the Sons of Art have their commission, as it were, given them : they write and
teach according to that permission which the Creator of all things hath given . . .
And truly it is not our intent to make the Art common to all kinds of men : we
write to the deserving only, intending our books to be but as way-marks to those
who may travel in these paths of Nature ; and we do what we can to shut out
the unworthy. Yet we write so plainly that as many as God hath appointed to
this Mastery shall certainly understand us and have cause to be thankful for our
faithfulness herein. This gratitude we shall receive from the Sons of this Science,
whatever we have from others : our books therefore are intended for the former,
but we do not write a word to the latter. Moreover, we write not our books for
the information of the illiterate, as though every vulgar mechanical distiller,
alchemist or sophister should readily carry away the Golden Fleece. Nor do we
intend that any covetous man—who makes gain his utmost ends—shall readily
gather the Apples of the Hesperides ; nor yet that any, though learned, should
by once or twice careless and slight reading of our books be straightway made a
philosopher. Nay verily, the majesty of this Science forbids so great impiety :
it is the gift of God and not of men. Our books are for those who have been or
intend to be employed in the search of Nature : we hint the way ; prayer to God
and patient persistence in the use of means must open these doors." And then,
most significantly as a light on the purpose in hand, it is added : " Let therefore
profound meditation, accompanied with the blessing of God, furnaces, coals,
glasses and indefatigable pains be thy interpreters. So I did, so I advise thee ;
and may the blessing of God attend all studious, virtuous searchers in this way."—
Ripley Revived, pp. 20–22.

of Sulphur, which is the Secret Fire. This is the Trinity, and these are called the body, the soul and the spirit. The body is the dead earth, which increaseth not without the celestial virtue ; the spirit is the soul of our air [1] or chamelion, which is also of a two-fold composure, yet made one inseparably; the soul is the bond of Mercury, without which our Fire never appears—nor can appear, for it is naked ". There is more to this purpose, but it does not call for quoting, the sum of the theme being (1) that in the first mixture there are three natures, and (2) that " the Work is carried to perfection according to the virtue of a body, soul and spirit ", the reason being (1) that " the body would never be penetrable were it not for the spirit ; (2) that the spirit would not be " permanent in its super-perfect Tincture " except for the body ; and (3) that these twain could not act on one another without the soul, because " the spirit is an invisible thing, nor doth it ever appear without another garment,[2] which garment is the soul ". So far as this exposition is concerned by analogy with the three-fold nature of man it is to be observed that it belongs to Eirenæus and not to Ripley, who as a priest of the Latin Church knew of no distinction between soul and spirit in our nature and was a stranger above all to any doctrine or hypothesis of a psychic body. The latter belonged at the period to occult philosophy.

The *Preface* proceeds to affirm that the Stone is in every place, that it is brought unto man alike by fowls and fishes, and finally that it is " in thee and me ", to which Eirenæus adds on the authority of Morien that it is found also in the dunghill, while according to *Novum Lumen Chemicum*—which is also cited—it is only the fool who cannot believe that it is in gold. But it is not " in thee and me " according to Ripley because Alchemy is concerned with the mode of our spirit's return " to God Who gave it " : on the contrary it is because the alchemist of Bridlington is speaking of his Philosophical Mercury. It is this which is in all and everywhere, or as he says in his dreadful measures : " without which nothing being is ". Now, Eirenæus in his commentary explains that this Mercury is " a concrete of water " and

---

[1] It will be seen that this is a confusion of images, interblending the trinity of Alchemy with the trinity of man.
[2] The body being an external vesture.

passes as such "through the whole family of concretes", whence it is said to be everywhere. "Moreover, the Stone, being the system of the world, doth in some way or other represent everything which is or can be perceived by man." [1] For Ripley, however, it is nearer in some things than in others, and for the philosophical practice of Alchemy the principle of the "material Stone" must be sought in the "Mercury of metals", otherwise, as Eirenæus says, that "true natural heat, in the acuation and stirring up of which is the whole secret of the Mastery", or in Ripley's formula "the potential vapour of metals". Finally, as a direct answer to the direct question, what is our Stone?—Eirenæus affirms "that it is gold digested to its height of purity and perfection through the co-operation of Art and Nature". It must be turned, however, into vapour and this means into Mercury, which is the seed of gold and has Sulphur hidden within it—otherwise, Fire of Nature.

Ripley's *Compound* itself is divided into twelve Gates, which at the same time are one and have one only lock, and to this there is a single key. (1) The first is Calcination, whereby the Stone—meaning its Matter—is purged, using a temperate heat for a year, or even more. (2) The second is Dissolution, a dissolving of metals into mineral water which does not wet the hand : it is performed in one glass, egg-like in shape and well closed. (3) The third is Separation, dividing the subtle from the gross and the thick from the thin, but the work is that of Nature and not of the operator's hands, manual separation appertaining to fools. It draws forth incombustible oil and water. (4) The fourth is Conjunction, which joins opposites in perfect unity, so that they never flee from each other : its variant name is Copulation, as of water and air, of earth and fire, of male and female, matter and form, Mercury and Sulphur-vive. But it is also of body, soul and spirit, a trinity which must be brought into unity : it belongs to the administration and regulation of the fire, which is at once continual and temperate. (5) The fifth is Putrefaction, without which no seed can multiply, and it is brought about by the continued action of a moist heat in a proper furnace or athanor. (6) The sixth is Congelation, in which the elements of the Stone are said to flow together, the result—

---

[1] *Op. cit.*, p. 27.

according to Eirenæus—being " a perfect powder impalpable " which has ingress into all metals and alters them radically.[1] He describes it further as a " whitening of the bodies ". (7) The seventh is Cibation, a feeding of the dry matter with milk and meat moderately. (8) The eighth is Sublimation, in which bodies are made spiritual and spirits thereafter corporal. It must be done without violence and not to the top of the vessel. The object in view is to cleanse from original filth. (9) The ninth is Fermentation and is said to be of three kinds, two being of clean bodies and the third most secret. It is an incorporation of soul and body. Gold is fermented with gold and silver with silver. (10) The tenth is Exaltation, by which bodies are augmented with the spirits of life. (11) The eleventh is Multiplication, otherwise augmentation of the Elixir in goodness and quantity, both for the White and Red. It is declared to be infinite, for the Medicine is fire and will never die. (12) The twelfth and last Gate is that of Projection. Therein the worth of the Medicine is proved by projecting a small quantity on metal or alloy, using " cleansed and very pure bodies ". A *Recapitulation* at the end affirms that " our Red Man " and his wife do not tinge until they have been tinged themselves. The work is performed " in one glass " and according to a single regimen. The Elixirs for Sun and Moon are termed Oils which convert all bodies—meaning metallic bodies—into gold and silver.

We see therefore that the Great Work of Ripley and Eirenæus is distinguished from that of which Mrs. Atwood dreams by the fact that it was not a work of the hands and that hers was, while their transmutation was performed on metals and not, as she imagined, in the soul of man. At this advanced point of our investigation it seems difficult to speak of such views with an air of seriousness and not forfeit the claim on any sense of humour. I will end therefore in respect of Ripley by saying that on the authority of his text the *Compound of Alchemy* was finished in 1471.

The *Ordinal* of Norton is a tract in high favour because of its supposed spiritual concern through all its length of measures. Our excellent friend Hitchcock is haunted by the

---

[1] *Ripley Revived*, pp. 386, 387. So is the end of the work forestalled half way.

rhymer's notion of " one thing " which is called Magnesia and the memories of *Est una sola res* in the other alchemists. He dwells also on Norton's " concords ", which are necessary in the work of the Stone, and allegorises thereupon at his will and pleasure, without one true star to guide him. But he is certain that he is on the right path, leading to an intelligible doctrine respecting the conduct of life when the alchemist's son and heir of knowledge is taught that the Stone is one—though three according to its principles—and that Philosophical Sulphur is a vital spirit which raises bodies from death, for such is that Divine Spirit which quickens the souls of men and leads them in a perfect way.

It came about also that Norton is quoted again and again in the *Suggestive Inquiry* because he testifies to the " profound philosophy " and " subtle science of holy Alchemy ". The Orient Water which he characterises as *lux umbra carens* is a " miraculous product of the spiritual poles of mind in sublime conjunction at their source ".[1] He leaves his operator to choose as he will among a multitude of vessels but adds that the best is one which agrees with that of Nature and quotes pseudo-Albertus as follows : *Si Deus non dedisset nobis vas nihil dedisset.* This is glass, says Norton, which means for the *Inquiry* that " the Spirit finally constructs its own vessel and vitrifies it ".[2]

But if we turn to the *Ordinal* itself instead of mere citations made therefrom, we shall find that its holy science which comes only by grace is that of making " fine gold and silver " out of " foul copper ". Here is the Art and Craft which

our Lord above
Has given to such men as He doth love,

and it will be observed that this statement, fantastic as it seems, is in the manner of all the alchemists, the work in mines and crucibles being as much under the direct wardenship of Divine Providence as the flight or fall of a sparrow. It is affirmed at the beginning that the *Ordinal* is a book on the increase of riches, a book of the needy for putting poverty to flight, it being imposed on the true seeker to avoid adulterated metals, albifications and citrinations which cannot abide a searching test. It is discovered only by the grace

---

[1] *Inquiry,* edition of 1920, p. 410.
[2] *Op. cit.,* p. 444.

P

of God or the goodwill of a teacher who has attained himself the Mastery, in which case it can de delivered in fullness only by word of mouth, being so glorious and wonderful : the communication even then is under a sacred oath.

In opposition to the unanimous voice of all the witnesses, it is affirmed that metals, as elementary objects, possess no seed, and there is hence no growth or propagation in this kingdom. Silver and gold are produced only by the Medicine of the Philosophers, and with this Medicine the Art of Alchemy is concerned. As regards its components, they are two, though the Stone itself is one. That of the White Tincture is called " our chosen Marcasite " and it must be prepared by those who seek it, being sold in no city of Christendom. In contradiction hereto it is termed a thing of small price, esteemed lightly by merchants, and no one who finds it cares to pick it up. That of the Red Tincture is named Magnesia, and it is found on the peaks of very high mountains, but also in the lowest depths of the earth : it is glorious, fair, bright, and an ounce may be obtained in most places for about twenty shillings. It is affirmed that no other substances than these are needed, which notwithstanding Norton proceeds soon after to say that the classification of intermediate minerals is one of the most difficult experiments in the Gross Work, as the different media that are used must be all in a highly purified state if the business is to reach its term, a Tincture— that is to say—which imparts perfection to all things and must contain nothing therefore which is foul and vile. The length of the whole process is fixed at three years, understood as a minimum, but thereafter those who are skilled in the art of augmenting the Medicine will have no need to undertake it a second time. The sense of sight in the observation of successive colours, as these arise in the process, of smell and even of taste are all invoked to guide the operator in his task, and he has also to watch over the fluxibility of the liquid. Though it does not seem in concurrence with what has been described previously, the White and Red Tinctures are affirmed towards the end to be composed from the same substance, in the same vessel and by the same methods ; but this is only till " the living matters have been mortified " up to which stage apparently the so-called Marcasite and

Magnesia are prepared together. But at the time of writing his *Ordinal* Thomas Norton had never prepared the Red Tincture, having been disheartened by being robbed of his chemical materials and implements.

He says that he had all his experiments in proper train when some thievish servants left him an empty laboratory. At another time he composed an Elixir of Life, of which a merchant's wife bereft him. On a third occasion he had procured a Quintessence, with other preparations of price, and was robbed of them by wicked men. He dilates frequently on the heavy cost of the process and on the number of assistants required, so that it is an Art to be followed by the rich of this world alone. The Stone, moreover, is not to be discovered or perfected, except through intense devotion. It remains to say that the *Ordinal* was begun on its own testimony in the year of our Lord 1477, and there is a tradition that Norton died in this year, very poor, according to Fuller, but so he had also lived, in the judgment of the. same deponent. He has been termed *alchemista suo tempore peretissimus* and alternatively *nugarum opifex in frivola scientia*. According to one of the stories, he undid himself and all those who advanced money for his researches. " It helpeth a man when he hath need ", poor Norton says of his Stone, and this is the kind of help. It must not be forgotten that the *Ordinal* is full of stories, now of the writer's own master, now of the pledges which bound him, and now of other adepts, besides vain pretenders. It is a picture of Alchemy at his period, as well as his own picture. There is a story of Briseus the money-changer, who caused loss to many but delight to some, and this leads up to " an almost miraculous event ", the same bed in a house near Leadenhall Street being occupied successively for ten days by three Masters, each of whom possessed the White and Red Tinctures. The eldest uttered many prophecies, and one among them averred that there should be joy in all parts of England after great sorrows : it would come to pass when the Cross was honoured by night and by day in the Land of God and the Land of Light. The Art, it was added, will be revealed then to a King.

There is another and less unconvincing account, which concerns Thomas Dalton, a man of religion, who was alive in 1450 and presumably about that time was taken from his abbey by Thomas Herbert, described as a squire of King Edward, and brought into the royal presence. There he was confronted by Debois, another squire, to whom he had once acted as chaplain. Outside this spiritual ministration Debois alleged that in less than twelve hours Dalton had made him a thousand pounds of good gold, and he attested the statement on oath. Thereupon Dalton exclaimed, looking at Debois : " Sir, you are forsworn." The betrayer confessed that he was pledged never to reveal the benefit which he had received, but he deemed that for the King's sake and the good of the commonwealth he should do wrongly by keeping his oath. Thereupon Dalton addressed the King and affirmed that he had received the Powder of Projection from a Canon of Lichfield on condition that he did not put it to the test till after the death of the donor, and since that event he had lived in such disquietude and danger on account of his possession that he had destroyed it in secret. According to Norton, the King dismissed Dalton, presenting him with four marks to carry him back whence he came. Herbert, however, lay in wait for him, and he was conveyed to the Castle of Gloucester and there immured, in the hope of inducing him to make the Philosophical Tincture. The scheme failed, and after four years of imprisonment the story goes that Dalton was brought out to be beheaded in the presence of Herbert. He came with smiling countenance, not only in resignation but joy, saying : " Blessed art Thou, Lord Jesus : too long have I been kept from Thee. The science which Thou gavest me I have reserved without abusing. I have found no one apt to be my heir, wherefore, sweet Lord, I render Thy gift to Thee." It is said that tears poured from the eyes of Herbert, and the execution did not proceed. But it was in reality a last device to wrest the secret of the adept, for the threat, like the imprisonment, was apart from royal knowledge, and Herbert would not have dared to proceed. Dalton rose from the block with a heavy countenance, grieved at the prolongation of his earthly exile. Herbert died shortly after and Debois himself came to an untimely end. The requirements of poetical justice were thus fulfilled.

While it would be idle to investigate the foundations

of this story,[1] it may be pointed out that a Master of Art in possession of the Philosopher's Stone could have secured his own safety by naming conditions with which his persecutors would have complied in their greed and could have protected his secret also by simple artifice. What is more, however, to the purpose is the fact that neither in the days of Norton, nor after or before, could any reasonable person pretend that the art of transmuting metals was a Mystery of Christ, except for purposes of evasion. But it was perfectly well known at the time that there was a Christ-secret, which is a Mystery of God.

Thomas Charnock's *Breviary of Philosophy* and the *additamenta* thereunto deserve a passing word, it being understood that he was another of the Hermetic poets included by Ashmole in his *Theatrum Chemicum*. The *Breviary* is the life of an alchemist to whom the Great Secret had been communicated, but a fatality pursued him on three several occasions in his attempts to perform the work, and this was the position of affairs when the metrical tract was written. It describes the vessels and instruments, with the regulation of the philosophical fire, but says nothing of the secret itself. The date of composition is said to be 1557. The additional matters are an *Enigma* belonging to 1572 and a memorandum dated 1574, in which the writer affirms his attainment of the transmuting powder when his hairs were white. Charnock had a master in the first and second year of Queen Mary's reign, and at his death the " unlettered scholar "—as the author calls himself—became heir of the adept. There is a full enumeration of all vessels and instruments, it being specified that they are obtainable in England. The requisite craftsmen are a potter, joiner and glass-blower: of these last there is one at Chiddingfield in Sussex. The business of the joiner is to build a tabernacle to hold the vessels, in shape like unto a hutch and secured with lock and key. These are unpromising materials for any metaphysical construction, but they did not baffle Mrs. Atwood, who leaves

---

[1] The personalities may be historical, but the alleged date is wrong. In 1450 King Henry VI was in the middle period of his long reign, and Edward IV, the only English monarch of this name during the entire century, did not succeed him till 1483. According to Stow's *Annals*, Sir John Debois' fell at the battle of Tewkesbury in 1471, and two days after his son James was taken, with others of the Lancastrian party, from a church where he had found sanctuary and was beheaded on the spot.

over the tabernacle but finds the potter to her purpose, including a counsel to stand by him in his work and see that he does as required.[1]

There ought to be something in Bloomfield as his *Camp of Philosophy* is cited three times by Mrs. Atwood: (1) on the titles of the Elixir, (2) on critics of the Art, and (3) on the Magistery itself, which is 3, 2, and 1, or the " animal, vegetable and mineral Stone ". The fixed, variable and fugitive are three also, and they have to be joined in one. For the rest, there is dark before dawn, mourning prior to joy, but Orient Phœbus comes, from which it follows that he who can work wisely shall in fine attain. The tract begins with a vision, in which Bloomfield was rapt into heaven and beheld the Blessed Trinity. A voice taught him to understand the dark sayings of philosophers concerning the altitude, latitude and profundity of the Stone, three in substance and one in essence. The quintessence of visible things is a strange priority abiding unseen in every substance, after the manner of the innermost Divinity : it is in things vegetable, animal, mineral and comes from God. It is made sensible to some of the elect. The vision ends and Bloomfield receives the Key of Knowledge from Father Time. But, *pace* the *Inquiry*, all this machinery is devised and set at work to reveal what we have learned otherwise by the evidence of all the alchemists, namely, that the First Matter is everywhere.

Pierce the Black Monk wrote on the Elixir and provides a dark recipe, though it is plain enough as to the end in view. The instruction is to take Earth of Earth, Earth's Mother, Water of Earth, Fire of Earth and Water of the Wood. These are to lie together and then be parted. Alchemical gold is made of three pure souls, purged as crystal. Body, spirit and soul grow into a Stone, wherein there is no corruption : this is to be cast on Mercury and it shall become most worthy gold. The last sentence offers a clear issue. But it is said elsewhere in the jangle that a sperm is taken from a body " in the which is all "—meaning the First Matter— and that a marriage is made by Water of the Wood, for which reason the Black Monk proceeds to affirm that

---

[1] *Op. cit.*, edition of 1920, p. 444. The *Suggestive Inquiry* has unfortunately no sense of humour.

Therefore there is no other way
But to take thee to thy beads and pray . . .
All you that have sought many a day,
Leave work, take your beads and pray.

So we hear much about prayer on the part of the *Suggestive Inquiry* and of its efficacy in spagyric works, all which notwithstanding, it behoves us to remember that the Stone of the Black Monk is cast on Mercury and produces gold.

The *Work* of John Dastin—as his tract is called—is one of mineral prudence. The symbolism is the Mystery of Salvation applied to metals, and the Sun is apparently their saviour. The Moon was first his mother and then his wife, from whom he is conceived a second time and a second time also brought forth, she having devoured her husband. This figurative mystery was too much for Mrs. Atwood and she does not quote it. . . . The *Work* of John Carpenter ordains the extraction of a Tincture from Titan Magnesia, Red Gum and Sulphur Vive. A marriage is to be made by the help of Mercury, in the conjunction of the Sun and Moon, the Water of Life acting apparently as celebrant. Care must be taken lest the fume escape, and the fire must be equal to the beams of Phœbus in June and July. That which is produced is denominated the Animal Stone and it is richer than the Mineral, which is said to be found everywhere. It would appear, however, that the Animal Stone, or its prime substance, is also ready to hand for those who can find it, since fowls in the air, fishes in the sea, the red and the white grape, souls of beasts and also the reason of angels

All bring to their house
This noble Stone so precious.

The author says that he found his key in the tract ascribed to Mary the Prophetess. . . . In *De Lapide Philosophorum*, Thomas Robinson reduces the whole Art within the limits of twenty-six lines. The symbology is that one produced four, from which came a second unity, described as " a grit ". The first unity is the Corner Stone, and the second cannot be had without it. In other words *Materia Prima* produced the Four Elements, from which comes *Lapis Exillis*, the slight or slender Stone, otherwise " that Great Stone which many seek and miss ". But at the very end, or after six thousand years,

all shall rest eternal and divine,
And by the beauty of the Godhead shine.

So far as I am concerned, this is surrendered to the casuists —I mean, this last message—-that they may make of it what word they can.

It is not to be supposed that these summaries exhaust the " famous English philosophers " who wrote on the Art in verse and were edited by Elias Ashmole. There is a *Hunting of the Green Lion* which is quoted in the *Suggestive Inquiry* " by way of recreation ", and I propose to leave it at that. There is an anonymous tract on *Experience and Philosophy,* which says everything that we have heard previously about the omnipresence of the First Matter. There is the well-known section of Gower's *Confessio Amantis* concerning three Stones : the Vegetable, which is to salve man : the Animal, which has virtues proper to eyes, ears, nose and mouth, serving therefore the same purpose ; and the Mineral, which purifies metals and transforms them, so that they assume the nature of gold and silver, by the help of fire. There are in fine anonymous fragments, extracts from Chaucer and Lydgate, as also from Dee and Kelley ; but these last will be mentioned again in their place. Those which are left over are like those with which I have dealt, testimonies throughout to the concern of English alchemists in that which engrossed their ancestors and co-heirs everywhere, from Byzantium in the early Christian centuries to Germany on the threshold of the Reformation.

CHAPTER XV

ALCHEMY AND EXPLOITATION

IF we look back upon the records of the past, being those that have been passed in review, it must be said that so far the characteristic of Latin Alchemy has been a certain authentic note which stands at least for apparent personal conviction on the part of writers. There are seals of sincerity even upon the myth of Flamel which I can only account for to myself by inferring that its inventor regarded the famous Hieroglyphics, then in full evidence, as belonging to the Great Work, and hence he devised a story to account for what he actually believed. That whosoever wrote the *Triumphal Chariot* was not in his own view walking by faith but science, however mistaken on the central point of fact, seems to be utterly certain, and I have made in days gone by too long a study of Paracelsus to have any doubt about his supreme conviction. The *Ordinal* of Norton conveys the same impression, while I have presented the personal stories of him who was called *par excellence* the good Trévisan and of Denys Zachaire at such full length that readers can judge for themselves. It is precisely this note of conviction, this seal of perfect sincerity that constitutes a real problem of alchemical literature. Had the writers been testifying to anything but an unknown subject couched in symbolical language, there would have been surely no challenge of a claim thus made through the centuries. But as the chequered sixteenth century drew to its close amidst reformation and rumours of reformation, above all amidst facilities of printing, the claims on adeptship multiplied and our next story moves in a different sphere, being that of the exploitation of Alchemy.

" I venture to hope," said the subject of this study, in his tract *De Lapide Philosophorum*, " that my life and character will so become known to posterity that I may be counted among those who have suffered much for the sake of truth." The justification thus desired modestly by Edward Kelley has not been accorded him by the Supreme

Court of Judgment to which he appealed. Posterity has continued to regard him in much the same light as he was looked at by some at least of his own generation and by most of that which succeeded it : in other words as a fraudulent notary—or what not—who was deservedly deprived of his ears, if a common report was true ; as a sordid impostor who duped the immeasurable credulity of the learned Dr. Dee, whether or not he involved his victim also in certain traditional transactions, the rumour of which has soiled a name which ought to have shone brightly in Elizabethan annals ; as, finally, a pretended transmuter of metals who was only too leniently treated by an Emperor whom he deceived. For example, the Astrologer in Butler's *Hudibras* :

> had read Dee's Prefaces before
> The Devil and Euclid, o'er and o'er ;
> And all the intrigues 'twixt him and Kelley,
> Lescus and th' Emperour would tell ye.

This is unjust so far as Dee is concerned, but it voices the verdict of posterity, in so far as the latter has concerned itself with the subject. It is in particular the verdict of biographical dictionaries, which have transcribed from one another after the method that prevails among them in dealing with seers and alchemists, as generally with other oracles of the borderlands. There is no need to add that on those rare occasions when it glances for a moment at borderlands, unerudite public opinion has been formed by the dictionaries, at least until the revival of interest in occult claim and pretence led up to some serious research.

Edward Kelley appears to have been born at Worcester, the event occurring, according to Anthony à Wood, about four o'clock in the afternoon on the first day of August, 1555.[1] This was in the third year of Queen Mary's reign. He was educated—however it may have been—in his native city until the age of seventeen, when—according to some accounts —he repaired to Oxford ; but the registers of this University contain no record of any Edward Kelley, either at or about the period in question. It has been proposed, however, that

[1] *Private Diary of Dr. John Dee*, edited by J. O. Halliwell. Camden Society Publications, 1842. See p. 1.—*Athenæ Oxoninses*, ed. of 1813, pp. 639–643. The best authority for the date is Dee's horoscope of Kelley, printed in the *Faithful Relation*, edited by Méric Casaubon in 1659.

his real name was Talbot, and three persons bearing this designation were entered at Gloucester Hall *circa* 1572.[1] The debate is not worth pursuing, as the story which connects him with Oxford adds that he left abruptly after a brief stay and, it is suggested, under a cloud.[2] Another account states that after his schooling, he became an apothecary's apprentice and in this way acquired some knowledge of chemistry, presumably at Worcester.[3] It might be subsequent to this that he has been said to have studied law and to have made a professional beginning therein, either at London or Lancaster. There is no evidence that he settled in the capital, while it was in Lancaster that his troubles began, according to report. He was a skilful penman, who had been also at the pains to acquaint himself with old documents, and by the help of these accomplishments he was accused of producing forged title-deeds, in the interests of a client or otherwise. The indictment is vague enough and is changed over by some deponents into a charge of coining. The alleged result in either case or in both testifies that he was pilloried at Lancaster [4] and—as I have intimated—that he was deprived of his ears. There does not seem much doubt that he fell somehow into grievous trouble and that almost to his life's end he was less or more in fear of English law ; but that the penalty which several of his biographers have meted out to him—whether condign or not—was in some way evaded it would seem more reasonable to think. His subsequent relations with Dee, the life which they led together through long years abroad, the distinguished

---

[1] The amanuensis of Thomas Allen, *temp.* Wood, of Gloucester Hall, said that Kelley spent some time in that house.

[2] The evidence is of course wanting. If one of the three persons named Talbot was Edward Kelley we cannot distinguish between them, while if one of them left in disgrace there is nothing to shew that it was Kelley.

[3] "Mr. Lilly told me that John Evans informed him that he was acquainted with Kelley's sister in Worcester, that she shewed him some of the gold her brother had transmuted, and that Kelley was first an apothecary at Worcester ".—Elias Ashmole, MS. 1790, quoted by Halliwell in his note to p. 1 of Dee's *Private Diary.*

[4] See Nash's *History of Worcester*, 2 vols. 1781. I do not know whether this is the first source of the story, but Nash took no especial pains concerning it, failing even to furnish a date for the alleged occurrence. Supposing that it took place at Lancaster, it would seem unlikely that Kelley should be willing to return thither at the bidding of a spirit seen and heard in a crystal on March 21, 1581. But we have Dee's authority for this in the *Book of Mystery*, part of which was printed by Halliwell in the *Private Diary.* The spirit ordered Kelley to fetch certain books belonging to Lord Monteagle from the Lancaster district, on the ground that they would perish otherwise.

position which he held subsequently at the court of the
Emperor Rudolph would have been scarcely possible to a
man who had lost his ears. Credulity on the part of the
learned and of royalties at the end of the sixteenth century
may have been prepared to condone much in the past of those
alchemists whom they protected, but scarcely to put faith
in an adept who had been visibly branded by law. An
alternative story is therefore to be preferred on the surface,
and this says that Kelley found refuge in Wales.

The field of dubious history is left at this stage for one
which has all the aspect of romance, of occult adventure
and invention : yet it proves to have something behind it,
or at least a residuum of fact. Kelley is pictured as embracing
a nomadic life and working his way from Wales into Somerset
and the neighbourhood of the Abbey of Glastonbury. He
put up among other places, at a lonely hostelry in the hills,
and there it came to pass that he was shewn an old manuscript, of which nothing could be made in the village. Kelley
may have had good, if somewhat mournful reason to be well
acquainted with the mysteries of archaic writing, but this
document was equally unintelligible to himself, being solely
in hieroglyphics.[1] He may have seen, however, that it
belonged to the records of Alchemy, and as a result of inquiries
he learned that it was found in conjunction with two small
caskets of ivory, containing respectively a red and a white
powder. There could have been few educated persons at
that time who, in connection with Alchemy, had heard nothing
of the White and Red Tinctures which were the efficient
instruments of the Great Work. Apothecary's apprentice
or otherwise, Kelley knew enough to be anxious for the
whole curious collection and he became possessed of them in
due course.

The nomadic life ends at this point and the alleged forger

[1] Compare Elias Ashmole's note on the metrical tract entitled *Sir Edward
Kelley's Work*, printed at the end of *Theatrum Chemicum Britannicum*, p. 481 :
" 'Tis generally reported that Doctor Dee and Sir Edward Kelley were so strangely
fortunate as to find a very large quantity of the Elixir in some part of the ruins of
Glastonbury Abbey which was so incredibly rich in virtue (being one upon 272, 330)
that they lost much in making projection by way of trial before they found out
the true height of the Medicine. . . . Whether they found it at Glastonbury . . .
or howsoever they came by it, 'tis certain they had it," and Ashmole proceeds to
tell the story of a transmutation performed by Kelley at Trebona, to which we shall
come in due course. We shall be able also to compare the present account of the
Powder with that of Sir Thomas Browne.

or coiner emerges at last into full light of day, not as yet,
however, in the character of an alchemist. He is presented
to Dr. Dee under the name of Talbot, in the Thames-side
house of Dee at Mortlake,[1] his qualifications being those of
one who could communicate with " spiritual creatures "
and " shew something in spiritual practice ".[2] He was
attempting, moreover, to entrap his host into a confession
of dealing with evil angels on his own part. This was at the
end of 1581, but we have Dee's recurring assurance that he
neither did nor would ever be concerned in such criminal
follies. They were and remained, however, the popular belief
about him from the year 1553, when he was charged with
sorcery by one George Ferrys, was imprisoned at Hampton
Court and tried in the Star Chamber for directing enchant-
ments against the life of Queen Mary. In the end he was
honourably acquitted, but suspicion was strong against
him, and was justified sufficiently for the ignorant mind
when twenty years later and over it began to leak out that
he was engaged in dealing with spirits, by the mediation of
successive seers or skryers, in conformity with his admitted
desire " to have help in my philosophical studies through
the company and information of the blessed angels of God ".
It was White Magic for Dr. Dee but sorcery, witchcraft and
devilry for the superstitious and vulgar crowd. There is
accordingly his own evidence that it termed him " a conjuror,

---

[1] Sloane MS., No. 3188, i.e., so-called *Book of Mystery*. The introduction was
made by one " Mr. Clerkson ", on March 8, 1581.

[2] He had considerable experience therein if we are to take at its face value
the tale of his necromantic performance given in Weever's *Discourse of Ancient
Funereal Monuments*, 1631, pp. 45, 46, and reproduced by Ebenezer Sibley in his
Illustration of the Occult Sciences, with a full-page plate illustrating the alleged
occurrence. The story is that Kelley exhumed the corpse of a peasant, then recently
buried in the churchyard of Walton-le-Dale, otherwise Wotton-in-the-Dale,
Lancashire, and thereafter evoked the spirit for the purpose of obtaining an answer
to several questions. A certain Paul Waring assisted at these proceedings, the
chief object of which, according to the exaggerated and falsified account of Sibley,
was to extract information on the whereabouts of " a considerable sum of money "
which the deceased had hidden. " They entered the churchyard at exactly
12 o'clock at night . . ., exorcised the spirit of the deceased by magical spells
and incantations till it appeared before them and not only satisfied their wicked
desires . . . but delivered several strange predictions concerning persons in that
neighbourhood, which were literally and exactly fulfilled." Waring is said to
have acted as companion and associate in all the conjurations of Kelley, and
there is, against expectation, some evidence that he was not alone in the Walton
experiment. See an original letter to Anthony à Wood signed *Anonymus Philo-
musus*, preserved among the Tanner MSS. in the Bodleian Library : it affirms that
Weever's authority was an accomplice of Kelley at the time of the necromantic
transaction.

a caller of devils, a great doer therein, and so (as some would say) the arch conjuror of this whole kingdom ". For Dee it was " a damnable slander ", but it brewed mischief and this ultimately was wreaked upon him.[1]

Whatever his views and hopes respecting the cipher manuscript and the vials of supposed Tinctures it does not appear that Kelley said anything respecting Alchemy in the first days which followed the meeting at Mortlake. Dee's interest of the moment was solely with the " spiritual creatures ". The Talbot alias was dropped, and they set to work on experiments with the crystal, to obtain communications and visions of good spirits therein. It is to be understood that

---

[1] As every species of magic was considered Satanic at that period it would follow that Dee's intercourse with spirits by means of crystals, whether obtained directly or by the mediation of a skryer like Kelley, would be counted as commerce with devils. There is the fullest evidence that Dee was innocent by intention, but it was otherwise with the Walton necromancer. In this connection there is a notable entry in the Diary of the *Faithful Relation* as follows : " April 13, 1584, *circa 3 horam.* After a short request made by me to Christ for wisdom and verity to be ministered by Nalvage "—i.e., one of the spirits in the crystal—"he appeared and spoke much to E. K. which he expressed not to me ; but at length confessed that he gave him brotherly counsel to leave dealing as an idolator or fornicator against God, by asking counsel of such as he did." Thereupon " E. K. confessed that he had been dealing with the devil ". In whatever sense this admission must be understood, it is certain that the evil reputation which ignorance fastened on Dee by reason of his own doings was increased by the rumours which went abroad in respect of his associate. I have mentioned the exaggerations of Sibley some two centuries later, but they represent probably the gradual growth of legend rather than personal invention, and as himself a profound believer in astrology and magic his account of the partnership is worth quoting. " Edward Kelley was also a famous magician, and the companion and associate of Dr. Dee in most of his explorations and exploits, having been brought into unison with him—as the Doctor himself declares in the preface to his work on the Ministration of Spirits "—that is, the *Faithful Relation*—"by the angel Uriel. But Dr. Dee was undoubtedly deceived in his opinion that the spirits which ministered to him were executing the Divine Will and were the messengers and servants of the Deity. Throughout his writings on this subject he evidently considers them in this light, which is still more indisputably confirmed by the piety and devotion he invariably observed at all times when these spirits had intercourse with him. And further, when he found his coadjutor Kelly was degenerating into the lowest and worst species of the magic art, for the purposes of fraud and avaricious gain, he broke off all manner of connection with him." The last point is a misreading of printed documents on the part of Sibley himself, but that which precedes belongs, I think, to the legend. It is this also—and the hearsay of the eighteenth century—which represents Kelley, when "rejected and discountenanced by the doctor ", as betaking himself to " the most mean and vile practices " of magic ; as having " many wicked and abominable transactions " on record against him, " performed by witchcraft and the mediation of infernal spirits "; as outliving " the time of his compact with the devil "; and as being at length " seized at midnight by some infernal spirits, who carried him off in the sight of his own wife and children, at the instant he was meditating a mischievious scheme against the minister of his parish, with whom he was greatly at enmity ". Kelley had no children and died abroad, as we shall see, under very different circumstances ; but these facts were unknown generally in England at Sibley's period, and he depended on mythical tales.

the seer was Kelley and that except on two or three occasions the instigator of the whole procedure himself saw and heard nothing. We must receive as we can and interpret also as we can what occurred actually when, according to the records, the Angel Michael appeared in the seering stone and presented to Dee a ring bearing a seal : it is immaterial for the purposes of this notice whether the visions of Edward Kelley were genuine—in the psychic sense—or not. It is much too late in the day to deny that a state of lucidity can be induced in suitable subjects by the mediation of crystals and other transparent substances, while it is not less evident (1) that such gifts of inward vision presuppose nothing corresponding to the word spiritual or even a tolerable morality on the part of those who see ; and (2) that beyond the bare fact and any logical inference that may attach thereto, nothing of real moment has resulted from such experiments. Edward Kelley may have been pilloried and lost his ears for forgery, coining and uttering, or may have deserved these penalties, and he may have been a genuine clairvoyant notwithstanding; while alternatively he may have been guiltless and unaccused of any illegal transactions but may have imposed shamefully upon his friend through a long series of so-called psychical experiments. It must be admitted that he was either a clairvoyant of an advanced grade or a man of most ingenious invention. Between the period of his alleged withdrawal from Oxford and the completion of his twenty-sixth year, he has been accused of so many crimes, not one of which could have been perpetrated without a considerable apprenticeship, that, assuming an unusual capacity for misdeeds, it is not easy to believe he could have accomplished so much in so comparatively short a time.

There is only one question of consequence for this notice, whether Edward Kelley came into possession, no matter where or how, of the two traditional Tinctures of Hermetic Philosophy. Convict or martyr, seer or cheating conjuror, knave or saint—all these matter little in comparison. At the beginning we have nothing but stories which appear to be pure invention, or for which at least no authority is cited or found. According to Lenglet du Fresnoy, Kelley was a notary in London, with Dee as an old neighbour and personal friend. When the Tinctures came into the former's hands, they set out to work in common, namely, in a goldsmith's laboratory, and in the month of December, 1579, they accomplished a transmutation of metals, which proved the capacity of Kelley's tincture to be "one upon two hundred and seventy-two thousand two hundred and thirty"; but it is added: "They lost much gold in experiments before they knew the extent of its power."[1] There is nothing in the very large autobiographical materials left by Dr. Dee, whether printed or unprinted, either to authenticate this story of doings in London, or even to leave room for it as a possibility. On the contrary we have seen that Kelley was brought as a hitherto unknown visitor to the Mortlake philosopher at his Thames-side house two years later than the supposed Hermetic event. Another account—as we have seen—represents Dee and his skryer as together at Glastonbury and there jointly discovering the alchemical treasures. But this is also a flight of imagination, for which the first person who cited it offers no evidence and names no authority.[2]

The first allusion in any of the Dee Diaries to Kelley's possessions occurs in a record of April 1582 and is found in the following note: "After coming from the Court"—that is, from Richmond, where Queen Elizabeth was then staying—"I thought I would try to discover the cipher of the paper E. K. brought me, as willed to do, found at Huet's Cross,[3] with a book of Magic and Alchemy, to which a spiritual creature led them."[4] The second allusion occurs a little later and puts on record the fact that a new spirit in the crystal counsels Kelley to inform his employer respecting the book and powder, as well as "the rest of the roll", on the ground that true friends should hide nothing from each other. According to this dubious passage, it would seem that the paper in cipher and the treatise on Magic and Alchemy were in neither case to be identified with the manuscript supposed to have been obtained at Glastonbury. The cipher baffled the skill of him who examined it, and we cease to hear concerning it, while the *Book of St. Dunstan*

---

[1] Compare my note *ante*, p. 220.

[2] Ashmole depended probably on current rumours, like the astrologer Sibley long after. It is not the story told him by Sir Thomas Browne.

[3] I have sought in vain to identify this place.

[4] The identity of the persons referred to does not appear, nor do we learn whether Kelley was one of those who found.

—as the Glastonbury discovery is called—seems to have remained another unresolved mystery.[1] About the fact of its existence there is not any question whatever, though the Dee memorials afford no clue to the circumstances of its finding and Glastonbury is never mentioned in this or any other connexion, so far as I have been able to trace.

There is, moreover, nothing to indicate that the advice or ordinance delivered from the crystal by the supposed spirit Il produced its result in Kelley, except that the alchemical manuscript—whichever it may have been—was henceforth in the hands of both but served the purpose of neither, for we have the authority of Sir Thomas Browne, writing to Elias Ashmole on information received from Dr. Arthur Dee, that it contained " nothing but hieroglyphics ". and that Dee senior " bestowed much time " upon it, but he adds: " I could not hear that he could make it out."[2] There is, for the rest, no indication that the Tinctures were exhibited by their owner or that there was an attempt to test their value during the considerable period that he was under Dee's roof at Mortlake. It would appear, however, that then—

---

[1] It continued, however, in evidence—as will be seen later—and may have remained cryptic only in the sense of every alchemical text.

[2] We are faced in this manner by a bibliographical problem which seems past finding out: it is that of the various memorials concerning the Great Work which came into the hands of the partners and are mentioned in the records of Dee. They are (1) certain books of Lord Monteagle at Lancaster, which must be rescued to save them from destruction: it is beyond question that they were either alchemical or magical and perhaps both, or the associates would have troubled little about them ; (2) the book said—in reports other than those of Dee—to have been found at Glastonbury or in its vicinity ; (3) the Cipher MS. found at Huet's Cross, with a Book of Magic and Alchemy ; (4) the scroll and book which Kelley brought to Mortlake from Islington, together with some " powder ", according to *Liber Mysteriorum, s.v.* June 5, 1583: there were metal bands across the cover of the book, which bore also a cross and was fastened by a single clasp. These may be identified, tentatively at least, with the book, powder, and " the rest of the roll " mentioned by the spirit *Il* more than twelve months previously. Now, it seems certain that the cipher treatise mentioned by Sir Thomas Browne was not the Cipher Roll, because it is described as a book, and it is very much more certain that it was not the *Book of St. Dunstan*, for this last was evidently not in cipher, and Kelley had made extracts from it, as appears by an entry far on in the *Faithful Relation, s.v.,* December 12, 1587. It is the record of a Kelley experiment, in the course of which a lamp was overturned and set fire to some spirits of wine. The result was a conflagration of books, including *Extractiones Dunstani* which Kelley had " extracted and noted out of Dunstan his book, and the very Book of Dunstan was but cast on the bed hard by from the table ". We shall see that in July, 1607, when he was on the threshold of death, an angel promises Dee that the secrets of the volume shall be " made known to him ", but this is a reference to the true meaning of a cryptic text and not to the decoding of a manuscript in hieroglyphic characters.

and afterwards abroad—Dr. Dee was far more deeply interested about visions in crystals than over the Great Work of Alchemy. His references to the latter at this time and for several years to come are few and far between, but the communications with angels, planetary spirits, and indifferently with all sorts and conditions of unseen intelligences—*ex hypothesi* on the good side—were recorded in writing with scrupulous and exhaustive fidelity. It was consequently as a seer in the crystal that Edward Kelley posed chiefly before the doctor of Mortlake and that he chiefly influenced his companion.

In the month of March 1583 there come on a visit to Queen Elizabeth the Count Palatine of Siradia, Prince of Poland, named Adalbert Alaski,[1] who sought acquaintance with Dee, became interested in the crystal experiments and with such results that in the following September he started on his return journey to Cracow accompanied not only by Dee and Kelley but their wives and Dee's three children. It is suggested (1) that the Prince was deeply in debt, (2) that he was hoping for relief in gold furnished by spirits, and (3) that the same helpers might secure him the crown of Poland, on which it is thought that he had an eye previously, though he had assisted in placing it on the head of Stephen Báthory, a Transylvanian Prince, in 1576. The evidence for these hopes does not emerge in the Diaries of Dr. Dee, and may exhibit the bankruptcy of speculation more plausibly than the likelihood of things. The continental journey was performed by slow stages, Prince Alaski's castle in Cracovia being reached only on March 13, 1584. Its long story does not concern us here, save only to say that the party had scarcely arrived in the North of Germany before Dr. Dee is said to have had intelligence—psychically or otherwise—of the destruction which had befallen his priceless library at Mortlake by the fury of a fanatical mob, which took advantage of the supposed sorcerer's absence to destroy

---

[1] There is one account of Alaski in Miss Charlotte Fell Smith's *John Dee*, 1909, pp. 97–99. But see the *Private Diary*, under date of May 1, 1583: *Albertus Laski, Polonus, Palatinus Scradensis, venit Londinem.* Compare MS. Donce 363, fol. 125: "The year of our Lord God 1583, the last day of April, the Duke or Prince of Vascos, in Polonia, came to London and was lodged at Winchester House." It was at half-past seven in the evening of May 13 that Dee made his acquaintance. He became a frequent and even continual visitor at Mortlake. King Stephen reigned in Poland from 1575 to 1586.

his effects.[1] The skryings were resumed when they were settled at Cracow itself in a house hired by Dee, but it was only in a more methodical sense, for they recur continually in the records, and a little prior to this the actors were asking instructions from a spirit *sub nomine* Gabriel about the use of the Red Powder, so the fact of the vials and Tinctures was known to Dee.   It does not appear that they obtained any satisfaction, nor later on from the expected revelations of Ave, another spirit, on the subjects of healing medicines and the uses of metals.

The business of the Prince took them in 1584 from Cracow to Prague in expectation of favours from the Emperor Rudolph II.   There all men talked Alchemy and numbers practised it, while supposed processes were as many as the adepts and claimants.   By the ordinance of a spirit Dee wrote to the Emperor, who desired to see him, but that which he carried to the audience was a message from the Angel Uriel, bidding him cease from sin and turn to the Lord.   It was received tolerantly and on the surface even with favour, but an intermediary was commissioned to deal in future on the royal behalf.[2]   It came about therefore that the same Intelligence directed Dee to communicate again with his Sacred Majesty, affirming that he could exhibit the Philosopher's Stone, and this behest was fulfilled by letter accordingly, the writer acting presumably on his faith in the Spirit, but fortified perhaps by assurances on the part of Kelley, who was about to assume a new rôle and merge skryer in adept.   Rudolph II was an amateur in Alchemy, but this offer produced no result, and in the absence of Alaski—who was about his own affairs—the adventurers, in the words of the record, were " brought to great penury ".   They were joined by their wives and children, coming over from Cracow ; but this city was revisited by Dee and Kelley in April, 1625,

---

[1] The date of the disaster is unknown : it is said to have been followed by the sequestration of his rents and property, but this is a myth, for much as she neglected her astrologer Dee remained in the good graces of Elizabeth, whether in his absence or presence.   For an account of the books, MSS. and scientific instruments at Mortlake see Dee's *Compendious Rehearsal*, edited by James Crossley, and published by the Chetham Society in *Autobiographical Tracts of Dr. John Dee*, 1854.

[2] It was a weird interview, belonging to a weird period. Dee related his life and claimed that he was commissioned by God : his own salvation was at stake if he spoke otherwise than his just cause ordained.   He was not actuated by personal ambition and he was neither dotard nor dreamer.

and there Alaski joined them.   By his instrumentality Dee
had three audiences with King Stephen and offered to compose
the Philosopher's Stone, if the King would bear the cost,
but explaining that he relied on the angels, on their power
and will to teach him, not on his own knowledge.   The overture
in this case also came to nothing, and the ambassadors of
occult arts returned to Prague, where in place of Polish
indifference they found that doubt and suspicion had turned
to open hostility.   On May 25, 1586, an edict of Pope
Sixtus V banished Dee and Kelley from Prague.[1]   They
proceeded to Erfurt, Cassel, Gotha and ultimately found an
asylum of peace and plenty at the Castle of Trebona in Bohemia
as guests of Count Rosenberg, the Emperor's Viceroy in
that country.

There, on December 19, Dee puts on record that " E. K.
made projection with his powder in the proportion of one
minim (upon an ounce and a quarter of mercury) and produced
nearly an ounce of best gold ; which gold we afterwards
distributed from the crucible ".   There is not one particle
of evidence throughout the records to indicate that Kelley
had at any period since they were brought together at
Mortlake an opportunity of exploring the mysteries of
alchemical experiment apart from Dee, but at the same time
there is neither question nor comment on his discovery of
the Great Secret independently of his own collaboration.[2]
For the time being it was evidently to remain a secret, and
as the influence of Rosenberg had persuaded the Emperor
to quash the Papal decree, Kelley revisited Prague from time
to time to pursue experiments at the Viceroy's house in
that city, where the eye of his partner could not follow him.
But whatever their worth otherwise the operations of the
Great Work did not furnish either current coin or its
equivalent in bars of precious metal, and it came about therefore

---

[1] The edict was dated May 29, 1586.

[2] Prior to this event Dee was invited by the Russian Emperor Feodor Ivanovich
to reside in his court at Moscow, reports of the astrologer's learning and wisdom
having come to his knowledge. See Hakluyt : *Principal Navigations*, 1903, vol. iii,
pp. 445–48. The Emperor is said to have desired Dee's counsel respecting " discoveries to the North-East " and other reasons are hinted vaguely. These have
been supposed to imply a very obvious ground of interest in rumours of the Great
Secret being known to the English scholar, but so far as any evidence goes the
question remains open. The offer on the surface was advantageous in every way,
but it was not entertained.

that Kelley made journeys into Poland to obtain financial help from Alaski. That he was successful in this quest is indicated by the fact that he paid over some five hundred ducats to Dr. Dee.

There came, however, a day, being May 10, 1587, when the latter puts on record that E. K. " did open the Great Secret to me, God be thanked ". Again, on August 24 : *Vidi aquam divinam demonstratione magnifici domini et amici mei incomparabilis D. Ed. Kellei ante meridiem tertia hora.* And lastly, on December 14th : " Mr. Edward Kelley gave me the water, earth and all." [1] On the speculative assumption that the quondam skryer had become possessed of anything authentic, it is an irresistible inference from his character and life, as they appear throughout the Diaries, that about the last person with whom he would share his knowledge was the associate of so many intimate years, and this being so that either he hoodwinked Dee or could deliver false processes only. The view is borne out by his treatment of Dee otherwise, Count Rosenberg being taken into his confidence as one who might at least share the experiments, his friend and old adviser ostracised. [2] There was something to be gained from the Viceroy of Bohemia, not from the occult philosopher of Mortlake, though Emperors and Kings had honoured him.

The breach between the partners widened from day to day, notwithstanding the efforts of many and above all of Dee himself. It is noted under date of February 4th, 1588, that he transferred to Kelley " the powder " and certain books, among other things specified, obtaining a discharge in writing. On the 16th of that month Kelley left Trebona for Prague, and the ill-assorted associates never met again. On March 11th Dee and his family began their return journey to England, while his former confederate, presented no doubt by Rosenberg as one who to his certain knowledge possessed the Great Secret of Alchemy, was welcomed and honoured by Rudolph. He received not only a grant of land and the freedom of the city but became a Councillor of State and

---

[1] See Halliwell's edition of the *Private Diary*, based on Ashmolean MSS., Nos. 487, 488.

[2] It is borne out more especially by the fact that even to his life's end Dee remained on the search for the Great Secret and the recipient of pseudo-angelic promises that he should at length attain it.

Eques Auratus : with or without his ears, he was henceforth Sir Edward Kelley.

An eccentric as he was and one who crossed ultimately the border-line between rationality and madness, it is very certain that these rewards of science were not conferred by the Emperor in the absence of colourable evidence respecting the science itself, and it follows that some of the wild stories of Kelley's transmutations at Trebona and Prague [1] are not without foundation in the plausible appearance of things. We hear that the Austrian potentate was dazzled by his achievements ; that Kelley was transmuting everywhere, as, for example, at the house of Thaddæus de Hazak, the imperial physician; that a fellow alchemist, Nicholas Barnaud,[2] also witnessed the process ; and that many well-known persons can be cited as bearing testimony, including Gassendus.[3]

But the tale of wonder ran the course which is familiar in the annals of Alchemy. Diminished by excessive projection, the powder approached exhaustion and was squandered further in futile attempts to increase it. We are told on doubtful authority that the Emperor commanded his guest to produce it in ample form, but all experiments failed. And yet Kelley had boasted no doubt his adeptship : he was not the mere heir of the Stone ; he was a master of the science. The Emperor may have believed this and may have gone on believing it to the end, in which case the impotence of the exhausted alchemist was attributed to obstinate resolve. There are several alternative explanations of the next event in his history, but in a sketch like the present they are not

---

[1] They are the coloured accounts of continental writers, who knew little enough of what occurred actually at Prague to Dee and Kelley, in their private life and relations. The whole party is represented as becoming exceedingly and suddenly affluent, great in their extravagance and magnificent in their retinues. Dee is no suppliant seeking an audience of Rudolph, but he and Kelley are invited to Court and repair thither, to dazzle that potentate by their prodigal transmutations.

[2] See my *Brotherhood of the Rosy Cross, cap.* iii, pp. 75–78.

[3] The only discoverable testimony of Gassendus is contained in *De Rebus Terrestris Inanimis*, 1658, vol. ii, *Lib.* iii, *cap.* vi, p. 143 : *Deinde manifesta sunt genera varia imposturarum, quibus versutiores fumivenduli illudere solent non modo simplicioribus, sed nonnullis etiam ex iis, qui se putant oculatores*—he has spoken already of the credulity of believers, more especially with regard to the forgeries of alchemical literature—*dum nempe non satis attendunt ad conditionem aut operantis, aut manus opus peragentis*, etc. Such is the preface to a reference couched as follows : *obque asservatam, ut memorant, Pragæ intra Thaddæi ædeis Mercurii libram in aurum conversam, infusa a Kelleio Anglo unicá liquoris rubicundissimá guttulá, cujus adhuc vestigium sit, qua parte facta fuit infusio.* This is hardly a testimony of Gassendus.

worth reciting. For whatsoever reason the honoured and titled guest was cast suddenly into prison at the Castle of Pürglitz by Prague and there remained till some time in 1591, when he was apparently restored to favour, under what circumstances we are never likely to know. It did not last long, for we have his own evidence [1] that he was interned a second time, and the next certain information concerning him is under date of November 25th, 1595, when Dr. Dee enters in his Diary the news received that " Sir Edward Kelley was slain ". Contrary to the popular accounts, it was not apparently by the hand of another or by the Emperor's decree.[2] The explanation is that he attempted to escape by a rope and fell from a considerable height, sustaining such injuries as resulted in his death at the age of forty years.[3]

After a long tarrying at Bremen Dee reached England in 1588 and took up his abode in the rifled house at Mortlake, bent on " alchemical exercises ", seeking and obtaining a royal permit, that they might be pursued without hindrance. It does not appear that the plans came to anything, or anything at least that called for record on his own part. He had nearer subjects, alike to heart and hand, in the provision of bare necessities for himself and his family. Following a succession of vain promises and some seven years of waiting, Elizabeth granted him the Wardenship of Christ's College, Manchester, and thither he proceeded, to the confusion and doubtless suspension of all Hermetic experiments. We hear nothing concerning them till there is a renewal of angelic visions in 1607, when Dee on the brink of the grave was told by Raphael (1) that he should be restored to bodily health,

[1] Kelley's tract on *The Stone of the Philosophers* opens with these words: " Though already I have suffered chains and imprisonment twice in Bohemia—an indignity which has been offered to me in no other part of the world—yet my mind, remaining unbound, has exercised itself all this time in the study of that philosophy which is despised only by the wicked and foolish."

[2] Note, however, Dee's use of the word " slain ".

[3] One authority for the attempted escape is Dee's son Arthur, cited by Sir Thomas Browne in the letter to Ashmole which has been mentioned previously : " He said also that Kelley dealt not justly by his father and that he went away with the greatest part of the powder, and was afterwards imprisoned by the Emperor in a castle, from whence attempting to escape down the wall, he fell and broke his leg, and was imprisoned again." It would seem therefore that he did not die of his injuries ; but Browne confuses the account by adding, on the same evidence, that Queen Elizabeth sent certain emissaries " to get Kelley out of prison ". They drugged his keepers, had horses held in readiness and Kelley made apparently a second attempt ; " but the business unhappily succeeded as is before declared," which stultifies the previous story. Compare *Athenæ Oxonienses.*

(2) that he should go on a journey to friends beyond the sea, (3) that the Secret of the Philosopher's Stone and the Book of St. Dunstan should be at long last revealed to him. A little later he is told on the same authority that the powder in his keeping, " the which thou dost make account of as no better than dust," shall come into its own by a proper practical use.[1] But John Dee fell asleep in the faith of his angels, *anno* 1608, being aged eighty-one.

So far as this study is concerned, the recurring and insistent question which arises for consideration in the lives of Dee and Kelley is the alchemical book or manuscript referred to the restorer and first Abbot of Glastonbury. I do not know when it was first pretended that St. Dunstan was an alchemist or how he came to be regarded as the patron of goldsmiths [2]; but an anonymous compiler in manuscript of the seventeenth century affirms that he " had no other Elixir or Philosopher's Stone than the gold and silver which by the benefit of fishing was obtained, whereby the kingdom's plate and bullion was procured. For the advancement of the fishing trade he did advise that three fish days be kept in every week, which caused also more abstinence, and hence the proverb that St. Dunstan took the devil by the nose with his pincers ". The *Book of St. Dunstan* is mentioned several times by Arthur Dee, especially in his *Fasciculus Chemicus*.[3] The British Museum contains also the Latin manuscript of another tract by the son of the philosopher of Mortlake, under the title of *Arca Arcanorum*, and this is followed by *Tractatus Maximi Domini Dunstani, Episcopi Cantuariensis, veri Philosophi, de Lapide Philosophico*.[4] Several extant manuscripts, both

[1] We have seen that he is supposed to have " transferred " the powder to Kelley in 1588.

[2] He is said to have been an artificer in metals—gold, silver, iron and copper— but as an amateur, not a craftsman and in the days of his youth, when he was trying many paths of skill and art and learning. He was a native of Glastonbury or was educated at least in that place by a colony of Irish monks. As he was born *circa* 925 A.D. and died on May 19, 988, when Latin Alchemy had scarcely come into existence, we are in a position to judge out of hand the authenticity of the tract which bears his name and which—so far as I have traced—is heard of for the first time in the records of Dee and Kelley. Dee at least would have known whether it was an old manuscript which came into his hands.

[3] The first edition of this tract is cited by Lenglet du Fresnoy as appearing at Basle in 1575 and again in 1629, the first date being the year of Arthur's birth. It was reprinted at Paris in 1631. There is the utmost confusion about it, including its ignorant ascription to Dee himself.

[4] It is to be regretted that there is no space for the examination of this manuscript, which is neither worse nor better than the multitude of things in its likeness

in Latin and English, widely at variance in their dates and in the nature of their contents, are attributed otherwise to St. Dunstan, the first printed text appearing at Cassel in 1649.[1]

I have given space to this record at length as of no inconsiderable importance for the general claims of transmutation, alike in itself and by comparison. We have been able to separate in the first place the facts of the claim and their history from a crop of later inventions, and this opportunity arises but rarely in the annals of Alchemy. There is before us one faithful witness, who recorded on the spot at the time of the various events and with full first-hand knowledge. We have afterwards that of his son, who wrote on the subject of the Art with the uttermost conviction in respect of its validity [2]; and there is further at its value, seeing that it is not direct, the testimony received by Sir Thomas Browne from Arthur Dee and communicated to

but is of extraordinary interest because it is attached to a treatise by Arthur Dee. The suggestion is that he inherited the mysterious *Book of St. Dunstan* from his father, though it might have been included, one would think, among the " certain books " made over to Kelley at Trebona, as already seen. We have found, however, that the revelation of its meaning was promised by an angel to Dr. Dee in 1607, and this signifies that it was still in the philosopher's keeping. See also *ante*, p. 225, where the fact that Kelley made notes from the Dunstan MS. justifies an inference that it was not his property. The notes are described by Dee as " 40 leaves in 40 "—that is, in quarto—entitled *Extractiones Dunstani*, "which he himself extracted and noted out of Dunstan his book." The *Tractatus* attached to Arthur Dee's *Arca Arcanorum* may by possibility have been therefore a transcript of the original text. But we do not know the history of the *Arca* MS. and—alternatively—it may be that the two texts were bound together by some subsequent owner. The fact that a *Book of St. Dunstan* was prized by Dee and his son does not connote, I must add, that it was intrinsically of alchemical value. Most of the supposititious Dunstan tracts are worthless, considered from their own standpoint, that is, as contributions to the Art of Alchemy. I printed one of them in my *Alchemical Writings of Edward Kelley*, and it is a case in point.

[1] Miss Fell-Smith—*op. cit.*, p. 193—mentions this edition as if it were Dr. Dee's " very book of Dunstan ", but this is nonsense. When Alchemy was regnant in the sixteenth and seventeenth centuries, to notify a mysterious book on the subject was to insure its production and printing sooner or later. The Flamel *Book of Abraham the Jew* is of all things imaginary and fable of all fable ; but it " came out " notwithstanding, symbolical designs included.

[2] I refer to *Fasciculus Chymicus* and *Arca Arcanorum*; but their note of certitude belongs to a period when the point of apparent fact was producing incessantly a sincere and lively faith, which was built, however, on sands, for want of critical inquiry into the fact itself. Arthur Dee may have played—like Rosenberg—with quoits which were originally of base metal but had been transmuted into silver. Did child or man test them, to see that they were more than silvered on the surface ? No, certainly not : at least there is no record that they did and none that they thought it needful. But Alchemy is full of such slipshod testimonies, at once sincere and worthless.

Elias Ashmole.[1] " I have often heard him affirm, and sometimes with oaths, that he had seen projection made,
and transmutation of pewter dishes and flagons into silver,
which the goldsmiths at Prague bought of them ; that
Count Rosenberg played at quoits with silver quoits, made
by projection as before ; that this transmutation was produced
by a powder they had, which was found in some old place,
and a book lying by it . . . ; that his father, Dr. John Dee,
presented Queen Elizabeth with a little of the powder, who,
having made trial thereof, attempted to get Kelley out of
prison ". It is added by Browne that Arthur Dee was so
inflamed by the wonders seen with his own eyes that he
" fell early " on the study of Alchemy " and read not much
all his life but books on that subject ".

We have evidence otherwise that Dr. John Dee returned
from his experiences abroad to take out a licence in Alchemy
from the Queen herself, so that his faith in the matter
remained, notwithstanding his treatment by Kelley.[2] It is
only in his last days that the Mortlake philosopher raised
no protest when the voice of the crystal told him that he
had come to regard the precious powder as so much dust.
The desire of Dee to persevere in experiment is stronger than
this silence. If, however, after such manner and to such
extent only, he is a witness by inference to the actuality of
Kelley's transmutations, he can be cited merely to set aside.
Kelley pretended to tell him the true process—Matter,
Water and all—but evidently kept it to himself. Being
therefore not in the secret, his explicit testimony to the
authenticity of operations performed at Trebona and Prague
would count for little ; but it is to be noted that there is none
in his Diaries.[3] When Arthur Dee certifies that projections

---

[1] I am indebted here to Miss Charlotte Fell-Smith in one of her appendices to
the Life of Dr. Dee, having been unable to carry it further, as she gives no reference.
The value of her interesting work is sometimes discounted by failure of this kind,
and throughout by her citation of dates according to days of the month but
omitting years, which too often cannot be supplied by working back through the
text.

[2] The licence was duly granted, but it legalised the proposed experiments of a
seeker, not the transmutations of an adept, and Dee continued to weary the heaven
of Windsor and other Court abodes with prayers for patronage.

[3] In like manner he was anxious above all things to deal only in the crystal
with holy angels; but where was his canon of distinction and where his test of merit?
A time came when one of them made infamous proposals, which were discussed
and accepted, at least tentatively.

were performed and transmutations accomplished by means of the supposed Glastonbury powder we have to remember that at the time of these events he was only eight years old and that his affirmations *qua* legal evidence are wanting on every issue. It does not appear that he was an eye-witness of even a single experiment : what he saw was apparent results—for example, things that looked like silver. There is no need to say that he would not know how to test them or dream of so doing, his father in the last respect being evidently in like case.

Here is the position of the alleged Kelley transmutations : it is evident that he produced things in the likeness of gold, silver, or both ; but what they were in reality there is no knowing.[1] The strongest point cited in their favour by Arthur Dee is that Prague goldsmiths bought them ; but we have nothing to shew whether he knew this at first hand or only heard it. The story, in conclusion, of the two vials containing Red and White Tinctures is utterly fascinating ; but we have to remember that it was Kelley's and unsupported apart from him. Now I conceive that no reasonable person would believe Kelley, on his strongest oath or otherwise, independent confirmation apart.

The story of Dee and his partner is after its own manner a faithful picture of the time in the matter of occult arts and

---

[1] The tract entitled *De Lapide Philosophorum*, published at Hamburg in 1673 and again in 1676, together with *Theatrum Astronomiæ Terrestris* is dedicated and addressed to the Emperor Rudolph, while Kelley was in prison, if not in the chains which he specifies, and no doubt implied an appeal for release, if not restoration to favour. It claims that the " imperial mind " can be guided thereby " into all the truth of the more ancient philosophy ". But it is only a long series of citations from the works of adepts in all ages to prove that Mercury is the First Matter of metals, and the sole suggestion that something other than ordinary quicksilver is intended occurs in an extract from Rhasis regarding " our Mercury ", which is said to be found at its purest in gold, silver and common *argentum vivum*. The tract is otherwise the work of a mere compiler. It is followed by certain fragments which claim to be drawn from letters of Kelley, and in one of these he affirms that " our gold and silver " are a certain " hermaphroditic water " and " not those which you can hold in your hand ". We hear also of animated quicksilver, and quicksilver which " has no life ". A discourse on *The Humid Path* terms Mercury, Sulphur and Salt " the first substances of all minerals ", but in different proportions, as minerals differ from each other. They are found not in these only but also in vegetables and animals. There are pretended processes for making the Stone, preparing the Tincture easily and producing Potable Gold. The *Theatre of Terrestrial Astronomy* proposes to " untie all the difficult knots of the ancient sages ", though " God alone can enlighten the eyes ". It sets out to explain a number of crude figures, one of which exhibits the Green Lion or Dragon, a " hidden and incomparable treasure ", the knowledge of which comes only from a master or by revelation. It is left to these in the texts, and so are knots untied.

practices; but I have introduced it more especially because it belongs to the epoch which preceded immediately that of the Rosy Cross in Germany. I have said previously that transmutations were everywhere, so far as pretensions and memorials are concerned in the Teutonic Fatherland of those fantastic days. The revelation of the Great Mystery took place almost from week to week in tracts and pamphlets. A great trade was driven in this unprecedented industry, and as no one possessed a key to the cryptic language of adeptship and its cloud of counterfeits, there was no means of distinguishing between the brummagem wares and those which were genuine—whether by intention only or otherwise. Meanwhile a very different school of thought on the Hermetic subject was beginning to emerge in Germany. One year after the death of Dr. Dee the posthumous *Amphitheatrum* of Heinrich Khunrath appeared for the first time, and if ever there was a text of purely spiritual and mystical Alchemy it was surely comprised within the covers of that old Latin folio. Moreover, while Edward Kelley was performing transmutations at the court of the Emperor Rudolph or undergoing imprisonment because he could transmute no longer, Jacob Böhme was beginning already to unfold within him the high and deep searchings belonging to his gift of seership: it was destined to find expression in theosophical books which are imperishable as curiosities of the soul in vision and have occasionally higher titles. The seership of the Teutonic theosopher and of Kelley the skryer, as he appears in the *Faithful Relation*, are at uttermost poles asunder; but as there are no revelations to compare with those of Böhme in his psychic states, so there is no skrying of any age or in any language which is in the same category as that of the seer of Dee. But, as I have intimated, Böhme was beginning only, and partly on this account and—for the rest—of the Rosy Cross, we stand in 1608 on the threshold of new things—within sound of their voices.

CHAPTER XVI

The New Light of Alchemy

THERE are texts, as it seems to me, which stand apart from all others in alchemical literature for their note of extraordinary certitude and for a certain inspired accent. They are those of the *New Light of Alchemy*,[1] under the name of Michael Sendivogius, and of the *Open Entrance to the Closed Palace of the King*, under that of Eirenæus Philalethes.[2] They might almost pass for the work of the same hand, were it not that some sixty years intervened between their respective dates of publication. Moreover, a cosmopolitan claim[3] was arrogated to himself by both of these writers, as persons who were abroad in the world to proclaim the gospel of Alchemy, the first by ocular demonstrations in private and public, the second apparently by the scattering of texts in manuscript. Eirenæus was more especially a Cosmopolite in the sense—as he termed himself—of a fugitive over the face of earth, to escape from the hands of those who sought undue knowledge of his secret treasure. He is without exception the most problematical person in Alchemy: (1) by his claim on attainment at the age of twenty-two as a result of individual studies and its virtual stultification in respect of the second clause when he appealed to the vows which bound him; (2) by his long confusion with a mystical alchemist who was in evidence at the same time, who was almost unquestionably born in the same year and who adopted a similar but not identical pseudonym[4]; and (3) by the fact that he is more difficult to identify than the true author of the *Letters* of Junius, all attempts having indeed

---

[1] *Novum Lumen Chemicum*, first published at Prague and Frankfurt in 1604, at Paris in 1606 and Cologne in 1610. The editions and translations are numerous.

[2] A full discussion of his position and claims will be found in Chapter XIX.

[3] The *New Light* was *ab origine* referred to a writer termed *Cosmopolita*, while Eirenæus subscribed himself—or was denominated by his editors—*natu Anglus, habitatione Cosmopolita*.

[4] That is, Eugenius Philalethes, for whom see Chapter XVIII, *sub nomine* Thomas Vaughan.

failed. About the author of the *New Light* the position, if not so utterly obscured, is but little better. The name of its self-accredited writer is hidden on the title page in an anagram which decodes as Michael Sendivogius [1]; but it has been settled long since—whether for once and all is another question—that this personage made a false claim on the text and that it was the work in reality of a Scotchman named Alexander Seton, about whom nothing whatever is forthcoming prior to his travels in Alchemy, which I will now proceed to relate.

In the summer of 1601 it is said that a Dutch vessel was wrecked on the coast of Scotland in proximity to Edinburgh and that some of the crew, its pilot included, were saved by the help of one Alexander Seton, who received them into his house, situated on or near the sea-shore, treated them with great humanity and provided them with the means of returning to Holland.[2] In the following year Seton visited James Haussen, the pilot in question, at Enkhuysen in that country.[3] The mariner received him with joy and detained him for some weeks in his abode, during which period he was an astonished witness of several transmutations performed by his guest, who confessed that he was a Master in Alchemy.[4] It does not appear explicitly that the pilot had been pledged to secrecy, but in any case he could not refrain from confiding his experiences to a certain physician of Enkhuysen,[5] who was a man of integrity and prudence. To him also the pilot presented a piece of gold which had been produced from lead in his presence on 13th March, 1602.[6] This curiosity came

[1] The anagram is *Divi Leschi genus amo* = I love the divine race of Leschus. There is also a later tract on Sulphur, in which Sendivogius is concealed under the veil of another anagram: *Angelus, doce mihi jus* = Angel, teach me the right. *De Sulphure* is regarded as his own work and not stolen goods, as alleged of *Novum Lumen*.

[2] The names Seton and Seatoun have been given as those of the village in question, but in Camden's *Britannia* Seton appears as the name of the house itself. The alchemist himself is myrionimous, figuring as Sethon, Sidon, Scotus, Sitonius, Sidonius, Suthoneus, Suethonius and even Seehthonius.

[3] See Theobaldus (but should be Ewald) ab Hoghelande: *Historia aliquot Transmutationis Metallicæ, pro defensione Alchimiæ contra rabiem hostium.* Cologne, 1604.

[4] As regards the alleged wreck, compare Georg Morhof: *Occasio notitiæ, quæ Scoto cum nautâ fuit, è naufragis orta est. Nauta enim ad littus Scoticum eô tractu, quo prædia ille habebat, ejectus, humaniter ab illo habitus, hospitio Enchusam venientem exceperat.*

[5] *Medicus Enchusanus.*

[6] It will be observed that this statement reposes solely on the veracity of the pilot.

into the hands of the doctor's grandson, who shewed it to
George Morhoff, by whom it is mentioned, with its history, in
a remarkable and indeed historical letter on the transmutation
of metals.[1]

From Enkhuysen Alexander Seton proceeded to Amsterdam
and Rotterdam, embarking subsequently for Italy, where
he stayed a short time only, passed thence into Switzerland
and so reached Basle, accompanied by Wolfgang Dienheim,
an adversary of Hermetic Philosophy whom the alchemist
convinced of his error by ocular demonstration in the presence
of several distinguished persons of that city. To this adversary
we are indebted for a description of Seton, who is said to
have been very spiritual in appearance, short in stature
but very stout, having a high colour and a beard in the French
style. He calls him Alexander Sethonius and states that he
was a native of Molier, " in an island of the ocean." [2] As
regards the particular transmutation, the lead required was
brought by a certain Jacob Zwinger from his own house ;
a crucible was borrowed from a goldsmith ; while common
sulphur was purchased on the road to the place where the
operation was to be performed. During the whole course of
the experiment Seton touched nothing himself, supplying
only the small packet which contained the Powder of Projection, by which the base metal was changed into gold of the
purest quality and equivalent to the original lead in weight.[3]
The experiment was repeated on a second occasion with the
same success, and in addition to the testimony of Dienheim
there is that also of Zwinger, who is described as respected
in the German history of medicine.[4]

---

[1] See Danielis Georgii Morhofii *De Metallorum Transmutatione Epistola*, published
originally at Hamburg in 1673 and reprinted by Mangetus in the first volume of his
Bibliotheca Chemica Curiosa, which I have cited on several occasions. So far as I have
been able to ascertain, Hoghelande is the chief witness, for the particular romance
of Alchemy which is that of Alexander Seton. Morhof derived from him and his
letter was addressed *ad virum nobilissimum Joelem Langelotum, Serenissini
Principis Cimbrici Archiatrum*. The doctor's grandson was Johannius Antonidæ
van der Linden.

[2] Dienheimius Medicinæ Doctor et Professor Freiburgensis in Brisgovia *De
Lapidis Philosophici Veritate*, otherwise *De Minerali Medicina*, Argentorati,
1610. It was on the journey from Zurich to Basle that Seton and Dienheim met.

[3] So far as evidence is concerned, out of the mouth of two witnesses, whose
records remain, this alleged transmutation is of considerable importance
historically.

[4] Jacob Zwinger wrote *Principiorum Chimicorum Examen*, published at Basle
in 1606. He is to be distinguished from Johann Jacob Zwinger, who wrote

Alexander Seton departed from Basle and went under an assumed name to Strasbourg, whence he proceeded to Cologne and took up residence with a student of Alchemy named Anton Bordemann,[1] by whom he was brought to the knowledge of other seekers in that city. He began a kind of alchemical crusade among them, exposing his knowledge and powers to credulous and sceptical alike, and producing on one occasion six ounces of precious metal by means of a single grain of his Philosophical Tincture.[2] Leaving Cologne in amazement, he betook himself to Hamburg, where his further projections are described by Morhoff; but at Munich, being the next stage of his pilgrimage—in place of transmutations—he disappeared suddenly with the daughter of one of its citizens, whom he seems to have married legally and to whom he was henceforth devotedly attached. About this time the fame of his performances attracted the attention of Christian II, the young Elector of Saxony, who invited or summoned the alchemist to appear before him. But the Hermetic propagandist was now merged in the lover and he sent William Hamilton, his apparent domestic but in reality a confidant and friend, to convince the Elector by ocular evidence as to the validity of alchemical claims. A successful projection was performed by Hamilton in the presence of the whole Court, and it is affirmed that the gold so manufactured withstood every test.[3]

The Elector had been previously a sceptic, and he was now more than ever desirous to behold the adept. Seton consented reluctantly and at this juncture seems to have been deserted by his ally.[4] He was received with distinction and presented

Specimen Physicæ Electrico-Experimentalis, issued at the same place in two volumes, 1707. The reference in my text is, however, to an *Epistola ad Doctorem Schobinger*, printed in the *Ephemerides* of Emmanuel Konig.

[1] See Figuier, *op. cit.*, p. 233. But no authority is given in this case and Bordemann I have failed to trace otherwise.

[2] Theobald de Hoghelande: *Historia Aliquot Transmutationis Metallicæ, pro defensione Alchimiæ contra Hostium Rabiem*, Cologne, 1604.

[3] It should be obvious even to an unversed reader that statements like this are worthless from any evidential standpoint. There is no means of checking them, as they are never accompanied by a reference to any source, and it must be said that the records—if any, outside general history—of the Court of Saxony at the end of the sixteenth century are beyond the length of my cable-tow, having followed too many chases of this kind and reaped no profit. It is desirable also to know something of the tests applied and of those who performed the task. See Galdenfalk's *Alchemical Anecdotes*.

[4] He is not at least heard of subsequently, for example, as coming to the aid of Seton in the evil days that followed.

a small quantity of the powder to Christian II, who of course sought to get possession of its whole secret.[1] Seton refused to gratify him and proved deaf to persuasions and menaces ; but the Elector—after the manner of German princes— convinced that he was in possession of a living treasure, determined to overcome his reluctance, whatever the means employed. He imprisoned the alchemist in a tower, apparently somewhere in Dresden and guarded by forty soldiers who had orders to watch him continually. ·The ill-starred adept was subjected to every torment which greed and cruelty could suggest. He was pierced with pointed irons, scorched with molten lead, burnt by ordinary fire, beaten with rods, racked from head to foot : yet his constancy never forsook him. At length he outwearied his torturers, and was left in solitary confinement.

About this time Michael Sendivogius, a Moravian gentleman generally resident in Cracow, chanced to be tarrying at Dresden. He is described as a skilful chemist who—like others of his period—was in search of the Philosopher's Stone and took a natural interest in the case of Alexander Seton, though it does not transpire how he came to hear of it. He is accredited, however, with some influence at the Court of the Elector and had permission to see the alchemist. After several interviews, during which the adept is represented as exceedingly reserved on all that concerned his science, Sendivogius proposed to contrive his escape. There is no need to say that the tortured prisoner consented and promised future assistance to his deliverer's Hermetic pursuits. The resolution thus formed, Sendivogius repaired to Cracow, sold his house in order to raise money and returned to Dresden, where he established himself in the vicinity of the prison and gained the favour of the guards by his prodigality. At length a day came for the execution of the plan proposed ; the guards were regaled royally and when they were all incapable Sendivogius carried Seton—who could not walk—on his back to a post-chaise, in which they set off unhindered. They called at the house of Seton for his wife, who was in possession of a quantity of the transmuting

---

[1] He is said to have been only some twenty years old at this time and to have given already evidence of a cruel disposition.

R

powder,[1] and then made haste to Cracow. There Sendivogius required from the alchemist a fulfilment of his promise, but only to be refused blankly : he was referred to God, on the ground that the revelation of such an awful mystery would be a heinous sin.[2] " You behold what I have suffered," said Seton. " My nerves are shrunk, my limbs dislocated ; I am emaciated to the last degree and my body is almost decayed : in order to avoid all this I did not disclose the secrets of philosophy."

Sendivogius was not destined, however, to be deprived of every compensation for his pains and risks. Alexander Seton did not long enjoy the freedom which his friend had secured for him, and on his death—which occurred two years after the escape—he bequeathed to his preserver the remains of the transmuting powder.

There is considerable material for the life and titles of Michael Sendivogius, but it is a mass of invention, one of his biographers being an anonymous German who claimed to have been his advocate but produced a romance rather than a history.[3] Among other fictions, he represented his hero as sent to the East by the Emperor Rudolph II, where he received from a Greek patriarch the revelation of the Great Secret.[4] There is, however, no reason to suppose that Sendivogius had anything but an amateur's ambition for alchemical knowledge before his acquaintance with Seton. He is said to have been the natural son of a Polish nobleman, named Jacob Sendimir, and to have been born in Moravia about 1566, in which case he would have been some thirty-eight years of age on the death of his taciturn master. Having almost exhausted his fortune to secure the escape of the latter and being credited with a taste for extravagant living, he is represented—not to speak of other and better reasons—

[1] It is of all things most unlikely. The wife of Seton would not have been otherwise than a public fact in Dresden, and if the cupidity of Christian II could drive him to such measures in respect of the alchemist, it is evident that his house would have been searched and his wife examined.

[2] The awful mystery of turning lead into gold by means of a powder ; one is disposed to speculate whether the history of Seton is yet another romance of Alchemy, or at least to question whence his materials were derived by Theobaldus ab Hoghelande.

[3] The true name of Sendivogius is said to have been Sensophax.

[4] Could we trust all the stories, it would seem that the eccentric monarch in question had alchemists by the score at his command, but the *Faithful Relation* of Dee knows nothing concerning them.

as unsatisfied at merely possessing a supply of transmuting powder, the sight of which made him more eager than ever to penetrate the mysteries of Hermetic Art. He married the widow of Seton but she knew nothing of secret processes, her only possessions being two manuscripts, of which Seton was the presumable author, one of them being the famous treatise to which I have referred already as *A New Light of Alchemy* and the other a *Dialogue* between Mercury, Nature and an ignorant, pretentious alchemist, both of which Sendivogius appropriated and issued presently as his own.[1] Meanwhile he believed himself to have discovered by their study a method of augmenting the powder but he succeeded only in reducing it.

Having regard to his alleged straitened circumstances it might be imagined that the remainder would have been used solely to produce gold for his personal use, but according to his story it was wasted in sumptuous living and in acquiring the reputation of an adept by repeated projections. Their number may have been, however, exaggerated. In any case he presented himself at Prague to the Emperor Rudolph II, whom he enabled to produce the gold of transmutation on his own part and in the presence of several nobles, the achievement being celebrated in verse by the Court Poét Mardochie de Delle.[2] Overjoyed at his success in the operation Rudolph appointed Sendivogius a Councillor of State. It is affirmed also that a marble tablet was erected in the chamber where the conversion was performed and that it bore the following inscription :

> *Faciat hoc quispian alius*
> *Quod fecit Sendivogius Polonus,*

---

[1] The *Dialogue* begins as follows : *In illo tempore convenerunt Chemistæ et consilium fecerunt, quomodo Lapidem Philosophorum facere ac præparare deberent, et sic per vota quilibet suam opinionem ut dicere constituerunt.* The majority are in favour of Mercury as the First Matter of the Stone, but Sulphur is acclaimed by some and other substances are cited also in the debate. In the midst of their dispute a high wind is said to have scattered the concourse through the four quarters, and the story turns to the imbecile experiments of one who believed that the matter was Mercury and proceeded to torture it by all kinds of processes and by combining it with foul substances. Mercury and Nature protest, but it is to no purpose. The tract is a satire on the innumerable follies of experiment at the end of the sixteenth century.

[2] I have failed to find any trace of this poet, who seems to have had none of his works printed and has been forgotten by biographical dictionaries.

which appears obscure as it stands and calculated to puzzle posterity.[1]

The chronology of alleged events is not easy to clear up, but it is thought that Sendivogius followed up this performance, as a further proof of his mastery, by printing at Prague the treatise ascribed to Seton under the name of Cosmopolita,[2] taking care that it should pass as his own work—as we have seen. Some time after he produced a tract on Sulphur, to which reference has been also made. There were discrepancies between this little text and the twelve treatises which make up the work of Seton, and this was observed by Sendivogius, so he altered accordingly in a second edition of the shorter work.

From the Court of Rudolph II the alchemist proceeded to Poland ; but as he passed through Moravia on his way a lord of the country, who had heard of his projections at Prague and suspected that he was carrying supplies of the transmuting powder, laid an ambush for him on the road and gained possession of his person, vowing that he should never be liberated till he divulged the secret of his treasure. Fearing with good reason the fate of Seton, Sendivogius contrived to cut through the iron bars which secured the window of his dungeon and making a rope of his clothes he escaped almost naked from the power of the petty tyrant.[3] The latter he summoned before the Emperor's Court, by which a fine was imposed upon him, and one of his villages was confiscated in favour of the alchemist, who gave it subsequently as a dower with his daughter at her marriage— all of which reads like fable.

Sendivogius made several projections at Warsaw and his powder was visibly diminishing, which notwithstanding

---

[1] "That which Sendivogius the Pole accomplished let him copy who can." Rudolph was mad enough for this or any other inscription, but I do not imagine that the story has any ground in fact.

[2] It will be remembered that the story of Seton opens in 1601, with the wreck on the coast of Scotland, and that the rescued pilot received him in Holland early in 1602. Amsterdam, Rotterdam, Basle, Cologne and Hamburg were visited in rapid succession, activities to be followed (1) by the sudden marriage of Seton, (2) his imprisonment and sufferings at Dresden, (3) his escape and death, (4) the marriage of his widow by Sendivogius and (5) finally by the publication of the *New Light* in 1604. It is not an impossible chronology, but the rush of events was great.

[3] It is obvious that this account is mythical, for Sendivogius inevitably would have been accompanied by his Powder of Projection and—also inevitably—it would have fallen into the hands of the robber-lord who attacked him. But the alchemist had his treasure with him as usual when he reached Poland.

he accepted an invitation to the Court of Würtemberg, where he performed two other transmutations in the presence of the Duke Frederic, who conferred on him the territory of Nedlingen, to place him on the footing of a prince of the blood,[1] as it is averred somewhat wildly. It happened, however, that an alchemist was installed already at the particular German Court, much as there may have been a Court Fool, and that he felt his position imperilled by a rival with a brilliant record behind him. In the first place therefore he advised Sendivogius that Duke Frederic was maturing plans which menaced the freedom of his guest and the security of his treasured powder. In the second place when, as doubtless anticipated, Sendivogius fled precipitately—with the fate of his master recalled once more, a vivid picture, to his mind—the treacherous brother in Art overtook him with twelve others, well armed and mounted, arrested him in the name of the prince, robbed him of his powder and caused him to be cast into prison. Behold thereafter the infamous souffleur performing transmutations which vied with those of his victim and more than restoring whatever was his former credit. But the plot transpired, the duke figured as a party and the wife of Sendivogius appealed to the King of Poland, by whom his freedom was secured.

It was not the end of the matter, for on his part the alchemist appealed to the Emperor, who demanded the person of the souffleur from the Duke of Würtemberg, and the possessions of Sendivogius were restored, the precious powder excepted, of which all knowledge was denied. The souffleur was hanged by the Duke; but from this time the pupil of Seton was aware of his star descending. The story is that he had now only a minute quantity of powder in his possession [2]; but even so, being ever in search of notoriety, he dissolved some of it in rectified spirits of wine and astonished the physicians of Cracow, whither he had returned, by the cures which he performed with this preparation as a medicine.

---

[1] The stories of Alchemy recall the romances of chivalry in the great *largesse* which may characterise princes at one time and another; but—as in the romances—they are liable to change quickly.

[2] As it has been stated definitely that the jealous fellow-craftsman " robbed him of his powder "—not, be it observed, of a part—we are entitled to ask how Sendivogius came to have any in his wallet. But we may search the deponents in vain.

Desnoyers moreover—another of the alchemist's biographers and the Queen of Poland's secretary—affirms that he was in possession of a crown piece which Sendivogius had dipped red-hot into this liquid and which was transformed partly into gold in the presence of the King of Poland, Sigismund III.[1] The Elixir finally relieved the same monarch from the effects of a serious accident.

But the end came according to those who regard the operator as merely the heir of a treasure which Seton left behind him. Every particle of the powder was at last expended, and Sendivogius is represented as degenerating into a mere charlatan who obtained large sums on the pretence of manufacturing a powder of projection. On one occasion he is said to have descended so far as to silver a piece of gold, after which, claiming that he possessed the Elixir, the silver was removed by a chemical process, exhibiting the gold beneath, and this was palmed off on the ignorant as a conversion of Luna into true Sol by Alchemy. The device may have been practised commonly enough in public spagyric operations. The mountebank of all classes had skill in those days, as he has skill now, and Rosicrucian apologists of the early seventeenth century have left us the benefit of their judgments on the German trade in *Alchemia*, as indeed has been seen previously.[2] So far as Sendivogius is concerned we have to reckon, however, as we choose with yet another biographer and this time with one who claims to have been his confidential servant, that is, Johann Bodowski.[3] He explains that his master's apparent impostures were in reality calculated devices to conceal his real attainments, he having learned from experience the necessity of evading the violence of covetous men. For the same reason Sendivogius feigned poverty on occasion or remained in his bed, attacked with imaginary

---

[1] See Desnoyers' Letter in Lenglet du Fresnoy: *Histoire de la Philosophie Hermétique*, vol. i, pp. 334-349. Borel, in his *Gallic Antiquities*, recounts that he saw this crown-piece, as did many others at Paris. He describes it as partly gold—so far that is to say, as it had been steeped in the Elixir. The part of gold is said to have been porous, though it was specifically more compact than in its silver state. There was no appearance of soldering and—so it is affirmed—no possibility of deception.

[2] The reference is again to my *Brotherhood of the Rosy Cross*, caps. v, vi, and elsewhere.

[3] There is a French version entitled *Vie de Sendivogius, tirée de la Relation de Jean Bodowski*, on which see Morhof as follows: *Relatio Budovskii œconomi Sendivogani fidem non meretur.*

gout and so forth. It is argued that by these means he diverted general suspicion, preferring to pass for an impostor rather than for one in possession of the Philosopher's Stone and hence of illimitable wealth. He travelled frequently in a footman's livery, concealing his red powder under the step of his chariot and causing one of his servants to sit inside. The alleged prudence inspired him very late in the day, and the authenticity of the *apologia* as a whole may be tested by one of its counts : a common trickster pretending to make gold stood in precisely the same danger at that period as a true adept would stand, or for that matter a tyro enjoying the gift of the Stone and making displays thereof. It is to be understood, however, that Bodowski poses throughout as one who had personal knowledge that his alleged master was in possession of the Great Secret. He tells us further that he kept a supply of transmuting powder in a small gold box and with a single grain of it would convert so much mercury into gold as would sell for five hundred ducats. How he contrived to dispose of it without creating suspicion is forgotten in this story.[1]

We owe also to the self-styled servant and confidant the outline of another episode which redounds to the credit of the adept. He was at his castle of Groverna on the frontiers of Poland and Silesia when he was visited by two strangers, one of whom was old while the other was young.[2] They presented him with a letter bearing twelve seals and addressed to Sendivogius. He declared that he was not the person whom they sought but was persuaded at length to open the packet, when he learned that his visitors were a deputation from the Rosicrucian Brotherhood, which desired to initiate him. He pretended not to understand them when they began to speak of the Philosopher's Stone, but he was drawn ultimately into discourse on several abstruse subjects. To the end, however, he declined the advantage which they came to offer.[2]

---

[1] The letter of Desnoyers, already cited, is a sufficient commentary on all these pictures, including the futile attempts of Sendivogius to manufacture gold after his powder was exhausted. Two cases are cited with the names of those who provided the cost of the proceedings on a considerable scale.

[2] There is obviously no need to go in search of rebutting evidence in respect of a story like this, but it appears to be concerned with the closing years of the alchemist's life, when the Rosy Cross was to all appearance in complete abeyance and was scarcely to be heard of again till 1710.

Michael Sendivogius died at Parma in 1646, aged eighty-four years, having been Councillor of State, it is affirmed, to four emperors successively. We have seen that he endowed his daughter on the occasion of her marriage, but we are told otherwise that it took place against his will and that he left her nothing but a *Treatise on the Salt of the Philosophers*, which, it is added, has been never printed and must be distinguished therefore from a spurious published work ascribed to him under the same title. But if the latter is of fraudulent attribution, as may well enough be conceded out of hand, the former in all probability existed only in the imagination of the deponent.[1]

One thing at least seems certain, namely, that the putative Sendivogius—otherwise, the real Seton—never contributed one jot or tittle to the science which we call chemistry and still less—were such a thing possible otherwise—for the instruction of any one who in those days desired to transmute metals. Like other texts before it, the *New Light* postulates the propagation of metals by means of mineral seed, a seed of all metals, generic to the whole group, including mercury, and affirms that it is known only to the sages.[2] Whosoever would produce a good thing must work with this sperm:[3] Here is the *sine qua non*. But what in reality it is and how it is obtained is not divulged in any of the twelve tracts which make up the famous work—so at least that it can be understood and followed. The next instruction however is: " Take the living male and the living female, and join them in order that they may project a sperm for the procreation of a fruit according to their kind ". Again : " You must produce one thing out of two by natural generation ". But of the begotten one and the antecedent two which generate there is nothing put into our hands whereby we should know them. It is said only that the seed of minerals is water, " in the very centre of their heart and life ",[4] and that the kidneys

---

[1] The *Chymische Schriften* of Sendivogius, published in 1718, includes fifty-five letters which are also certainly spurious.

[2] *Naturam accipere oportet Metallicam, et hoc in mare et fœmina, alias nil efficies.—Tract. Primus. Minerale semen a Philosophis cognoscitur.—Tract. II.*

[3] *Unaquæque res in mare et fœmina multiplicatur. . . . Divisio sexus nil creat vel producit, sed debita illius conjunctio profert novam formam : semina vel spermata ergo, non corpora, sunt accipienda.—Tract VI.*

[4] *Aqua in mineralibus semen est in centro cordis eorum et vita.—Tract VII.*

of its digestion are fire, while the receptacle of the watery seed is affirmed to be air. But all this tells us nothing, more especially as according to a later contradictory statement the seed itself is air. We learn otherwise (1) that iron may be transmuted readily into copper, tin into quicksilver and lead into silver, because in the celestial heavens Mars is higher than Venus, Jupiter than Mercury, and Saturn than Luna— an argument which is sheer nonsense; (2) that there is one metal which has power to consume all others except gold and silver and that its name is Chalybs = steel; (3) that steel is ameliorated by gold and silver; (4) that if gold emits its seed into steel, the latter conceives and brings forth a son much nobler than the father; (5) that if this son fertilises his own mother, her womb becomes " a thousand times better fitted to produce excellent fruit "; but (6) that there is another Chalybs, " created as a thing of itself by Nature," and this can " elicit from the rays of the sun that which so many have sought and which is the chief principle of our Art ".[1] As regards this desideratum, we hear nothing further concerning it.

With respect, however, to gold it is to be understood that there is no seed in the common kind, and this has therefore to be matured and ripened, when it will produce a sperm—otherwise the Tincture of Philosophy: here is the work of " a wise and judicious artist, who knows how to assist Nature ".[2] The kind of work is dissolution, which must be performed naturally, by opening the pores of the metallic body in " our water ", which " does not wet the hands ". It is described as a heavenly water and yet is not rain. When the dissolved body of gold has produced its seed it is said that " our silver "—which is not common—

---

[1] *Unum datur metallum quod habet potentiam alia consumendi, est enim fere ut aqua eorum, et fere mater. Unica tantum res, humidum radicale, Solis videlicet et Lunæ, resistit ei, et melioratur per illud: sed, ut detegam, Chalybs vocatur. Si undecies coit aurum cum eo, emittit suum semen, et debilitatur fere ad mortem usque; concipit Chalybs et generat filium patre clariorem. Postea cum semen jam nati imponitur in suam matricem, purgat illam, et facit millesies aptiorem ad patiendum optimos fructus. Est et alius Chalybs qui assimilatur huic, per se a natura creatus, qui scit ex radiis Solis . . . elicere illud quod tot homines quæsierunt, et operis nostri principium est.—Tract IX.*

[2] The affirmation is: *Lapis Philosophorum seu Tinctura nil aliud est quam Aurum in supremum gradum digestum: nam Aurum vulgum est sicuti herba sine semine. Quando maturescit producit semen: sic aurum quando maturescit, dat semen seu Tincturam.—Tract X.*

conceives therefrom.[1] The seed is then digested by one continuous fire for seven or even ten months, the result of which is that " our infant of the second generation is born ". So far all this belongs by its hypothesis to the theory of the work, and the practical preparation of the Stone follows in yet darker terms.[2] The instruction is to " take our earth, our gold and by means of our fire " to draw forth a water from that earth : it is called Mercury of the Sages, as also Menstruum of the World. It comes from the sphere of the Moon and is so rectified that it can calcine the Sun.[3]

This is of the end, however, but that which belongs to the beginning is that which constitutes the prime object of research, " to find a certain hidden thing, from which—by a marvellous artifice—there is obtained a liquid, the office whereof is to dissolve gold as gently and naturally as ice is melted in warm water ". So is that seed manifested, the hypothesis concerning which was with us at the beginning. On the surface of alchemical literature it lies before us as a fundamental postulate belonging to the natural history of metals from the Hermetic standpoint. It was manifest that in the animal and vegetable kingdoms every species is propagated by means of seed, and it was obvious that in the bowels of the earth there was some method by which Nature produced minerals and metals. What could be more plausible —one might almost say irresistible—in those days of untutored speculation, ever along wonder lines, untrammelled by rigid distinctions between organic and inorganic, than to hold that what obtained in the two visible domains must obtain also in the third. It followed that there was a sperm of metals, and could this be discovered, together with its proper matrix, there was no question that gold and silver should be begotten by an artifice which was not apart from Nature. The seed is sown in earth and corn comes up, and when Alexander Seton talks of placing sperm of gold in some mineral substance which he elects to veil under the designation of another

[1] *Corpus est aurum quod semen dat : Luna nostra est (non argentum vulgi) quæ recipit semen auri.—Ibid.*

[2] It is comprised *ex hypothesi* in the last two tracts.

[3] I may add that, according to *Novum Lumen*, two vessels only are used in the work, the first round in shape, while the second must be of glass and somewhat smaller in size, the form being that of a vial or egg.

Chalybs, he is formulating a process in metallic husbandry, to be followed *ex hypothesi* in due course by a tillage of gold.[1] Generation is hence the key-word rather than transmutation. It seems to me possible that this notion—so plausible apparently for past centuries—is the touchstone by which we may distinguish serious books belonging to physical Alchemy from the hosts of misguiding texts which are either records of blind groping or are of those purely fraudulent products which are a recurring source of complaint on the part of authentic writers.

As an addendum to this chapter there may be given at its value the account of a respectable goldsmith, named Gustenhover, who is said to have resided at Strasburg in 1603. At a time of great peril he sheltered a certain Hirschborgen, who is described as good and religious. On taking leave after a considerable stay this person presented his humane host with some Powder of Projection and then departing on his journey was heard of no more. The fatality of his unexpected possession set to work in its usual manner, Gustenhover imprudently making transmutations before numerous people, till the facts were reported to the Emperor Rudolph II, that recurring figure in so many alchemical histories. He wrote to the magistrates of Strasburg, demanding the person of the goldsmith, who was arrested thereupon and placed under a strong guard. When he ascertained that the intention of his imprisonment was to deliver him at Prague into the Emperor's keeping he divined all that it signified and he invited the magistrates to meet, bringing crucible and charcoal for melting lead in his presence, he being kept at a distance. For this purpose they had recourse to musket balls and, the metal being molten, he handed them a small portion of red powder, which they cast into the crucible, the result being a considerable quantity of pure gold. The object of this exhibition does not emerge and in any case it did not prevent the magistrates obeying the Emperor's behest. Gustenhover explained to the tyrant that he had not prepared the powder and knew nothing of its nature or constituents. But the so-called " German Hermes ", a ruffian in training for madness, looked on this tale as a subterfuge, the goldsmith

[1] Compare Patrick Scot: *Tillage of Light*, London, 1622.

protesting in vain. His material was soon exhausted but he found himself still set the task—now impossible—of making gold. He sought refuge in flight but was overtaken and immured in the White Tower for the rest of his life. The so-called Hirschbergen who rewarded his benefactor with the perilous gift is identified with Alexander Seton, then errant *ex hypothesi* under various disguises in Germany.

CHAPTER XVII

THE REFORMATION AND GERMAN ALCHEMY

PARACELSUS aimed at a reform in the School of Medicine, as did his contemporary Luther in that of Religion, and they were heralds of change to come in their respective realms of dedication. If we look back upon the path that has been travelled, it will be found that the purposed intimations of high spiritual intent on the part of alchemists are without consequence for ourselves since their physical concern emerges unaffected throughout. From my own point of view it is a key to the spirit of the times that those who went down into the mines appealed to God for guidance, that the day and night vigils over crucibles were often vigils of prayer, as well as of work with hands ; but it remains that the end in view was to transmute metals and not, as it has been suggested, to transfigure souls. Now, at the end of the sixteenth century and thence onward we begin to distinguish the uplifting of occasional other voices amidst the clamour of adepts and pretenders ; but we must be careful not to overstate the import if it seems that there is another message. It must be remembered that at this period—above all in Germany—the claim of transmutation was everywhere but the evidential fact nowhere, while the trades driven in the subject by booksellers and their craftsmen in pamphlets had nauseated serious persons and led to something like a declaration of war on the part of the Rosy Cross in the second decade of the seventeenth century. The records of this are in one of my recent works and need not be recited here.[1] When another way of regarding the alchemical mystery arose at the same period in the Teutonic Fatherland and England under the names of Böhme and Fludd there is no question that it attained a certain vogue, to put my point at the lowest. There came a day in the problematical Brotherhood when it was preached almost like a gospel,[2] though it contributed nothing to the dreams of Mrs. Atwood

[1] *Brotherhood of the Rosy Cross*, pp. 125, 150, 154 and elsewhere.
[2] *Ibid.*, pp. 305, 306, 312, 478, 481, and elsewhere.

and her *Suggestive Inquiry*, while it signifies little in the reality of things if Hitchcock might have found himself here and there justified in his own speculations or here and there rather curiously forestalled.

But there was an earlier witness than these and earlier than Jacob Böhme, though the folio in which it is enshrined did not see the light till after the author's death. I refer to Heinrich Khunrath, about whom I have written elsewhere and—so to speak—at full length.[1] He may be approached here from a somewhat different angle, and it shall be that, in the first place, of an absolute believer in the literal transmutation of metals : he looked also through another glass of vision and—something after the manner of Robert Fludd who came after him—beheld in his fantasy the whole cosmos as a work of Supernal Alchemy, performed in the crucible of God. He has, however, a more serious side, for which man is the Subject of Art and the proper understanding of Alchemy an *Ars Magna Sciendi*.

The Prologue of *Amphitheatrum* directs the Aspirant to the Temple of Everlasting Wisdom, the sum of which is to know God and Jesus Christ Whom He hath sent, to know also himself and the Mysteries of the Macrocosm. The treatise is purely mystical. There are seven steps leading to the Gates of Universal Science, and they are described in a commentary on portions of the *Book of Wisdom*. The Stone of Philosophers is said to be identical with *Ruach Elohim*, Which brooded over the face of the waters during the first period of creation. It is termed otherwise *Vapor Virtutis Dei* and the internal form of all things. The Perfect Stone is attained through Christ and, conversely, the possession of that treasure gives knowledge of Christ.[2] The deep things of inward experience are shadowed forth herein ; but it will be seen that the thesis is substantially that of Paracelsus, as exhibited in my twelfth chapter.

[1] *Ibid.*, pp. 61–70.
[2] It will be observed that this doctrine differs from that of Robert Fludd, who unfolded his theosophical considerations from Scripture and for whom therefore the Stone was Christ, not a revelation concerning Him. It should be remembered also that according to Thomist theology the soul is the form of the body, and if that which is called Stone is the internal form of all things it is probably a reference to the soul of the world. But that which would follow herefrom cannot be outlined here, as it would demand a whole chapter and would take us, moreover, far away from Khunrath and his book on Eternal Wisdom.

It is said that Nature is ruled by the Elohim and that the Son of Nature—otherwise the Stone of Wisdom—is the Magnesia of Philosophers, regarded as movement and light. The science of Nature and the knowledge of this Son, constituting true wisdom, have been vouchsafed to Khunrath, apparently by the mediation of ministering angels; he has been constituted in this manner the servant and organ of God; the Treasure of Divine Benignity has been set open in his favour by the Father of Lights; and as a faithful lover of Theosophy he delivers that which has been received by the inspiration of Jehovah. The reward promised to readers who are or become under his auspices as true Sons of the Doctrine is not less signal than appears the claim itself, being (1) Knowledge of God and of Jesus Christ Whom He has sent; (2) self-knowledge; (3) that of the macrocosm; and (4) the science of its Son, the Magnesia already mentioned, which is the predestined perfect subject of the Philosophical Stone. More explicitly, the *Amphitheatre of Eternal Wisdom* unfolds the inward meaning of Solomon's apocryphal book and can communicate his great riches in the physical as well as in a spiritual and intellectual sense, because Divine Wisdom is the giver of all things, alike in oratory and laboratory. " The Voice of God is in all things, in and by all, and comes from all to all."

. But as the Rosicrucians affirmed later on that the secret of metallic transmutation was the least of their hidden possessions, so do gold and silver occupy the lowest place, according to Khunrath, among the fruits of the Stone: the highest are in the soul of man, regarded as *Mens Divina*, and the gates of his symbol are gates which lead up into union between the soul and God. The secret of attainment is in theosophical prayer and work, looking with the eyes of the soul towards that light, infinite and eternal, which became incarnate in the Saviour, which gives also that other light abiding in the Blessed Stone—indwelling, that is to say—for those who have stripped off the vestures of evil life. It is the way of regeneration, the way of the soul in God, Himself the Eternal Soul Which gives eternal life. There is an age-old Salt of Wisdom and a catholic Vitriol of Nature which are found in the mine of wisdom: to possess these is to know all in all. Herein is the glory of Theosophy; and this wisdom is the Stone of Truth, solid and immovable, the veridic type of which is the Philosophical Stone in the great work of Nature.

It will be seen that notwithstanding a confused parade of words and all the mixture of images, the Stone which is Christ is not exactly the Stone which transmutes metals, but apart from the first—as I have shewn—it is held impossible to find the second. The counsel is therefore to seek first the Kingdom and this—like all other treasures—shall be added unto you. Unfortunately the mode of adding does not emerge anywhere, but the recommendation is made categorically.

The thesis is connected also with the doctrine of regeneration, the method or way of which is one of reduction to the simplicity of the Monad ; for " man should and can be born again, restored in his integrity, divinely led back to God, from Whom he has been separated by his own dissension. He can be made a new man, espoused, illuminated and united to God, even—as it were—deified ". It is then added that those who are wise may learn hereby concerning the regeneration of the Catholic Stone of Philosophers. In a word, it is the royal way.[1] But the way to the Stone itself—I mean, the Physical Stone—remains under its invariable veils : its First Matter is Magnesia, and this discloses nothing ; its very uses are concealed, because it is not permitted to " break the celestial seal of occult revelation and to divulge the Mysteries of God ". The Sons of the Doctrine are referred to the symbolism of " the waters which were above the firmament " in *Genesis* I, 7. As a sufficient exhibition of his point of view we must be content therefore when Khunrath affirms that the Blessed Catholic Stone is that by which " inferior metals are converted really into those which are superior, that is to say, into silver and gold ", adding that they are transmuted " fruitfully ", alike in essence and in form. It is added somewhat banally that this notwithstanding health and long life are preferable to pecuniary wealth. There is thus in his theosophical reverie Khunrath's notion of the

---

[1] Mrs. Atwood cites the *Amphitheatrum* some nine times in the course of her inquiry, but in no case from the passages which I have drawn together on the subject of being born again and that which may follow therefrom in the Hermetic reveries of Khunrath.

Stone which is Christ—drawn from New Testament symbolism —and there is the Stone of which Magnesia, so called, is the basis ; but the imagery that belongs to the one is transferred too often to the other. Moreover, in a certain *Isagoge*, appearing as a supplement in explanation of one of the plates by which the work is illustrated, there is a long consideration devoted to the supposititious Physical Stone, the certitude of its existence, that which it is—but this escapes in the verbiage—why it is so named, and lastly its three aspects, which are Divine, Macrocosmic and Microcosmic. In the first of these it is typical of the Christ-life on earth, from birth to ascension, besides being the formula of our own regeneration and a perfect mirror of the Sabbath to come, which is that of our eternal beatitude. It signifies nothing to my purpose that all evidence for these statements is wanting, since we hear nothing of the Stone in its confection. The imagery is so far fairly distinct, as of type and antitype, the similitude of Divine Things and the Divine Reality. But when we hear in the last words that the Stone of Philosophers is the Sea of Eternal Goodness, of the Wisdom and Omnipotence of God, there is no question in the logic of things that type has been merged in antitype, though the context indicates that it is a confusion of terms only.

It remains to say that from a study of the work at large it emerges with compete certainlty that Khunrath is concerned solely with an *itinerarium mentis in Deum* and that because he was an alchemist he used things seen, imagined or reported in the process of the Stone to illustrate—as he understood them—the states and stages of the soul's ascent upward. To adopt popular terms, it follows that *Amphitheatrum Sapientiæ Æternæ* is a Book of Divine Alchemy, and it is of great importance, not only because the physical aspects of the Art dissolve continually and are intended to merge in the spiritual, but most especially because it is the very first of the kind. In the study of Spiritual Alchemy Khunrath is therefore our real point of departure. He wrote and was published prior to Jacob Böhme, prior to Robert Fludd and the other Rosicrucian apologists. There is no question that his remarkable thesis was known to all : it was only " the shewing of a vision ", for I do not see that it carries any special seals of personal attainment, but it did its work

s

among them. Regarded solely as a record of conceptions formed in the mind, it is far more significant than a few other texts of the period which seem on the surface to look at the spirit of Hermetic quest rather than at the body of Alchemy.

Some of them connect with the great debate which grew up about the claims of the Rosy Cross, and though belonging as such to the first decades of the seventeenth century, in so far as any one or more may call for consideration, they are left over by necessity to the very end of our research. There is, however, a single tract which demands a word of notice in this place because it is commended by Böhme to one of his correspondents as containing " much truth " and being—moreover—clear. This is *Aquarium Sapientum*, otherwise the *Sophic Hydrolith* or *Water-Stone of the Wise*.[1] It is notable for direct derivation from Paracelsus in his commentary on pseudo-Hermes and recalls Khunrath in his *Amphitheatrum*. Grasseus, its accredited author—under a sacramental title—is also, like Khunrath, an implicit believer in the fact and virtues of the Physical Stone, though he rules—also like him—" that he on whom the Most High has conferred the knowledge of this Mystery esteems mere money and earthly riches as lightly as the dirt of the streets ". He is in search of the heavenly reality, and the *Wisdom* of Solomon, on which his predecessor depended, is cited in this connection. We hear also of the Stone as Christ, with all the familiar quotations from Holy Writ. After the same manner and in the same spirit, it is affirmed that " the Precious, Blessed and Heavenly Stone agrees most wonderfully with our earthly, corporal and philosophical Stone. The correspondences are set out at full length in limpid language, a striking contrast to the fuliginous terminology of the *Amphitheatrum*. But it is all to the same purpose, the one text being like a transcript of the other : if one cares to say so, it is the second witness in the world of Alchemy. It is also the voice of one crying : " Ye must be born again ". The distinction, however, between the Earthly Stone and the Stone of Heaven is keen and full

---

[1] The first edition appeared at Frankfurt in 1609, the attributed author being Johann Ambrosius Siebermacher of Nuremberg ; but nothing is known concerning him.

and clear ; but it is the Stone which is Christ that matters. It can be left, I think, at this.

There were alchemists of a spiritual mind in that clouded day who were aware of the correspondences which have been thus held up before us, but not to the same extent.

No investigation seems likely to elucidate the obscurity which envelopes the life of that strange Hermetist who called himself Benedictus Figulus and is distinguished otherwise by himself as poet, theologian, theosophist, philosopher, physician and—more curiously still—as eremite of Utenhofen and Hagenau. The second term of his assumed appellation signifies a potter, and it has been conjectured accordingly that his real name was Törpffer. There are no biographical data available in support of this or any other speculation. He comes before us as an ardent and devout disciple of Theophrastus Paracelsus, collecting his works eagerly, to redeem them from destruction on the one hand and from perversion and mutilation on the other. As an original writer he seems to have accomplished little, either for Alchemy or general literature. He is editor, commentator, translator, and these only—except for his brief prefaces or an occasional excursion in compilation. That he had aspirations above these humble, though not undiscriminating efforts is exhibited in a *Prolocutory Discourse* prefixed to his *Golden and Blessed Casket of Nature's Marvels*, a memorial of considerable interest, for it is a history of his mind in outline, its aspirations and its early struggles. The distinction which he desired to attain seems, however, to have been denied him and he has been catalogued badly in his obscurity by one of the chief bibliographers of Alchemy, Lenglet du Fresnoy, who probably knew him at second hand alone. His collections are exceedingly scarce, and it remains only to be added concerning their author that his name has been cited as a witness to the existence of Secret Hermetic Societies anterior to the appearance of *Fama Fraternitatis*, the first Rosicrucian manifesto. It happens unfortunately—as I have had occasion to point out elsewhere—that there is no ground for this rumour, though it has been transmitted by one to another for over a hundred years. Moreover, his works shew [1] that

---

[1] All the collections of Figulus with which I am acquainted belong to the year 1608, and probably exhaust the list, though he was also connected editorially with

Figulus belonged to the Catholic School of Alchemy and herein
if not otherwise, he differed from the militantly Lutheran
College of Mysteries which was represented by the Rosy Cross,
as well as from Khunrath himself. He has left us indeed
a curious example of a Hermetic Mass, containing variations
in the Introit, Collects, Antiphons and other divisions of the
Ordinary, which are converted into invocations for the Gift
of Divine Illumination on the Secrets of Philosophy. It
may be compared with a Mass for the Soul of an Alchemist
printed at a later date in one of the Hermetic Museums.

There is no ground for supposing that Benedictus Figulus
ever attained, even in his own estimation, the Great Mystery

some other authors who do not belong to Alchemy. An enumeration of the
Hermetic ingamerings follows. I. *The Heavenly Tripartite Golden Treasury:
That is, a Heavenly and Golden Treasure of many choice Rarities, wherein lieth
concealed the Ancient, Blessed and Great Carbuncle* . . . *Divided into Three Parts.
*(a) *The Magical Secret of D. Phillippus Theophrastus Paracelsus ; also of Bernard,
Count of the March ; and the Apostle's Creed, elucidated Kabalistically.* Item.
*Fr. Vincentius Koffsckius : Concerning the First Vegetable Tincture and the First
Matter.* (b) *The Hermetic School, wherein may be learned the Preparation of the
Royal Oriental, Transparent Ruby of the Blessed Astral Magnet of the Magical
and Chaldean Tingeing Stone.* (c) *The Light Shining in Darkness, of Raymund
Lully, being an aid to investigate the Highest Secret of Nature and to educe it from
concealment into light, according to philosophical usage.* Item : *How also to prepare
the Blessed Stone of Philosophers and the Secret of its Philosophical Augmentation
in Virtue. Now dedicated* . . . *to all Lovers of Divine Truth and Hermetic Philosophy.* . . . *By Benedictus Figulus of Utenhofen,* etc. Frankfurt, 1608.

II. *The New Olympic and Blessed Rosary : That is, a fresh, living, philosophical
Garland of Roses.* Part I, *shewing from King Solomon the Wise, H. Solomon
Trismosin, H. Trithemius and Dom. Theophrastus how the Blessed Golden Bough and
Treasured Tincture are to be obtained from the* . . . *Tree of the Hesperides, by means
of the Grace of God. A Faithful Revelation to every Son of the Hermetic Doctrine
and Lover of the Teaching of D. Theophrastus.* Part II. *A Book* . . . *of Laurentius
Venturus Venetus, Doctor of Medicine, On the Blessed Stone of the Philosophers.
Faithfully translated for the first time from the Latin into the German tongue. By
Benedictus Figulus of Utenhofen,* etc. *Printed at the cost of the Author.* Basle, 1608.

III. *Hortulus Olympicus Aureolus : That is, a Heavenly, Golden, Hermetic
Pleasure Garden, planted by old and new Philosophers, giving an Instruction for the
Disintegration of the celestial* . . . *sulphur-red and scarlet-blue of* . . . *the tingeing
Carbuncle Stone, whereby human, vegetable and metallic bodies attain their renovation
and highest perfection.* . . . *Now presented* . . . *to all Sons of the Doctrine by
Benedictus Figulus,* etc. . . . Frankfurt-on-the-Maine, 1608.

IV. *The Golden Hermetic Paradise, flowing with Nectar and Ambrosia, by* . . .
*which we may learn how the Golden Apples of the Hesperides can be plucked from the
Philosophical Tree. Hitherto concealed but now unlocked* . . . *for the benefit* . . . *of
Sons of the Chemico-Spagyric Doctrine. By Benedictus Figulus,* etc. Frankfurt, 1608.

V. *A Golden and Blessed Casket of Nature's Marvels, concerning* . . . *the Philosopher's
Stone. Containing the Revelation of* . . . *Hermes Trismegistus, translated by our
German Hermes.* . . . *A. Ph. Theophrastus Paracelsus. Also Tinctura Physicorum
Paracelsica, with an excellent Explanation by* . . . *Alexander Von Suchten, M.D.
Together with certain hitherto unpublished Treatises by this Author.* . . . *Now
published for the use and benefit of all Sons of the Doctrine by Benedictus Figulus,*
etc., 1608.

of Adeptship; but he was a zealous student and one who regarded his ultimate success with a certain pious confidence. Thus, in the *Discourse* already mentioned, he will be found covenanting to reward those who would assist him now in the discovery of Paracelsian MSS. with a grateful compensation " when we (D.V.) shortly reach our goal in Philosophy and Medicine ". Taken altogether, Benedictus Figulus, though admittedly a minor figure, is one who should not be overlooked because of his fervent and religious devotion to the Art itself, as well as to those whom he counted among its Masters.

In so far as Alexander von Suchten is more than a mere name in alchemical literature, especially in England, it is due to Benedictus Figulus, who included some of his memorials in the *Golden Casket*, and this has been translated. His life, like that of his editor, is not so much involved by mystery as simply unknown, though in a certain *Dialogue* between Alexander and Bernhardus he may be regarded as perhaps affording indirectly—like Figulus—a few gleams of personal information. In this case he left wife and child at home to go seeking Hermetic knowledge at Basle, Cologne, on the Rhine, in the Marches of Brandenburg, Silesia, Switzerland, and among disciples of Paracelsus in Denmark. He " heard great argument about it and about ", but his variant on Omar, and it reads like a transcript, is that " as I came to them, so I left them ". They could tell him only what he had read long since in Paracelsus, concerning the Quintescence and Potable Gold. Moreover, they understood all things literally and had no mind for Hidden Mysteries. It fell out therefore that neither in these nor in other places did he find anyone to teach him, whence—on a chance encounter—he appealed to his old friend and fellow-student in the Schools, who—at least on account of his name—recalls Bernard Count of the March Trévisan. They discoursed of many things—of Medicine for the astral part of man, medicine for his part of flesh, of Mercury, Sulphur and Salt. At the close of the long colloquy Bernhardus tells Alexander that he is too deep in the letter, which blinds his eyes, but, this notwithstanding, " at the time of the New Birth I will not forget you ", more especially as to the Earth of Philosophy, " into which flow all the influences of the whole firmament."

Alexander von Suchten carries on the tradition, almost

universal in Alchemy, that the processes of the Great Work are strictly analogous to those which are attributed by *Genesis* to the creation of the greater world. The Philosophical Stone is therefore a *minutus mundus*, which corresponds also to the microcosm of man. Whatever essential value may or may not attach to these parallels, Suchten not only exhibits a clear and liberal mind but one that penetrated the letter and sought the hidden meaning which abides therein. He had emerged also from current belief in the astrological operation of sidereal forces. " The Sun and Moon which I see above me can influence me neither for good nor evil; but the Sun, Moon and Planets with which God's providence has adorned the heaven within me—and this is the Seat of the Almighty— these have power to rule and reform within me, according to their course ordained by God." [1]

If Alexander von Suchten was physician as well as alchemist it was apparently by reason of the Grade of Mastery which he had attained in the latter realm : the Stone at its highest, the Perfect Medicine of Metals communicates at least by analogy the Perfect Medicine of Men ; and alternatively if behind the whole Mystery, or in its best understanding, there is, veiled in alchemical allegory and illustrated by its Hermetic symbolism, a Mystery of Attainment in the Soul or Spirit of Man, then those who can say of it *absque nubis pro nobis* may not only enjoy on their own part *mens sana in corpore sano* but can heal others in the body and perhaps in the mind also. The Stone which is tinctured is tingeing, and the soul transformed in God may well be and is also a channel of saving grace in soul and flesh to others. It is not my intention to suggest that although this is Hermetic hypothesis liberated from all its trammels and imagery there is evidence that the grade of attainment which it connotes was reached by anyone according to Hermetic history, and much less by the

---

[1] The posthumous tracts of Suchten in the *Golden and Blessed Casket* are (1) *Concerning the True Medicine*; (2) *Man, the best and most perfect of God's creatures*; (3) *A Dialogue* and a sequel thereunto, called (4) *Extracts from the Book of the Three Faculties*; (5) *An Explanation of the Natural Philosopher's Tincture*, according to Paracelsus. The following enumeration of other writings rests on the authority of Lenglet du Fresnoy : (1) *Mysteria Antimonii*, Basle, 1573, and anteceding therefore the *Currus Triumphalis* of Valentine ; a German translation appeared in 1613 at Nuremberg. (2) *De Secretis Antimonii Liber*, described as translated from the German into Latin, Basle, 1575, and this is said to have been reprinted at London in 1675. Both editions were probably the *Mysteria* with a variant title. (3) *Clavis Alchimiæ*, Montisbelligardi, 1614.

German theosophical philosopher. Some of his intimations, however, are worth noting.

The chief secret of medicine, which he believed himself to have derived from his master Paracelsus, would appear to have consisted in an application of " the soul of the world " to the universal healing of humanity. The prescriptions of an exoteric pharmacy are in themselves useless; herbs have no real virtue, but they are signs of the True Medicine for physical necessity, after the same manner that Church ordinances direct us to the Fountain of spiritual health for man but are not themselves the Fountain. The Soul of the World—which is said to be the source of all riches as well as bodily health—is identified with the Spirit of Truth that the world cannot comprehend without revelation or the instruction of those who know.[1] It is also the Spirit of God, but the term is to be understood in the sense of Divine Breath or Divine Immanence manifested in Divine Activity, and its centres seem to be the Sun and Moon of the Macrocosm, to which correspond the interior Sol and Luna of the lesser or microcosmic world.[2] At the same time this *essentia secreta* is identified elsewhere with the Mystery of the Incarnation, the opening of Heaven to St. Stephen and the rapture of St. Paul. For this and for other reasons enumerated in the text it is not permissible to reveal it.[3]

There are perhaps few things imbedded in confusion to the extent of *theosophia reformata* in the immediate post-Lutheran period. We know the difficulties which have hindered for three centuries any general study of Jacob Böhme, but

---

[1] The authority is Paracelsus, and I could cite at length from his writings, but I will refer only to the *Revelation of Hermes*, as edited by Benedictus Figulus. " As the Soul moves all limbs of the body, so also is this Spirit in all elementary created things. It is sought by many and found by few; it is beheld from afar and is near; it exists in every thing, in every place, and at all times. . . . Its action is found in all elements, and the qualities of all things are therein, even in the highest perfection. By virtue of this essence did Adam and the Patriarchs preserve their health and live to an extreme age." See the English translation of *A Golden Casket*, edited by myself in 1893, p. 37. See also *ante*, p. 182.

[2] *Ibid.*, p. 52, *Concerning the True Medicine.* It is said also, p. 53, that " the heat of the Sun and Moon is extracted, by a wonderful and occult art, from those things through which matter is most simply generated by the great and good God from the Spirit of the World, for the restoration and conservation of human nature." As regards the Divine Breath, compare Khunrath on *Vapor Virtutis Dei.* The Incarnation of Christ and its Mystery referred to in the text exhibit another quality of correspondence between Suchten and Khunrath, but it is to be observed that when Suchten wrote the *magnum opus* of the latter was still unpublished.

[3] *Ibid.*, p. 168, s.v., *The Book of the Three Faculties.*

he is a lucid well by comparison with Valentine Weigel and Ægidius Gutmann, not to speak of the occult philosophers. It is not easy to characterize the intellectual condition which permitted Suchten to identify the Spirit of Truth with the " source of all riches ", meaning material wealth, and thereafter connect this source with the Mystery of the Incarnation. But amidst all the muddledom of images and the welter of distracted thought he was groping his way through the morass of alchemical reverie to a realisation of the Stone spiritualised, and he is therefore one of the precursors. It is for such reason only that a place has been found for him among the personalities of the present chapter.

CHAPTER XVIII

Thomas Vaughan

IF the seventeenth century school of English Platonists had been also a School of the Rosy Cross in a secondary sense, or had at least included some of the latter *alumni*, I do not think that it would have seemed strange at that epoch of religious, metaphysical and even mystical speculation and debate, more especially when we remember the contributions of Henry More to the *Kabbala Denudata* of Baron Knorr von Rosenroth, about which More was concerned so seriously that he was at the pains of producing several distinct tracts. There are things in Rosenroth's *Apparatus*, placed either *sub nomine Rosæ Mysticæ* or scattered through Zoharic excerpts, which might have recalled Robert Fludd and Joachim Fritz to his remembrance, while the *Æsh Mezareph* —that sole Kabalistic treatise on the Great Work of Alchemy [1] —embodied in his German correspondent's vast collection, might have drawn him to the Spiritual Alchemy and supernal gold of those English Rosicrucian apologists of the generation which preceded his own. It happened, however, that in the day of the Great Rebellion there was but one theosophist who in all his dreams and dedications—as indeed in his eccentricities and extravagance—may be said to have represented the Brotherhood, to have been made in its image and likeness. He came out of Wild Wales, the brother of a Silurist poet, wrote under the sacramental designation of Eugenius Philalethes and was named Thomas Vaughan.

The intellectual and literary life of Thomas Vaughan belongs to a period which, so far as Wales—his native country—is concerned, must be called vacant in respect of preoccupations that were similar to his own. But in England there were mystical interests clothed in puritanical vestures and there were manifold concerns and activities of the occult kind, in common with those parts of Western Europe which

[1] See Appendix II.

were most in communication, mentally and otherwise, with Britain. There is neither need nor occasion here to dwell upon Vaughan's external life, about which I have written fully in another and representative memorial.[1] Moreover, the known facts are few and they offer practically no landmarks regarding his inward dedications, as these are exhibited in the writings with which I am alone concerned. The compass of his literary work is small : he produced little books, truly minute tracts, in place of those tomes in folio which were published by Robert Fludd a generation or so previously, and he issued everything within the limit of six years. There is no means of gauging what impression his work produced in its own day, for the hostile animadversions of Henry More cannot be counted except as the formulation of an individual judgment, while a satirical allusion in *Hudibras* cannot be counted at all. Vaughan, after his manner, was an alchemist, or he would have no place in these pages, and it is certain that a century or so after his death he was disesteemed in this particular *rôle*, as alchemical bibliographies make evident. This is to be explained readily, for the makers of such lists reflected the feeling among those who were groping after the physical work in metals, and Thomas Vaughan —in spite of fitful experiments and certain obscure reveries— was too much on the metaphysical side to be appreciated or indeed understood in such circles and at such an epoch in England. If the year 1850 can be said to mark among us a renewal of Hermetic concern because of the *Suggestive Inquiry*, it marked also a change in the estimation of Vaughan. When Alchemy began to be regarded, under Mrs. Atwood's ægis, as the illustration of a purely spiritual mystery within the veils of physics, Eugenius Philalethes was accepted as a typical example of the true artist, comparatively close at hand in time as well as in place. He was exalted at once to a seat " beyond mortal thought ", and as criticism of a different kind can be scarcely said to exist he has so remained to this day—at once prized among the few and neglected by all others.

---

[1] *The Works of Thomas Vaughan, Eugenius Philalethes, edited, annotated and introduced by Arthur Edward Waite.* In earlier years I had edited *Lumen de Lumine* and still earlier the first four tracts of Eugenius Philalethes, under the title of *Magical Writings of Thomas Vaughan.*

Apart from either alternative, it is my proposal to examine the purport, horizon and inferences which belong to one of his texts, which may be taken to stand for the whole and thus ascertain his place among expositors of the Hermetic subject. *Lumen de Lumine* is in several respects the most considerable tract which has appeared under the name of Eugenius : it is much more important—within his proper measures— than *Euphrates, or The Waters of the East*, although this was his last work ; and it is much more mature, as a fruit of thought, than the little things that preceded it, though they are individual enough in their way, and like all that came from his pen have a certain charm of style which is not altogether to be explained by their archaic flavour. Those who read them will be met with a difficulty of two kinds. The first is initial on the surface and therefore superable : it attaches to the general terminology of occult literature in English of the seventeenth century. To write on its subjects in the vernacular was still something of a new experiment : we may remember how Fludd avoided it. That which had been expressed obscurely enough in the universal medium of the Latin tongue fared worse in the unaccustomed vesture. But Vaughan, it has been said, was an alchemist, whence his texts have the further and essential difficulty of that symbolical language which prevails indifferently in every tongue and dialect which has contributed its resources to the expression of Hermetic Mysteries.

I have noted elsewhere that some books are written within and without, and we know of one which is so described under the most mystical of all conditions, concerned as it is with that epoch when the last things of time will suffer dissolution into eternity. Among others which in a lower sense correspond to this definition there are a few that seem to be written after an inverted fashion, so that to get at their message it may be better to begin at the end and to work backwards. Thomas Vaughan's *Lumen de Lumine* looks like a case in point, though it does not follow that he had recourse to this cryptic plan consciously. In any case I have broken up its veils to my better satisfaction by proceeding as indicated. The tract is offered by its title as a new magical light communicated to the world : let us see therefore what he has to say about Magic. Those who understood it in the past,

according to his view, divided it into three parts—elemental
or physical, celestial or astrological and spiritual. The first
and second are not to be understood in any conventional
sense, for Vaughan despised common processes of Alchemy—
to cite a single example belonging *ex hypothesi* to the elemental
branch—and furthermore he did not consult almanacs
or ephemerides either, which would connect with the second
division. At the same time there were aspects of practical
Alchemy which he respected and proficiency in which he
sought. He recognised also the subtlety, the power and the
universal diffusion of stellar influences, wherein, under God,
both soul and body—except in complete regeneration—
would have been said by him to live and move and have
their being.   But hereof was his Natural Magic on the
astrological side. As regards the third division, it is plain
throughout the discourse that an alternative designation
of Spiritual or Divine Magic is that root and mode of
experience which lies behind the mystical doctrines of theology.
Having reached this point it should be unnecessary to add
that Vaughan's Magic was a Secret Wisdom distributed
after definite manners and was not evocation or necromancy,
dealing with angels or demons, trafficking with elementary
spirits, the confection of talismans or sigils, or anything
connecting—at whatever distance—with the dregs and lees
which have been gathered into Keys of Solomon, Almadels,
Arbatels and Grimoires. The intellectual fools of these
subjects and devices he left to their foolishness, and the
cultus-mongers of diabolism to the disease of their black arts.

The three divisions which I have cited are said to be
intermarried, and it is held essential that they should so be
for the fulfilment of any great work. But this is when they
are comprehended at their height, for normally they are
now dismembered. Once they were united in a single Natural
Subject ; but man separated them, with the result that
they became ineffectual and are called dead. As our mystic
does not speak further, or at least from the same point of
view, concerning this Natural Subject, and as we know
otherwise that there is one and one only to which these
branches of experience and implied attainment are attributable,
I conclude that Man is the synonym thereof, his body the
ground of the occult physics, his soul—or psychic part—the

one sphere in which the stars can be read with a true judgment, and finally that of things divine the criterion or key of discernment is in the high spirit of man. If therefore it pleases anyone who would set up a veil of words to term the knowledge of this subject Magia, it will be scarcely worth while to dissuade him, always on the understanding that he can shew such reasons for concealment as may excuse recourse to veils under any circumstances. At the close of this particular study we shall have to glance at the veils which encompass some of the so-called hidden sciences, at the claim that they may cover an experience about which it is unsafe to talk openly in the public day and decide whether we can make a guess at its nature. We shall then have received that magical light which Thomas Vaughan set out to communicate in his tract ; we shall be in a position to judge whether his veils failed him as a warrantable and catholic medium, and how far he was hampered by the inchoate physics of his period, as well perhaps as by his personal limitations, which may prove substantial factors.

We can say at once that *Lumen de Lumine*, in any precise understanding of the respective terms, is an alchemical rather than a magical discourse, and out of this arises the initial question of our concern, namely, whether Vaughan's Alchemy is after all or not that of the mines, or whether it is that of the inward spirit of man. For this purpose it will be useful, as stated, to begin near the end of his little book on the subject. In that day which was his, as he tells us, there was one section of a perverse generation [1] which commonly called themselves chemists, and these abused the Great Mystery of Nature by applying thereto the name and nonsense of *Lapis Chemicus*, whereas the gold and silver of the philosophers are a soul and spirit, while the common metals of Alchemy, as it was known to the Latin Geber, are in no wise adaptable to the purposes of masters in the Art.[2] We can recognise, I think, here that Vaughan is again talking—and still in the

---

[1] It is termed " scribbling " and " ill-disposed ", a concourse of persons who would " gain an opinion of knowledge ", but they are full of " whimsies and fancies ".

[2] See my edition of the *Works*, p. 303. Compare *Anima Magica Abscondita*, *ibid*, p. 95, on applying the " narrow name of *Chemia* " to " a science both ancient and infinite ". I have cited this statement often, as occasion arose, because it summarises in a sentence the doctrinal position of Thomas Vaughan on the fact of an Alchemy which was not that of metallic transmutation and dealt with no substances which are brought up from earthly mines.

language of subterfuge—on that subject which we have agreed conditionally to regard as Man. His Medicine is a spiritual substance, his gold is wisdom, his Stone is the touchstone which transmutes everything. And again, the Medicine can only be contained in a glass vessel, but this on our hypothesis must be understood as the purified body of the adept.[1] Connected with this there is the theory of a metempsychosis, which is the last transmutation, and thereby the mercurial nature of man is endowed with the constancy of symbolical gold.[2] The Key of all is the Kabalistic Septenary of man, it being understood that these distinctions of faculty are without division of essential personality. The Septenary is composed of two triads and unity in the middle thereof; or, seeing that such distributions are essentially fluidic, there is an alternative key which is formulated as one ruling over three, three over seven, and seven over twelve, the Name of the One being *Deus Rex Fidelis*, the Divine Part of Man in its union with the Divine in the universe, governing and co-ordinating the triad of its chief phases, the heptad of its gifts or faculties and the duodenary of its fruits in manifestation. "This and no other," says Vaughan, "is the truth of that science which I have prosecuted a long time with frequent and serious endeavours."[3]

---

[1] It is to be realised that I am seeking to present an intelligible notion of a cryptic thesis and not making a dogmatic contribution: it is hypothetical, as my text states. I have shewn elsewhere that "notwithstanding the 'narrow name of *Chemia*' and the derision of *Lapis Chemicus* there was, in the hypothesis of Vaughan, "a literal Art of Alchemy which would 'pass the test royal without any diminution'." *Introduction to Works*, p. xlvi. Fortunately, Vaughan has nothing to say on metallic transmutation performed by magic or on its psychic manufacture as the result of a second birth. He speaks once of regeneration as one of three supernatural mysteries, the others being incarnation and resurrection. See *Anima Magica Abscondita, ibid.*, p. 108. Also Mrs. Atwood's view, *ante*, p. 209.

[2] It belongs to Vaughan's doctrine concerning the "radiant body" or "body of adeptship" of which I have given a summary in my *Introduction, ibid.*, pp. xxxi–xxxv. It is the state of Moses on Mount Horeb, of Enoch and Elias in their translation, "splendid as the sun and moon." See *Anima Magica*, p. 110, and *Cœlum Terræ*, p. 230, on a Medicine which is "in Heaven itself".

[3] This is the concluding message of *Lumen de Lumine, ibid.*, pp. 304, 305. It is Vaughan's cryptic way of presenting the soul's progress, which is that of "an essence royal", *Anthroposophia Theomagica, ib.*, p. 5; its passing from mode to mode, *ib.*, p. 6, after quitting that primeval state when it was "planted in God" and there was "a continual influx from the stock to the scion", *ib.*, p. 10. The essence is not to be found in "the texture of the great world", because it is supernatural and divine", *ib.* p. 33, a "wind of the Divine Spirit and breath of the Divine Life", according to Arius Montanus. It is that which Vaughan terms elsewhere the "hidden intelligence", above the "rational spirit", even as this is superior to the ethereal or sensual part of man. *Anthroposophia*, pp. 41, 42.

We may seem already to stand in the upper room of a high-erected palace, with windows looking out over a far country; but to translate the cryptogram in the sense which is here attempted cannot be termed sufficient in itself to justify Vaughan or our especial concern in his reveries. If a given cipher decodes in the official language of a theosophy which is already familiar, we have had our pains to no purpose. But we shall see at the end whether in his concealed fashion the author intimates anything concerning that *Rex Fidelis* by which his Kingdom may be declared with power in the consciousness of the heart.[1]

Proceeding a little further in our reverse process, we shall come to understand more openly the sacred and religious nature of that metempsychosis—or soul transfer—which is here under notice, because its alternative word is designated very simply as transmutation, while salvation itself is nothing but the synonym of both. When it is understood that these three are one, their product is yet another familiar term which stands for them all—that is to say, conversion, of which we have heard so frequently in these pages and must understand in anything rather than the vague, word-encompassed sense of Mrs. Atwood, or in the simplicity and primitive protestantism of Hitchcock, but rather as a deep, mystical, substantial change, by which " the hard and stubborn flints of this world " can become " chrysolite and jasper in the eternal foundation ". It is the same process as that which is connoted by the old Rosicrucian counsel: *Transmutemini, transmutemini de lapidibus mortuis in lapides vivos philosophicos.* It is in this sense that *ars chemica transmutoria*—according to its vulgar understanding—was in the mind of the Rosicrucian Brotherhood the least and most negligible of their secrets. Through the virtue and effect of such conversion, it is said by Vaughan that we may ascend from our present distressed Church, which is in captivity with her children, to the Jerusalem which is above and is

The soul in fine is a " vast and infinite capacity, which is satisfied with nothing but God, from Whom at first she descended ". *Ib.*, p. 47.

[1] Alternatively, whether the *Secretum Artis* of *Lumen de Lumine, ib.*, p. 285, is indeed *margarita pretiosa* or merely a philosophical, metaphysical or religious truism. The little books of Vaughan and the books—big and little—of two or three mystical alchemists claim to put seekers on its track, though it is a thing " never published " and never written on paper by any adept.

the mother of us all. Man attains thereby the state of the Septenary, which is the true Sabbath, the rest of God wherein the creation shall itself enter at the end of the great symbolical week.[1]

But Thomas Vaughan is like some schools of the mystics which are working at this day and draw their oracles of interpretation from many branches of symbolism, artificially combined and indeed confused together. He discourses now of physics, now of astrology, now of Alchemy, when often he means in reality that highest conception of religion which he has been able to attain ; and he pauses there and here to visit a righteous vengeance on those who have sophisticated and degraded these " sciences ", which in their proper understanding are aspects of the one science of sanctity. So also, and as a particular excursus in divergence, he introduces that convention attributed to Zoroaster under the name of Prester[2] which has come to have rather ridiculous associations at this day. He is seeking to shew, in his halting and ineffectual way, that the earth itself is not only the Lord's —as well as the fullness thereof—but that it is bright with the glory of God and glowing with His intelligence. To that which thus animates and enlightens he ascribes the name of Prester, otherwise the fire-spirit of life or—according to pseudo-Zoroaster—" the priest that governeth the works of fire." This, says Vaughan, is an influence from Almighty God, that is to say, it is Life of life, and it comes from the Land of the Living, signifying the Supernatural East and the Second Person of the Divine Trinity. The elucidation offered is that Eternal Light was first manifested in the Second Person—or, literally speaking, in Christ—even as the sun is first manifested in the East, morning by morning.

I believe, and it is indeed certain, that all this is an allusion to the work of Christ in the soul[3] ; but again we shall have got no further than we had reached very long and long before we had opened the closed gates of *Lumen de Lumine*, unless— as the term of all—he has something so far undemonstrated

---

[1] *Lumen de Lumine, ib.*, p. 302. The subject under consideration is *Vita nova* and regeneration by water and the Spirit, while the dogmatic principle is *unum-quodque habet in se semen suæ regenerationis*, which is referred to Trismegistus— apart, as usual, from any citation of text.

[2] *Lumen de Lumine, ibid.*, pp. 294-300.

[3] Life and spirit are said to come from the figurative Supernatural East.

to tell us of this operation and that which lies behind its experience at first hand. It is in the true sense of this oracle that Vaughan explains also the Kabalistic maxim which affirms that every good soul is a new soul coming from the East.[1] It comes, that is to say, from the *Sephira* called Wisdom, and this, according to the Christian Kabalists, was Messias the Son of God. The school of Christian Kabalists may be said to have been founded by Picus de Mirandula and carried some steps further by William Postel, while at Vaughan's own period it was putting forth a great light of arbitrary reasoning in Germany. It dwelt on the mystery concerning birth in God. Such birth and rebirth, however, are not exactly an operation belonging to time, or of God in the soul, while the soul is still dwelling in an earthly body : they connote a theosophical doctrine of emanation ; in other words, the descent of the soul is from God by way of the Second Person, and in this sense it is antecedent to the night of the body.[2]

Vaughan, however, was not especially versed in Kabalism : he wrote prior to the publication in Germany of Rosenroth's *Kabbala Denudata*, and as I have intimated he did not —even when his intention is at its best—express himself too clearly. Against his apparent contradictions, which will be found at this point in the text, it should be understood that there are variant accounts in the *Zohar* [3] : according to one view the descent of souls took place by way of the two Sephirotic Pillars in the Tree of Life in Kabalism : at the head of the one there is the Supernal *Sephira Chokmah* on the Mercy side, while that of *Binah* is at the other, being the side of Severity. Respectively these are Wisdom and Understanding, answering by the Christian hypothesis to Christ and the Holy Spirit, but in reality to *Abba* and *Aimah*, who are in no sense these Divine Persons of the Christian

---

[1] *Omnis anima bona est anima nova veniens ab Oriente.—Conclusiones Kabalisticæ*; No. 41.

[2] *Animæ a tertio lumine ad quartam diem inde ad quintum descendunt : inde exeuntes corporis noctem subintrant.—Ibid.*, No. 8. On the basis of this text Vaughan contradicts himself and shews the descent of the soul from the Holy Spirit, referred to *Binah* in his Christian Kabalism, *Binah* being presumably the third light.

[3] See my *Secret Doctrine in Israel*, 1913, c. xiii, which may be compared with my *Doctrine and Literature of the Kabalah*, 1902, Book ii, § 7, on the *Doctrine of Pneumatology*, pp. 82–8.

T

Trinity. To put it shortly, there was emanation or creation from both sides of the Tree. Among later Kabalists no two excogitated along precisely the same line and criticism is disposed to regard most of the scholia and commentaries as works of reverie.[1] But the independence of each consideration in respect of antecedents is in the spirit of the *Zohar*. The Christian Kabalists added their own inventions, and if there is anything which emerges clearly out of the general chaos it is the fact that the doctrine of the soul's descent from the Divine according to Sephirotic Theosophy scarcely adjusts itself to Christian interpretation, the scheme being much more involved than appears by the latter, the exposition of Vaughan included. It must be said also that as he proceeds in his short thesis he moves further and further away from recognised mystical philosophy, more especially in his statement that it was the Most Holy Spirit Which breathed into Adam the breath of life.[2] He registers another misconception when he seeks to justify this view by identifying the Third Person of Christian Theology with the Kabalistic river flowing forth from Paradise and with the Kabalistic *Mater Filiorum*. The Sephirotic *Binah* or Understanding has nothing to do with any river symbolism in the Sephirotic scheme, its *fons et origo* being the *sub-Sephira* which is called *Daath* or Knowledge, while the principle of womanhood in the Christian Divinity does not reside in the Third Person but in the First, as I have sought to explain elsewhere.

For our present purpose it signifies little in the last resource whether Vaughan confused or even if he embroidered Kabalism, and I should have dwelt much more briefly—if indeed at all—on this part of his subject were it not that we approach through it what may be termed his personal

---

[1] *Doctrine and Literature*, Book vi. See p. 291 for the doctrine of the soul according to Moses of Cordova ; pp. 299–303 for the soul's revolutions according to Isaac de Loria.

[2] *Lumen de Lumine, ib.,* p. 296. To confuse the issues further Vaughan says that " the Holy Ghost could not breathe a soul into Adam but He must either receive it or have it of Himself. Now the truth is He receives it, and what He receives that He breathes into Nature. . . . He is also called Mother of Sons, because by this breathing He is, as it were, delivered of those souls which have been conceived ideally in the Second Person. Now that the Holy Ghost receives all things from the Second Person is confirmed by Christ Himself "—quoting St. John, xvi, 13–15. I am afraid that this is Vaughan at his worst : it is neither Kabalism nor Christian Kabalism : it is not Christian doctrine, but the product of a confused mind in riot among the tokens of symbolism.

presentation of Secret Doctrine, which will be now stated substantially in his own words, leaving the necessary developments till all is collected at the end. The first intimation begins fantastically enough by a comparison of souls to flowers in the Land of the Living, and it is said to be for this reason that the Prester is called in the *Oracles* a flower of thin fire. The reference of course is to flowers in a world of light, and this world is presented as the supernatural centre upon which Nature was founded at the beginning, or the Throne of Quintessential Light. Now, it is said that the operation of what Thomas Vaughan has elected to call *Magia* is to attain this centre,[1] while its Supreme Mystery or Practice— the *modus* of the operation in question—is to multiply, which means to manifest, the centre.[2] The reference which is here intended is not to that centre which gives up no form —the abyss of Saint-Martin—but rather to the circumference thereof, which is the foundation of all forms, and of him who enters therein it is affirmed by *Lumen de Lumine* that he will know why the fire descends and, having found a body, why it again goes up to heaven, this being an allegory—one perhaps out of several—of the soul's outward progression and ultimate return within. An alternative, correlative formulation of this mystery in doctrine affirms that the Prester is the " Secret Light of God ", while its knowledge is that also of the Hidden Intelligence and the Vision of the Inexpressible Face.[3] Herein is a categorical statement of Vaughan's claim upon the inward mystical experience, whether in the rational mind or in further deeps of being. It is therefore the evidence that we seek as to his place in the chain of witnesses ; but if it must be expressed plainly the doctrinal theory is insufficient without a guide to the practice.

---

[1] " To come at last to the Prester, which is the Candle and Secret Light of God." *Ibid.*, p. 299.

[2] *Ib.*, p. 300.

[3] *Ibid.*, p. 299. It is said also that we shall know " the secret love of heaven and earth and the sense of that deep Kabalism : ' there is not an herb here below but he hath a star in heaven above ; and the star strikes him with her beam and says to him : Grow.' " There is again nothing to guide us as to the source of this citation, but Vaughan proceeds to affirm (1) that we shall know how the fire-spirit hath his root in the spiritual fire-earth and receives from it a secret influx ; (2) why " all influx of fire descends—against the nature of fire—" coming downwards from heaven ; and (3) " Why the same fire, having found a body, ascends again towards heaven and grows upwards."

In several respects the spiritual philosophy of Thomas Vaughan is like that of his period : it recalls Robert Fludd, Reuchlin and other Christian Kabalists, from each of whom something was drawn, and many more who possessed in their day certain lights for the exposition of the mystery of the soul, who were conscious also of an uninspired, feverish anxiety to probe the mysteries of Nature and carry to its last consequences the Hermetic doctrine that things which are above correspond to things below, that the macrocosm is summarised in the microcosm and that the first is only the second on a greatly extended scale. The hypothesis passes through a wide world of fantasy and yet it has a heart of truth, because the means of Divine Grace are abroad in Nature, though the correspondences between Nature and Grace are not understood in their confusion but in their parallel distinction.

It happens also that Thomas Vaughan, who confesses everywhere to a policy of concealment, is liable to be credited with more subtlety than he possesses, for his method of expression is as much unintentionally involved as it is wilfully cryptic. His discourse on the ether [1] offers a case in point. It is said to be that of the lesser world, of the microcosm, and he likens it to the Heaven which Anaxagoras called his country, believing that he would return thither after death, so that, within the limits of theoretical philosophy, though not in reality, we seem to have moved beyond the microcosmic region. The ether heats but does not burn ; its region is above the stars, in the circumference of the Divine Light. It is the empyrean which receives warmth direct from God and conveys it to the visible heavens and the inferior creatures : it is the reflection of the First Unity.[2] On the surface all this is crude enough, as it is also pre-posterous enough, even on the understanding that Vaughan is thinking in his heart of Divine Offices in the soul, using primitive language of physics. That his concern is this and not, except far away and in virtue of dubious analogy, a reverie on light of the spirit passing into material

---

[1] *Lumen de Lumine, ibid.*. pp. 289-293. Among denominations ascribed to it there is that of " the air of Paradise ". It is distinguished from the First Matter, with which he has been dealing previously.

[2] That upon which it is reflected is called the celestial cube.

light on reaching the material world, is made evident when
he says that the microcosmic office of the ether is to bring
news of another world and to show that we live in a corrupt
place. What else can this signify except the descent of
Divine Light into human consciousness, that light being
obviously understood in a figurative sense only ? When therefore the alchemist Sendivogius—or alternatively Alexander
Seton, standing behind his disciple as the true author of
the *New Light of Alchemy*—affirms that with this ether he
watered the . lunar and solar plants, he would be held by
Vaughan to be speaking of the powers and graces of the
soul and spirit, of the seven gifts of the spirit and the twelve
fruits thereof. And when the Kabalist, also quoted, says
that this ether is divine, that if joined with Divinity, it makes
divine substances, I conceive again that hereof is the work of
God in man's soul.[1] The ether is therefore Divine Virtue
immanent in the macrocosm and in the microcosm, other
intimations being wilful verbiage or undesigned confusion.
And I suppose further that its identification with the so-called
mineral tree of alchemical philosophers [2] is the one or the
other as whosoever may please to regard it. In reality it is
perhaps both, and out of these two there comes a third
as their natural issue, for I have intimated already that
according to theosophical cosmogonies of this kind and of
this period the creative work in the mines is like the formative
work in the soul, and God raises plants and vegetables to life
as he restores the inward man from bonds of corruption
into the life of the spirit. So also, as Luna is held to correspond
with the psychic part of man in virtue of a nature-born
symbolism which seems almost as old as history, so Vaughan
says that there is a Luna of the mines ; and as there is a Sol
which is the spirit within us, in the same immemorial correspondence of symbolism with Sol in the greater world, so also
our Mystic supposes an *Astrum Solis*, a mineral sun, to which
in his obscure fashion he attributes power that he calls
spiritual. There is no need to say that the institution of
such analogies could not help physicists or the seekers after

---

[1] Neither the Kabalist nor his text can be identified ; he is termed a Jew
simply, and his words read thus in the Latin : *Ex mari meo oriuntur nebulæ,
quæ ferunt aquas benedictas, et ipsæ irrigant terras et educunt herbas et flores.*
[2] It is said to grow like vegetables, bearing leaves and fruits in the very hour of
its nativity.

metallic transmutation, and Eugenius Philalethes fell therefore reasonably into disrepute among them.

It would seem that enough has been gathered by way of quintessence from the mixed elements of *Lumen de Lumine* to shew that its author, though he elected to write of eternal and divine things under the regrettable term of Magic, was concerned above all with these and was therefore before all else a mystical philosopher. I have thus established a certain canon of criticism and have secured a *terminus ad quem* for the whole discourse. We can now proceed to a short consideration of his tract in its opening sections, leaving to the last a Rosicrucian document which is not his work, but by which it is in a sense justified and wherefrom it arises as an elaborate commentary. I have intimated that Vaughan was also an occult philosopher, and as such he carried the warrants of his school at the period for an explanation of the cosmogonical universe. To this end he had the one Catholic and Hermetic axiom for a root principle of philosophy, being the doctrine of correspondences as established by the *Emerald Table*. It is not only of universal acceptance in all branches of Hermetic Theosophy but it is at the root of mystical religion, which explains Nature by Grace, man by God, that which is without by that which is within and the things that are seen by means of things which are invisible. It is *par excellence* the universal sacramental doctrine ; but it is to be distinguished on the one hand from any thesis of pantheistic identity and on the other from aberrations which characterised the occult philosophy of physics in the seventeenth century, though it was thought that they drew from Nature.

Having unfolded in the light of his masters certain spiritual principles which illustrated mystically the dealings between God and man, and, moreover—if we care to think so—having passed through certain grades of inward experience, which he expounds hermetically, and comprehending thus, within his particular measures, how the soul grows under the light of Divine Grace, he proceeds to theorise physically along the same lines, with results which are readily intelligible, seeing that in such matters he was in the rear rather than the van of any science of his period. He speaks therefore on the authority of similitudes connoting things which are within concerning that which is without, and declares in the macrocosm who should declare in the microcosm only. This is how at the beginning of their wisdom the wise exceed their measures. He had many of the modes and dilections of the great subjects, and he knew also that there is a mystical marriage to be made between things without and things within. But it was not given him to proclaim the banns, and he went astray accordingly, as others have done before and after this illuminated disciple.

It is almost impossible to extract anything consecutive from the continual superincession which he effects between spiritual and physical works. As a theoretical alchemist, who was not apart from occasional practice, he went astray also, and amazingly, in his dreams about the generation of metals. He began his occult concerns as a follower in particular of Henry Cornelius Agrippa, and it was no doubt in this manner that he came to call his bizarre philosophy of things by the name of Magia. But he passed further afield and into the realm of Alchemy, which became his dedication, chiefly in its symbolism transferred from mineral to spiritual quests, but still with an eye on the mines. The latter was a preoccupation which he condemned loudly but never overcame, and this is why it is not merely so difficult to separate what is highest in his memorials from the chaffer and clatter of crude physical reveries but why the former secures so little by comparison in residue.

In some respects it is certain that he was taught of the spirit, though he stood on the threshold only, but the spirit told him nothing that is or was of moment about the material world. I believe that he had what for him counted as a true theory on the spiritual side, and he spoke of it no less darkly than did other adepts about their great " practical " work. His only extant manuscript is positive proof that he had not advanced far in physical experiments, even as they stood at his period, nor is there any reason to conclude that he was on the right track or met with decisive success even in respect of the *minima*. He attempted to apply his spiritual theory in the physical order, accepting his own tentatives with high seriousness, as occult philosophers did. He describes how he obtained recognition and credentials from Thalia, the Spirit of Nature, as a reward of his zeal and service. In the course of a visit paid in her company to the mineral kingdom, she communicated to him some of her mysteries under the seal. It does not transpire what they are in any clear manner; but he returned with two gifts, of which the first is an hypothesis concerning the generation of minerals and metals in the bowels of the earth after a mode analogous to that of animals and vegetables, this being an old story; but the second is that cryptic similitude in virtue of which he and others borrowed the language of Alchemy to speak of the soul's transmutation. As regards both, it is certain that the one was taken over by Thalia from Paracelsus and the chemists of his extensive school, while the other looks like a draft on open account from Jacob Böhme, though otherwise there is little evidence that he was especially known to Vaughan.

There is only one thing more to say of this wonderful interview, which went into things so deep and yet suffers anti-climax from a *mise-en-scène* of light sentiment couched in indifferent verse and rather suggesting comic opera than the centre of things physical in the course of their solemn exploration. It is certain again that Vaughan is adapting his mystical doctrine by the help of Hermetic correspondence to the physical world; he is really endeavouring to get at the First Matter and the principle of metallic life; he is not therefore discoursing of spiritual mysteries under a veil. At the same time, and bacause he is applying a spiritual principle to things external, there is here also superincession in his language: in other words, he is talking of one subject in the technical terms of another. It would be possible to reconstruct the visit *ad interiora terræ* so that it would read like a formulated mystery of introspection, a visit *ad interiora animæ*, characterised by the chief signs which are presented symbolically at their reception to the initiates of certain Instituted Mysteries. We should find the great but not hostile darkness amidst which such experiences and ceremonies so often open; the hush of expectant anxiety; the breathing of the spirit; a light which goes before ritual manifestation in the spirit; the approach to the sanctuary; the intimations concerning a way of ascent and descent; and so forward. The sanctuary and altar at the centre would become those which in figurative language are withdrawn in the deep place of our own inward nature, from which the fire goes up

towards a higher mode of being; and as no man knew better
than Vaughan that the way of the soul is indeed a way within,
his spiritual dedications may have been scarcely less present
—without conscious intention—to his picture-making mind
when he talked of the growth, transmutation and tincture
of physical things than when his subject was in all frankness
the coming down of the soul into generation.[1] Here and
there he seems to offer profound suggestions that we have
not touched the fringe of that great and mysterious Providence
which was at work in the traditional fall of man. He mentions
here and there an ascent and fermentation which, whether
he thought or not that it had a root in the material side,
is unintelligible except as the *ascensus mentis in Deum* and
as the ferment of the new life.[2] In fine he seems to hint at
the repose of the body in ecstasy and recalls the Sabbatic
Rest of the soul, as it is described by the great Kabalists,
in the hour of translation.[3]

Speaking generally, it is because of his recurring preoccupations of the better kind that when he is least to our purpose
in his actual matter we find allusions and side-lights in
Vaughan's writings which are true and rare and precious.
I think that he realised, for example, the Divine Presence
and the Divine Immanence at the centre and root of material
things; and he may after all have recounted his symbolical
journey to the mineral region as if he were passing into
the realisation thereof. For him the Immanence was declared
externally in Nature; for him it was at work everywhere—

---

[1] *Lumen de Lumine, ibid.*, pp. 303, 304. He speaks of a bodily fermentation and
elects to term it a descent, but there is a spiritual fermentation also and this is
an ascent. The first is performed by multiplying tinctures; the second seems
synonymous with incorporation and is performed by projection on molten gold,
for Vaughan is dealing apparently at this particular point with the work on metals,
though he opens the subject with that reference to the nonsense of *Lapis Chemicus*
which I have cited in another connection: his pendulum swings perpetually
between the two subjects.

[2] The fact does not prevent him from applying the same symbolical language
to the physical work, as he does at the point referred to in my previous note.
But his real concern, when he was Eugenius Philalethes at his best and not Thomas
Vaughan " operating strong mercury "—in the course of which he met his death
at last—is one only and always, that of a possible ascent to " the invisible, supernatural Monad ", *Monas unitissima*, in which state the soul is united to " the
First, Eternal, Spiritual Unity ". *Anima Magica Abscondita, ibid.*, pp. 87, 88.

[3] He has been quoting an unknown Rosicrucian philosopher who is said to have
been called *Sapiens* by his brother-adepts, and then adds: " This is the pitch and
place to which if any man ascends he enters into chariots of fire and is translated
from the earth." *Ibid.*, p. 106. The translation is said to be one of soul and body,
because of Enoch and Elijah, but he cites also St. Paul, whose rapture was obviously
in the soul only.

in generation, even in corruption. It was shewn forth also in man by that light of conscience wherein we abide under the shadow of the Divine Light. Thus the first matter of the spiritual work is always within us; we are thus wonderfully made; an inner Heaven and an earth are ours, even by Nature. If naturally also we are comparable in the spiritual sense to a realm without form, there is a cosmos to be declared within us, a desirable term in harmony to be manifested. If Vaughan recognised the hand of God in any physical work, it was because in the spiritual order no other power obtains or counts for anything. If he affirms that the secret fire to which he refers so often has the place of its abode in the Divine Nature, it is because this is the root and essence, the life of all our life: as such his theoretical intention was perhaps an inquest beyond the regions of knife and scalpel into the very heart and marrow of our being. He dealt, and only too often, with other matters; but he knew that the true subject of philosophy is the man within. And he was by no means alone in his school over this dedication, for even some physical alchemists, who sought for the gross elixir, had held this notion before them, and their minds were so polarised—if I may use such a strange term—that they could scarcely help combining man's physical and spiritual welfare. The Divine Experience could occur to man in flesh; his higher part is indeed a holy ground; it is the vessel and recipient of Heaven, the Mystical Horeb on which the Law is promulgated, whereon falls the Divine Seed. Vaughan's reference to the Hidden Intelligence, which I have mentioned already, looks very much like getting to the Palace of the King. For a brief moment he seems himself a prophet, who has seen God manifested in a burning bush and comes down from the Mount of Vision, that he may apply his great experience to the explanation of every cosmos. How far he could have expressed the position to himself in this direct language I do not know; but he is speaking continually, to the extent that any power has been given him, concerning the mystery of a grace above all normal grace made known in the heart.

I believe therefore that I am within the reason and the evidence if I repeat that Thomas Vaughan was *per essentias* a mystical philosopher and that his school as such was ostensibly of the Hermetic Tradition, with derivations from other and especially Kabalistic sources, the whole Christianised. But *per accidentia* he was a Hermetic philosopher in the school of metallic transmutation, and he worked upon a fantastic understanding of the Divine Promise contained in the Divine Counsel: " Seek first the Kingdom of God and His justice, and all other things shall be added unto you ".[1] That notebook of his, to which I have alluded, exhibits his devotion to certain lines of experimental research which he never left and of which he died ultimately, at a comparatively early age. It seems evident from the manuscript that he proceeded largely by guesswork, which he may have regarded as a kind of inspiration ; and the fact that he was once successful in performing a specific experiment was no guarantee that he could repeat it. On one occasion he failed through forgetting his materials ; but another inspiration came, and then he remembered and achieved. It is not after this manner that the Great Work was performed—if performed indeed— in physical Alchemy. He was otherwise a man of transparent sincerity, and so it should be added and noted that he never claimed final attainment in respect of the mystery which absorbed him on the outward plane: so also he arrogated nothing to himself in the grades of mystical attainment, but he had reached after some manner the degree of intellectual certitude.

The points which remain over are now few in number, but they are the main points of my thesis—its term and conclusion. Intellectual certitude or conviction on the basis of experience, if alternatively he had reached this stage, what is the message which he bequeaths to those who study and are concerned with him only as a mystic ? He has illustrated the hopeless nature of the material quest when he says that, although nothing can be effected in its absence, the *Secretum Artis* has never been published and remains a Secret of God.[2] But there is another Hidden Mystery,

---

[1] We have seen that it was understood simply and literally—so to speak, at its face value—by generations of alchemists : it was implied in all their counsels, when it was not quoted, as the qualification in chief of the quest : it was expressed ever and continually in individual forms of language.

[2] It is mentioned that Flamel wandered in a wilderness of errors for three years and Madathanus for five because they knew not this secret. Both attained it in the end according to the stories which pass under their names, but we know that one of them is a myth. We shall come at a later stage to the evidence which the second bore in his own case, namely : *Post sextum annum clavis potentiæ per arcanam revelationem ab omnipotente Deo mihi concredita est.*

which is called *Donum Dei* and is presumably dispensed more readily to those who are prepared and seek it, the aspirant being counselled, before all things, to beware of sin. It is said that while repentance is possible in such case, the super-efficacious grace which is the tincture of this gift is lost thereby, or alternatively has been turned to poison, and there is no record of its second reception.[1] It is obvious that this reference can be only to a state of the soul which is above the two states recognised by official theology, namely, sufficing and efficacious grace. There is, I believe, an exotic theology which admits of a sudden *élan*, a sudden illustration, a call and response so instantaneous and unconditional that the soul overleaps everything, even repentance,[2] and does not merely partake of sanctity but becomes it. This is the condition of the Tingeing Stone, which diffuses what it has and is, and in the spiritual sense sanctifies by its presence. If such a state is ever reached— God knoweth—I should suppose that sin is impossible, for the soul is no longer under the law of positives and negatives but under the law of union. On such hypothesis, the condition descried or experienced by Thomas Vaughan lies somewhere between a region which we can look at only through a glass darkly and the world of efficacious grace. I suggest that it responds to the first-hand realisation in consciousness of the most approximate *locus* of the Divine Immanence—which *locus* is within us. The bond between that Immanence and the great Transcendence is the link and chain by which we are " bound about the feet of God ". Herein is the recognition—and after some high manner, the manifestation—of the *Deus Rex Fidelis*, the sight of " the secret light of God " and the " vision of the Inexpressible Face ". Assuredly, those who have received these gifts

---

[1] This is not the testimony of Vaughan, but is quoted by him in a Rosicrucian Epistle to which I shall recur immediately. The notion concerning a second reception is, in my view, to be rejected utterly.

[2] My readers must be content to take the statement on trust. as I cannot recall the written source from which I derive : it is not perhaps in what is called orthodox theology. There is another witness, however, outside that of any document, for as God is known of the heart so is this state known in respect of possibility. It is the hidden mystery of Divine Love—*Secretum Artis* indeed and *Donum Dei*. But it is seen only from afar, albeit those who see cannot understand why the distance intervenes and why it cannot be crossed—in a moment, as in the twinkling of an eye. See *ante*, p. 43.

can never sin willingly : such gifts are health of the body, health of soul, pearls without price.

Now the key of which we are in search to unlock these mysteries further is not given by Vaughan, as on his own authority, but is found in a certain *Letter of the Rosy Cross* which is cited in *Lumen de Lumine*, and of which his visit to the mineral region is a variant or reflection on a kind of external plane. The *Letter* describes, under the allegory of a mountain, a certain profound state of introspection, the experience of which, in one or other of its aspects, is shewn forth, like his own allegory, by the pageants of some Instituted Mysteries.[1] Once more, the darkness is always there, the guide is there also, and so are the symbolic Dwellers on the Threshold, who are conquered by complete purgation, even as the presence of the guide is insured by a preparation which answers to the mystic prayer of aspiration in the highest state thereof. The revelation comes in a stillness which is as if after a tempest : it is then that the darkness dissolves, the sun rises and the treasure is found. That treasure is, according to Thomas Vaughan, a Mystery of Christ, and according to the Rosicrucians it is the deep secret of a Meeting in the Spirit—that is to say, where the House of the Holy Ghost lies hidden from the world. It is the " secret incubation of the Spirit of God " upon the chaos of the natural man. It follows from the context of the *Letter* that the practice is a work which is done by a man on his own part, proceeding from his own basis. To attain therein I conceive that it is essential and imprescriptible that at any and every hour we should abide—at least by conformity of the will—in communion with the Divine, and that whether we eat or drink, whether we are dejected or exalted, we should never permit any lesser interest to interfere with that communion, because there is nothing to be gained in the whole world which is of any value in comparison with the Gift of God, wherein He offers Himself and is received. But this is the high commonplace of eternal truth.

There are three other things only : the concealment

---

[1] *Lumen de Lumine, ibid.*, pp. 259–263. Vaughan terms the Rosicrucian Mountain a Mount of God, the mystical and philosophical Horeb, in the sense presumably of a place of revelation.

practised by Thomas Vaughan, the unity of that mystery which is the subject of cryptic writing in Christian times, and after what manner it is rooted in Christian doctrine. These three are intermarried by an underlying bond, and as they can be taken in any order, while the exhaustion of one will almost determine the other, I shall begin by speaking of a peculiar artifice of language which is adopted in *Lumen de Lumine*, so that it shall at once intimate and cover the parts that are most vital in the subjects of discourse. I have scarcely occasion to say that this art was less or more common to the whole school of occult philosophy or that to all intents it was a creation of Christian times. There is no proper sense in which it can be said to have existed in old Greece or Rome. Plato was deep and suited little enough to men and women of the crowd ; Plotinus was perhaps deeper still ; we know also that there are the so-called *oracles* of Zoroaster and that there is so much as has passed into writing, by reflection of otherwise, of original Pythagorean Wisdom. They were not of this order. The Instituted Mysteries were never made known in the open day ; but there were no concealed literatures. There were no subjects which, by claim or attribution, were exceedingly high, even as a *gloria in excelsis*, and about which for some inscrutable reason it was necessary to write books that dealt with the subject from a standpoint of intimate familiarity, while they never made it known. It was, of course, *Hekăs, hekăs, este bébéloi* for those who were foreign to the sanctuary, and the schools of philosophy were protected from intrusion by a graduated scheme of instruction ; but there is no analogy between these facts and the successive production, for centuries, of books on Alchemy. Except in the sense that all great books are cryptic—that is to say, are mysteries of art and yield up the inward essence of their meaning to those who have inward ears—there is no concealed writing at the present day. If I, for example, had such a predisposition and so pursued it that I learned how to transmute metals, I should either make known my process or reserve the fact of its discovery. I should not write mystery theses to announce that I possessed the secret and place it under impassable veils, while affirming that I revealed the whole Art.

I am not in the seat of judgment in this matter *per se*,

and though I know that all this was done in the past, I am
not prepared to say—except upon a single assumption, to
be specified later—how or why it appealed to those who
adopted it in the old days. But as Alchemy is not the only
concealed literature and as it has two aspects from the days
of Khunrath onward, while in respect of its more exalted
part it does not differ manifestly in the descried term from all
spiritual traditions, the question arises whether there is a
mystic secret, the existence of which can and should be
intimated but is at the same time too vital to speak of openly,
either from the danger which may attach to it, apart from
certain conditions, or from its possible abuse ; either because
it is only transmitted by initiation or because its formulation
is not possible in terms of the logical understanding. I feel
that the first set of alternatives offers no adequate explanation
though it was used on both sides indifferently by the
alchemists. In the second set I do not care to entertain
definitely any question of things which are held to exceed
expression because of the wilful obscurantism which may
seem to be implied thereby to the normal mind. It is obvious
that thoughts conceived in the brain can pass into the
symbolism of language and are not otherwise delineated.
By the hypothesis, however, we are dealing with experience
which lies behind the common field of consciousness and
records concerning it will be understood in a living sense
only by those who have shared it. The hindrance is not
therefore solely in respect of formulation but of the interpreting
mind. Moreover, the cryptic literature does not confess to
inability through the failure of language, while on the other
hand it alludes and testifies plainly to restriction imposed
by duty.

When Eirenæus Philalethes claims that he has spoken
more openly than any adept who preceded him, he admits
also that he was ever in fear of his vow, lest he should betray
that part of the mastery which he had covenanted not to
record.[1] We find everywhere the intimations of a hindrance

---

[1] It is to be understood that he stultified himself flagrantly as one text followed
another : he had attained the Art by nothing but his own studies and the grace
of God, yet he was bound by a vow, as others are bound by a spell : he testifies
that one of his books is of truth in the Art only, that it clears all clouded issues,
yet he affirms later on in another work that he has spoken doubtfully—in the willing
sense—in all his previous writings.

belonging to this order; and though again I do not care to regard a matter of experience as communicated always and so communicable solely in a Sanctuary of Initiation or even from master to pupil only, and although there is no trace of such initiation in the books of Thomas Vaughan, if he is to be classed among adepts, the process of exhaustion may seem to leave no other explanation open, and this therefore is the assumption to which I have once referred. If we accept it the whole position is simplified: we have no longer to consider whether the law of concealment was itself justified and much less whether it was essential, for we are dealing with a code of honour which lay between the hands of a secret tribunal or an individual master, presumably in a position to enforce covenants. As the mystery was received, so it was also passed on, and the texts came into being, demonstrably or otherwise, to keep alive the tradition. It will be asked, after what manner? How could they act as recruiting sergeants? Supposing that one of them fell into hands prepared, how did the simple fact and how did the untutored study bring such a person to the door of any secret circle or into the presence of a qualified teacher? It may be suggested that the student was put thereby upon the quest and that if he followed it with untiring zeal, he came at length to the right quarter and the right people or person. This is how the hypothetical case stands in respect of physical Alchemy, and if I do not think that it can be held tentatively it is because of a veiled implication. It presupposes—as it seems to me—that physical Alchemy was an authentic secret science and did or could communicate a real knowledge to its initiates. On the other hand, supposing that there were transmission of a spiritual kind to spiritual aspirants from another and very different circle it may be thought that what Eckartshausen terms an "inner sensorium" was opened by reflection and zeal of quest; that at a certain point a seeker was joined to the chain of tradition; that he entered and took his place in the Secret Church, Company or Assembly. In a word, he grew up into the Sanctuary. Individual initiation included, this seems the only intelligible construction in such a hypothetical case. We know how our meetings come about naturally and everywhere in the normal consciousness and how our consanguinities are declared. But if—as we can and may know—there is an experience possible in a higher form of consciousness, then it is reasonable to suppose that therein are other meetings, as of those who have grown up into the same degree, and that there other bonds are declared.

Those who have followed the path of astral workings, and who are acquainted with the kind of encounters which take place in that region, should understand well enough that very different doors may be opened in the world of sanctity. Those also, and such still more, who in the repose of the heart receive intimations of the Union will not need that I should add more hereon or concerning the communion of saints in a common medium of experience. They understand that we need not go either to the East or the West to reach our peers or masters. The experiences are spoken of diversely in all the schools [1]; but I have not found that the draperies conceal other than the same form; and I end as I began therefore, by affirming that it is one mystery concerning one experience and the deeps and the heights thereof. It does not differ in Thomas Vaughan, who set out to use language that he might hide his thoughts, or in Jacob Böhme, who had assuredly no pledges to maintain but is darker still, because in the heights and the deeps he saw indeed plainly but found no adequate tongue. And I place these two cases in apposition to shew that initiation is one thing and by the hypothesis may be a shorter road, but the work of the Spirit is not confined within such limits, and the high experience is everywhere. The great mystics of the Latin Church reached attainment in experience which it was given them to unfold more fully than the exponents of most other schools. But these confess also how language failed them respecting that which the physical eye has not seen nor has the sensible ear heard. So there is something—as those who have undertaken the great journey will be aware otherwise—to allow for impediments which are of this nature as well as for the holy jealousy which is special to the Secret Sanctuaries.

[1] It must be said that in so far as they unfolded and infolded under the veils of alchemical symbolism they are most difficult of recognition, and it is hardly possible to feel certainty except along broad and very general lines. There are doubtless errors of interpretation in what has been attempted here and whatever is of detail is put forward under all reserves, though I hold that there is no question as to the real concern of Vaughan.

U

In this manner we begin to understand why the " mystic and adept philosophers " had recourse to their veils : there was the difficulty of initiation under covenants and there was the difficulty of translating an experience of the deeps into the terms of the surface. It may be that Vaughan spoke often enough as he best could, subject to the personal confusions which made his veil a patchwork ; and it may be that to those who are seekers on their own part of mysteries which are within he will bring reports concerning the work of God in the soul which are more pregnant than those of the general cloud of witnesses, unless they are his peers and brothers. And this is the summary which arises out of the present examination, that the holy centre is manifested in consciousness, or as Thomas Vaughan says in his crude terminology, the Prester is multiplied—that is to say, " the influence of Almighty God " and the Life of Life. To conclude therefore : he testifies on many occasions and in all his books that his mystery is in Christ and that Christ is the Key thereto. The Incarnation [1] is the Key in particular of his mystic chaos. I should add that the schools to which some of my subsidiary references are made were also Christian schools ; but because the first-hand experience of what spiritual alchemists called the fount of Nature is of all tongues and nations and ages and climes I think that the Divine Saviour has been known by other names in many places of God. He is the ground of union, which union has been attained everywhere. It is in this wide sense that all His sheep are not of the same fold, and Christ delivers up the Kingdom to His Father in all regions of the Universe. But that Kingdom has been revealed within us and has been established there ; the *Rex Fidelis* has entered to reign therein, and I think that Thomas Vaughan does in his strange manner of language help us to understand how it may be declared with power in the consciousness of the heart. Yet it is nothing so new, so rich and passing strange, above all it is nothing so encompassed with perils as to make his veils needful : and here I leave it.

---

[1] " Remember that in the incarnation of Christ Jesus the *Quaternarius* or four elements, as men call them, were united to their Eternal Unity and *Ternarius*." *Lumen de Lumine*, p. 302.

CHAPTER XIX

The Cosmopolite

EIRENÆUS Philalethes, who described himself as *natu Anglus, habitatione Cosmopolita*, is the chief adept in evidence, by the fact of very numerous writings and vital force of claim, during the second half of the seventeenth century, or from 1667 onward, when his first and most notable tract was edited by Langius and issued at Amsterdam. I have no intention of retracing a ground which has been travelled on several previous occasions in my various monographs and studies of his predecessor, Eugenius Philalethes, with whom he was confused so long and frequently. I will take up therefore the question of his identity at the point where it was left in the year 1919 when I edited for the first time the complete *Works of Thomas Vaughan*. In a prefatory excursus to that collection it was determined, to the best of my knowledge and belief, that he neither was nor could have been that twin brother of Henry the Silurist who wrote memorable Hermetic tracts between 1650 and 1655 under the sacramental name of Eugenius Philalethes. The position thus formulated has not been challenged and remains, as it seems to me, beyond dispute. I could have almost wished otherwise, or perhaps that I had been able to exhibit a satisfactory reason why there is no record of Thomas Vaughan being buried by Thames at Albury, as his story states, namely, that he did not die in 1665, but went over the world wandering—to the Americas and otherwhere—and wrote yet further treatises, manuscript copies of which he left there and here, but himself printed nothing. I mean that to have done this, if possible, would have been more interesting to the sense of romance than shewing how Vaughan perished through a chemical explosion at the house of a dissolute parson and how impossible it is to recognise the hand of Eugenius in the writings of Eirenæus Philalethes.

In the same year that I published at London the *Works of Thomas Vaughan* in the collected form which I have mentioned Mr. G. L. Kittredge issued through the University Press of Cambridge, U.S.A., a considerable pamphlet entitled *Dr. Robert Child the Remonstrant.* It is of importance from two points of view (1) for the light which it casts on personalities and events in America of the seventeenth century, (2) for the concern in Alchemy exhibited on the part of the group with which the pamphlet deals. I was reminded on my own part of a point which is noted in my preface to the *Works*, pp. xix, xx, namely, that a memorandum in an old hand inscribed on a copy of the *Marrow of Alchemy* in the British Museum affirms that the name of Eirenæus was Child. It is not the only ascription in connection with the same text. Sloane 2558 is a transcript of the printed *Marrow* and has a similar entry facing the title page and saying : "It is supposed Eirenæus Philalethes' name was Bartlett, who was acquainted with Dr. Child." Mr. Kittredge is familiar with the second and not apparently with the first attribution, but his account presents Child as a less or more zealous amateur of the Hermetic subject and cites one of his letters, dated 13th May, 1648, to prove that " he had never solved or pretended to solve, the momentous problem of transmutation "—a sufficient distinction, one would think, from the position assumed in his writings by Eirenæus Philalethes.

Mr. Kittredge puts forward another concealed author in the person of George Starkey, who printed the *Marrow of Alchemy* in 1654 as the work of Eirenæus Philoponos Philalethes, a pretended friend and pupil of Eirenæus the Cosmopolite. As I have dealt otherwise with Starkey [1] I need only say here that—under the variant of Stirk—he was one of the Boston group who belongs to the story of the Remonstrant and that when he migrated to London *circa* 1650 there is good reason for agreeing with Mr. Kittredge that he carried a considerable number of Philalethes MSS. We have his own authority for the fact that they were in his keeping. Starkey's story, which appears in the work mentioned, was that he received them from the hands of the supposed pupil, in the existence of whom I have registered

[1] Preface to *Works*, pp. xx, xxi.

my disbelief,[1] and Mr. Kittredge has reached independently the same conclusion. Another point of agreement between us is on the significance of the fact that Starkey betrayed himself by using subsequently Eirenæus Philoponos Philalethes as his own pseudonym. Our concurrence ends here, for I regard Starkey as author of the first part or poem in the *Marrow*, not of the second, which is the work of a different hand, and still less of the *Open Entrance* and the other notable tracts under the name of Eirenæus. Mr. Kittredge, on the contrary, affirms that the " splendid fiction " of this anonymous and unknown adept was invented by his emigrant from Boston and he is " prepared to prove " it, though Cooper, Starkey's publisher, was unacquainted with the fact. Unfortunately, at this vital stage he leaves the question in suspense because the evidence is " too long and complicated to give ". adding, however, that he will return to it one of these days. Meanwhile he produces the Starkey pseudonym as a " decisive fact " in favour of his view. But I have shewn already the narrow measures within which, if anywise, it can be called decisive, though I should not have ventured on my own part to use so strong a term. It is evidence for me that he was the imaginary pupil of *Marrow*, Book I, but by no means the concealed master.

For the rest, Mr. Kittredge makes two citations, from which it follows that his speculative hypothesis was put forward in the seventeenth and again in the eighteenth century. He quotes a contribution to the Breslau *Ephemerides* of 1676 or 1677,[2] made on the authority of a letter " received from our English College ". It certifies (1) that the Philalethes Anonymus was named George Starkey ; (2) that he received the White Elixir from Dr. Child ; (3) that he brought it to England, together with the titles of twelve tracts composed by the said Child, who was the adept behind him ; (4) that on account of his hypocrisy Starkey was cut off from all communication with his master ; (5) that thus debarred from further progress, he used the Child titles for twelve tracts of his own and thus " caused many evils " ; (6) that the writer became familiarly acquainted with him only when he

[1] *Ibid.*, p. xx.
[2] It was written by Johann Ferdinand Hertodt von Todtenfeld, described as a Moravian physician. The correspondent from the " English College " is not identified by name.

had exhausted the Tincture; (7) that he and his friends " discovered the emptiness of his words "at their proper cost.[1] Such is the deposition in summary : it is in error over the adept behind Starkey ; it is on the surface utterly gratuitous in proposing the existence of twelve treatises composed by Child which no one has seen ; and the sole evidence offered for the notion that Starkey forged other works under the same titles is that the unknown witness had seen a copy of one of them " done from Starkey's autograph " whatever that may be held to mean. I have shewn [2] that copies must have been fairly numerous. Langius printed the *Open Entrance* from a Latin text and said that it was a faulty copy ; Cooper produced his English version from one which was admittedly not the autograph, and there were other transcripts extant. If one of them was in the writing of Starkey it proves nothing.

The second citation is from Joh. Conrad Creiling in *Dic. Edelgeborne Jungfer Alchymie*, 1730, and is given thus : " Certain it is that Georgius Starkey, an apothecary in London . . . , published the tracts in question and perhaps wrote some of them himself ". On the contrary, all the works of Eirenæus Philalethes remained in MS. till after the death of Starkey [3]—as it is said, in a debtor's prison—

[1] If Mr. Kittredge and I are correct in supposing that the " pupil " Eirenæus Philoponos Philalethes was an invention of Starkey, these things follow : (1) that this sacramental name was his own designation and was in use long prior to the publication of the *Open Entrance* ; (2) that in addition to the *Marrow of Alchemy* Starkey refers two other tracts to the mythical personality created by him ; (3) that these are *Brevis Manuductio ad Campum Sophicum* and *Elenchus Errorum in Arte Chemica Deviantium* ; (4) that the first of these is suspiciously like *Brevis Manuductio ad Rubinum Cælestem* which Eirenæus Philalethes affirms that he wrote in Latin : see his preface to *Ripley Revived* ; (5) that at the end of an *Exposition upon Sir George Ripley's Epistle to King Edward V*, being the first tract in *Ripley Revived*, William Cooper, its publisher, places a catalogue of books by Eirenæus Philalethes, and among thirteen of which he was unable to find copies there appears the *Elenchus Errorum* ; (6) that this list is followed by a general catalogue of books printed and sold by Cooper which reproduces the available Philalethes writings ; (7) that among these are enumerated the *Marrow of Alchemy*, the *Brevis Manuductio* to which the cosmopolite confessed, and finally *Vade-Mecum Philosophicum, sive Brevis Manuductorium ad Campum Sophiæ*, a variant in title of the tract which is fathered on Philoponos by Starkey. It follows that in the opinion of Cooper, who should have known if any man knew, outside Starkey himself, that Philoponos was a veil for the Cosmopolite. It follows also that Starkey is not the true Eirenæus because if he had invented the latter to veil himself he would not have invented Philoponos also as an intermediary semi-adept, because there was no need.

[2] Preface to *Works of Thomas Vaughan*, pp. xiv-xviii.

[3] After 1654 he was engaged in the publication of his own works, for a list of which see *Bibliographical Sketches of Graduates of Harvard*, by J. L. Sibley, 1873, vol. i.

with the sole exception of the *Marrow*, for the second part of which he may have been responsible or not. A little bibliographical knowledge would have made such a proposition impossible, and I suggest that Mr. Kittredge himself will do well to consider this aspect of the question carefully before he produces his alleged proofs, " when time serves."

The appeal on my own part is meanwhile to the literary sense, and judgment based thereon will determine the subject in the same manner as I have disposed of it in the case of alleged identity between Eugenius and Eirenæus Philalethes.[1] It is impossible that *Ripley Revived* should have been written by the author of *Lumen de Lumine*. So also, in view of the fact that George Starkey wrote *Pyrotechny Asserted*,[2] not to speak of his tract on the *True Oil*,[3] he could not have produced the magisterial and inspired work which is called *Introitus Apertus*. Eirenæus Philalethes remains therefore as he was, pseudonymous and utterly unknown. I proceed now to a short consideration of his testimony, respecting the fact and matter of Alchemy, as well as his experience in accomplishing the Great Work. A testimony concerning himself is in the preface to the *Open Entrance*.[4]

" I, being an adept anonymous, a lover of learning and a philosopher, decreed to write this little treatise of medicinal, chemical and physical secrets in the year of the world's redemption 1645, in the three and twentieth year of my age, that I might pay my duty to the Sons of Art; that I might lend my hand to bring them out of the labyrinth of errors; that I might appear to other adepts as their brother and equal; and that those who are bewrayed by deceits of sophisters might return safely, seeing and embracing the true light. Now therefore I presage that not a few will be enlightened by these my labours: they are no fables but real experiments which I have seen and made and know, as every other adept will conclude from these lines. And because I write for the good of my neighbour, let this my confession be enough that no one heretofore has testified

---

[1] *Works of Thomas Vaughan*, pp. xiii, *et seq.*
[2] It was published at the White Horse in St. Paul's Churchyard, 1658. A French translation by Jean Pelletier appeared at Rouen in 1706.
[3] See *Collectanea Chymica*, published by William Cooper in 1684.
[4] I have used Cooper's English text of 1669, abbreviating here and there.

in this Art so clearly. In truth many times I laid aside my pen, designing to forbear from writing, being rather willing to have concealed the truth under a mask of envy; but God compelled me to write, and Him I could in no wise resist, Who alone knows the heart and unto Whom be glory for ever. I believe undoubtedly that many in this last age of the world shall be rejoiced with the Great Secret because I have written so faithfully, leaving of my own will nothing in doubt for a young beginner. I know many already who possess it in common with myself and am persuaded that I shall yet be acquainted with many others who are destined for its attainment in the immediate time to come. May God's most holy will be done herein. I acknowledge myself all unworthy of bringing these things about, but in such matters I submit in adoration to Him, to Whom all creation is subject, Who created all to this end and having created preserves them." The preface ends at this point and that which follows is abbreviated from various parts of the thirteenth chapter.

"Alchemical books—almost without exception—abound with obscure enigmas, sophistical operations, or with rough and uncouth terms. I have not followed these courses, herein resigning my will to the Divine Pleasure, which—in this last period of the world—seems about to open out these treasures. I fear therefore no longer that the Art will be disesteemed, for true wisdom will defend its own honour. I could wish that gold and silver were in as mean esteem as earth, instead of the great idol adored by the whole world. Then we who know these things should not need so studiously to hide ourselves, who unto this present are as if there had fallen upon us the very curse of Cain. We are driven, so to speak, from the face of the Lord, from the pleasant society of friends which we could enjoy once without fear. We are tossed up and down, as though beset with furies, nor can we hold ourselves safe in any place for long. We make our complaint unto the Lord: "Whosoever shall find me will slay me." We pass through many nations like vagabonds and dare not assume the care of a family or possess any certain habitation. Although we possess all things we can use but few. Wherein is therefore our happiness, save in satisfaction of the mind? Many strangers to the Art believe that if

they attained it they would be about this and that, as I
also in my time; but being grown more wary by the hazard
that we all have run we have learned a more secret way:
whosoever has stood once in great peril of his life will be
wiser thenceforth. I have found great wickedness in the
world and scarcely one therein who does not propound
privately to himself some base and unworthy end, howsoever
he seems in public. Moreover, he who will practise works
of mercy, if he stands alone, may run the hazard of
his head, as I myself have found, in foreign places, where I
administered the Medicine to some at the point of death.
They having recovered miraculously, there was presently a
rumour spread abroad concerning the Elixir of the Wise,
and on one occasion I had to fly by night, after changing
clothes, shaving my head, putting on a wig and passing
under another name. Otherwise I had fallen into the wicked
hands of those who lay in wait for me on mere suspicion,
filled with the greed of gold. I could cite many such incidents
and some of them might seem ridiculous in the opinion of
those who believe that they would manage much better and
differently if they possessed the Stone, not realizing that they
may find their match in those who are on the watch for masters.
The iniquity of men is so great that some have been strangled
with a halter on the false suspicion that they were acquainted
with this Art. Be warned therefore, you who are in truth
adepts: you shall hardly stir a foot, except you wish to be
betrayed. If you have much gold or silver and would sell it
there will be questioning as to whence it came and how it is
of such fine quality: the best is from Guinea or Barbary,
and is in the fashion of smallest sand; but this is yet better
and in a massy form. Be sure that there will be notable
rumours, sufficient to bring you misfortune. And if you
sought to adulterate it the law of most nations is against you,
for this may be done only by a licensed metallurgist. On
a time, and in a foreign country, I would have sold so much
pure silver worth £600; but although I was dressed like a
merchant they said unto me presently that the said metal
was made by Art. When I asked their reason it was answered:
'We know the silver that comes from England, Spain and
the other places; but this is none of these kinds'. On
hearing this I withdrew suddenly, leaving the silver behind

me as well as its price and never returning. Being taught
by these difficulties, I have determined to lie hidden and
will communicate the Art to those who dream about it and
observe what good they do with it when it has come into
their hands.

" I have made the Stone : I do not possess it by theft
but by the gift of God. I have made it and daily have it
in my power, having formed it often with my own hands.
I write the things that I know. The Searcher of all hearts
knows that I write the truth, nor is there any cause to accuse
me of envy, because I write with an unterrified quill in an
unheard of style, to the honour of God, to the profitable
use of my neighbours, but in contempt of the world and its
riches. Elias the Artist is already born, and now glorious
things are declared of the City of God.[1] I dare affirm that
I possess more riches than the whole known world is worth,
but cannot make use thereof because of the snares of knaves.
I disdain, loathe and deservedly detest this idolising of gold
and silver, by the price whereof the pomps and vanities
of the world are celebrated. Ah, filthy evil, ah, vain nothing-
ness : believe you that I conceal these things out of envy ?
I protest that I grieve from the very bottom of my soul
that we are driven, as it were, like vagabonds throughout
the earth. But what is the need of words ? The thing which
we have seen, taught and wrought, which we have, possess
and know, this do we declare, being moved with compassion
towards the studious, and with indignation towards gold,
silver and precious stones, not indeed as they are creatures
of God, for in that respect we honour them. But the people
of Israel adore them as well as the world, wherefore let them
be ground to powder as the brazen serpent. I hope and expect
that within a few years money will be like dross and that
this prop of the anti-Christian beast will be dashed in pieces.
The people are mad, the nations rave, an unprofitable wight
is set up in the place of God. These signs will herald our
long expected and suddenly approaching redemption, when
the New Jerusalem will abound with gold in the streets ;

[1] It is to be observed that this is not a reference to the Elias of Helvetius and
his famous *Vitulus Aureus,* to which we shall come in due course. The tract in
question appeared at the Hague in 1667, and the *Introitus Apertus* of Eirenæus
was issued at Amsterdam in the same year, but had been written—according to
its claim—*circa* 1645.

the gates thereof shall be made with entire stones, and these most precious ; the Tree of Life, in the midst of Paradise, shall give leaves for the healing of the nations. I know then that these my writings will be to most men even as purest gold and that because of them gold and silver will become vile as dirt. Believe me, ye young men, and ye fathers also believe me, because this time is at the door. I write not of vain conceit but of what I see in the spirit. Then shall we who are adepts return from the four corners of the earth, nor shall we fear any further snares laid against our lives ; but we shall give thanks unto the Lord our God. My heart whispers unheard-of things, my spirit beats in my breast for the good of all Israel. As a preacher I send forth into the world these tidings, that I may not be as one buried unprofitably therein. Be this my book therefore a forerunner of Elias, preparing the kingly way of the Lord. I would to God that every ingenious man in the whole earth understood this Science : then would no one esteem it—gold, silver and gems being so exceedingly abundant—except so far only as belongs to knowledge. Then at length, naked as it is, virtue would be held in great honour for its own lovable nature. I know many that possess the true science,[1] all of whom have vowed a most secret silence ; but, as for myself, I am of another judgment, because of the hope that I have in my God. Therefore I wrote this book without the knowledge of my adept brethren, with whom I converse daily.[2] For God gave rest unto my soul by a most firm faith, and I do believe undoubtedly that in such manner I shall serve the Lord my Creditor and the world my neighbour, chiefly of all Israel,[3] by this use of my talent. And I know that none can put out his talent to so great interest, for perchance some hundreds will be illuminated by these my writings : wherefore I consulted not with flesh and blood,[4] nor sought

[1] So also in his earlier day, when many gates were beginning to open, Alexander Seton testified that many persons, both of high and mean estate, had seen Diana Unveiled.

[2] It is not, on the surface at least, an intimation that Eirenæus had been drawn within a circle of initiation. By his own hypothesis, he had accomplished the Great Work alone and wholly unaided, except by God and certain books of the philosophers. Later on he spoke of pledges, but he writes here as one who is his own warrant and whom none on earth shall hinder.

[3] Meaning the Israel of catholic election : it is not to be inferred that *Introitus Apertus* was the work of a Jew.

[4] Compare St. Paul, alike in spirit and letter.

after the consent of my brethren in treating hereof. God grant that it be to the glory of His Name, that I may attain the end to which I look : then will the many adepts who know me rejoice that I have published these things.''

It will be seen by the next extract that the preface to *Ripley Revived* is important for the writer's own studies and for bibliographical particulars.

" For my own part, I have cause to honour Bernard Trévisan, who is very ingenious, especially in the letter to Thomas of Bononia, where I seriously confess that I received the main light in the hidden secret. I do not remember that ever I learned anything from Raymund Lully. Some who are not adepts give more instruction to a beginner than one whom perfect knowledge makes cautious. I learned the secret of the Magnet from one, the Chalybs from another, the use of Diana's Doves from a third, the Air or Chameleon from another, the gross preparation of the dissolvent in another, the number of Eagles in another ; but for operations on the True Matter and signs of the True Mercury I know of none like Ripley, though Flamel be eminent. I know what I say, having learned by experience what is truth and what is error. I have read misleading, sophistical writers and made many toilsome, laborious experiments, though but young ; and having at length, through the undeserved mercy of God, arrived at my haven of rest, I shall stretch out my hand to such as are behind. I have wrote several treatises, some in English, but especially in Latin ; one English treatise touching the Stone, very plain but not perfected : unfortunately it slipped out of my hand, and I shall be sorry if it comes abroad into the world ; two in Latin, *Brevis Manuductio ad Rubinum Cœlestem* and *Fons Chymicæ Philosophiæ*—these, for special reasons, I resolve to suppress.[1] Two other Latin treatises I lately wrote which perhaps you may enjoy, namely, *Ars Metallorum Metamorphoses*,[2] and *Introitus Apertus ad Occlusum Regis Palatium*.[3] I wrote two poems in English

[1] They appeared notwithstanding at Amsterdam in 1668 ; at Frankfort in *Museum Hermeticum Reformatum et Amplificatum*, 1677, 1678 ; and in Mangetus : *Bibliotheca Chemica Curiosa*, 1702.

[2] Included in the publications mentioned in my previous note.

[3] At Amsterdam in 1667, as already seen ; at Frankfort in *Museum Hermeticum*, 1677 ; at Venice in 1683 ; at Jena in 1699 ; at Cologne in Mangetus, *op. cit.*, 1702 ; at London and in English, 1669 ; at Amsterdam and in German, as *Abyssus Alchimiæ Exploratus*, 1705.

which are lost [1]; also in English an *Enchiridion of Experiments*
a *Diurnal of Meditations*, with many receipts declaring the
whole secret and an *Enigma* attached. These also fell into
the hands of one who, I conceive, will never restore them."[2]

There is a sense in which I have now provided a representative portrait of Eirenæus Philalethes. We know that for
which he stands, the end for which he worked and his high
certitude that he had not worked in vain. The cup of his
success was not only full but overflowing, and the material
wealth of the world was at his call. From one point of view
it was a gift of God, but it came as a reward of work and
not by revelation. He thinks that even in the case of Solomon
—if Solomon possessed the Stone—it was because his hands
had made it. Let us turn now to the last chapter of the
Open Entrance, for his final message to those who have
attained like him—perhaps by his mediation—and also for
his last words on the Catholicon and all its virtues.

" He who hath once, by the blessing of God, perfectly
attained this Art, I know not what in the world he can wish
but that he may be free from all snares of wicked men, so
as to serve God without distraction. But it would be a vain
thing by outward pomp to seek for vulgar applause : such
trifles are not esteemed by those who have this Art ; nay,
rather they despise them. He therefore whom God hath blessed
with this talent, hath this field of content. First, if he should
live a thousand years and every day provide for a thousand
men, he could not want ; for he may increase his Stone at his

---

[1] See my preface and Introduction to the *Works of Thomas Vaughan* on the
question whether these lost poems are or are not contained in the *Marrow of
Alchemy*, published at London by Eirenæus Philoponos Philalethes, i.e., George
Starkey, in 1654. The seventeenth century suggestion that Starkey wrote these
poems presumably after coming to England is ridiculous in the light of this statement ; he would scarcely say in a later forgery that things were lost which he had
actually printed and published.

[2] The *Enchyridion* is included among manuscript works of Philalethes, a long
list, which follows the enumeration of printed books under the same pseudonym
in the bibliography of Lenglet du Fresnoy, *Hist. de la Phil. Herm.*, vol. iii, pp. 264–6.
I select a few of the apparently more important items : (1) *Expositio in Arnoldi
Villanovani ultimum Testamentum* ; (2) *Cabala Sapientum, sive Expositio Hiero-
glyphicorum Magorum* ; (3) *Opus Elixiris Aurifici et Argentifici* ; (4) *Brevis Via
ad Vitam Longam*—but my impression is that this was printed subsequently ;
(5) *Expositiones in sex posteriores Portas Alchimiæ*, referring to the Gates of Ripley.
The *Commentary* of Philalethes on the first Six Gates was issued by William Cooper,
who advertised also for that on the remaining six, which he was unable to find.
The list of Lenglet du Fresnoy is drawn from one of Cooper's, but the latter confesses
that he knew of them by report only.

pleasure, both in weight and virtue, so that—if a man would—one man that is an adeptist might transmute into perfect gold and silver all the imperfect metals that are in the whole world. Secondly, he may by this Art make precious stones and gems, such as cannot be paralleled in Nature for goodness and greatness. Thirdly and lastly, he hath a Medicine Universal, both for prolonging life and curing of all diseases, so that one true adeptist can easily cure all the sick people in the world : I mean, his Medicine is sufficient. Now to the King Eternal, Immortal and sole Almighty, be everlasting praise for these His unspeakable gifts and invaluable treasures. Whosoever enjoyeth this talent, let him be sure to employ it to the glory of God and the good of his neighbours, lest he be found ungrateful to God his Creditor—Who hath blessed him with so great a talent—and so be in the last day found guilty of misproving of it and so condemned."

Thus did Eirenæus Philalethes open the Palace of the King for those at least who held his key of symbols. A final citation shall present in the next place the story of George Starkey and the beginnings of his experiences in the path of Hermetic Knowledge.

" I have now to assert from my own experience facts of transmutation of which I was an eye-witness. I was well acquainted with an artist, with whom I have often conversed on the subject, and I saw in his possession the White and the Red Elixir, in very large quantity. He gave me upwards of two ounces of the White Medicine, of sufficient virtue to convert 120,000 times its weight into the purest virgin silver. With this treasure I went to work ignorantly upon multiplication and was caught in the trap of my own covetousness, for I expended and wasted all this Tincture. However, I made projection of part of it, which is sufficient for my present purpose, enabling me to affirm the possibility of the Art from occular demonstration. I have tinged many times hundreds of ounces into the best silver. Of a pound of mercury I have made within less than a scruple of a pound of silver ; of lead, little more waste ; but 'tis wondrous to see tin : although a dross was burnt from it, its weight increased in the fire. I essayed the Medicine on copper, iron, even on brass and pewter, on spelter, solder, tinglass, mercury, and on regulus of antimony : I can say with truth that it conquers all metallic things and brings them all to perfection. I found that there was nothing akin to it which it would not tinge into pure silver. Even perfect gold was penetrated and changed into a white glass that would transmute—but in small quantity—inferior metals into silver; but when this silver was assayed it was found to abide aquafortis, cupel of antimony, and it weighed as gold, so that it was white gold. This was because the White Tincture had been fermented with Red Earth and both virtues, coming into projection, produced silver-coloured gold, or silver equalling gold in perfection but wanting its hue. I did not know the value of this silver till my gold had nearly gone and sold eight ounces of it at the common price, though it was as valuable as gold. I projected the Medicine on pure silver and had a crystalline metal like burnished steel or a mirror, but there was no increased virtue in this : it tinged only so much as it would if it had not been projected on silver.

" The artist who gave me this is still living : I prize him as my own life; I wish him happiness, for he has been a sure friend. He is at present on his travels, visiting other artists and collecting antiquities as a citizen of the world. He is an Englishman of an ancient, honourable family, who live now in the place wherein he was born. He is scarcely thirty-three years of age and is rarely learned. You cannot know more of him from me: my own acquaintance with him was as unexpected as his love was cordial. I had seen often by experiment that he was master of the White and Red before he would vouchsafe to trust me with a small bit of the Stone, nor would I press him, trusting to his courtesy soon or late ; and this I received shortly—as appears by what I have said of the White Medicine—and also a portion of his Mercury. He told me that this was a matchless treasure, if God would open my eyes to the use of it : else I might grope in blindness. With this dissolvent —which is the Hidden Secret of all masters—he multiplied exceedingly his Red Stone. I saw him put a piece of the Red, by weight, into that same Mercury, which thereupon digested, dissolved and caused it to change colour, so that in three days it passed through the process of Black, White and Red.

" I thought that if the Red and White could be multiplied, one lineal process led to either, and on this false ground I destroyed ten parts in twelve of my Medicine. Nor did this loss suffice me, for I mixed the remaining two parts with ten times their weight of Luna and fell to work again, hoping to make up for my first error. Thereafter I began to think upon the maxims of the old books, revolving in my mind the agreement of my work with the laws of Nature, and at length I concluded that each thing must be disposed according to its condition. When I found that my vain attempts only wasted the Tincture I stopped my hand, resolving to keep the few grains left for some urgent necessity, and for its preservation I mixed it with ten parts of Luna. I tried some of the Mercury before mentioned on gold, my desire being to see the work carried forward to Luna—if not to Sol. This, then, I projected on mercury. After having alloyed it with silver it tinged fifty parts and I strove to imbibe it, but in vain, because I had let it cool. I expected foolishly to obtain the oil by imbibition. However, Nature carried on the work into blackness, the other colours and whiteness, which yet was far short of what I looked for. In these trials I wasted nearly all my Mercury likewise, but I had the witnessing of transmutations to console me, and those extraordinary processes which I beheld with mine own eyes and blessed God for seeing.

" After some time I met my good friend and told him all my mishaps, hoping that he would supply me as before. But, considering that my failures had made me wise, he would not trust me with more, lest I shoul pluck the Hesperian Tree as I chose, for my own and other men's hurt. He said to me : ' Friend, if God elects you to this Art, He will in due time bestow the knowledge of it ; but if in His wisdom He judge you unfit, or that you would do mischief with it, accursed be that man who would arm a maniac to the harm of his fellow-creatures. While you were ignorant I gave you a great gift, but so that it should destroy itself if so heaven ordained. It is not right, I see, that you should enjoy it at present : that which Providence denies you I cannot give, or I should be guilty of your misconduct.'

" It must be confessed that this lesson in divinity did not please me : as I had hoped so much from him, his answer was a disappointment. He said further that God had granted me knowledge but for the present withheld its fruit. I gave him then to understand how I had discovered the skill of the Water, by which I might obtain in time that which he denied and was resolved to make the attempt. 'If so,' he replied, 'attend to what I say, and you may bless God for it. Know that we are bound severely and by strong vows never to supply by our Art any man who might confound the world if he held it at will, and that all the evil which he should do would be left at the doors of any adept who was so imprudent. Consider what a prize you had, alike in the Stone and the Mercury. Would not any one say that he must be mad who threw all of it away without profit ? Had you been guided by reason you might have had enough in what I gave you. Your method was to add but a grain of the Stone to the purest gold : in fusion it would unite thereto, and then you might go about the business with your Mercury, which would mix speedily with that gold and shorten the work greatly : this also you might govern easily to the Red. And as you saw how I wedded new gold to such Sulphur and such Mercury, as you saw the weight, time and heat, what more could you have wished ? Seeing also that you know the Art of preparing the Fiery Mercury, you might have as much store as anyone. But you do not perceive by this that God is averse to you and has caused you to waste the treasure which I gave. He foresees perhaps that you would break His holy laws ; and though He has imparted so much knowledge, I discern plainly that he will keep you for some years without the enjoyment of that which you would probably misuse. Learn that if you seek this Art without a ferment, you must beware of frequent error : notwithstanding all your care, you will stray from the right path and may not in the course of your life attain this treasure, which is the alone gift of God. By the straightest course it will take you a year to arrive at perfection ; but following wrong ways you shall be left often behind, to renew your pains, repenting your loss in much pain and peril, with an expense that can hardly spare. Attend therefore to my counsel, and I shall disclose the secret conditionally. Swear before the mighty God that you will for such a time abstain from the practice, nor shall you thereafter, even if you are at the point of death, disclose some few points that I shall reveal to you in secrecy.

" I swore, and he unlocked his mind to me, proving that he did not deceive by shewing me those lights which I shall recount honestly, so far as my oath will admit."

It follows from this account, which is clear and simple at its non-evidential value, that George Starkey was in direct communication with Eirenæus Philalethes—who corresponds to the description given—not with an intermediary or pupil of that master. But this pupil appears in Book I, Part 2, of the poem which follows and the account is at issue not only with Starkey's preface but with the testimony of Eirenæus Philalethes concerning himself.

My last word on the Cosmopolite, based on the evidence cited, shall affirm that the most important expositor of Alchemy in the second half of the seventeenth century was an adept, by the hypothesis of his claim, in the transmutation of metals and in nothing else. Those who have sought to understand his texts after another manner have testified to their own distraction.

CHAPTER XX

John Frederick Helvetius

IN the autobiographical narrative of Bernard Trévisan it is possible to accept everything at its face value except the issue of his story, according to which—and at the close only of a long life of failure—he discovered the Great Secret by comparing alchemical texts, and in this manner was enabled to transmute metals. In view of the texts themselves there is nothing *a priori* more unlikely, while, as we have seen, in his concluding and pseudo-practical part he takes refuge in allegory, a device in which his work is stultified as a record of serious research. We are practically in no better position with Denys Zachaire, who owes everything at the end to the illumination of a single text. On the other hand, the striking evidence of an independent witness like Picus de Mirandula on things done in his presence produces no conviction because it does not appear that he had taken any precautions against deception. Outside the professed alchemists themselves a question therefore arises whether there is any case of transmutation performed or alleged to be performed by any known and responsible person who did not claim to be an adept on his own part ; and the answer is that John Frederick Helvetius is an example ready to our hands, with a record of extraordinary fullness which I will give in the first place, practically as it stands in the original Latin text.[1] We shall see also that there is John Baptist Van Helmont, testifying in 1648, but his particulars are few in comparison with those of Helvetius.

" On December 27th, 1666, and in the forenoon, there came a certain man to my house who was unto me a complete

---

[1] The full title is *Vitulus Aureus quem Mundus adorat et orat, in quo tractatur de rarissimo Naturæ Miraculo Transmutandi Metalla, nempe quomodo tota Plumbi Substantia, vel intra momentum, ex quavis minima Lapidis veri Philosophici particula in Aurum obryzum commutata fuerit Hagæ Comitis : Autore Joh. Friderico Helvetio,* 1667. There were later editions in 1702 and 1705, the earlier of these being in the collection of Mangetus : *Bibliotheca Chemica Curiosa.*

stranger, but of an honest, grave and authoritative mien, clothed in a simple garb like that of a Memnonite. He was of middle height, his face was long and slightly pock-marked, his hair was black and straight, his chin close-shaven, his age about forty-three or forty-four and his native place North Holland, so far as I could make out. After we had exchanged salutations, he inquired whether he might have some conversation with me. It was his desire to speak of the Pyrotechnic Art, as he had read one of my tracts, being that directed against the Sympathetic Powder of Sir Kenelm Digby, in which I implied a suspicion whether the Great Arcanum of the Sages was not after all a gigantic hoax. He took therefore this opportunity of asking if indeed I could not believe that such a Grand Mystery might exist in the nature of things, being that by which a physician could restore any patient whose vitals were not irreparably destroyed. My answer allowed that such a Medicine would be a most desirable acquisition for any doctor and that none might tell how many secrets there may be hidden in Nature, but that as for me—though I had read much on the truth of this Art—it had never been my fortune to meet with a Master of Alchemical Science. I inquired further whether he was himself a medical man, since he spoke so learnedly about the Universal Medicine; but he disclaimed my suggestion modestly, describing himself as a brass-founder who had always taken great interest in the extraction of medicines from metals by means of fire. After some further talk, the Artist Elias—for he it was [1]—addressed me thus: ' Seeing that you have read so much in the writings of alchemists concerning this Stone, its substance, colour and wonderful effects, may I be allowed to question whether you have yourself prepared it ? ' On my answering this in the negative, he took from his bag an ivory box of cunning workmanship, in which there were three large pieces of a substance resembling glass or pale sulphur, and informed me that here was enough of the Tincture to produce twenty tons of gold.

" When I had held the treasure in my hands for some

---

[1] We have seen that the Artist Elias was a prophet of Alchemy whose advent was promised by Paracelsus and who was to reveal all secrets of the Art. The mysterious visitor of Helvetius was of course an Elias for him.

fifteen minutes, listening to an account of its curative properties, I was compelled to return it, not without a certain degree of reluctance. After thanking him for his kindness, I asked why it was that his Tincture did not display that ruby colour which I had been taught to regard as characteristic of the Philosopher's Stone. He replied that the colour made no difference and that the substance was sufficiently mature for all practical purposes.[1] He refused somewhat brusquely my request for a piece of his substance, were it no larger than a coriander seed, adding in a milder tone that he could not do so for all the wealth which I possessed, not indeed on account of its preciousness but for another reason that it was not lawful to divulge. Indeed if fire could be destroyed by fire he would cast it rather into the flames. Then, after a little consideration, he asked whether I could not shew him into a room at the back of the house, where we should be less liable to observation.[2] Having led him into the state-parlour—which he entered without wiping his dirty boots— he requested me to produce a gold coin, and while I was finding it he took from his breast pocket a green silk handkerchief wrapped about five medals, the gold of which was infinitely superior to that of my own money.[3] Being filled with admiration, I asked my visitor how he had attained this most wonderful knowledge in the world, to which he replied that it was a gift bestowed on him freely by a friend who had stayed a few days at his house,[4] when he taught him also how to change common flints and crystals into stones more

---

[1] The statement is not in accordance with the concensus of alchemical testimony on the colours which succeed one another in the evolution of the Alchemical Stone. There are, however, a few examples of alleged transmutation by means of a yellow powder.

[2] The sequel shews that no purpose was served by this request, as he who had exhibited the Stone itself in a room facing the street produced subsequently nothing but gold medals.

[3] The evidence does not emerge. Had Helvetius subjected the medals to any test of the period he would have registered the fact beyond doubt. He must have trusted therefore to the eye, as it does not appear that he took them even in his hand. It follows that either Helvetius was not a very careful recorder, when uttermost care was needed, or that he pronounced judgment on practically no warrant.

[4] It is to be noted that, according to his description, as given in *Vitulus Aureus*, the so-called Elias was in 1666 apparently of the same age as Eirenæus Philalethes, and the question arises whether Helvetius could have mistaken the cosmopolite English adept for a North Hollander, in which case the story of a master who taught the said Elias was camouflage, if we accept at its face value the claim of *Introitus Apertus*.

precious than rubies, chrysolites and sapphires. 'He made
known to me further,' said the artist, 'the preparation of
crocus of iron, an infallible cure for dysentery; of a metallic
liquor, which was an efficacious remedy for dropsy; and of
other medicines.' To this, however, I paid no great heed
as I—Helvetius—was impatient to hear about the Great
Secret of all. The artist said further that his master caused
him to bring a glass full of warm water, to which he added
a little white powder and then an ounce of silver, which
melted like ice therein. 'Of this he emptied one half
and gave the rest to me: its taste resembled that of fresh milk,
and the effect was most exhilarating.' I asked my visitor
whether the potion was a preparation of the Philosopher's
Stone, but he replied that I must not be so curious. He
added presently that at the bidding of his master he took
down a piece of lead water-pipe and melted it in a pot,
when the master removed some sulphurous powder on the
point of a knife from a little box, cast it into the molten lead,
and after exposing the compound for a short time to a fierce
fire he poured forth a great mass of liquid gold upon the
brick floor of the kitchen. 'The master bade me take
one-sixteenth of this gold as a keepsake for myself and
distribute the rest among the poor, which I did by making
over a large sum in trust for the Church of Sparrendaur.
In fine, before bidding me farewell, my friend taught me
this Divine Art.' [1]

"When my strange visitor had concluded his narrative,
I besought him in proof of his statement to perform a
transmutation in my presence. He answered that he could
not do so on that occasion but that he would return in three
weeks and if then at liberty to do so he would shew me
something that would make me open my eyes. He returned
punctually on the promised day and invited me to a walk,
in the course of which we spoke profoundly on the secrets
of Nature in fire, though I noticed that my companion was
exceedingly reserved on the subject of the Great Secret.
But he discoursed gravely about the holiness of the Art,

---

[1] It will be observed that Elias obtained the Great Secret in an exceedingly
easy manner, as if at the hands of a person who—like Eirenæus—had acquired the
Art by his own unguided efforts and was hence under no bonds. But on the faith
of his story he was evidently pledged himself.

as if he were the minister of a church.[1] The sum of it was that God had ordained the initiates to make it known only to the deserving. At last I asked him point blank to shew me the transmutation, begging him to return and dine with me and to spend the night at my house. My entreaties and expostulations were in vain, and when I recalled his promise he retorted that it was conditional on permission being given him to reveal the secret.[2] When I prayed him, however, to entrust me with a morsel of his precious Stone, were it no larger than a rape-seed, he delivered it like a princely donation. When I expressed a doubt whether it would be sufficient to tinge more than four grains of lead he demanded it eagerly back. I complied, hoping that he would exchange it for a larger fragment, instead of which he divided it with his thumb, threw half into the fire and returned the rest, saying : ' It is yet sufficient for you.' I was more heavily dejected than ever ; but he bade me take half an ounce of lead—or even a little more—and melt it in a crucible. While protesting my inability to believe that so minute a quantity could convert so large a mass, I had to be satisfied with his gift, and my chief difficulty was now about its application. This led me to confess that when I held originally his ivory box in my hand I had contrived to purloin a few crumbs of the Stone, but they had only changed lead into glass instead of into gold. He answered laughing that I was more expert in my thieving than I had proved in using the Tincture. ' You should have protected your spoil with yellow wax, when it would have been able to penetrate the lead and transmute it into gold. As it was your Medicine evaporated by a sympathetic process in the metallic smoke, all metals being corrupted by the fumes of lead, and degenerated into glass. I shewed him my crucible, and he discovered the yellow Medicine still adhering thereto, whereupon he promised to return the next morning at nine o'clock, when he would demonstrate that even now it would serve for transmuting

[1] Mrs. Atwood passes over this rather pregnant statement in her casual allusions to Helvetius : *Inquiry*, 3rd edition, pp. 66, 321.
[2] If Elias really derived from a master and was in a position to communicate with him at short notice, it follows that the still more mysterious adept must have been somewhere in the Hague district in 1666, and that Elias got no permit to intruct his new acquaintance, if indeed he had sought it, which of course does not appear.

lead into gold. With this promise I had to declare myself
satisfied but prayed him to favour me with some particulars
about the preparation of the Mastery. As to cost and time
he would tell me nothing,[1] but in respect of substance he
affirmed that it was prepared from two metals or minerals,
the latter being better because they contain a larger proportion
of mature Sulphur. 'The solvent is a certain Celestial Salt,
by means of which the sages dissolve the earthly metallic
body and thus elicit the precious Elixir of the Wise. The
work is performed from beginning to end in a crucible over
an open fire [2] : it is consummated in four days and its cost
is only about three florins. Neither the mineral from the Egg
nor the Solvent Salt is very expensive.'

I pointed out that his statement contradicted the
testimony of sages, who specify seven or nine months as the
period of the work, but he replied that their words were to
be understood in a philosophical sense [3] and that no uninformed
person could grasp their real meaning. I besought him that
as a stranger had made known to him this priceless mystery,
so he would extend the same boon to myself, or give me at
least sufficient information to remove the greater difficulties.
Were there certitude on one point, its connections would be
discovered more easily. But he answered : ' It is not so
in our Magistery : if you do not know the whole operation
from beginning to end, you know nothing at all. I have indeed
told you everything [4] : yet you do not see how the crystal
seal of Hermes is broken ; how the Sun colours it with the
great splendour of his metallic rays ; in what mirror the
metals behold with eyes of Narcissus the possibiblity of their
transmutation ; or from what rays the adepts collect their
fire of perfect metallic fixation.' Reiterating his promise to

[1] Compare the statement which follows immediately and according to which
the time of the process is four days, the cost being three florins, on the authority
of the adept himself. It is surely a very careless record.

[2] Not by the magic of Paracelsus, not by Jacob Böhme's transcendental powers
appertaining to the second birth of the mystic, or those conferred in trance by
operators belonging to an age-old School of the Mysteries.

[3] One is inclined to suggest that the work would be obviously longer or shorter
according to the skill and knowledge of the Operator. In the case of those who,
like the alleged Elias, were instructed by a friend in the whole process it
might be done much more rapidly than by those who, like Eirenæus, are said to
have taught themselves.

[4] A possible reference to the discourse between Elias and Helvetius when they
went out walking together, though the adept is said to have been reserved on the
subject of the Great Secret.

return the next morning, he left me there and then. At
the stated hour he did not redeem his promise ; but a stranger
called later, saying that his friend had been detained but
would be with me in the afternoon at three o'clock. I waited
until half past seven but he failed to appear, and my wife
would have persuaded me to attempt transmutation myself.
Though I was by now almost convinced that my visitor
was an impostor, I resolved to wait till the morrow, but
ordered my son to light the fire meanwhile.

" When the morrow came in its course I asked my wife
to put the Tincture in wax, I preparing meanwhile six
drachms of lead, on which presently I cast the Tincture, duly
enveloped. As soon as it was melted there was a hissing
sound and a slight effervescence ; and after fifteen minutes
I found that the whole mass of lead had been converted into
the finest gold. Before this transformation took place, the
compound became intensely green, but when poured into
an ingot it assumed a hue like blood. On cooling it glittered
and shone like gold. We took it at once to a goldsmith,
who declared it to be the purest that he had ever seen and
offered to buy it at the rate of fifty florins for an ounce.
The rumour spread next day like wildfire through the city,
and I was visited by many illustrious students of this Art.
The Master of the Mint came also, with some other gentlemen,
and asked me to place at their disposal a small part of the
gold that it might be put to the usual tests. My consent
given, we proceeded to the house of a silversmith named
Brechtil, who submitted it in the first place to what is called
the ' fourth test '. Three or four parts of silver are melted
in a crucible with one part of gold and then beaten out into
thin plates, on which strong aquafortis is poured. The usual
result is that the silver dissolves, while the gold sinks to the
bottom in the shape of a black powder but resumes its former
state after the aquafortis is poured off and it has been melted
again in the crucible. As a result of this experiment it seemed
at first that half of the gold had evaporated but on the
contrary two scruples of silver had changed into the more
precious metal. We tried then a further test, being that
which is performed with a septuple of antimony. On this
occasion it looked as if eight grains of gold had been lost,
but in reality not only was our original increase maintained,

but the unconverted silver was much improved in quality
and malleability.   I performed this infallible test three
further times, at the end of which it remained that every
drachm of gold had produced an increase of a scruple.   I have
unfolded in this manner my whole story from beginning
to end.   The gold is still in my possession, but I cannot tell
what has become of the Artist Elias.   Before he left me—on
that last day of our friendly intercourse—he stated that he
was on the point of undertaking a journey to the Holy Land.
May the Angels of God watch over him wherever he is and
long preserve him as a source of blessing to Christendom.
This is my earnest prayer on his and on our behalf."

Helvetius adds in a later part of his tract that there was
left in his heart by the Artist a deeply seated conviction
that " through metals and out of metals purified by highly
refined and spiritualised metals, there may be prepared the
Living Gold and Quicksilver of the Sages, which bring both
metals and human bodies to perfection ".   Furthermore, he
learned from his instructor that the Chalybs of Sendivogius [1]
was " that true mercurial metallic humour which—apart
from any corrosive—would suffice to separate the fixed rays
of the Sun and Moon from their bodies [2] and to render them
volatile and mercurial for the dry Philosophical Tincture ",
being that which he had shewn to Helvetius and that with
which the latter had performed transmutation.   The Artist
testified (1) that metals are produced by the same method
in the bowels of the earth ;   (2) that metallic sulphur mixed
with saltpetre may be converted by gentle heat successively
into solid earth, air, limpid water and glass of a most beautiful
colour ;   (3) that there is a sympathy between certain metals,

[1] " There is one metal which has power to consume all others for it is, so to
speak, their water and almost their mother : it is resisted only by the radical
humour of gold and silver, and is ameliorated also thereby.   This metal is called
Chalybs."   New Light of Alchemy, Tract Nine.   Chalybs is steel, but the term is
understood philosophically.   It is said also that there is " another Chalybs ",
created as a thing apart by Nature : it can elicit " the chief principle of our art "
from the rays of the sun, meaning presumably alchemical gold.

[2] Compare ibid., in the prefatory part : " But as many, either from ignorance
or from a desire to conceal their knowledge, are daily teaching and inducing others
to believe that the soul of gold can be extracted, and then imparted to other
substances, thereby enticing numbers to incur great waste of time, labour and
money : let the Sons of Hermes know for certain that this extraction of the
essence of gold is a mere fond delusion, as those who persist in it will be taught
to their cost by experience."

between gold and quicksilver, silver and copper, and that such sympathy is the rationale of transmutation ; (4) that there are also metallic antipathies, as between lead and tin, iron and gold, lead and mercury; (5) that an accurate and comprehensive knowledge of these sympathies and antipathies is the qualification in chief of every man "who aspires to be a master of this Art". The valediction of Helvetius follows in these words : " If anyone doubts the truth of my statements, let him but live a pious and Christ-like life here below, and he will learn the truth of all things in the New Jerusalem above ".

It may be added that the story of Helvetius concerning his Artist Elias is prefaced by brief recitals of other notable transmutations.[1] There is the testimony of Kuffler concerning his conversion to a belief in Alchemy as the result of an experiment which he had been enabled to perform himself ; but we do not hear how he obtained the powder and no reference is given. Secondly, there is an account of a silver-smith named Gril, who, in the year 1664 and at the Hague, converted a pound of lead, " partly into gold and partly into silver," using a tincture obtained from a weaver named John Caspar Knöttner. This was done in the presence of many witnesses and Helvetius examined the precious metals produced. Thirdly, there is the evidence of John Baptist van Helmont, in his treatise *De Vita Æterna*, which shall be quoted from the work itself : " I have seen and handled more than once the Stone of Philosophers : in colour it was like powder of saffron, but heavy and shining, even as pounded glass. There was given to me on a certain occasion the fourth part of a grain, or the six-hundredth part of an ounce. Having wrapped it in paper, I made projection therewith upon eight ounces of quicksilver, heated in a crucible,

---

[1] We may compare with these and with analogous tales of transmutation the following account which is given by Claude Berigard of Pisa, an Italian philosopher, in his *Circulus Pisanus*. " I did not think that it was possible to convert quick-silver into gold, but an acquaintance thought proper to remove my doubt. He gave me about one drachm of a powder nearly of the colour of wild poppy, having a smell like calcined sea-salt. To avoid all imposition, I purchased a crucible, charcoal and quicksilver, with which I was certain that no gold was mixed. Ten drachms of quicksilver which I heated on the fire were transmuted on projection into nearly the same weight of good gold, standing all tests. Had I not performed this operation in the most careful manner taking every precaution against the possibility of doubt, I should not have believed it : as it is, I am satisfied of the fact."

and immediately all the quicksilver—having made a little noise—was congealed into a yellow mass. This being melted in a strong fire, I found eight ounces, *minus* eleven grains, of most pure gold. It follows that a full grain of this powder would have transmuted nineteen thousand one hundred and fifty-six grains of quicksilver into excellent precious metal ". On another occasion, and after an acquaintance of a few days only, he affirms that he was presented by an adept with half one grain of the Powder of Projection, with which he transmuted nine ounces of quicksilver into pure gold. Nor are these his only stories, for he mentions several occasions on which he performed a similar operation in the presence of a large company, and always with success. On these grounds he affirms his belief in the certainty and prodigious resources of the Art, citing also his acquaintance with yet another adept who had so much of the Red Stone that he could have produced gold to the weight of two hundred thousand pounds. The Secret of the Art was unknown to Van Helmont, but not that of the alcahest, with which it is claimed that he prepared efficacious medicines.

It is to Van Helmont also that we are indebted for some particulars concerning an alleged Irish gentleman, named Butler, who was a prisoner at the Castle of Vilvord in Flanders for reasons which do not emerge and while so immured effected strange cures by means of Hermetic Medicine. For example, a Breton monk, who was one of his fellow prisoners, had severe erysipelas in his arm and was restored to health in an hour by drinking " almond milk " in which Butler had merely dipped the Stone of Philosophers. A report of this circumstance brought Helmont—who was either staying or living in the neighbourhood—to make investigations at the Castle, accompanied by several noblemen. In their presence Butler cured an aged woman of the " megrim " by dipping the Stone into oil of olives and then anointing her head. There was also an abbess who had suffered for eighteen years with stiff or paralysed fingers and a swollen arm, which difficulties were removed by applying the Stone a few times to her tongue.[1]

[1] J. Baptist van Helmont: *Ortus Medicinæ*, Amsterdam, 1648, republished as *Opera Omnia*, Leyden, 1653. He is confused sometimes with his son, Franciscus Mercurius van Helmont, whose *Oriatrike, or Physic Refined* was translated into English and published in 1662.

From sources outside Van Helmont [1] we hear that Butler attracted attention in London during the reign of James I by several transmutations performed prior to his Vilvord experiences. He is represented as a traveller, and during one of his voyages the ship in which he took passage was captured by African pirates and brought into some unnamed port, where he was sold as a slave to an Arabian. The latter proved to be at work on Alchemy, apparently with knowledge of the true process. Butler was called to assist and, being " ingenious ", took part in some difficult operations. Though it is pretended that he did not acquire the whole secret, he knew all that was at stake, and when the work was completed he arranged for his ransom—as it is said with an Irish merchant—or alternatively made his escape, in either case carrying off a large portion of the Red Powder.

In the course of the London transmutations a physician formed a plan for discovering the secret. He presented himself as a servant in search of a place and was engaged by Butler, who proved so circumspect, however, that there was nothing to justify public report of his treasures until the spy was sent to buy lead and quicksilver in quantities. The disguised doctor executed his commission with despatch and subsequently pierced a wall in his master's room, to watch what followed. He saw Butler remove something from a box, place it on molten lead, and then deposit the box in a secret place contrived in the floor. At this juncture the table and chair on which the doctor was mounted gave way, and the clatter of his fall brought Butler from his business. In this manner the false servant was discovered and was on the point of being despatched by his master's sword. The fact that he was spared or escaped did not prevent him denouncing Butler as a coiner, but a search of his premises discovered only a crucible : the apprehended alchemist was therefore set free.

So much by way of subsidiary examples, and it remains now to sum up. After making every allowance for that of Seton, corroborated by two witnesses, the one transmutation story which stands forth among all, and as if apart from all, is that of Helvetius. Unless we are prepared to say that he bore false testimony, the circumstantial account in *Vitulus*

[1] See *Lives of Alchemysticall Philosophers*, 1815.

Aureus is on the face of it irrefutable and can mean only that he who was neither alchemist nor believer in the Art as possible converted lead into gold, with the help of a powder obtained from an anonymous and unknown person, the nature of such powder being also unknown. In certain notes on his account I have shewn the difficulties, such as they are, which attach thereto: they are mainly matters of wording, questions of care in words. On the terms of the story no modern chemist can indicate any substance which added to molten lead in the proportion certified might have produced something which at the period would have passed as gold. The proportion was as a rape-seed is to half an ounce of lead. The product obtained stood the known tests of the seventeenth century and I do not infer that they would be challenged seriously now. More incredible perhaps than the transmutation itself is the statement that, weight for weight, there was more gold obtained than there was lead originally: what in such case was the density of that powder, in size as a seed of rape?

A conjuror's criticism will invoke an explanation from something corresponding to sleight of hand, when an adept operated himself, and we can suspect trickery of the kind in the case—say—of Edward Kelley; but a shorter and simpler way is to affirm that all accounts of transmutations are pure fiction, as to which I should spare none that—by any possibility—are open to this view—for example, the case of Butler. But if we accept the Helvetius story, it is obvious that we accept bodily the whole thesis of alchemical literature and history. It will follow, moreover, that at least several other accounts of metallic conversions which do not offer such a clear issue between affirmation and denial may be veridic also. The evidence of Van Helmont and Isaac of Holland belong to this category, but of the former more especially, whose testimony to repeated transmutations performed by himself is stronger as such than the one case of Helvetius but is minimised by its utter lack of detail. If cumulative evidence can be held to count for anything in such a subject, one would feel disposed to think that metallic transmutations have taken place in the past, though in any legal sense the best individual testimony—that of Helvetius—falls to the ground because it is uncorroborated.

Had the author of *Vitulus Aureus* possessed any notion of evidence and its scientific value, he would have operated in the presence of witnesses and taken their depositions. It must be admitted, however, that if this would have strengthened his case from the legal standpoint, it would have left him open to the charge of having tricked his audience. In other words, there is no way of demonstrating the truth of physical Alchemy on the faith of its witnesses, because —by its own hypothesis—the alleged science was secret and the cards were not on the table.

There are three things to be said in conclusion, and the last is personal to myself: (1) It is suggested from time to time that modern science is likely to end by transmuting metals, but it seems quite certain that this will not be accomplished through the addition of x, in size a coriander seed, to molten lead, in the proportion of six drachms. (2) On the hypothesis that Helvetius bore true testimony, within the measure of his abilities, on the bare point of fact, is there any scientist who can suggest any substance by which, bearing proportions in mind, molten lead could be given such an appearance that it would look like gold to careful or even casual observers of the past ? This question is asked because it has been alleged that the old operators were deceived by appearances in the work of their own hands, such appearances not corresponding, however, to surface tinctures. (3) In case any of my readers should desire to be acquainted with my own position, it is immaterial to me whether metallic transmutations took place in the past, except in the sense that its demonstration would add one more fascinating item to the " curious things of the outside world ". I am an old student of alchemical literature but am not on the quest in metals.

CHAPTER XXI

An Alchemist of Mitylene

JOHN FREDERICK HELVETIUS passed from this life in the year 1709, and it is impossible to say whether he had been preceded or not by the great professional alchemist Eirenæus Philalethes. Whether of adepts or witnesses in the forefront of ordinary physical science, no other voice arose sounding an authentic note in respect of metallic transmutation. Sincerus Renatus—*id est*, Sigmund Richter—was to issue in 1710 his *Perfect and True Preparation of the Philosophical Stone*; but this was according to the method of the Golden and Rosy Cross, and Rosicrucian Alchemy is not only least of all evidential but has some appearance, as we shall find, of belonging to another category. However this may be, Renatus has not been held to count except as marking a revival of the mysterious Hermetic Society.[1] The canon of Alchemy had of course by no means closed, and we shall come presently to its consideration from a new standpoint; but Eirenæus as a physical alchemist found no successor in literature, and no accountable person appeared after Helvetius to say that any particle of the Stone had come into his hands, but much less that it had been used by him to vindicate the validity of claims concerning it. There was destined, however, to be witnessing of another kind, a portent at least and a rumour which in some respects is stranger than anything that preceded, as if after all the theses and all the written testimonies, the matter of fact itself was to be paraded almost publicly before the face of the world.

The story of Lascaris has so much of the character and atmosphere belonging to a romance of occult history that one might be disposed to speculate whether it is not of fiction rather than of fact. There is no question about its decoration,

[1] See my *Brotherhood of the Rosy Cross*, c. xiv, *passim*.

especially in French hands,[1] but by reference to German sources [2] it becomes fairly clear that a mysterious adventurer was going about under this name in the early years of the eighteenth century, much as if he were the emissary of some Hidden House of Adeptship, House of the Rosy Cross or *Occlusum Regis Palatium*, commissioned to proclaim the Mystery of Hermes in the Teutonic Fatherland; but so only that he remained himself unknown. The last condition at least was fulfilled with such fidelity that his real name, age and place of birth, with all that concerns his private life, have eluded any research which has been attempted concerning them, somewhat far in the past. He is said to have adopted several appellations and to have claimed an oriental origin, but he spoke Greek fluently and—because of his chief alias—was rumoured to be a descendant of the Royal House of Lascaris.[3] He appears to have represented himself as archimandrite of a convent in the Island of Mitylene, but the story that he bore letters from the Greek Patriarch of Constantinople is probably invention. His mission in the West was ostensibly to solicit alms for the ransom of Christian prisoners in the East,[4] but there is no record that he pursued it, and no pretence could be more idle for those who can accept what is told of that which he carried in his wallet.

A man seemingly between forty and fifty years, he has been described as of attractive mien, agreeable in manner and fluent in conversation.[5] On one occasion, the date of which is uncertain, he either was or, for an ulterior reason, pretended to be indisposed at Berlin [6] and sent for a certain " apothecary ", who was unable to come in person but was represented by a pupil or apprentice at the bedside of the stranger. A sort of acquaintance sprang up between this

---

[1] The reference is to Louis Figuier and his work on *L'Alchimie et Les Alchimistes*, Paris, 1856. There were stories to tell, and they are told too often in the pseudo-historical manner.

[2] I refer more especially to Carl Christoph Schmieder's *Geschichte der Alchimie*, Halle, 1832, but there is something also in Siegmund Heinrich Güldenfalk's *Sammlung von mehr als hundert wahrhaften Transmutations geschicten*, etc., of 1784.

[3] An ancient Byzantine family, which gave two emperors to the Greek throne in the thirteenth century.

[4] It may have been one of the precautions which he took to conceal himself.

[5] The authority is Democritus Christianus, i.e., Johann Conrad Dippel, but I have failed to trace the reference, which is to *Aufrichtiger Protestant*, Berlin, 1733.

[6] Schmieder, *loc. cit.*, c. xv. The account of Figuier is taken so largely from this source that in many parts it is little more than translation and the debt should have been acknowledged.

Y

youth and Lascaris, for it transpired that the apothecary's assistant had read Basil Valentine and even attempted some experiments along lines laid down by this alchemical master. The putative patient recovered in due course, and on the eve of quitting Berlin the story is that he presented his attendant with a quantity of the Powder of Projection, imposing silence as to whence it was derived and forbidding the recipient to use it till a stated time after the donor's departure. For the rest, Lascaris affirmed that when unbelievers beheld its amazing virtues no one would be able to regard Alchemy as a delusive art.

The name of the young man who was thus dowered unwisely —though not perhaps by one who had no foresight—was John Frederick Bötticher, and intoxicated at the acquisition of the unexpected treasure, ready made and without labour, he determined to adopt Alchemy as his sole profession. The master-apothecary would have dissuaded him from a pursuit which he considered chimerical, but his assistant astonished him and his friends alike by producing gold from silver in their presence. The experiment was repeated with mercury for the pleasure of an acquaintance of Bötticher, after which there is no need to add that the news went round, till it is said that the apothecary's pupil became the lion of Berlin, above all as he circulated a report that he himself could compose the Philosophical Tincture. He was summoned by Frederic I, who desired to witness his performances ; but he had heard—it may be—how alchemists and their substitutes were apt to fare at the hands of royal patrons, and he fled to an uncle at Wittenburg. He was claimed from the authorities of that town as a Prussian subject, but he was now a prize of value : the Elector of Saxony put in a counter-claim for the care of his person, and Bötticher decided on proceeding to his court. He was welcomed warmly, and when his transmutations had been witnessed there was conferred on him the title of Baron : it was difficult to escape such honours in those days and places when gold gleamed in the crucible. He took up his residence at Dresden, living in a magnificent style till the Powder of Projection was expended to its last grain, when he was left saddled with debts, even to his servants, who are supposed to have spread a report of his intended flight. The Elector

declined to regard this sudden failure of resources as a proof
that Bötticher was unable to compose or augment the
Philosopher's Stone : his house was surrounded with guards,
with him imprisoned therein.[1] At this juncture Lascaris,
still errant in Germany, seems to have heard of the misfortunes
which had befallen his young neophyte in the merchandise
of Hermetic Mysteries, and he took some thought upon them.
He endeavoured also to extricate him from the embarrassing
position, not indeed by direct intervention but by means of
a tool in the person of a young doctor named Pasch, who was
a personal friend of the ennobled apothecary's boy.[2] Their
manœuvres resulted in the imprisonment of Pasch at the
fortress of Sonnenstein,[3] while the Castle of Kœnigstein put
an end to the adventures of Bötticher for the time being.
Two and a half years passed away, and then Pasch succeeded
in making an escape at the cost of his limbs : he died a few
months later, complaining bitterly that the adept Lascaris
had deserted him in the hour of peril.[4] Bötticher remained
in confinement, with every opportunity afforded to compose
the Stone of the Wise, which however he failed to accomplish.
But between his apothecary's training and his prison researches
he had become skilled in several branches of chemistry. He
discovered a process for producing red porcelain and white
somewhat later, both superior in quality to the substances
then passing under those names. The avaricious potentate
was enriched by these inventions, if they did not produce
the illimitable wealth suggested by the White and Red
Tinctures. Bötticher was restored to his favour and again
enjoyed his baronial title ; but he returned in his liberty to
luxurious and extravagant ways : as he expended the Powder

[1] The account of Figuier may be compared with that of Schmieder, the matter
being identical in both and the arrangement varied only. For example, Figuier
having mentioned Bötticher at the beginning of his story of Lascaris transfers the
account of his adventures to a separate and much later section, rather to the
disadvantage of both narratives.

[2] Pasch was a little dubious about the success of his commission and especially
regarding a ransom of 800,000 ducats which Lascaris was willing to furnish for the
liberation of Bötticher; but he was convinced when a transmutation was performed
by the adept in his presence.

[3] At the same place and much about the same time the strange semi-mystical
Hermetist who wrote Mystère de la Croix and is said to have been named Douzetemps
tells us that he suffered imprisonment, but without stating the reason.

[4] Lascaris had promised to make him as rich as Bötticher, if he could deliver
the latter.

of Projection previously, so now he expended life itself, with the result that he died in 1719 at the age of thirty-seven.[1]

Bötticher was by no means the only youth or the only apothecary's pupil who was enriched by the Powder of Lascaris and despatched to preach the Gospel of Alchemy with practical demonstrations. Godwin Hermann Braun and Martin of Fitzlar are mentioned among uninitiated messengers who shone till their stock-in-trade was exhausted and then passed out of view.[2] In the meantime Lascaris himself was not idle. On February 16th, 1709, he is believed to have changed mercury into gold and gold into silver, a double transmutation which has been held to signify a very rare grade of mastery. Liebknackt, Counsellor of Wertherbourg, is cited as a witness of this achievement.[3] In the same year a goldsmith of Leipsic [4] was visited by a mysterious stranger who is identified with Lascaris and who showed him a lingot which is declared to have been manufactured by art and which proved in assaying to be gold of twenty-two carats. It was purified by the goldsmith with antimony and part of it was presented to him by the unknown, as a memorial of the event.[5]

At no long time after a lieutenant-colonel in the Polish army, whose name was Baron Schmolz von Dierbach, having inherited from his father a belief in alchemical Art, was talking on the subject at a café,[6] when he was accosted by a stranger who gave him presently some Powder of Projection —for there was much largesse in those days. It was of a red colour and a microscopic examination revealed its crystalline nature.[7] It increased the weight of metals in

---

[1] Schmieder's authority for the misfortunes of Pasch is J. C. Dippel, in the work already cited. See also Güldenfalk, *loc. cit.*, c. liii, pp. 79–91.

[2] See Schmieder, *loc. cit.*, pp. 479, 480.

[3] *Ibid.*, p. 481. Schmieder, citing Struve : *Bibliotheca Antiqua*, pp. 163 *et seq.*

[4] That is, Georg Stolle. I do not know why Schmieder produces this story as there is no evidence that the stranger was in fact the adept Lascaris or that the lingot was gold obtained by way of transmutation.

[5] That is, two out of seven circular pieces into which the lingot was cut by the stranger's order. They are said to have been inscribed thus : *Tu Alpha et Omega vitæ spes es post mortem* ♄ *revivificatio* ☉ ☽ ; and *O unicus amor Dei in Trinitate miserere mei in æternitate. Per* ♆ ♀ ☿ *fit Lapis Philosophorum.* As it is not said that the lingot was itself inscribed with sentences which could be preserved intact after cutting, it seems obvious that Georg Stolle must have been responsible for their presence in the case of his own coins.

[6] At Lissa.

[7] The authority throughout is Dippel.

transmutation to an extent which hostile criticism declares impossible. The recipient made use of his gift generously, distributing to friends and acquaintances the gold produced by projection. Here also the undeclared donor is identified in the imagination of German writers with the mysterious Lascaris, who in the same anonymous and unaccountable manner is supposed to have enriched the Baron de Creux with a box of the precious substance and to have gratified the Hermetic aspirations of the Landgrave of Hesse Darms- stadt—Ernst Ludwig—through the simple medium of the post.[1] In a word, every unidentified adept who appeared at this period, in or about Germany, is supposed to have been the alleged Greek Archimandrite of a convent in Mitylene.[2]

The too facile method of attribution involves, however, an earlier activity on the part of Lascaris, the first of whose debtors or victims is supposed to have been Domenico Manuel—son of a Neopolitan goldsmith—who was put in possession of a small quantity of White and Red Tinctures under mysterious circumstances in the year 1695.[3] As it was not sufficient to enrich him by the process of simple conversion, he decided to trade after another and more cautious manner ; and he is said to have obtained large sums from wealthy amateurs for the privilege of witnessing the consummation of the Great Work. When it is to be presumed that he had offered evidence enough in Italy, he travelled through Spain, Belgium and Austria, plying the same business but now claiming that he could prepare the Stone himself.[4] In this manner he imposed on the Emperor Leopold and the Palatine Elector, as well as on private persons. In different places he assumed names that were different : now he was Count Gaetano, now Count de Ruggino : at other times he called himself Field Marshal to the Duke of Bavaria, Commandant of Munich, a Prussian Major-General, and so forth. In 1705 he appeared at Berlin, where he hoodwinked the Prussian King, but only for a brief period : he failed in

---

[1] Güldenfalk pp. 285–287.
[2] That is the feeling of Figuier and is given less or more in his words.
[3] Schmieder, pp 484–487, citing Dippel. Compare Figuier, pp. 332–339. It does not appear where he received the gifts, nor where he charged fees for exhibiting his experiments, as he is said simply to have been on his travels through Italy.
[4] The Spanish Ambassador at the Court of Vienna is said to have accused him in public of stealing fifteen thousand piastres from the Ambassador's cousin.

ratifying his covenants to transmute metals and as this constituted treason, by the hypothesis of Prussian royalty, he was hanged on August 29th, 1709, *ad majorem Regis gloriam*.[1]

As an illustration of the involved stories which may be found in the byways of transmutation there is that of the rustic Delisle.[2] We must begin by supposing an anonymous personality believed to be in possession of the Philosopher's Stone, somewhere in Provence. He took into his service the rustic, who became in this manner acquainted with alchemical experiments; but the operations are described vaguely as falling under suspicion, and the adept had to leave France. At the next stage of events he had retired into Switzerland accompanied by Delisle, who is held to have assassinated him in the mountains and to have obtained in this manner a considerable quantity of transmuting powder. However this may be, the rustic returned to France —in disguise, as it is said—and about the year 1708 attracted general attention by changing lead and iron into silver and gold. He travelled through Languedoc, the Dauphiné and his own Provence, meeting at Sisteron with the wife of a certain Aluys, and she appears to have shared his fortune for the space of three years, during which his notoriety increased, owing to the simplicity of his methods. He spread powder and oil over iron, thrust it into the fire, and that which came forth therefrom was a bar of gold. He distributed nails, knives and rings in a state of partial transmutation and was successful also in experiments with common steel. How he profited by these proceedings and how he subsisted otherwise are matters belonging to the story behind the story.

[1] I have shortened this account considerably, for it is that of a mere knave who had learned a few devices as a goldsmith's apprentice. So far as evidence goes, there is not the least reason, to suppose that he had ever met with Lascaris or any other adept, but much less that he had received a gift of Tinctures. The latter claim would be transparently his own invention and his transmutations a conjuror's tricks. It may be mentioned that he was imprisoned for two years at Grünerwold in Bavaria by the elector Maximilian Emmanuel. He succeeded in convincing Dippel by changing mercury into silver. See Schmieder, pp. 486, 487, and Guldenfalk c. lv.

[2] The authorities are Lenglet de Fresnoy in his *Histoire de la Philosophie Hermétique*, ii, pp. 68–98; Schmieder, *loc. cit.*, pp. 502–506; and Louis Figuier, *loc. cit.*, pp. 317 *et seq.*, who draws from both. Schmieder supposes that the mysterious figure of Lascaris stood behind the philosoper of Provence, who was only a recipient of the tinctures from the Greek Archimandrite.

There came a day when some old gentleman—named M. de la Palud—offered Delisle a retreat in his own chateau, where the supposed alchemist, surrounded by admirers, received daily visits from the curious. But over and above these there was the Bishop of Senez,[1] and he appointed Cerisy, Prior of Chateauneuf,[2] to collect evidence for the truth or otherwise of the marvels. We do not hear how he fared, but the Bishop wrote ultimately to the Minister of State and Comptroller General of the Treasury at Paris, giving account of things heard and seen, affirming his initial scepticism and present inability to resist the evidence of actual transmutation performed in his own presence and before other vigilant witnesses, who took every precaution against deception. There is further a Report of M. de Saint-Maurice, President of the Mint at Lyons, who testifies to the following points : (1) That he was accompanied by Delisle into the grounds of the Chateau de Saint Auban in May, 1710, where he uncovered a basket buried in the earth; (2) that in the middle of this basket there was an iron wire, at the end of which there was something wrapped in linen; (3) that he took possession of the bundle, carried it into the dining room of the Chateau, and by the direction of Delisle exposed its contents—a blackish earth, about half a pound in weight—to the solar rays; (4) that after fifteen minutes the earth was distilled in a retort over a portable furnace; (5) that when a yellow liquor began to flow into the receiver, Delisle recommended the removal of the recipient before a viscous oil, then rising, should enter therein; (6) that two drops of this yellow liquor, projected on hot quicksilver, produced in fusion three ounces of gold, which were presented to the Master of the Mint; (7) that subsequently three ounces of pistol bullets were melted and purified with alum and saltpetre; (8) that Delisle handed Saint-Maurice a small paper, desiring him to throw in a pinch of its powder-content and two drops of the oil used in the first experiment; (9) that this admixture was covered with saltpetre, kept in fusion for fifteen minutes

---

[1] He is said to have been an eye-witness—*a vu toutes ces choses de ses propres yeux*—and so describes himself.

[2] The correspondence which arose in this manner is printed by Lenglet du Fresnoy—*loc. cit.*—and reprinted by Figuier. It gives a graphic account of Delisle and his performances, one of the stories affirming that his chief ingredients were derived from the plants known as *Lunaria major et minor*.

and then poured on a piece of iron armour ; and finally (10) that the said armour became pure gold, bearing all assays. A conversion into silver was performed in the same manner with white powder, the Report which testifies to these occurrences being signed officially on December 14th, 1710.[1] Part of the gold supposed to have been made by Delisle was refined, it is said, at Paris, three medals being struck from it : one of them was placed in the King's cabinet and bore the inscription : *Aurum Arte Factum.*[2]

His seeming alchemical skill notwithstanding, Delisle was unable to read or write, besides being rude, untractable and fanatical in disposition. He was invited to Court but pretended that the climate in which he lived was essential to the success of his experiments, as his preparations were vegetable. The Bishop of Senez suspected him of unwillingness rather than inability, endured his subterfuges for the space of two years and then obtained a *lettre de cachet*, which led to the arrest of the alchemist. On the road to Paris his guards endeavoured to extort his supposed riches and wounded him severely in the head. He arrived at the Bastille in this state and was compelled to start alchemical operations but soon refused to proceed, tore off his bandages, and finally poisoned himself in the following year.

His illegitimate son, *sub nomine* Aluys, is supposed to have inherited some of the powder from his mother. He wandered through Italy and Germany, performing transmutations. On one occasion he made projection before the Duc de Richelieu, then French Ambassador at Vienna, who assured Lenglet du Fresnoy that he not only saw the said operation performed but operated himself, producing gold on two occasions and silver forty times.[3] Aluys is said to have made a considerable collection of gold coins, ancient and modern, during a journey through Austria and Bohemia. At Aix,

[1] It is given *in extenso* by Lenglet du Fresnoy and Figuier.
[2] This is on the authority of Du Fresnoy. Altogether it seems tolerably clear that the Provençal rustic was in possession of a Tincture which no common art could have furnished—either of his own or another's. I do not know why he is termed continually an impostor by Figuier. If we sift the available evidence, we know only that he produced either veritable conversions of lead and steel into gold or else alloys which deceived the Mint at Lyons. How he came by his Tincture is another question, the murder story being without anything to support it, that of the philosopher whom he served being possibly his own invention to confuse inquiry, and that of Lascaris no better than speculation.
[3] *Histoire de la Philosophie Hermétique,* ii. 98–103.

on a certain occasion, he presented himself to the President of Provence, who desired him to call again on the following day ; but suspecting a design to arrest him Aluys fled in the interim. Later on he was imprisoned at Marseilles but escaped and reached Brussels. It was here, in 1731, that he gave Philosophical Mercury to M. Percell, the brother of Lenglet du Fresnoy, and though the recipient fermented it imperfectly he succeeded so far as to convert an ounce of silver into gold. The death of a certain M. Grefier shortly after some operations on corrosive sublimate, by which Aluys proposed to instruct him in Alchemy, compelled the latter to depart, and he was heard of no more.

There are other stories of unknown persons in possession of supposed or veritable transmuting powders in the generation and day of Lascaris, and therefore identified either with himself or with his emissaries. The stranger who called on the Baron de Creuz at Hamburg in 1715 and left some of it behind him ; the fugitive who took refuge with a Countess d'Erbach at her castle in the Odenworld, to escape the Palatine Elector, and changed her household silver into gold, in recognition of her hospitality ; the anonymous adept who made gold on three occasions in the presence of J. G. Joch, an amateur of Dortmund, *anno* 1720 ; that other Master of Art who had the Red and White Tinctures and performed a transmutation at Amsterdam in the presence of Democritus Christianus, afterwards cutting up the product to shew that his copper had been changed into gold within, not merely tinctured without [1] ; and finally the anonymous unknown who reached Vienna in July, 1716, convoked notable persons in the palace of the commandant and changed copper coins into silver by making them red-hot, putting powder upon them and plunging them into an unknown liquid.[2]

It will be seen in this manner that the chequered canvas of alchemical history presents at one time the portrait of a prodigal adept who distributes transmuting powder with a free hand to novices and almost boys, but at another the

---

[1] The copper was changed into silver by means of the White Tincture and then into gold with the Red. The account is second-hand, as in the absence of J. K. Dippel's *Aufrichtiger Protestant*, 1733, I have derived from Figuier, who gives no date for the occurrence.

[2] The full minutes of the proceedings were drawn up by Councillor W. P. Pantyzer of Hesse and are given by Schmieder in full.

mere shadow of a master in the background of the picture, while in front is one who possesses the Stone either as his heir or otherwise, including acts of theft. It looks sometimes as if the manifest user had invented a concealed master the better to dissemble his own knowledge. A possible case in point is Richthausen, of Vienna, behind whom stands the alleged adept Busardier,[1] who is said to have lived at Prague with a certain lord of the Court.[2] There came a time when. Busardier fell sick and feeling his end at hand he wrote to his supposed friend, Richthausen, begging him to come that he might receive from him the Stone in person, and be present during his last moments. The latter set out at once, but when he reached Prague it was to learn that the adept was no more, and inquiry elicited that he had left nothing behind him but certain powder which the Court noble seemed anxious to preserve but which his steward, who gave the information, did not know how to use. Richthausen, however, had apparently learned what he wanted and managed moreover to secure the powder, after which he departed. But the nobleman heard of the transaction and threatened to hang his steward if he did not recover the treasure. The latter pursued Richthausen, judging that he was the culprit, overtook him on the road and presented a pistol at his head, swearing that he would shoot him if he did not give back the powder. Richthausen complied in order to save his life,. but he had prepared apparently for the event and a substantial part of the treasure remained in his hands.[3]

This is the first act of the drama, and it bears all marks of fiction. In the second Richthausen is at Prague, professing Alchemy at the Court of the Emperor Ferdinand III, who called in the aid of his mine-master, Count Russe, and, taking every precaution, made projection himself with some of the abstracted powder. It is said that a single grain sufficed

[1] Otherwise Labujardière according to Figuier, but evidently a misreading of La Busardier, the variant of Schmieder. This story begins prior to 1650.

[2] The earliest account with which I am acquainted is in a work under the pseudonym of Chymiphili, entitled *Offenbarung Chymischer Weisheit*, published at Nuremberg in 1720. See *cap.* lxvii. The story is retold by Schmieder and borrowed from him by Figuier, who had recourse also to other sources, of which there are several.

[3] This is in one account, but others say that he retained the whole treasure and surrendered a worthless substitute; in either case the supposed steward might have done more wisely.

to convert three pounds of mercury into gold, thus exhibiting
" the force of this tincture as 1 upon 19,470 ". It is affirmed
further that the Emperor caused a medal to be struck,
bearing on the obverse an effigy of Apollo holding the caduceus
and inscribed with the motto : *Divina metamorphosis exhibita
Praguæ, Jan. 15, anno 1648, in præsentia Sac. Cæs. Majest.
Ferdinandi Tertii.* The reverse bore another inscription,
namely : *Raris hæc ut hominibus est ars ; ita raro in lucem
prodit, laudetur Deus in æternum, qui partem suæ infinitæ
potentiæ novis suis abjectissimis creaturis communicat.*

Richthausen is represented as being ennobled by the
fantastic title of Baron Chaos, and this—so far as I have
traced—is properly the end of his story, which may signify
that he passed his remaining days in ease and not in the
persecution which befell alchemists so often at the hands of
royal masters.   We hear indeed that other transmutations
were performed with the same powder, but I will cite one
only, which belongs to the year 1651, when the Elector of
Mayence is supposed to have made projection under the
immediate auspices of Baron Chaos, possibly at that place,
possibly otherwhere.   An unspecified quantity was enclosed
in gum tragacanth and put into the wax of a taper, which was
lighted, and placed at the bottom of a crucible. These preparations were made by the Elector himself, who afterwards
poured four ounces of quicksilver into the vessel and set
it in a charcoal fire by which it was entirely surrounded.
They began blowing to the utmost and on raking off the
coals in about half an hour, the content of the vessel proved
to be " over red, the proper colour being green ". When the
Baron said that the matter was yet too high and that silver
must be added, the Elector took coins from his pocket,
which were liquefied and then combined with the substance
in the crucible. When this was in perfect fusion it was poured
into a lingot and, after cooling, proved to be very fine gold,
but rather hard.   After a second liquefaction " it became
exceedingly soft, and the master of the mint declared to his
highness that it was more than twenty-four carats and that
he had never seen so fine a quality of the precious metal ".

An end may be made of the stories at this point, it being
understood that many are omitted, and we may look back now
upon the theses out of which our inquiry has originated.

All Alchemy testifies to the fact that the so-called Philosopher's Stone was a physical object composed of certain material substances by those who had claims to adeptship and certified otherwise as such by persons who had seen and handled it. Moreover, those who made it are never backward in telling us the ingredients of which it is fabricated, though they bear their " faithful witness " from a chair of camouflage, rather than the chair of truth. Now, it is possible to grind individual Stones in the mill of destructive criticism and scatter them as fine dust ; but there is remarkable cumulative evidence that a Stone was going about in the fifteenth, sixteenth and seventeenth centuries, and more ostentatiously still from the period of Seton to that of Lascaris. As according to the records it was a physical object, so that which it effected was the physical transmutation of metals : it was done in laboratories and palaces by unknown superiors and those who had abstracted or received in deed of gift a portion of that Powder of Projection which *en masse* is termed the Stone. It follows that metallic conversions—if any—were not performed by Magic : on specific occasions they were accomplished, under direction, by persons who knew nothing of the Art, had never seen the tingeing substance previously and never saw it again. For the same kind of reason it was not effected by the powers of the soul in man : it was done by apothecary boys, if they had a piece of the Stone. When it is called from time immemorial a Stone and not a stone, it does not mean that the use of this word is to be understood symbolically, as if it were the Stone Which is Christ or the mystic cube with a New Name written therein. It was not a stone, in the sense that it was neither flint nor granite, neither pebble nor marble, but a moderately concrete mass of dry powder which could be broken up with the hand and scraped with the finger-nail.

The story is that particles so detached were competent in a due proportion to transmute metals. Now no substance known to modern science is capable of communicating, e.g., to lead, a fallacious appearance of solid gold, except by way of plating, and still less is there any which can produce gold from lead. If ever the Stone existed a question arises therefore as to how it was made. If anyone cares to cite the case recorded by Kircher, in which the materials were revealed in dream,

I care nothing, for the point still to be determined is what the materials were. It remains also if another prefers to say that they were communicated to earnest seekers by God Himself, because such is the witness borne in numbers of the old records. The meaning, of course is that, like the Scholar Gipsy, they " waited for the spark from heaven to fall ", the sudden inspiration towards right procedure. On the claims of Paracelsus and Böhme it is sufficient to say that the records in both cases are against them, each and all. Yet if Magic could make the Stone, or the Grace of God abiding, there arises yet and again the unescapable question, on what did the sorcery work, or what was " the dark, disesteemed " substance, " of a grey colour " into which the regenerated soul, *Deo adjuvante,* infused the tingeing power ?   It has not been suggested so far by any zealous disciple of " the noble and beloved monarch " that *Abracadabra* in its efficient pronunciation will convert lead into gold, nor has any scholiast on the *Suggestive Inquiry* as yet intimated that the *Epiclesis* Clause in the mouth of one who is reborn will manifest *Aurum Fluddanum,* a Gold of God, visibly and materially to eyes and hands of sense. The proper characterisation of such views would be in terms corresponding to the diagnosis of Bedlam states. For the rest, it happens that in their moderation and sanity Alchemy according to the alchemists was a work of Art, however essential it was that " the spark from heaven " should fall or a master alternatively should appear and teach.

CHAPTER XXII

The Mystic Side of Alchemy

I HAVE spoken of new voices which began to be uplifted soon after the Reformation of Luther had become an accomplished fact : they were voices of a new spirit making its presence known, as if a gate had opened suddenly on new paths of doctrine or a sealed fountain had been loosened and its figurative waters were flowing through many minds of the age. I trust that this imagery will not suffer confusion or give birth thereto. If we care to affirm that the Reformation was itself a light, it was stained and clouded ; if we think that it made for liberation, it was more especially the freedom to forge new chains and bonds ; if we look to the land of reform for the fruits it bore, we shall find that the period which intervened between the death of Luther and the Thirty Years' War was filled in the German Fatherland with a raging strife of sects. It would seem that the Holy Scriptures had come into the hands of everyone only to beget chaos : prophets, reformers and zealots sprang up on every side ; and perhaps the most sorry cohort in all the fustian pageant was that which fell a prey to Second Advent mania, seeing portents in stars of heaven and omens innumerable in imagined meteors of mind. I am presumably the only person in English-speaking countries who has seen with his own eye the *Naometria* of Simon Studion [1]—from the date of its completion in 1604 to this present day of grace ; and that unprinted document offers unawares an eloquent picture of its epoch, the spirit and mentality of which are reproduced and sometimes exaggerated in printed works by the score : a madder world, my masters, there never was through all the Christian centuries.[2]

---

[1] *Brotherhood of the Rosy Cross*, c. ii and Appendices.

[2] We may take Valentine Weigel and Ægidius Gutmann as typical cases in point on the side of their extravagance ; but there are many others. Perhaps indeed it is scarcely fair to quote them, for they are not so open to the charge of irredeemable dullness which characterised the general mania.

But there were also some great lights and by contrast with those about him, from his birth even to his death, I suppose that Jacob Böhme was a luminary of the first magnitude, who might also shine largely in this our own hour, could he be stripped of his ill-made vestures. We have seen that he belongs to Alchemy as one who unfolds a deep searching concerning its path and terms, as one who had quick things and pregnant to present upon it, though in a particular direction he offered a fantastic key. From that time onward there are evidences of a change which came over the literature and grew from more to more. It becomes increasingly difficult to determine the real purport of certain texts, and I have spoken at some length of one which, a little prior to the epoch of Böhme, had set a new fashion of consideration in which Alchemy was transfigured and became a Spiritual Mystery, the more remarkable because he who performed the work was himself a physical alchemist in the practical sense and not in hypothesis only, like the Teutonic theosophist. I refer of course to Khunrath, and in this connection it should be added that we need a critical examination of his writings outside the famous *Amphitheatre of Eternal Wisdom*.

The new spirit, if it may be so called correctly, reflected somewhat into the later memorials of physical Alchemy, into the records of Michael Maier, into those even which pass under the names of Sendivogius and Eirenæus Philalethes, while Thomas Vaughan, who figures almost unconditionally on the arch-natural if not the mystical side, was drawn persistently by the work on metals, much as he condemned it with his lips. In this manner he recalls his contemporary Elias Ashmole, who knew enough to hold his tongue but, on his own confession, not enough to speak, who was therefore by profession an amateur as regards the Art, an antiquary and editor as regards some of its memorials. We know, however, that he was more than this, for he believed himself to have received from an adept and his individual master the secret of the Great Work.[1] Whether on the basis of this revelation or from other sources, he was of opinion that the making of gold is " the chief intent " of the alchemist, but that it is

---

[1] I have quoted otherwise the supposed *Memoirs*, being the *Diary* of Ashmole, and its references to the alchemist William Backhouse.

" the lowest use . . . made of this *materia* ".[1] He recognised indeed four aspects or kinds of Philosophical Stone, being (1) mineral, (2) vegetable, (3) magical, (4) angelical, though he offers no intimations as to the nature and offices of the last three. The question does not signify in any manner that can be called essential, but the implicits of his enumeration have been set out fully elsewhere on my own part.[2] Those who know Ashmole will be aware that a mystical understanding of Alchemy lay far beyond his measures, that his notion of magic would correspond broadly to the occult philosophy of Cornelius Agrippa, while that which he terms angelical would answer to communion with spirits. Behind both theses there lay modes of practice, of which the *Heptameron* and *Arbatel* are examples in the one case, while the crystal seerings of Dee and Kelley are instances ready to our hand in the other. We are confronted therefore by a thesis that there was for Ashmole (1) a method of transmuting metals, corresponding to the symbolism of a Mineral Stone; (2) a way of preparing a secret Medicine of men, otherwise an Elixir of Life, which he terms the Vegetable Stone; (3) a psychic faculty which was exercised in the business of magic; and (4) a closely related faculty which opened to those who were prepared the world of unseen intelligences. The last may or may not have belonged to crystal gazing, for as everyone knows the gift of clairvoyance is evoked in many ways. His use of the term Stone to characterise each division of his subject is obviously a symbolism borrowed from metallic Alchemy. He would mean in this case the Powder of Projection; he may have regarded the Vegetable Elixir as also in a dry form; his Stone of Magic may have belonged to the old theory of talismans; while the Angelical Stone was a figurative method of presenting the all and sundry devices for the induction of lucid vision.

I have surveyed the Ashmole thesis from a point of view which may be called intelligible, comparatively speaking at least: it will be understood readily by those who are acquainted with occult literature, with Gaffarel and his " unheard of curiosities " concerning the Talismanic Magic

---

[1] Compare *Fama Fraternitatis R∴C∴*, which counted the Medicine of Metals as least among the treasures in their Holy House of Initiation.

[2] *New Encyclopædia of Freemasonry*, vol. i, pp. 359, 360.

of the Persians, with the clouded wells of *Philosophia Sagax*, discovered and sounded by Paracelsus, with the vast record of Dee's *Faithful Relation* of dealings with highly supposititious angels, as seen in the crystal and heard *ex hypothesi* in some psychic state developed in the course of the visions. They will understand so well that none of them will need to be told of the insensate folly which sought to establish relations between things like these and the Philosophical Stone of Alchemy. It was, however, a day of such marriages, and there is no other way in which the Oxford virtuoso and antiquary could have understood his own story. Mrs. Atwood knew him well enough and was not restrained as a rule by normal considerations belonging to the law of probabilities; but even she did not venture to suggest that his Four Stones were one quadripartite, emblematic and mystical *Lapis* resident in his own regenerate nature and variously projected to perform the psychical conversion of physical metals; to produce "a potent spiritual medicine" for material body and mind; to contemplate hidden cosmic virtues and adapt them magically to the will and purpose of adeptship; to open in fine the inward eye of the higher mind, that it might contemplate the Divine in the universe and be joined therewith.[1]

Poor Ashmole, eaten up with aches and pains, quarrelling with Lady Manwaring, feasting with astrologers, attending Masons' Hall and ever—like Anthony Wood—hungering after antiquities, would have been dismayed indeed at the suggestion of such possible powers within his weakly frame and not too brilliant head. But he knew Cornelius Agrippa and the forged "fourth book", which most probably he thought genuine; he knew about talismanic magic and modes without end of divination, not excepting perhaps the *Verus Jesuitarum Libellus*, if it belonged to that date. He had edited—as we have seen—alchemical poets, and William Backhouse—a little later on—divulged to him his personal notion on the First Matter of Alchemy. He had listened not only with great reverence but with a believing heart, and he did—nothing. When he testified therefore concerning four manners of Stone, his meaning lay within the measures

---

[1] We have seen indeed that Ashmole is never mentioned in the *Suggestive Inquiry* except as editing *Theatrum Chemicum Britannicum*.

of his book-knowledge and reflections thereupon. It is
of no consequence whatever, except as illustrating the change
which had come over the mind of reverie in its concern for
the Great Work : it could not dispense with Alchemy,
it would not set aside the evidence of valid transmutations
operated in the realm of metals ; but it could do no longer
with the subject as this came down from the past, in part
because it was brought up always against an unscaleable
wall, and in part because for many there seemed much
ado about little in the making of gold.

We have to ascertain now whether there were directions
in which this spirit unfolded further ; but I propose in the
first place to glance at a text belonging to the early seventeenth
century and one of many that illustrate the difficulties
besetting our path of investigation. It deals with the Great
Work and it exhibits—as it seems to me—in an eminent degree
the fact that alchemists were not less concerned at times—and
indeed often—with the investigation of physical secrets because
they appear to approach them as if they were Mysteries of
the Soul and God : those who have held otherwise have
applied a false canon of criticism in the majority of cited
cases, if not indeed in all. We may take an example from the
famous *Arcanum* of John d'Espagnet, which proceeds as
follows : " The light of this knowledge is the gift of God,
which by His freeness He bestoweth upon whom He pleaseth [1] :
let none then set himself to the study hereof until, having
cleared and purified his heart, he be devoted wholly unto
God and emptied of all affection to things impure. Those
that are in public honours and offices, or are ever busied with
private and necessary occupations, let them not strive to
attain the top of this philosophy, for it requireth the whole
man, and being found possesseth him, and being possessed
challengeth him from all long and serious employments,
esteeming all other things as strange unto him and of no
value. [2] Let him that is desirous of this knowledge clear

[1] In the same manner *The New Light of Alchemy*, ascribed to Sendivogius,
declares that " the most commendable Art of Alchemy is the gift of God and
truly is not to be attained but by the alone favour of God enlightening the understanding, together with a patient and devout humility, or by an ocular demonstration from some experienced master."

[2] If, however, the Art is that of the search after God and His righteousness, as
proposed by Hitchcock, there is no person in his senses, and much less one who is
experienced in the quest, that will recommend the man of affairs or the bread-
winner to put it away from his thoughts.

his mind from all evil notions, especially pride, which is abomination to heaven and the gate of hell. Let him be frequent at prayers and charitable, have little to do with the world, abstain from over much company—keeping and enjoying constant tranquillity, that the mind may be able to reason more freely in private and be more highly lifted up. For unless it be kindled with a beam of Divine Light it will be hardly able to penetrate the hidden mysteries of truth." The Masters of Spiritual Life know well enough that its attainments are not the reward of reason but of utter dedication in abiding love, and he proceeds to make plain the kind of work on the darkness of which he looks for a light from heaven to fall. " A studious tyro of quick wit, constant mind, inflamed with the love of philosophy, acute in *philosophia naturalis*, of a pure heart, perfect in manner and mightily devoted to God may enter with confidence the highway of Nature and peruse the best philosophers, even though ignorant of chemistry." [1] The meaning is obvious, namely, that he will learn his chemistry as he goes, though it might be better if he had been grounded previously. Were he about to be engaged on the antithesis of physical work, it would be ridiculous to introduce the reference.[2]

The final instructions to the neophyte are (1) to seek out an ingenious companion and not despair of his desire ; (2) to read but few of the philosophers, choosing those of note and experience ; (3) to suspect things that are understood quickly, since truth lies in obscurity, and the wise never write more " deceitfully " than when their words are plain, nor more veridically than when their words are dark. The last caution is repeated from mouth to mouth through all generations of Alchemy, the loosely thinking and loosely talking *Adepti* failing to perceive that if they were taken according to the literal sense, it would follow that they were commending their pupils to *diabolus* when it was proposed

---

[1] The seventeenth century translation which has served my purpose in the text may be compared with the original, which says : *licet chemicæ praxeos ignarus*. It follows that a certain hindrance is implied by the want of knowledge but is not insuperable.

[2] Hitchcock goes utterly astray in his understanding of this passage. According to his *Remarks*, the operation is obviously not physical, the reason given begging the point at issue, namely, that the chief instrument of Alchemy is determined and concentrated thinking on the highest intellectual planes. It is nothing of the kind if the work is physical, and it is nothing of the kind also if the work is mystical, for man does not by concentrated thinking find out God.

that they should be dedicated to God and that the order of their particular recommendation on obscurity and plainness must itself call to be reversed.

There is one further citation which may be offered at the moment, for a reason that will appear in its place. " Whosoever attempteth the search of our Glorious Stone, he ought in the first place to implore the assistance of the all-powerful Jehovah, at the throne of His mercy." The explanation might well be that the Stone of the Wise is no other than the White Stone with a new name written thereon, *Lapis Dei et Christi*, and the Mystic Head of the Corner. But the instruction proceeds to explain that Jehovah is " the true and sole Author of all Mysteries of Nature ", presumably as of those which belong to the World of Grace. He is " the Monarch of heaven and earth, the King of kings, omnipotent, most true and most wise ". But, coming to the question in hand, He " not only maketh manifest in the microcosm " —that is to say in the mind of man—" the truth of every science to worthy philosophers, and liberally bestoweth both natural and divine knowledge on the deserving and faithful, but also layeth open his treasures of wealth and riches, which are locked up in the abyss of Nature, to those who devoutly worship Him." It looks therefore as if Alchemy were an Art of securing material wealth by the Law of Grace, as if those who led the kind of devotional life should be those to know of the doctrine taught by Hermes concerning the work of Nature in mines and of Secret Art in crucibles. The quest in any case is one of work in Nature, not in the Secret Temple of the Soul and not in the Hidden Divinity. The text goes on : " Forasmuch as none is permitted to touch the Mysteries of Nature with foul fingers, therefore it behoveth all who attempt such matters to lay aside their natural blindness, from which they may be freed by the light of Holy Scripture and a steadfast faith, this being the means by which the Holy Spirit doth clearly make manifest the most profoundly hidden light of Nature, which light alone lays open the way to the Wisdom of Nature and to unlock the most abstruse mysteries thereof." It is yet and again and for ever the one old theosophy : " Seek first the Kingdom of God and His Justice, and all other things shall be added unto you," not excepting the Philosopher's Stone.

The *Arcanum* of D'Espagnet is a post-Reformation document and it illustrates the deepening sense of spiritual things on the part of physical alchemists. But we have seen from the beginning of our research that in the view of the whole Art, considered in all its stages, an undevout alchemist was like the undevout astronomer of Young's *Night Thoughts*, or at least that, if he was not mad, he was remote from any path which led to attainment. The issue in most cases was exceedingly simple. Those who sought to penetrate the Great Secret by the unaided work of their hands, following the light of such text-books as were available in their day and generation, could succeed only in so far as their understandings were opened, because it was certain and foredetermined by their own testimony that *Secretum Artis* was not put into writing by any philosophers, and that " the blind work in metals " was not of itself likely to open the eyes of anyone. The " truth of the Art " was to be proved in some other manner : many would call it now the leading of a happy guess-work, but I have quoted preferably on my own part " the spark from heaven " of Arnold. The working of such an inward light was recognised on every hand, and it was termed Light of God. Those who would deserve it must live in the sense of that light, must qualify for its reception, or it would never dawn within them.

I speak in the spirit of that faith which ruled in ages of faith ; but over and above this there was the issue which belongs to communication, the transmission of an operative secret through the centuries. It proceeded from spiritual father to spiritual son, or such is the inference concerning it, for there is no trace—so far as I am able to see—of anything which would answer to a notion of corporate adeptship in the old records anywhere, except within those narrow measures of hypothetical possibility which have been set out in my prefatory words. The cases of an adept choosing his heir are few and far between ; but it is evident that when the right was exercised there was great care in selection. It accounts presumably for the recurring affirmation, to which I have referred otherwise, that the masters were bound by a vow, unless anyone prefers to assume, while admitting that direct evidence is wanting, the existence of that secret school to which I have just referred. In this connection it should be remembered that prior to the seventeenth century and thereafter—practically speaking—the witnesses to the fact and claims of Alchemy are successive and not concurrent : it might look therefore as if they were sent out one by one as witnesses to a hidden Art from a common centre. Rhasis, Alfarabi, Avicenna, Morien, Albertus Magnus, St. Thomas Aquinas belong to the mythical, supposititious period, for we have seen that the tracts passing under these names are almost certainly of fictitious allocation and generally of much later composition. It would look indeed as if the first historical alchemist in the West of Europe might have been Roger Bacon, in which case the second would be Arnoldus de Villanova, and the third that concealed adept who assumed the illustrious name of Raymond Lully. Ferrarius, Bonus and Johannes de Rupecissa are referred to the fourteenth century ; Basil Valentine, Isaac the Hollander and Trévisan are of the fifteenth, together with the English masters, Norton and Ripley. Paracelsus is the first great name of the sixteenth century, but there is that also of Denys Zachaire and thirdly of Heinrich Khunrath. Alexander Seton belongs to the first decade of the seventeenth century, his successors being Eirenæus Philalethes and the problematical Lascaris, who left nothing in writing. Considering the extent of the literature, it will surprise many to learn that this enumeration exhausts the list, which may be divided for the rest into (1) works of commentary ; (2) theoretical works ; (3) a large class of either undeclared authorship or of writers about whom little or nothing is known ; (4) a doubtful class, put forward in the name of the mastery but carrying no authentic marks ; (5) testimonies to the fact of transmutation by persons of consequence who had no claim on knowledge ; (6) works presenting or believed to present a spiritual side of the subject.

No critical account of Alchemy and its records has ever put forward previously the veridic position of the subject as it has been delineated here and now : that the succession of historical reputed masters is less than two score during a space of five centuries ; that the enormous literature which remains over can have therefore under any circumstances no evidence in its favour, unless it is of an internal kind ; and that such evidence is wanting because there is no key to the real meaning of a very long succession of cryptic texts. An intimate and ripe familiarity with the literature may enable a few to determine whether Document A should be referred to the physical side and whether Document B —supposing that it is post-Reformation—might be placed tentatively or definitely in the spiritual and mystical class ; but it can answer none of the vital questions which arise in the former case, while it remains to be seen whether anything valid can be inferred concerning the latter. It is certain meanwhile, so far as evidence goes, that—whether they came forth from a centre, whether certain masters found and taught their pupils, whether so-called happy guess-work profited some earnest students—as apparently in the case of Eirenæus—the line of messengers, heirs or discoverers on the physical side ended with the adept last mentioned, among those who left memorials, and with Lascaris, if we elect to regard him as a witness to the fact of transmutation. But it goes without saying that many seekers remained over and propounded in writing as many theories of the work which they may have regarded as valid in all seriousness of mind, some without putting to the test and a few in spite of failure. I feel less or more sure that Abbé Pernety and Baron Tschoudy in the second half of the eighteenth century wrote from conviction in terms of great certitude, but I doubt very much whether they made experiments or would have thought their speculations wrong if they had failed personally to demonstrate them in laboratory practice.

As regards the spiritual side it seems to have later records, the last apparent testimony coming from a hidden Temple of the Rosy Cross on the eve of the French Revolution. On its origin we may glean a little light by recurring once more to the parlous condition of Alchemy at the end of the sixteenth century, when it had become a commercial venture, so far as the literature is concerned. The pretended adepts were everywhere, above all in Germany, and their books in all the booths. No one held the key which might unlock their meaning, and none could distinguish therefore between purely fraudulent wares and those which might count as serious. The operators also were on all sides, with a thousand processes, not one of which led anywhere except to ruin. There is no question that when Jacob Böhme arose he became

a great light in the eyes of occult schools, though he was
cast out of Lutheran churches, and perhaps because of his
expulsion. He was in particular a light unexpected—indeed
after the manner of revelation—to hosts of earnest students
who had sat in darkness and in the shadow of death among
" the blind work in metals ", pinning their unprofitable
faith to " the narrow name of *Chemia* ".

Mrs. Atwood affirms that when Böhme's books appeared
the hidden masters of the Art concluded that they could
no longer keep under veils the secret of their vessel and of
the First Matter therein. The vessels were, however, well
known, and I do not find that a considerable mystery is
created about any one of them. The First Matter and the
Three Principles are everywhere in the work of Böhme,
but no one is brought nearer thereby to the nature or
composition of the dark, disesteemed Stone, of grey colour.
What he did in reality was to present the alchemical subject
under a new aspect, and it must have come to many in
Germany with great and strange appeal, if only because
it opened the door of mind to the conception of that new
birth about which my feeling is that Latin popular theology
said and knew little enough. But this is the beginning of
all in things of the spirit, as if the Matter of the Great Work
should be put into the hand of a tyro without instructions.
It happens, however, that Böhme put, as it were, a new Stone
into the hands of seekers, so that they could not help seeing
that, theosophically and mystically, it was all things and in
all things, within and without themselves, but for the true
alchemist was to be found and used within, there being
the secret of transmutation and there the place.[1]

---

[1] I have cited the *Threefold Life of Man* on several occasions concerning the
Stone and the Word in my first chapter, since writing which there has come to
my recollection an excellent summary in Edward Taylor's faithful and true digest
of the chief works : *Jacob Behmen's Theosophick Philosophy Unfolded*, 1691,
p. 298. It is put so clearly that it deserves the space of a note. " The Word was
and for ever is the only noble spiritual Philosopher's Stone, Christ. This Stone was
in all the holy men from Adam downward, whereby they both were good and did
good ; but the men of lower outside principles, or rationists, have a counterfeit,
scholastic, glittering, pleasant Stone, which they think is right, and they hotly
persecute the true precious Stone, to advance their own, which outside Stone of
theirs is only a Stone of the great building of this world ; for it initiated childhood
in wantonness and bravery, requiring covetousness and crafty guile to support
it. So they set the Paradisical garland of blossoming youth on the serpent's head,
learn to contemn them as simple who have the true Stone, because they live as
not of the world but childlike, and go through and out of the world weeping, yet
bearing precious seed."

The distinction seems to be maintained always between this Christotheosophical Stone and the secondary Philosophical Stone; but the latter passes continually from less to lesser, while always the former grows from more to more. For on the hypothesis that it is valid art and science the Alchemy of crucible and furnace can aim no higher than to produce that which answers to gold of mines, and this is nothing in comparison with that which is Gold of Heaven. " We see a rude stone lying on the ground, and in many there is best gold," which " glisters in the stone " ; but this is inanimate and knows not that which it has. " So also we are earthly sulphur," but therein is a sulphur of heaven, and they are " one among other " now, though they " operate not together ". The earthly man " is signified by the rude drossy stone ", while Sol answers to the Word which became man " and impregnates humanity in its corruption ". The explanation is that although indeed earthly, man has " the eternal centre of Nature " and longs after the gold of God. As the gold in the rude stone is liberated by the work of fire from that which is unworthy of it, so also there is a process of " dying and consuming " which sets free our eternal centre. " The earthly man is not worthy of the jewel which he carries," being " dark or dusky earth in respect of the Virgin Child born of God ". It seems to follow that in this sense of symbolism unregenerate man is himself the dark, disesteemed Stone of grey colour. But " as gold has a true body which lies hidden in the drossy stone, so also the Virgin-like Tincture in the earthly man has a true heavenly divine body in flesh and blood ", but not such as the earthly. " It can subsist in the fire, it goes through stone and wood, and is not apprehended." In this manner we are brought once more to the radiant body of adeptship, the arch-natural body of Thomas Vaughan and the others. It belongs to that mystery of new generation about which it is added that " man conceives the Word of Life which became man in Christ " and that the place in which he conceives is the virgin-like centre, the " eternal centre ", which is imprisoned in his corruptible body.[1] Of the new man brought forth in this new generation it is said elsewhere that " as the Son is one with the Father, so also thy new man is one in the Father

---

[1] *Treatise of the Incarnation*, Part I, cap. 14 : *Concerning the New Regeneration.*

and the Son, one virtue or power, one light, one life, one eternal Paradise, one eternal heavenly birth, one Father, Son and Holy Ghost, and thou His child ".[1] The instruction further concerning that heavenly body which is the vesture of the Heavenly Tincture affirms in yet another place that " the eternal flesh which is hidden in the old earthly man " is in truth *Lapis Philosophorum*, and " to whomsoever it revealeth itself he hath all joy therein, for there is no end of its virtue : he that hath it doth not give it away ; but if he doth impart it to any, yet it is not profitable to him that is lazy, for he diveth not into its virtue, to learn that ". But respecting the zealous seeker, he " findeth the Stone, with its virtue and benefit together, and when he findeth and knoweth that he is certain of it, there is greater joy in him than the world is able to apprehend ".[2]

When these citations are taken in connection with those of my first chapter it becomes evident that we have obtained our unquestionable point of departure for the fact of Spiritual Alchemy, on the understanding that Heinrich Khunrath was a kind of precursor by means of his posthumous book, published in 1609. It was in 1610 that Jacob Böhme began to unfold his revelations and produced the *Aurora, or Morning Redness*. That his inspiration was first-hand and *sui genesis* I am very certain and debate on the question would be idle, but many things act as a pretext, an occasion or aid to awakening, and there is no difficulty in believing that Böhme may have received a certain prompting from the *Amphitheatre of Eternal Wisdom*. There is othrewise no comparison whatever between Khunrath and Böhme : the one is so dwarfed by the theosophical Titan who succeeded him that it is more than a satisfaction to give him his just due as the first—so far as can be told—who proclaimed that the Stone is Christ. He is in contrast otherwise to Böhme— who had not gone to the *praxis*—for he affirms with unstinted

---

[1] *Three Principles*, cap. iv, § 9.
[2] *Threefold Life, cap.* vi, 97, 100, 101. See also *cap.* x, 3, which appears to be speaking of a work that may be done in metals by those who have abandoned the barren search after Mysteries of Nature " in the stars and elements ". It is said that if you " take the Spirit of the Tincture, then indeed you go in a way in which many have found Sol "—presumably gold of transmutation—" but they have followed on the way to the heart of Sol, where the Spirit of the Heavenly Tincture hath laid and brought them into the liberty, into the majesty, where they have then known the Noble Stone, *Lapis Philosophorum*, the Philosopher's Stone, and have stood amazed at men's blindness and seen their labouring in vain."

force of language that he had seen, handled and used the Philosophical Stone, while that in which he had used it was the work of transmuting metals.

It calls to be added that Böhme is not only the well-spring or fountain-head of Spiritual Alchemy; he is to all intents and purposes the one person who has said what matters on the subject. He can scarcely be termed the founder of a Spiritual School within the Academy of Hermes: in a very real sense he may be termed the School itself, for his works—which are long and many—embrace almost every department of the Hermetic subject, outside the physical *praxis*. They are of Alchemy in the cosmos, its First Matter and its Three Principles; of the alchemical work in man; of the threefold life in him and the four elements; of the Eternal Essence and the Tincture in man and Nature—the whole of course spiritualised. In this panegyric—if it needs to be so named—I have by no means forgotten Robert Fludd; but he exercised no such influence as his Teutonic contemporary, and when he was laid to rest at Bearstead the star of his repute went down, like his star of earthly life. The one was a man of revelation, a seer and prophet—whether we are able or not to receive his visions or regard his prophetic office as wholly authentic—the other was " a philosopher by fire " who was raised above his proper class and denomination from time to time by the operations of a spiritual mind.

But after Fludd and Böhme we are called to consider the output of occasional alchemical tracts which bear his marks upon them, whether—as in most cases—they are about the business of metallic transmutation or belong, actually or presumably, to a higher concern. We make our departure therefore and proceed through the seventeenth century, having the substantially concurrent testimony of three theosophical alchemists that the Great Work of Hermetism, in its proper understanding, was not in metals but in the soul of man. All of them are like gates which open on glorious vistas of Divine Experience, within and beyond their respective fields of realisation, while Böhme would repay the dedication of a whole book to this one theme.

It came about a few years before his death that among the great cohort of alchemical texts there began to appear a few which took a certain lead from his writings and spoke in their own manner of language about the Second Birth, as in the *Golden Age Restored*.[1] Its author remembers " God's great mercy and the Mystery of Regeneration ". He is apparently on the work in metals and derides those who look for their First Matter outside the mineral kingdom. He condemns also the innumerable " preparations, purgations, sublimations, distillations " and so forth " as no better than impostures, though Geber, Albertus Magnus and the general choir of philosophers impose these and many analogous things in their practice. The tripods, athanors, alembics, retorts and pelicans fare no better. It was in answer to daily prayers that his own mind was enlightened by the light of the Holy Spirit, so that he saw " with these eyes and held in these hands " the Great Mystery of the Sages. " The truth was borne in upon my mind and my eyes were opened like those of the disciples at Emmaus, who knew their Master in the breaking of bread." Hereof is " the Revelation of the Spirit " and the manifest " Arcanum of the Sages ". The tract is otherwise an allegory concerning a beautiful Virgin clothed in foul garments, which are cast aside, awaiting their purification by Art. Considered as such, it may be open to almost any construction which fantasy may place upon it, for it is only in a preface addressed to the Christian reader that there is any reference to metals.[2]

Another and far more elaborate tract in the same collection, under the title of *Gloria Mundi*, is really an ingarnering of many ancient dicta—including those of the *Turba*—with commentaries thereupon, but it is notable on several accounts and especially for its parallels between the Philosophical Mystery and the Mystery of Christian Faith.[3] There is no identification, like that of Robert Fludd, between *Lapis Philosophorum* and the Stone which is Christ, and there is no confusion between them while attempting to make a distinction.

---

[1] Henricus Madathanus, i.e., Adrian Mynsicht : *Aureum Sæculum Redivivum*, printed—apparently for the first time—in *Museum Hermeticum*, Frankfurt, 1625. This, however, was the year in which Böhme left this life. He was born in 1575.

[2] The allegory itself is left at a loose end, the garments are not cleansed and it is an unsettled question whether the virgin is dead or has been taken into the hiddenness. Moreover, the author's *famulus*, Herman Datichius, who produces an " epigram " as a colophon to the prefatory part, stultifies the condemnation of accepted processes by affirming (1) that he has many times purified, matured and joined together, as a result of which (2) he has found the Golden Tincture, which is the remedy for all metals and all sick persons.

[3] *Gloria Mundi, seu Tabula Paradisi.*

The Philosopher's Stone, when prepared in the right way, " is a pearl of great price and indeed the earthly antitype of Christ, the Heavenly Corner Stone. As Christ was despised and rejected in this world by the Jews, and yet was more precious than heaven and earth, so it is with our Stone among earthly things." The explanation is that " it is familiar to all men, both young and old, is found in the country, in the village, in the town, in all things created by God : yet is it despised by all. Rich and poor handle it every day ; it is cast into the streets by serving maids ; and children play with it. No one prizes it, though next to the human soul it is the most beautiful and precious thing on earth, and has power to pull down kings and princes. Nevertheless it is esteemed the vilest and meanest of earthly things.... Indeed it is the Stone which the builders of Solomon disallowed ".[1]

The First Matter of the Philosopher's Stone is said to become water by evaporation, but it is like no other water on earth. Now, as the Matter is everywhere it should follow that its evaporation can be effected in all places ; but with the inevitable contradiction which stultifies all the texts it is affirmed elsewhere in *Gloria Mundi* that " there is only one spring in all the world from which this water may be obtained". The spring is in Judea and is called " the Fountain of the Saviour or of beatitude ", but is apparently not in that land of Judah which is reached by journeying over this earth of ours, for it is said that no one can " discover the way " thereto or reach the secret spring, except indeed the sages, to whom it has been revealed by God. All this notwithstanding, the waters of the said fountain in the hidden place " flow over all the world " and are thus " familiar to all ". Which is the right spring and which the right water are mysteries of the Art and no one can attain the Art until he has stripped off their veils. Of those who so do and thus become masters it is said that they have (1) gold, silver and all the wealth of this world ; (2) perfect health as well as length of days ; " and, what is better still, (3) the comfort to be derived from a reassuring type of the bitter passion and death of our

[1] The allusion is possibly to some Talmudic tradition, for Zoharic Stone-symbolism does not involve the builders of the First Temple in an act of rejection. The reference is curious and should interest Mark Masons.

Lord and Saviour Jesus Christ, His descent into hell, His glorious and most holy resurrection on the third day, His victory over sin, death and hell, a victory that must bring joy to all who have the breath of life." The text gives no further light upon the analogy thus instituted—as I think— for the first time, though I have some recollection of meeting with it in several later examples of the literature, and it will recur here in the consideration of another text.

There are certain alchemical tracts which might have been passed over as *nihil ad rem nostram*, but they have been cited as if there were no question regarding their spiritual intent. One of them is referred to Nuysement, described as *Receveur Général du Comité de Ligny en Barrois*, and is a disquisition on Philosophical Salt.[1] There is no question whatever that it belongs to physical Alchemy, if ever a text belonged, but the " divine virtues " ascribed to the Philosophic Elixir did not fail to mislead Mrs. Atwood, who had a fatal facility in collecting everything into her casting net ; but Nuysement is speaking of things effected *ex hypothesi* by the mineral spirit when in a pure state. He delineates also the work of the artist in exalting the Elixir to the highest degree of redness, but he affirms that gold possesses in itself " a magnetic virtue ", and so the entire passage is annexed. Finally Nuysement counsels the artist to observe the rule of the work with great diligence, and a tacit assumption causes this to be cited in the particulars of a supposed " experimental method ", for the " kindling of Divine Ecstasy ".[2] Nuysement proved also to the purpose for Hitchcock on at least two occasions, but they are in connection with Swedenborg, whom he supposed to be a Hermetic philosopher. One of them, however, is not without bearing on our subject, as it reflects something from Böhme. "The body of the world lies open to our senses, but its spirit lies hid ; and within this spirit is the soul, which cannot be united to its body save by the mediation of the spirit, because the body is gross and the soul subtle, being far removed from all corporeal qualities.

[1] *De Vero Sale Secreto Philosophorum, et de Universali Mundi Spiritu, Latine versus a Ludovico Combacho.* Published at Cassel in 1651, and at Leyden in 1672, the original having appeared in French at the Hague, n.d., and at Paris in 1620. An English version was issued in 1657 under the title of *Sal, Lumen et Spiritus Mundi Philosophici, or the Dawning of the Day.*

[2] *Suggestive Inquiry*, 3rd edition, pp. 101, 158, 159, 309 and 322.

For the union of these two we must find a *tertium quid*, participating in both natures and, as it were, a corporeal spirit, seeing that extremes cannot be joined without an intervening ligament,[1] having affinity with both. We see that heaven is high and earth low, the one pure and the other corrupt. . . . At no time could these have been brought together and reconciled, except by the mediation of Christ Jesus, God and man, Who is the true attractive gluten of both natures." [2] It happens, however, that nothing follows in the tract from the analogy thus instituted between the mediatorial office of our Saviour as the bond of heaven and earth—meaning the Father and man—and a postulated link between the soul of the world and its visible, material body.

There is also another treatise on Salt which claims to be the work of an adept and is entitled *Lucerna Salis*.[3] It affirms (1) that the intent of the Art is to convert imperfect metals into gold after their purification; (2) that to this end they are fermented with gold most pure; (3) that this is the gold of the wise and not the vulgar metal; (4) that it is a clear and pure water which contains a fire called "lightning of the Lord"; (5) that all things have life therefrom; (6) that in its essence, however, it is not water or any other of the four elements, though it can become all of these; (7) that it is in every place and thing; (8) that it is known to none but the sages and is termed their Salt, extracted from their earth; (9) that common earth and vulgar salt have no part therein; (10) that it is rather Salt of the World and Salt of Life; (11) that it preserves man from all maladies in addition to transmuting metals; (12) that in its sublimation it becomes Philosophical Mercury, pure and clear; (13) that this Mercury contains a Red Sulphur; (14) that the whole foundation of Alchemy abides in these; (15) that the Water which at first is not water becomes the Stone, which is no stone; (16) that it turns white in the vessel, and this is the

---

[1] Hitchcock compares this ligament to Swedenborg's doctrine of Christ as the *nexus* between finite and infinite. See *Swedenborg a Hermetic Philosopher*, pp. 102, 103.

[2] I have adapted the English translation of 1657 under the name of Cambachius.

[3] *Lucerna Salis Philosophorum, secundum mentem Sendivogii, Geberi et aliorum*, Amsterdam, 1658. The author was Johann Harprecht of Tubingen. An English translation of Digby is cited frequently by Mrs. Atwood, but I have failed to trace it under that name or otherwise.

White Elixir for the White Work ; (17) that its earth has then become and remains black ; (18) that it is raised by fermentation to the Red State ; (19) that its tingeing virtue is magnified indefinitely by successive multiplications ; (20) that the knowledge of this Salt and its Mystery is vouchsafed only as a reward of toil, the personal work of the artist, preceded by study and fervent prayer to God, Who blesses those who invoke Him and hinders those who do not.

It will be observed that this thesis does not differ from other alchemical texts in any important matter, as to the theory or practice of the work, and that it certifies with particular clearness as to the end in view. It is therefore a typical case in point for the general term of the literature, and it cannot be cited continually in the defence of an alternative and diametrically opposite concern until it has been shewn that the objective of metallic transmutation is a veil and evasion by evidence to that effect. The fact of such evidence is affirmed but is produced nowhere by Mrs. Atwood and Hitchcock. The assumption of the first is that chemistry has nothing in common with Alchemy except " the borrowed terms ",[1] and of the second that not one of some three hundred volumes in his possession " could have been written by anyone in pursuit of actual gold ".[2] We have seen, on the contrary, that from the rise of the Art in Byzantium till its authentic records were closed, the alchemists were actually about their proper business, without deceit or evasion ; that they never concealed its object and symbolised only over the materials on which they were at work and the processes by which they hoped to attain their admitted end. When Khunrath and Böhme and Fludd rose up in witness to another and higher Alchemy they did not pretend that it had been practised by the old alchemists as such, and they did not question that metals could be and had been transmuted.

I pass now to the consideration of a text which has been

---

[1] *Suggestive Inquiry*, 3rd edition, p. 143.

[2] *Swedenborg, a Hermetic Philosopher*, p. 9. Compare, however, the counter-statement on p. 194 : " Most of the real adepts have written nothing at all "— in which case what and how did he know concerning them ?—while those who have recorded anything have limited themselves to very small tracts, published not so much with the object of making known a doctrine as to indicate to the initiated their claim to brotherhood, and these works have almost invariably been anonymous." It is the statement of one who did not know the literature.

regarded as bearing faithful and high witness to Alchemy as a Mastery in the Spirit. This is *Centrum Naturæ Concentratum*, in which are the well-known words : " I admonish thee, whosoever thou art, that desirest to dive into the innermost parts of Nature, if that thou seekest thou findest not within thee, thou wilt never find it without thee. If thou knowest not the excellency of thine own house, why dost thou seek and search after the excellence of other things ? . . . He who desires the primacy amongst the students of Nature will nowhere find a greater or better field of study than himself." For which reason it is added : " I will follow the example of the Egyptians, and from my whole heart and certain true experience, proved by me, speak to my neighbour in the words of the Egyptians, and with a loud voice do now proclaim : O Man, know thyself : in thee is hid the treasure of treasures."

This is a remarkable citation and is appreciated as such by General E. A. Hitchcock, who cites it at full length. Mrs. Atwood also appeals twice to the tract, but her citations or references are worded to suit her purposes and do not properly represent the text. Both writers accept the ascribed authorship without a shadow of question. It comes about in this manner that he is termed an Arabian by the one and a Moorish philosopher by the other. We cannot of course expect any critical discernment in either case, but it happens that *Centrum Naturæ Concentratum* is a production of at or about the period when its original publication took place and was never cited or heard of previously.[1] It is forgery pure and simple in respect of age and authorship, while it may be left to stand at its value in the matter of content,

---

[1] *Quadratum Alchymisticum, das ist : Vier auserlesene rare Tractätgen vom Stein der Weisen, etc.* . . . Hamburg, Verlegts Christian Liebezeit, Druckts Philipp Ludwig Stromer, 1706. The four tracts are (1) *Speculum Sapientiæ*, (2) *Centrum Naturæ Concentratum*, (3) *Discursus de Universali*, by Martinus de Delle ; (4) *Abyssus Alchymiæ Exploratus*, ascribed to Thomas de Vagan, but in reality the *Open Entrance* of Eirenæus. The sub-title of the second tract is : *oder ein Tractat von dem wiedergebohrnen Saltz, insgemein und eigendlich genandt : Der Weisen Stein. In arabischen geschrieben von Ali Puli, einem Asiatischen Mohren, darnach in portugisische Sprache durch H. L. V. A. H. und ins hochteutsche versetzt und herausgegeben von Joh. Otto Helbig, Rittern Chur-Fürstlichen Pfaltzischen Rath. Gedruckt im Jahr* 1682. Of the alleged Portuguese version there is as much and as little trace as of the original in Arabic. It should be added that *Quadratum Alchymisticum* is a made up collection, comprising separately printed and paged tracts. This accounts for the *Centrum* bearing an earlier date than that of the general publication. Were it otherwise, the Low Dutch translation mentioned in my text would be earlier than this in High Dutch.

A a

which is more curious than a single extract can indicate. It is not mentioned by Berthelot and was unknown to Lenglet du Fresnoy, who names the collection in which it appeared originally, but as one who had never seen it. As regards the accredited author, he is called Ali Puli.[1] It is said that he was a Mauritanian, born of Asiatic parents, and that he embraced Christianity. Various works are attributed to him, written in Arabic, but they belong to the romance of invention. The tract under notice was translated into " low Dutch " and published in 1694. Our National Library contains only an English rendering of this, by E. Brice, writing as " a lover of the Hermetic Science ". It belongs to the year 1697. The sub-title is " The Salt of Nature Regenerated, for the most part improperly called the Philosopher's Stone ".

It is proclaimed at the inception of the work that the seeker after gold should be driven from the entrance of that Temple which leads to Hermetic Knowledge, and that he shall not find what he seeks. A later explanation tells us that " those who desire to serve God, their neighbour and themselves, have no leisure for vain chemical experiments ". Seekers on this path should abandon such frivolities. The first work is a renewal of the heart in God, and the symbolism of this kind of conversion is put quite plainly when it is said : " Transmute your own souls, which have attracted the hardness, coldness and impurity of lead, the austerity and bitterness of copper, the inconstancy of *argent vive*, and by the Divine Spirit render them peaceful and better." This is part of the work which is termed a searching out and discovery of " the universal centre of all Nature ". That centre is man, in whom earth, air and water are said to meet. " He is placed in the middle, between that which is superior and that which is inferior, and *Ruach Elohim* was inspired into him "—or the Eternal Word and Life—together with an elementary or astral spirit. It is said further : (1) That he who has knowledge of the microcosm cannot long be ignorant of the macrocosm ; (2) That " the universal orb of the earth contains not so great mysteries and excellences as a little man, formed by God to His image " ; (3) that the world in which " the matter of the Sophy is

---

[1] Called Alipili in the English translation.

highest and best to be found is man " ; (4) that the term of our research is in our own body.

Now, all this stands forth clearly enough at its value as to the apparent inward nature of the work. This notwithstanding, the Dutch translator speaks of eye-witnesses who stated that " with a small quantity of his Regenerated Salt, Ali Puli transmuted a great quantity of base metal into good silver and gold ". And the alchemist testifies on his own part that " by the grace of God he has prepared a matter out of animals ", which " offered unto me one way animals, another way vegetables, again another way often minerals and metals ". This follows from his thesis that " animal, vegetable and mineral natures come from the same root ". The wording is exceedingly obscure and reminds one of the ridiculous processes on egg-shells and all kinds of refuse-matter which were attempted by groping amateurs and were derided by others who were better versed in the Art. But the thesis appears to be that as, by the hypothesis, there is a common basis of the animal, vegetable and mineral kingdoms, so each individual member of each kingdom carries within itself something that is a characteristic essence of the whole. It is on such assumption that Ali Puli proceeds to develop a theory of material transmutation in comparatively simple terms.

" If thou can'st make that spirit familiar to thee which by its energy in the animal creatures maketh all things that enter into thee to live an animal life, what and how great an effect dost thou think that spirit will produce, if thou joinest it for the Agent to a metalline nature ? " On the surface at least, there was never a more grotesque proposition than to take the animal power of assimilating and converting food and apply it to a metal for any purpose whatever. The meaning, however, is that " herb and grass " become man by their passage through him for his nourishment, and therefore, presumably, if we can endue gold with the power of assimilation we can feed it with inferior metals and they will be converted in turn. It is a grotesque argument from a forced analogy, and there is little need to say that any *modus operandi* is wanting, while it does not by any means follow from the writer's way of expression that he wished to be taken literally. He says, indeed, that the generation of men and animals is a better subject for consideration than that of gold.

If, however, in his references to " metalline nature " he could be regarded as speaking in parables which call to be understood mystically, a question arises as to that " spirit " which maintains the life of animals in the manner indicated ; and it happens that this is really the subject-matter of the text. What then is this spirit ? The answer is that it is the Salt of Nature, which is drawn out of the inward centre. It appears to be concealed everywhere—in " the inferior parts of the world " and in those also which are superior. He who can extract it is Magnus Apollo. That from which it is to be extracted is called " viscous water ", of which it is a concentrated centre. On the side of its natural history there are no further particulars, but on the theosophical side it is said cryptically that it is joined to " the invisible speaking of the Divine Word " by the light of which it is moved and nourished. This Salt of Nature was created by Christ, or the Word, and was that which He called good.[1] It is a spirit which " ascends up into the airy heaven and which again descends, which restrains the winds, and holds them in the fists of its power, which gathers together the waters into their places ". It is added that this Spirit of Salt is the medium of all things and that nothing in Nature can subsist without it.

When it has been regenerated by an artist, there proceeds from this Salt " a wonderful and noble thing. . . , which maketh every corrosive thing sweet, every weak and inferior thing sound and strong ". And again : " This thing giveth both riches and wealth ; and in this life it deserves the name of a most precious treasure. It is the type and image of the resurrection and immortality ". Finally, says Ali Puli, " I have seen by this thing how the Word was made flesh," together with His days of ministry, passion, death, burial, resurrection and ascension.

The supposed Arabian alchemist is not the only one of his fraternity who has compared the stages of the Great Work to that of the world's creation or to the mystical

---

[1] Christ being the Maker of the universe, on the authority of the Fourth Gospel : *per quem omnia facta sunt.*

pageant of the world's redemption in Christ. His incessant alternation between physical and material images is a curious feature of the discourse. If we suppose for a moment that he is really veiling a dream or a reality in physics, he is useless on that side, giving no key whatever. If he is veiling a spiritual mystery, we have heard on other authority of a Wisdom which proceeds from the mouth of the Most High and which disposes all things " strongly and sweetly ". We know also that the birth, life, death, resurrection and ascension of Christ constitute a scientifically accurate delineation of the soul's ascent and attainment. But again, on this understanding, the secret is useless, because it gives us no process, no suggestion of the path to follow. By the hypothesis of sacramental Christianity, under veils of bread and wine, the Eucharist communicates Christ and those who receive worthily are converted by Divine Nourishment. If the *Centrum Naturæ Concentratum* is an allegory of this Arch-Natural Graal, then the term of our research is indeed in our own body, but we find no aid to that term in the tract of Ali Puli.

To speak seriously, however, one puts up as one can with the false attribution of the *Tract on Mystical Theology* by pseudo-Dionysius, while remembering the pious fraud of one of those detached letters which pass under the name. That *Tract* is the fountain-head of all Christian Mysticism in the West and—on the faith of scholarship—this is how it began. We make our glosses on the subject and perhaps hoodwink though we scarcely convince ourselves. But I at least am unable to suppose that there may have been a high intention behind the production of an alchemical doctrine in the seventeenth century and its ascription to an eastern source far back in the past. I cannot think—as some in the occult circles might elect to do—that it was sent forth by masters for the purpose of indicating that there was a Divine Mystery lying somewhere in the deeps within the more open alchemical claims. I bequeathe therefore *Centrum Naturæ Concentratum* to those whom it may concern, preferring that Centre of which it is said that it " gives up no form " to one which produces impostures. For all that I know to the contrary, the tract may connote only the alchemical *colportage* of its period.

There are texts by the score which might be brought forward for consideration in succession to those which have occupied recent pages, and I confess that they are left over with regret ; but on the one hand they would make this critical study of inordinate length and on the other the most that they would exhibit would be that certain but not too defined change which came over the literature in post-Reformation times, with occasional traces of Jacob Böhme's influence.

Those who read Joannes Grasseus Cortalasseus and his *Arca Arcani Artificississimi* will find that his " lucid explication of the Philosopher's Stone " is set forth not only in respect of the soul of man but as appertaining equally to the work of converting metals : the business in hand is, however, that of transmuting. But the examination of text after text as the days drew on to the beginning of the eighteenth century exhibits that in proportion as the alchemical mind was more and more overbrooded and tinged by the religious and devotional spirit, the more clearly if possible emerges the physical term in view. It is all *Soli Deo Gloria,* but *mysterium magnum* is still *mysterium conficiendi aurum.* A disciple of Grasseus dedicates his *Mysterium Occultæ Naturæ* to illuminated students who are lovers of God. He affirms that the Word of the Father, *per quem omnia facta sunt,* is the True Heavenly Stone and tinges our souls for salvation or life eternal, but it is to turn his attention thereafter to that other *famosus et mirabilis Lapis* which is said to contain all things *præter cœlestia,* multiplying precious metals and producing Potable Gold. Claiming the grade of adeptship in Hermetic Wisdom, Pantaleon may dedicate his *Bifolium Metallicum* at great length to the Omnipotent Triune God, but his discourse is on the universal metallic Tincture and the method of obtaining it by the humid and dry ways ; and when he opens the *Tomb of Semiramis* in a later treatise it is for the discovery of Philosophical Mercury, that the species of metals may be transmuted after reduction into their First Matter. Here are casual illustrations from the long series and they must be taken to stand for the whole. Were there anything to the real purpose it would not be omitted over a mere question of space ; but as the first epoch of Spiritual Alchemy belongs to the early decades of

the seventeenth century,[1] so the second is on the threshold
of the French Revolution : it is confined to one circle, from
which issued a single book consisting largely of symbolical
designs.[2] This being the case, we are called to pass over the
intervening period and so proceed to the last stage of our
research.[3]

It takes us to the Brotherhood of the Rosy Cross at a
period immediately subsequent to the Reformation of 1777,
an epoch of extraordinary activity in Germany—especially
in the Kingdom of Prussia—and in the Russian Empire.
In my work on the Rosicrucian subject there is a representative account of this period ; but in that which follows
I have been able to draw upon sources unavailable for the
particular publication and still unavailable in England.
They confirm my view that in these circles of the
Order there was a moving spirit which, not only by
intention but practical work, especially in Russia, was
aiming at high things. We are concerned, however,
only with the Hermetic symbolism which appeared
in the Ritual Ceremonies and the instructions appertaining
to the Degrees. It will be understood that the Rosy Cross
in Russia derived from Germany and that my own sources
are German. The picture which they present is notable,
if not antecedently unlikely, for it proves that the Order, in
and about the year 1784, was following the alchemical
quest along the two paths which are at once contrasted and
harmonised by Heinrich Khunrath and Jacob Böhme, to

[1] In so far as there are intimations or evidences of Alchemy on its mystical
side in the open records of the Rosy Cross, I must refer to my work on the Brotherhood which has been cited already in notes on several occasions. It is obviously
impossible and undesirable to restate them here.

[2] I have relegated to an Appendix the consideration of two other and earlier
symbolical books for reasons which will appear in their place.

[3] I have not as an unaided student been able to take the whole literature of
Alchemy as my province, for many texts are unavailable to research in England.
There are some which suggest by their titles that they may belong possibly to our
concern : the following enumeration may prompt continental readers to afford me
some help with regard to their content and purpose. (1) *Lapis Metaphysicus,*
Paris, 1570. (2) *Cyriaci Lucii de Lithosophistica erronea quorumdam de Lapide
Philosophico disceptantium Doctrina, Religioni Christianæ incommoda, Observatio,
atque de Lapide Christosophico Admonitio,* Ingolstadii, 1582. A warning concerning
the Christosophical Stone prior to Jacob Böhme ought to be important.
(3) Henricus Nollius : *Methodus Metaphysicus,* Frankfurt, 1617. (4) *Arbre ou
Abrégé des Mystères de la Grace et de la Nature,* sine loco, 1646. (5) *L'Ayman
Mystique,* Paris, 1659 and 1689. (6) *Isagoge in veram Triunius Dei cognitionem,*
Hamburg, 1674. (7) *Lampas Vitæ et Mortis,* Leyden, 1678. (8) *Cabala Chymica,*
Hamburg, 1680.

some extent possibly also by Robert Fludd. The Great Work in its proper and plenary understanding is spiritual, and it is this only which matters for those who are on the quest of reality—transmutation performed in the spirit rather than that of physics.[1] It is affirmed categorically that the transmutation of human nature is Alchemy and that man must therefore be iron so that he may become gold.[2] He is iron presumably in uncoverted will and purpose ; it is this and all that is connoted in desire and mind which must be turned to Divine things, that " holy reunion between the Creator and the creature " may be in fine accomplished, the soul freed from vice, the heart dedicated to virtue, fear of God and the love of others.[3] It is said also that Knowledge of God is the first duty of every reasonable being.[4] The foundation of all things is the Spirit of God, from which it follows that material things are explained by spiritual and therein is their end and meaning. It comes about in this manner that " the highest unity is revealed in diversity " and that diversity must return into unity.[5] The real aim of the Order is to build up the Kingdom of Christ on earth and even to extend it further.[6] The aids in this work are " the Light of Reason, the Light of Nature and the Light of Revelation ",[7] in connection with which there is a recurring appeal to the tradition of a secret knowledge which came down from Adam through all the ages and was presumably now in the keeping of the Rosy Cross. It is from this source ex hypothesi that the chief metaphysical doctrine of the Order may be supposed to have been drawn, being expressed somewhat crudely as follows : " The soul is only an altered form of the spirit, while the body is an altered and grosser form of the soul." In the particular theosophy the soul is described as נפש, and this name—borrowed from Kabalism—is affirmed

---

[1] See *The Theoretical Grade of the Rosy Cross*, which appeared at Berlin in 1785. Its revelations caused confusion for a time in the secret circles, but it was preparatory only to the real ceremonial workings.

[2] Johann Gottfried Jugel : *Physica Mystica et Physica Sacra Sacratissima*, Berlin and Leipsic, 1782.

[3] From the Secret Preparatory Ritual or Ritual of the Novitiate, the qualification for which was the Grade of *Écossais Master*.

[4] *Freymaurerische Versammlungsrede der Gold-und Rosenkreuzes des Alten Systems, mit 12 eingreduckten Vignatten*. Amsterdam, 1779.

[5] *Physica Mystica*, etc.

[6] *Theoretical Degree*. Compare *Starke Erweise* of 1788.

[7] Ritual for Novices.

to signify " a branch broken off "—that is to say, from the
Spirit which is God. In this manner the mystical ground on
which return into unity is based emerges in a single sentence.
The supplementary doctrine that the soul builds up its own
body is old in theosophical speculation and will account
not only for Rosicrucian intimations concerning the body
of adeptship but for the fact that in the secret circles there
seem to have been notions concerning an Elixir of Life which
was not manufactured chemically.

If we compare these speculations with the veridic
experiences which built up the inward science of Christian
Mysticism, it will be seen that they are poor and vague ; but
it is just to add that they are pervaded by an earnest spirit
which has, I fear, evaporated in a bald summary : it suggests
that the teachings of the Order were very real to their
keepers in 1785. Whether it would be reasonably possible to
assume as much for the crazed speculations on physical
Alchemy is another question ; but they are in precisely the
same category as those of Jacob Böhme, and I conceive that—
like him—the Brethren may not have proceeded to the
praxis in any serious sense, though it is on record that they
had a laboratory. According to *Freymaurerische Versammlungsrede der Gold-und Rosenkreuzes*, the profane chemist
of those days was delighted when he was able to distil a
sweet oil from antimony, but this anonymous work of
Rosicrucian exposition and defence testifies that there was
ground for joy of a greater and truer kind " in finding a
friend who will open the way to the Temple of Wisdom and
to integration in the Invisible Fraternity ". Presumably,
like the early Brethren of the Rosy Cross, the art of making
gold alchemically was the least of their *magnalia Dei et
Naturæ*. But so far as I can follow the vague indications,
they had their hypothesis concerning it, though it does not
really emerge. There is a thesis that the Almighty Architect
created the sun, moon and planets, that " they might drive
the influence of the four elements into the centre of the
earth and cause the birth of the seven metals ". I infer
that the artist in Alchemy, when he was not about the Greater
Work of the Order, was held to be on the path of transmutation if he drove the seed of gold into the matter contained
in his crucible. It would appear also that this matter

corresponded—as so many others have said—to the original chaos, " a dark formless mass, composed of water and fire ", of which it is declared further that all things were contained therein. It is the age old story of Alchemy concerning the First Matter.

The affirmation with which I started has now passed into demonstration, namely, that the Order of the Rosy Cross was following the two paths of quest which are denominated Spiritual and Physical Alchemy, and it may be added that the novice passing through its various Grades was invited to study the writings of Jacob Böhme.

In the years 1785 and 1788 there appeared at Altona a folio of coloured plates and German letterpress which claimed to explain and illustrate *The Secret Symbols of the Rosicrucians* in the sixteenth and seventeenth centuries. I have dealt with the collection at length in my *Brotherhood of the Rosy Cross* but without reference to the two aspects of Alchemy which are the subject of the present work, and it calls to be regarded shortly from the standpoint offered by these. There is no doubt that it emanated from the circle about which I have obtained evidence *sub anno* 1784, and although there is no call to dwell upon the fact here, there is no doubt also that this circle was that which emerged from the reformation of 1777, our chief knowledge of which is derived from revelations by the so-called Magister Pianco and from his work entitled *Der Rosenkreuzer in seine Blosse.* There is proof abundant of this in the *Starke Erweise* of 1788. The influence of Jacob Böhme is found everywhere in the *Secret Symbols*, and I can trace also that of Khunrath, perhaps especially in the plates. Alike in plates and letterpress, the spiritual and physical works have been brought into such bonds of union that the material side has dissolved or remains only as a hypothesis faintly shadowed forth. In one place, the Celestial Sun, understood as that of Nature, is contrasted with the Terrestrial Sun of Philosophy, regarded as the Alchemical Tincture ; but the aids to reflection on this thesis are (1) that the light is " knowledge of the Glory of God in the face of Jesus Christ " ; [1] (2) that of Him, to Him and through Him are all things ; [2] remembering (3) that there is " one God and Father of all, Who is above all and through

---

[1] *2 Corinthians,* iv, 6.   [2] *Romans,* xi, 36.

all, and in you all "; and finally (4) that He is All in all.[1]
There is more to the same purpose in the exposition of another
plate, illustrating a symbolical river of gold and silver.
Jesus Hominum Salvator, the Divine Sun of Justice and the
Word made flesh, is contrasted with *Hyle*, the Natural Sun
of the Sages, which is a shadow of the Eternal Sun. The
Celestial Quintessence is distinguished from that of Nature,
while it is affirmed that God generates God, on the authority
of *Ps.* ii, 7 : " Thou art my Son : this day have I begotten
Thee." So also gold generates gold. The doctrine on the
one side is " He that hath seen me hath seen the Father " ;
" I am in the Father and the Father in me " ; " I and the
Father are one ".[2] On the other it is said derisively that the
fool is pleased by the glitter of gold, and therefore the four
elements must become a gold stone for the fool's sake.
According to St. Paul, all treasures of wisdom and knowledge
are hidden in Christ,[3] and in Him dwelleth all the fullness of
the Godhead bodily ; [4] but this is re-expressed to indicate
that the Holy Trinity resides in Christ as in a terrestrial
body. So also it is affirmed that in visible, tangible gold
there resides a natural and mundane trinity, which is Salt,
Sulphur and Mercury. He who understands this and can
explain it according to the Mysteries of *Alpha* and *Omega*—
otherwise, according to the Christ-Mystery—is a Master and
true Brother of the Rosy Cross.

The point is that these three Principles are the life of all
things. Mercury is denominated Dew of Heaven and a
terrene unctuosity. It is neither metal nor mineral, but is
the mother of minerals and metals and their First Matter.
According to another form of symbolism, it is the Blood of
the Red Lion and the Gluten of the White Eagle. It is
coagulated by Hermetic Art and produces a sweet Salt,
which is termed Manna.

In the coagulated state it is said to be like electrum or
clear amber. It is found in all things and is rejected with
contempt by the world. In the course of growth it is divided
into two branches, respectively white and red, springing from
one root. It is the most subtle part of earth ; but the Sun
is its Father, the Moon its Mother—as said in the *Emerald*

---

[1] Compare 1 *Cor.*, xv, 28.   [2] *St. John*, xiv, 9–11, and x, 30.
[3] *Colos.*, ii, 3.   [4] Ib., v. 9.

Table—and from these it received life, light and brilliance. Now, all this is familiar alchemical symbolism, but the commentary upon it, as added by the *Secret Symbols*, is (1) that *Jesus Hominum Salvator* is beginning and end of life, hope after death and regeneration ; (2) that the sole and only love of God in Trinity is our refuge in eternity ; and this is a typical example of the way in which things belonging to the physical Alchemy of the past are dissolved in the Spiritual Alchemy of the Rosy Cross. The key is put at the end of the particular page and reads : *Liber Vitæ Christus.* It will be understood therefore that when *Poculum Pansophiæ* is explained in a great diagram, that which is written about it is : *Omnia ab uno et omnia ad unum,* God and Nature, the three kingdoms and that which is *veritas simplex.* It is said elsewhere to be " the greatest medicine in the world ", and this medicine, this draught of healing is Jesus Christ. " Those who have the Spirit of Him " will receive " the Heavenly Manna and the Philosophical Stone." As regards this Spirit, another instruction teaches that there is " a triple birth of man "— presumably that of the body into the manifest world, the birth or wakening of the soul within the body, and the birth of the Holy Spirit of God within the soul. It is no doubt in the same sense that we hear otherwise of " the immortal children of God "—meaning the regenerate—being born of the Spirit, while " the perishable children of Adam "—the unconverted—are born of flesh. In its mystical understanding it is said that the number seven—compare the Gifts of the Spirit—is the Heaven of the Regenerated Children of God. It is also the Rosy Cross in theosophical understanding, for this is the manifestation of God in man—a clear issue in respect of the symbol, as understood by the Order at the end of the eighteenth century.

There is much more on the old birth which is into the death of darkness, on leading back through the Word to the Spirit and thus into a second birth, but this is unto light in Christ, as into eternal life and the heavenly Kingdom. " The old must go entirely. ' Behold, I make all things new.' Herein is the being born again of water and the Spirit . . . through the Word of Truth. A new creature is born of God ; Christ becomes flesh therein, arises in man and awakens him." It is He in us and we in Him, for we are told otherwise

(1) that the new being remains in Christ; (2) that this is regeneration and unification with God. Here also is the sense in which the alchemical Water of Life is represented as flowing from the Vine of Christ. "The true Christian is he to whom the Son of God becomes manifest"—meaning inwardly—"through the power of the Holy Ghost"; but this revelation "is to be sought in each other's love", the "spiritual love of God in man being the source of all beatitude." To make an end therefore: (1) "All wisdom is comprised in one Book", being the Book of Life opened by the Lamb in the *Apocalypse*; (2) "all power is in one Stone"—*Lapis reprobatus, Caput anguli*; (3) "all beauty in one Flower"—*id est, Rosa Hierachunti*; (4) "all riches in one Treasure"—beyond the moth and the rust, and beyond the reach of thieves: it is called Treasure of the Humble and Treasure of Benefits; (5) "all felicity in one good", being that of which it is testified that it fills the heart entirely; (6) "and this"—understood as these in their unity—"is Christ Jesus, dead and risen." *Introivit semel in sancta, æterna redemptione inventa.*

There is nothing before me in Germanic records to shew how far, if anywise, these things were taken into the heart, so that realisation was begotten therein and came forth into the manifestation of life and dedicated work. But there is evidence, and some of it has been given in my previous book, that the Rosy Cross in Russia lifted up a great light at the same period and poured a healing grace on an arid and traitorous time. The operation of such providence was, however, arrested quickly, for Catharine II reigned on the Muscovite Throne. The question is beyond my province in this place. That upon which I can rule, at the value of a personal judgment based on the literature at large, is offered to those whom it concerns in these concluding words. The ruling is that under all reserves arising from a tangled skein of symbolism and the confusions of a cryptic language, the *Secret Symbols* and that which lies behind them in circles of the Rosy Cross, represent the doctrines of Spiritual Alchemy at the furthest point of development. In so far as the doctrines connote a valid experience, and are not "about it and about" in words and pictures, this so-called Alchemy is brought into line with the authentic records of

Christian Mysticism. In relations between man and man, the maxim of the Mastery is : *Sois l'œil de l'aveugle, le bras du pauvre et le bâton du vieillard, et Dieu te dira le grand pourquoi de la vie humaine.*[1] In respect of the Divine in the universe and the Divine beyond the universe, the maxims of the Greater Mastery are : *Est una sola res*, of old repute in Hermetism, and that which I have quoted already : *Omnia ab uno et omnia ad unum*, the connotation of which, alike in doctrine and experience, is : *In omnia, omnis Deus.* But the realisation of this,[2] from more to more, is the path of regenerated life, the path of mystical death and the path to that resurrection which is in Christ. There is also one other maxim, the last which shall be cited, and it reads : *Amor via est.* There is a sense in which it is the message of all these *Secret Symbols*.

Hereof therefore is the scope and purpose of that which has been called Spiritual Alchemy, adopting an arbitrary designation, not too well or wisely. It is to be observed that it is a way of life and that between the age of Byzantine records and the age of Luther there is no vestige of its doctrine or practice in alchemical literature.[3] As a way of life, moreover, the most that could be offered by any Instituted Mysteries would be a shadow of path and term in figurative pageant ; but those which belong to history had no such scheme in view. Finally, the way is not more followed or the end attained by the aids of magnetic trance than by

---

[1] A dictum of Éliphas Lévi.

[2] It is to be regretted that the measures of my critical purpose do not permit the consideration of a diagram and connected letterpress on p. 51 of the *Secret Symbols*. A Cross surmounted by a Crown is superposed on two solid triangles, the inscriptions on which are (1) Faith, Hope, Charity ; (2) Way, Truth, Life. It is written also, in the words of the Psalmist, that " the Stone which the builders rejected has become the headstone of the corner ". Beneath the Cross is a Chalice, from which emerges a Sacred Host. The doctrine is that of Tauler : (1) " The true communion is the substantial, potent, omnipotent presence of Christ " ; and (2) " If we are penetrated and full of the spirit of Christ, then is Christ present within us, and we are in Christ." It is the Rosicrucian doctrine of the Eucharist in its clearest formulation. It is said otherwise (1) that the Spirit of God is the nutriment of the human soul, and (2) that the Body of Christ is an universal spiritual substance or principle which fills those who can receive it. The Law is Nature and flesh but the Gospel is grace and spirit. Herein is the contrast between Adam and Christ. It is the most important diagram in the whole collection and has no adventitious elements. It is said elsewhere of Christ that He feeds flesh with his own substance and transforms it into a new being—another of the Eucharistic references which recur so frequently in the records of the Rosy Cross.

[3] Our research has determined the historical quest-object in a very different sense, as a record—that is to say—of alleged experimental physics.

those of opium or heroin; and it is not of communication, automatically or otherwise, by man to man. In view of the fact that those texts which can be regarded as of mystical intent, and this only, are exceedingly few as well as exceedingly late, their testimony to a Hidden School is restricted within the measures of the Rosy Cross at its German centre towards the close of the eighteenth century.

APPENDICES

I

ANIMAL MAGNETISM IN 1850

THE "Rochester Knockings", which inaugurated the epoch of modern Spiritualism, were first heard at Hydesville, U.S.A., towards the close of the year 1848. They marked and set apart that year from all others for many thousands of believers—in truth many tens of thousands—during succeeding decades. We have seen that the *Suggestive Inquiry* bears in its original edition the same date on its title, and it has been stated incautiously that Mr. South and his talented daughter had experimented in Spiritism prior to the publication of that work. As they do not happen to have been discoverers of Spiritism or to have turned tables before the girls of the Fox family, it is obvious that this is a mistake; but among "curious things of the outside world" which characterised that period we have Mrs. Atwood's personal testimony that they were "greatly excited with mesmerism" and were "mixed up" with its chief exponents in England. Now, Mrs. Atwood wrote upon Mesmerism before she wrote upon Alchemy, and it is needful to register the fact of her pamphlet on this subject[1] because it is not unlike a prolegomenon to her extended dissertation on the Hermetic Mystery. We may glance in the first place at the kind of atmosphere which prevailed when both productions grew up in the mind of their writer.

The school of Mesmerism in England may be said to have originated in the course of the year 1829, with the publication, in the *London Medical and Physical Journal*, of some articles on the subject by Richard Chenevix, F.R.S., as the result of experiments which had been undertaken by himself. These experiments were witnessed by various members of the medical profession, and, among these, led to the conversion

---

[1] *Early Magnetism, in its Higher Relations to Humanity as veiled in the Poets and the Prophets.* By Θυος Μαθος. 8vo., pp. viii + 127. London: 1846.

of Dr. Elliotson, whose sufferings in support of the unpopular cause form an instructive chapter in its history. Some years passed away, and in 1836 J. C. Colquhoun published his once well-known work, *Isis Revelata*, which is a summary history of Animal Magnetism up to the year 1831, when the second French commission issued its memorable report on the subject. In the same year the Baron du Potet visited London, being perhaps the most successful operator who had yet appeared in France. Indeed, from Mesmer to Puséygur, from Puséygur to De Leuze, and from De Leuze to Du Potet, these are the three epochs, in so far as France is concerned, of that art which was affirmed by the most zealous of its followers to have done more towards the explanation of man and the universe than any other discovery of the century to which it belongs. Du Potet gave public demonstrations, and we notice again the presence of Dr. Elliotson, who now undertook some researches on his own account and published their result in the *Lancet*. The high position which he occupied at the time gave great prominence to his views, and they excited much discussion and bitter hostility, from which he emerged, professionally speaking, a ruined man. But, gifted as he was with a peculiar tenacity of purpose, and withstanding, if he did not overcome, all the opposition, he was the recognised centre of the movement, within which a small but useful literature began to grow up. Townshend's *Facts in Mesmerism*; Esdaile's Account of its Curative Powers, as proved by his Mesmeric Hospital in India; Elliotson's *Cases of Surgical Operation without Pain in the Mesmeric Sleep*; Gregory's *Letters on Animal Magnetism*, became and remain among standard works of reference, to which appeal on the subject is still made, and not without justice.

The English school sought its explanation of the phenomena in the hypothesis of Mesmer himself, namely, that animals exercise an influence one upon another, at a distance and otherwise, by the projection or diffusion of a subtle fluid which was compared to the action of the magnet on iron; and about this there was for a long time no division of opinion. Those who believed in the phenomena accepted the explanation concerning them, while those who rejected the latter challenged the alleged evidences. But in the year 1841 a remarkable innovation arose which was destined to throw a fresh light upon the experiments, and to inaugurate a scientific investigation, with, finally, a general acceptance of many facts which had long been the subject of derision on the part of scientific men. In that year the Swiss mesmerist, La Fontaine, came to England and gave public demonstrations all over the country, including the town of Manchester. There James Braid, a Scottish surgeon of some exceptional ability, had settled recently, and his curiosity, or rather his scepticism, drew him to the meetings of La Fontaine, with the object of discovering how the manifestations were produced. He found, however, that he was not in the presence of occurrences which were the result of collusion, as he had expected, but that some at least of the phenomena were genuine. Thereupon he betook himself to a first-hand study of the experiments, with the idea of ascertaining the agency at work in their production. Prior to his investigations, the peculiar pathological conditions understood by the mesmeric state were supposed to require of necessity the presence of an operator, and on the hypothesis of a projected fluid it would be impossible for it to be otherwise. But Braid discovered that an operator was not essential, and he produced, under the name of Hypnotism, similar effects, which at the time he regarded as identical, by simply fixing the attention of the subject on some bright object. When he published the result of his observations and his reflections thereupon in his little work on *Neurypnology, or the Rationale of Nervous Sleep*, he abandoned the identity of the conditions induced by the two processes, but from his later writings, there is ground for believing that he had not really reached any definite conclusion.

While Elliotson was a man, as we have seen, of very high reputation and position, Braid had only a local practice, with a certain more extended status through his skill in the treatment of club-feet. But the man of influence lost caste altogether, while the more humble surgeon became famous. The explanation is not to be sought in the cross-purposes of fortune : in the one case an unpopular cause was championed by a person who, except by the repetition of experiments, cast no further light thereon ; in the other an original genius found a new explanation which made it possible to accept at least a section of the facts, without reference to a hypothesis which was everywhere regarded as unscientific because it was thought transcendental. It would not be correct, however, to assume that Braid's discovery was at once welcomed in all medical circles. The chief organ of the profession may be said never to have mentioned it during his lifetime, though it took it for granted when his obituary appeared in its columns. There was silence also for years in another camp, which there is no need to say was that of the mesmerists. It does not follow that individual exponents of the older process did not recognise the importance of Braid's discovery, but it was disliked by the central authority. Dr. Elliotson had suffered too long and too severely to allow willingly a cause which, for him at least, had become sacred in his own person to be thus rationalised and explained away.

The hypnotic method, despite its professional welcome, and despite the opposition of the so-called transcendental school, was in connection with some of the tenets of that school more intimately than its discoverer imagined at the inception. He was not long, however, in learning or perceiving that his process was akin to other processes which rank among the wonders of the past. He came to realise that self-hypnotism had been performed more or less by Fakirs, Yogis, Ascetics and even Saints of every land and most religious dispensations. When he first entranced a subject by means of his gold pencil-case or the head of his lancet, he reproduced inadvertently the artificial method by which Jacob Böhme entered into what has been called the " interior condition " ; but the *éblouissement* and trouble of the eye is not the only means of passing either into that state or into the condition of hypnotism. When Braid laid stress on the necessity of engrossing the attention, he might have known that the fixing of the eyes was only a pretext or a safeguard. He learned this afterwards when he found that he could hypnotise the blind.

While the phenomena of artificial somnambulism and the cataleptic trance were being reduced by Braid into science, Animal Magnetism may be fairly described as running riot in America, so great was the confusion of operation and theory, so indiscriminate were the things concluded from the facts produced, so sensational were the claims, and possibly the honest beliefs, of its ill-balanced exponents. The hypnotic fluid of Mesmer became in their hands no longer an invisible projection from one animal to another. The whole universe was permeated with the substance which the operator was supposed to dispense to his subject, and God Himself was spoken of as the Universal Mesmerist, much as at a slightly anterior period, and in another school, the Great Architect of the Universe was denominated the First Freemason. Scarcely had the subject been rendered superficially scientific and respectable by a matter of fact explanation, which ruled out the so-called higher phenomena, than a new process crossed the Atlantic, to make shipwreck of all the proprieties, in the shape of Electro-Biology, a name chosen with the peculiar tact which governs American vocabularies, and involving a double misdescription, as the phenomena were not electric and not more exclusively biological than the process of digestion. This notwithstanding, the new nondescript, exotic of unreason as it seemed, really involved something which if not overlooked by Braid, had received little prominence in his researches, or was not at least regarded from the most salient point of view. This was suggestion in the waking state. There can be no doubt that Grimes, the supposed inventor of Electro-Biology, and the itinerant lecturers who had come over to demonstrate his process, at least assisted Braid to realise a point which he had shunned, and first under the spirit of vigilance as to his parental rights over his own invention, and next with something derived from his own unconfessed borrowers, he reduced the subject to its proper proportions. Unfortunately, or otherwise, for all the interests involved, hypnotism itself was destined to be made obsolete for the time being, almost at its commencement, by the discovery of anæsthetics, which are far simpler in their operation and far more certain in their results. Here it must be remembered that the new psychological agent was almost exclusively presented for its curative powers and for its aids to surgery. Within the professional sphere, Braid, however, was a man of open mind, and he recognised the advantage of ether and chloroform in these special respects, without at the same time abating the superior claim of his own agent in more important directions than those of mere facility.

Towards the close of his life the report of experiments by the Austrian Baron von Reichenbach reached this country. These were designed to demonstrate quite unconsciously the very antithesis of Braid's discovery, namely, the existence of a fluid or emanation given off by animals and human beings, and by other objects which need not be enumerated, but including the graves of departed persons. He conducted his experiments with a great number of subjects who, he found, had the faculty of perceiving the alleged emanations, and there is no doubt that his patience and care were infinite. He seems in particular to have avoided as far as possible any suggestion of that which he expected to his subjects, though none of these could enter into a second experiment without being aware of its object. This unavoidably was a weak point in his researches, and Braid took up the matter accordingly, exposing the fallacy of his conclusion, while paying an admiring compliment to his skill and to the importance of his facts within a more limited range, namely, that of suggestion. It was the fashion of the moment in England to reduce all medical theses to the smallest dimensions and to publish them in the most unobtrusive form. Braid's counter-experiments, after appearing in a second-rate journal, because the ruling organ of the profession would not have received them with welcome, reappeared in a minute pamphlet closely and painfully set. Beside the enormous volumes of Reichenbach it must have looked so unserious as to be little short of ludicrous, and the Austrian baron seems to have left the Manchester surgeon to be disposed of by his English disciples, among whom were Ashburner and Gregory. There was thus no explicit reply to the ingenious arguments and experiments of James Braid. Reichenbach continued to believe that he had demonstrated the existence of a new imponderable, and at the present day, the recognition of an aura encompassing persons and objects is the commonest of psychical phenomena, nor do I know whether any one but a complete sceptic would be at the pains of challenging the simple point of fact.

The lessons which may be derived from the early history of the several processes in England are at once encouraging and disconcerting. They illustrate that natural and, we may hope, ineradicable sobriety which so invariably disposes the

English mind to that middle way in which safety for the most part lies, and in which truth is found occasionally. Sobriety of this kind is essentially of the scientific spirit. But it illustrates also, and this is not less true because it is a commonplace, that the reticence and reluctance of the middle way, and the scientific caution which in itself is so salutary, are subject to observable excesses of intolerance, the results of which have been not infrequently regrettable. The treatment of Dr. Elliotson, at the hands of men who were professionally his brethren, must be regarded as an instance to the point, after due allowance for the fact that a peculiar temperament may have predisposed him to aggravate rather than disarm the hostility which took arms against him. Except for the moral it conveys, the personal question is not now of any real consequence ; it is now nearly true to say that, in England at least, ' no man suffers loss or bleeds ' for scientific experiments or theories. Moreover, the memory at least of Elliotson has in these later days received a tardy but altogether honourable exculpation. The great majority of his facts have been substantiated fully by research, especially in France, and it has been demonstrated therefore that he suffered mainly because he was in the right. There is no higher compensation for suffering than a demonstration of this kind. Unfortunately time has shewn also that in Mesmerism as in Hypnotism the field of experiment is restricted, so far as the medical standpoint is concerned, and the instinct which dissuaded the profession from recognising the one and which led it to welcome the other, because it reduced the one, is memorable to-day only as a point of view, though the instinct was true in its way, an illustration of caution in the face of new realms as yet imperfectly explored.

Mrs. Atwood was concerned in her pamphlet only in a secondary and almost negligible sense with any question of ordinary therapeutics, as her sub-title indicates, and the first question before us is whether and how far she derived a notion of Animal Magnetism in its alleged higher aspects from those who preceded her in the theoretical and practical investigation of all its claims. It is of common knowledge that the psychic state of many entranced subjects conveyed an impression of purity, refinement, beauty, as if the actual or comparative grosser part had been put to sleep for the time being. But this state is as far removed from the spiritual attainment envisaged by Platonic successors as are the records of trance mediumship from the realisations of Eckehart and Ruysbroeck, speaking in the light of the union. When J. C. Colquhoun produced his story of Animal Magnetism under the ambitious title of *Isis Revelata*, as if the girdle of all Mysteries were unloosed thereby and therein, we might be excused for thinking that he was Mrs. Atwood's precursor in a thesis of " intellectual reminiscence " and the hidden science of the soul transmitted from antique sanctuaries. That she turned in this direction—though it was to find nothing —there is good reason to suppose and she may have gleaned some notions from Ennemoser's *History of Magic*, which appeared at Munich in 1843 but was not translated into English till four years after the publication of the *Suggestive Inquiry*. It explained all wonders of the past by the aid of Animal Magnetism, and cites Schubert on the preparations and purifications of candidates for the Egyptian priesthood. It has something to say otherwise of healing temples in Greece and elsewhere, like those of Æsculapius, and the "houses of sleep " therein. But of Eleusis and its Rites, or of other Instituted Mysteries, save that alleged in connection with Egyptian sacerdotal ordination, there is no word anywhere.

II

Kabalistic Alchemy

THE attention of my readers is directed in the present excursus to an unfrequented byway of Hermetic research. It is exceedingly curious and will repay visitation on this account only, but it would not be offered for consideration on this ground alone: a connection between the Kabalah and Alchemy is a traditional notion which is taken for granted and is referred to frequently in the literature of transmutation, for which reason it must not be passed over entirely. At the same time, and with the exception of a single text, it is a matter of ascription only, for which reason I have placed this study in an appendix rather than in the body of my work. We are taken back in the first instance to Byzantine Alchemy, and it will be remembered that among the writings of Zosimus the Panopolite there is a tract entitled *The True Book of Sophe the Egyptian*, of which some account has been given. It appears to regard Lead—philosophically understood or otherwise—as the First Matter of the Physical Work and Copper as the Tingeing Agent. However this may be, the little text has a preamble of one paragraph concerning the Divine Lord of the Hebrews and the Powers of Sabaoth. This creates a noteworthy distinction between the science and wisdom of the Egyptians and that of the Jews. Both have come down from the far past; neither investigates material or corruptible bodies; the operation of each is sustained by prayer and Divine Grace; but that of the Hebrews is rooted more solidly in Divine Justice. There follows a passage which I have quoted already elsewhere [1] and which is the earliest example of a recurring comparison between the work of Alchemy and that of God in creation. " The symbol of chemistry is drawn from creation (in the eyes of its adepts), who save and purify the divine soul enchained

[1] See *ante*, p. 80, and compare my *Doctrine and Literature of the Kabalah*, 1902, pp. 451, 452.

in the elements and, more than all, who separate the divine spirit entangled with the flesh ". This is sufficiently remarkable as a definition of the work of adeptship, but I have reduced it within due limits when commenting thereupon. We have seen also that the tract proceeds promptly to its proper business, being that of transmutation, and affirms its thesis thus : " As there is a sun, the flower of fire, a celestial sun, the right eye of the world, so Copper, if it become flower (that is, if it assume the colour of gold) by purification, becomes a terrestrial sun, which is king on earth, as the sun is king in heaven ".[1]

My object in repeating these citations is not to shew that it is easy—as it is certainly—to find casual mystical aspects of Alchemy in the Greek remains, but to introduce my particular subject by proof positive that thus early in the records, we find the people of Israel accredited with science and wisdom like that of Solomon, namely, greater than the Egyptians, but—ex hypothesi—like theirs a science and wisdom which seems on the surface to have a supposed analogy with Alchemy. We may leave it, at least for the moment, as an open question whether the wisdom and science were purely mystical and transcendent or whether there was also what was thought to be a practical side in the sense of physics.

Here, then, and in any case, is our first intimation concerning the possible existence of a Kabalistic Alchemy at an early period of the Christian centuries. In the opinion of M. Berthelot, the tract—but more correctly there are two tracts—which Zosimus refers to Sophe, or Cheops, contains elements of considerable antiquity, belonging to the period of the oldest texts passing under the name of Hermes. It is not a very clear intimation, being confined to the statement of an alleged fact, from which nothing appears to follow. There is, however, as we have seen, a much longer treatise —by way of commentary on Zosimus and some other philosophers—referred by tradition to Olympiodorus, an Alexandrian philosopher, and possibly the preceptor of Proclus. In this it is affirmed that Democritus and the rest of the adepts, belonging to anterior times, concealed their science by the use of common and inappropriate terms, so that it

---

[1] Berthelot, *Collection des Anciens Alchimistes Grecs.* Greek text, pp. 213, 214; French translation, 206–208.

might be reserved to the Egyptian kings and that they, on their own part, might be enabled to maintain their rank among the prophets. The Jews notwithstanding attained knowledge of the practice and expounded it in clandestine books.[1] It is said further by Zosimus himself that the Jews, having been initiated, transmitted that with which they had been entrusted, namely, suitable processes in the mystery of natural tinctures.[2] So also he went in quest of a certain " instrument " but could find nothing concerning it till he had recourse to Jewish books.[3] Finally, under the pretext of describing furnaces and other apparatus, the same Zosimus gives an account of the vocation, habits and aims of philosophers which incorporates a very curious mysticism concerning man in his original perfection, the fall of man, his redemption and restoration to Paradise. All this he claims to have drawn out of Jewry, and it is not a little in the likeness of what we now understand as Kabalism, but permeated by Gnostic and Christian elements.[4]

Now it is difficult to think that these testimonies do not establish the fact that not only was the Secret Doctrine in Israel beginning to exceed the measures of Talmudic literature, but that there were at least a few alchemical treatises, presumably written in Hebrew, outside those of Maria the Jewess, to whom the Byzantine alchemists refer so frequently, it being understood, however, that they were not of necessity Kabalistic in the proper sense of the term. Zosimus, it should be remembered, belongs to the third century of the Christian era and pseudo-Democritus is referred by Berthelot to the very beginning of Christianity. The Hebrew literature is, however, lost—unless, after that manner which is dear to the heart of occultists, we prefer to say that it is in concealment.

Kabalistic Alchemy is represented at this day by a single tract, or rather by so much of it as can be found in a piece-meal translation into Latin of the late seventeenth century. The original has disappeared, and it is indeterminable whether it was written in Hebrew or Aramaic, though one

---

[1] *Loc. cit.*, Greek text, p. 90 ; French translation, p. 98.
[2] *Ibid.*, Greek text, pp. 242, 243 ; translation, pp. 233, 234.
[3] *Ibid.*, Greek text, p. 138 ; translation, p. 140.
[4] *Ibid.*, Greek text, pp. 229–233 ; translation, pp. 222–226.

of the modern editors has decided in favour of the latter, but without assigning his reasons. The text in question is called *Aesh Mezareph*, the " refiner's fire " of *Malachi ii, 3,* according to the Authorised Version, but translated *ignis conflans* in the Vulgate, and hence the alchemical work is called in the English rendering of 1714, *Purifying Fire.* It was put into Latin, as I have said, by the pains of Baron Knorr von Rosenroth and is incorporated into that great Lexicon or Apparatus which forms the first volume of his *Kabbala Denudata.* The incorporation has no pretence to completeness, which was not to be expected, having regard to the purpose in view; and the extracts are described by Rosenroth on his first title-page as forming a *Compendium Libri Cabbalistico-Chymici, Ash-Mezareph dicti, de Lapide Philosophico,* etc. When the unknown student who called himself " A Lover of Philalethes " made the English translation at the period I have mentioned, he collected all the excerpts scattered through the Kabalistic dictionary and reduced them into logical order, taking considerable pains. His work has been reprinted, with certain revisions and occasional notes, under the editorship of Dr. Wynn Westcott.[1] What proportion the collated text, as we know it, bears to the original seems likely to remain as it now is, a matter of speculation, though a preface to the latest English edition mentions that it is " still extant as a separate treatise ". About this there must be some misapprehension, unless it is in that state of hiddenness to which I have alluded. In any case it does not seem to have been available for the purpose of the edition in question.

In the absence of the original we are as much in the dark as to its date as we are about the comparatively unimportant question of its authorship. It is transparently that which it claims to be, a genuine remanent of Kabalistic Alchemy. At the same time, it belongs to late Kabalism, as it postulates the existence of ten *Sephiroth* or Numerations in each of the Kabalistic Worlds, and this is not countenanced by the *Zohar.* There is one reference to Geber, the Arabian philosopher, but, at least to my own mind, it suggests an acquaintance with the Latin tracts alone. The *Zohars* are rather numerous in Hebrew and there is mention of one of

[1] *Collectanea Hermetica,* Vol. IV, 1894.

them which treats of medicine, but this I have failed to identify and believe that it may be a confused reference to the anonymous *Zohar Al Harrephua*, or *Splendor super Medicinam*, which was printed at Venice in 1497. Could we rest certain that the " Lover of Philalethes " had made

1
KETHER
The Crown
White Head

3
BINAH
Understanding
The Mother

2
CHOKMAH
Wisdom
The Father

5
GEBURAH
Severity

4
CHESED
Mercy

6
TIPHERETH
Beauty
The Son

8
HOD
Glory

7
NETZACH
Victory

9
YESOD
Foundation
10
MALKUTH
The Kingdom
The Daughter

THE SEPHIROTH AND THEIR SIGNIFICATIONS.

all his extracts from Rosenroth correctly, the *terminus ad quem* in respect of antiquity might be settled out of hand, for *The Book of Purifying Fire* in its English form quotes *The Garden of Pomegranates*, which is a work of Moses of Cordova, and this Rabbinical Master flourished in the course of the sixteenth century, the date of his death being 1570. On referring, however, to the Latin text of Rosenroth it seems certain that a mistake has been made and that a short passage referable to the German compiler has been credited to the alchemical text. In this case, four lines at the head of Chapter III call to be deleted. I should imagine, in conclusion as to the point of date, that we shall be safe in assigning the *Aesh Mezareph* to the sixteenth century, or subsequently to the appearance of the *Sepher Ha Zohar* in its first printed forms at Cremona and Mantua, between 1558 and 1560. There is no doubt in my own mind that it was the publication of these editions which gave an impetus to the study of Kabalism, both in Christendom and Jewry ; for, although what I have called late Kabalism, largely an extension of Zoharic doctrine and its interpretation, had already begun, the works by which it is best known are of posterior date.

Having now finished with the preliminary and bibliographical part of my subject, I will take up the question as to the way in which the little Kabalistic treatise on Alchemy should be approached if we are to attain any clear notion of its symbolical content. In so far as it embodies Kabalistic elements regarded under a Hermetic light, we must have recourse to the *Zohar* for its study. Following *Sepher Yetzirah* or *The Book of Formation*, this great monument of Hebrew Theosophy postulates ten *Sephiroth* or Numerations extended through Four Worlds, beginning with pure Deity and ending with the manifest creation. There is neither place nor occasion to speak of them in detail here. In a broad sense the gulf between the Divine and the world of earthly elements was bridged by means of the *Sephiroth*, and hence they have been called emanations, but the Zoharic system is not, strictly speaking, emanationist, or at least it includes counter aspects which modify or perhaps cancel some apparent leanings in that direction. The *Sephiroth* are tabulated as follows : KETHER = The Crown ; CHOKMAH = Wisdom ; BINAH = Understanding ; CHESED = Mercy ; GEBURAH = Severity ; TIPHERETH = Beauty ; NETZACH = Victory ; HOD = Glory ; YESOD = The Foundation ; MALKUTH = The Kingdom. These titles are conventional, for the most part, and will be familiar to many, but they have been enumerated, this notwithstanding, for the purpose of the subject in hand. In ancient Kabalism the first three form the *habitaculum* of Deity, the essence of which is triadic. This is the world of *Atziluth, fons Deitatis,* the true region of emanation, but it is that of Divine Persons, proceeding one from another, though having very slight correspondence with

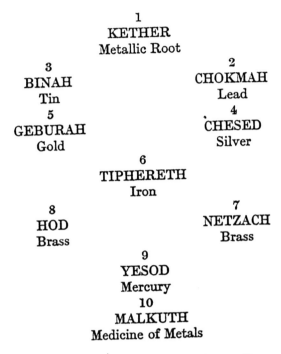

1
KETHER
Metallic Root

3
BINAH
Tin

2
CHOKMAH
Lead

5
GEBURAH
Gold

4
CHESED
Silver

6
TIPHERETH
Iron

8
HOD
Brass

7
NETZACH
Brass

9
YESOD
Mercury
10
MALKUTH
Medicine of Metals

THE SEPHIROTH AND METALS: FIRST SCHEME OF ALLOCATIONS ACCORDING TO AESH MEZAREPH.

the Christian Trinity. The next three *Sephiroth* constitute the world of *Briah,* or of creation. From one point of view, this world is archetypal, the pattern or idea in Divine Mind which became manifest afterwards; from another it is the realm of highest created intelligence, understood broadly as archangelic. The world of *Yetzirah* or Formation comprises three further *Sephiroth.* Under one aspect of symbolism, the universe was formed therein, but it was not externalised; from another standpoint it is the angelic world. *Assiah*, the factual, manifest, material world is constituted by the tenth *Sephira*, *Malkuth*. Here is one scheme of the Sephirotic system, but there is another of high importance which postulates *Briah* and *Yetzirah* as the body of the Divine Son

1
KETHER
Philosophical Mercury

3
BINAH
Philosophical Sulphur

2
CHOKHAH
Philosophical Salt

5
GEBURAH
Gold

4
CHESED
Silver

6
TIPHERETH
Iron

8
HOD
Copper

7
NETZACH
Tin

9
YESOD
Lead

10
MALKUTH
Metallic Woman
or Moon-Lady

THE SEPHIROTH AND METALS: SECOND SYSTEM OF ALLOCATIONS ACCORDING TO AESH MEZAREPH.

and *Assiah* or *Malkuth* as the Daughter of God. Between them they contain all created intelligence, from Seraphim to human souls, and the Daughter is more especially the Community of Israel, the synthesis of elect souls. So far concerning the *Zohar*, but the masters of rabbinical theosophy who discourse therein knew nothing of Alchemy, nor does the latter exhibit any connection or acquaintance with Kabalism of this kind.

Later Kabalism had, however, yet another classification, as I have intimated already, and this repeated the decade of *Sephiroth* through each of the Four Worlds. Now, it was possible obviously to say things about *Kether* in *Assiah* which were not possible about *Kether* in *Atziluth*, and so of the rest. But the author of *Aesh Mezareph* goes further even than this and affirms that the *Sephiroth* are found, from first to last, in the Mineral Kingdom; and on this basis he produces two further classifications, as they now follow. (1) *Kether* = The Metallic Root, from which all metals originate, as the remaining *Sephiroth* from *Kether* in the worlds above. (2) *Chokmah* = Lead, which is the first-born of the Metallic Root and is called Father in relation to the rest of the metals. (3) *Binah* = Tin, being of old evolution in the series, as shewn by its age. (4) *Chesed* = Silver, and the reason of this allocation is said to be the metal's colour and use. (5) *Geburah* = Gold, because in the late Kabalistic Diagram called the Tree of Life, *Geburah* is on the left or northern side, and according to *Job* xxxvii, 22, gold " cometh from the North ". With this rendering the Latin Vulgate agrees but our Authorised Version substitutes " fair weather " for the precious metal. (6) *Tiphereth* = Iron, because it is said to be like a man of war, presumably having the kind of beauty which belongs to the array of battle. (7 and 8) *Netzach* and *Hod* = Brass, because this is the hermaphrodite of metals and because the two pillars of Solomon's Temple were made thereof. (9) *Yesod* = Mercury, because it is the foundation of life, and quicksilver is a living water, which is the basis not only of metallic Art, but of Nature herself. (10) *Malkuth* = the Medicine of Metals, because they are metamorphosed thereby into gold and silver, under the auspices of Judgment = *Geburah* = Gold, and of Mercy = *Chesed* = Silver, on the right and left sides of the Tree.

The alternative classification is held equally acceptable for the reason that " all systems tend to the one truth ". According to this, the first three or Supernal *Sephiroth* represent the three alchemical Principles, thus *Kether* = Philosophical Mercury; *Chokmah* = Philosophical Salt; *Binah* = Philosophical Sulphur; *Chesed* = Silver; *Geburah* = Gold;

Tiphereth = Iron ; *Netzach* = Tin ; *Hod* = Copper ; *Yesod* = Lead ; and *Malkuth* = The Metallic Woman, the *Luna* of the Wise, the Water of Gold and that mysterious field " into which the seeds of secret minerals ought to be cast ". I should add that, his liberality notwithstanding, the author of *Aesh Mezareph* prefers the first classification, as it is that which he uses chiefly in the text.

The next question before us is that which we can learn from our text about metals and their allocations, the Three Principles, the Medicine, and the Water of the Wise. As a Kabalist, the author was quite naturally concerned with the tabulation of all important references to the seven metals found in the Old Testament. On these he allegorised, computed the sum of the numbers produced by the consonants of the names, and sought further light by comparison with other names and words from which the same numbers could be derived. Herein he followed certain familiar methods —I mean, familiar among Kabalists—but if I were to enter into this part of the subject and deal adequately therewith I might fill a volume. If anyone should be disposed to pursue it, I can promise him much that is curious, a few analogies which are striking, but he will not find that *latens Deitas* abiding, by the hypothesis, behind the processes —whether these are understood as belonging to mystical Alchemy, or as the secret of metallic transmutation.

It is possible, no doubt, to work so long at the decade of *Sephiroth* and dwell upon it so steadfastly that an enthusiast will see the desired thing everywhere. Had it not been for the saving virtues of sovereign reason, I might have been in such case myself, considering my years of immersion in Kabalism, its schools and its literature. The " adept anonymous and lover of learning " who discoursed of Purifying· Fire must have taken a high degree in this kind of persuasion, for he discovers the decade in Gold, which has ten orders or degrees, all derived from the Scriptures and beginning with the *Kether* of the precious metal, being that " head of fine Gold " celebrated in *The Song of Solomon*, v, 11, and ending with the " Gold of Ophir " mentioned in *Job*, xxxii, 25. Silver has also its decade, and if anyone is in search of its *Kether*, he will find it in *Exodus*, xxxviii, 17, where the chapiters of the pillars in the Court of the Tabernacle are said to be overlaid with this metal. But the *Malkuth* of Silver is that Silver " seven times purified " which is compared to the Word of the Lord in *Psalm*, xii, 6. The *Sephiroth* of Lead are in a state of Occultation, which means literally that the number of references to this metal in Holy Writ falls short of the decade, so that it has to be completed by splitting the reference in *Zechariah*, v, 7, 8, into two parts. Lead in alchemical doctrine is the Primordial Salt of the Wise. Now, as it is impossible to discover more than five references to Tin in all the Law and the Prophets, the author is in a position to elicit an exotic of Secret Doctrine to account for the inconsequence of this metal so far as the Work of Wisdom is concerned and he says therefore that it " remains separate from the Universal Medicine ". Moreover, vileness and tenuity are its conspicuous vices and hence—in addition to the obvious Scriptural reason already intimated—it is not suggested that Tin contains a Sephirotic decade. On the other hand, this is found easily in Brass, which term there is reason to believe signifies Copper ; but silence reigns concerning the decade in respect of Mercury or Quicksilver. The reason seems to be that this metal was unknown in ancient Jewry, though our Hermetic scholiast pretends that its mystery lies hidden in the name of Mehetabel, who was the wife of a king of Edom, according to *Genesis*, xxxvi, 29. I do not know why the decade of Iron is omitted from *Aesh Mezareph*, unless it be that this kind of invention maketh even the heart of the artist grow sick within him ; but we learn for our consolation instead that Iron is the Male and Bridegroom, " without whom the Virgin is not impregnated," which Virgin would seem to be the philosophical *Luna,* or Medecine of Metals, already mentioned. Turning for one moment to the second tabulation and in particular to the three alchemical Principles, no canon of distinction seems to be offered between *Mercurius Philosophorum* and mineral Quicksilver ; on Philosophical Sulphur I find nothing that lends itself to quotation ; while the discourse on the Salt of the Wise seems to be one of the lost sections.

So far it will appear that the intimations of *Aesh Mezareph* are remote from the practical side of things in Physical Alchemy ; they are an exaggeration in part of Zoharic principles of commentary, interpretation and so forth, while for the rest they draw upon the artificial and arbitrary devices of what is called the practical Kabalah. There is of course no reason to question that its domain is that of metals, literally understood, or at least that it begins therein. What it presents, however, in rough and broad lines is an hypothesis of evolution or generation from a Metallic Root, operating in several directions with various results, according to the places of the *Sephiroth* on the Tree of Life. As such, I consider that the first tabulation is almost manifestly incorrect; but if the second should be preferred to the first, it is not therefore unimpeachable. I have met with other attributions in more secret Kabalistic systems and these are still better, though not perhaps perfect; but they do not concern us now. To the hypothesis there is a process added for the production of the White and Red Tinctures, but I do not feel that it would serve any useful purpose to do more than register the fact. It rests on the authority of Rabbi Mordecai, though I do not find an alchemist of this name in the great bibliography of Bartolocci.[1]

Hereof is Kabalistic Alchemy, as it stands in the text, and I should think that scientific criticism would be disposed to turn and rend me, did I suggest that it should be taken seriously, or even as a contribution of any discernible moment to the most cryptic side of the literature. There is, however, another point of view, and to approach this we must set aside the wonderful but arbitrary verbal gymnastics of *Gematria*, *Temura* and *Notaricon*, in virtue of which Kabalism of a certain sort deduced anything that it wanted from the words of Scripture by the transposition of Hebrew consonants, the substitution of one for another and the computation of their numerical values. There are a few people in Israel who believe in these kinds of methods even at this day, but they are the antithesis of philosophical Kabalism. When the *Zohar* draws from the fountains of the higher mind, it knows nothing of such devices: indeed it knows and cares very little concerning them in moments of pure fantasy. It is arbitrary enough, very often and too often, after its own manner, but it has other tricks than these. The ill-equipped occultism of the late nineteenth century, when it betook itself to Kabalism in ignorance of the real authorities,

---

[1] *Bibleotheca Magna Rabbinica*, 4 vols., folio, Rome, 1675-93.

thought that there were great mysteries in all these follies of artifice.

We must set aside the putative process of *The Book of Purifying Fire*, and then there will remain the attribution of metals and their supposititious planets to certain *Sephiroth* in the Tree of Life, together with that of alchemical Principles and so forth to the *Sephiroth* which remain over. Now, I have followed the quest of the meaning which lies behind these ascriptions through no common paths of research, and I have found some things that belong to our subject on the possibly mystical side of the Hermetic literature. If metallic transmutation is possible, then—in the hope that it may become actual—we know enough to be certain that the experiment has to be approached from the direction of modern scientific chemistry and not from that of the old alchemical texts. There are seven planets of the ancients as there were seven metals; the names given to the planets in the Western world have become in the course of time almost interchangeable with those of the metals. At least this is certainly the case so far as Alchemy is concerned. The history of the interlinking is obscure and it is beyond my present horizon. I may say that it is not explicable by arbitrary analogies of ascribed colour, though there are certain thin correspondences, as, for example, between Sun and Gold. It is not entirely explicable by an hypothesis of astrological influence, as there seems nothing on the surface of this to connect Saturn and Lead. It is a western doctrine of similitudes, and as such has been extended to the Signs themselves; but this does not now concern us. The Hebrew names of these planets are not only entirely distinct from those of the metals, so far as the metals were known to ancient Jewry, but they were never interchanged with these. The seven planets were: *Sabbathaï, Tzedeq, Maadim, Hamâ, Nogâ, Cokhab, Lebanâ*; that is to say, Saturn, Jupiter, Mars, Sun, Venus, Mercury, Moon. This is on the authority of the *Zohar*, Part III, fol. 287*a*. The seven metals are: Lead = *Ophereth*; Tin = *Bedel*; Iron = *Barzel*; Gold = *Zahad*; Copper = *Nehuseth*; which, except in *Ezra* viii, 27, is always translated " Brass " in the Authorised Version; Mercury = *Aspirka*; Silver = *Cheseph*. The connection with which I am dealing between the metals and *Sephiroth* cannot be said to exist in the *Zohar*, though we are told in one place that Silver = *Chesed* = Mercy, and Gold = *Geburah* = Severity, or alternatively, Gold = *Binah* = Understanding, while Brass is the union between Severity and Mercy, which might be held to answer by way of reflection to *Netzach* = Victory and *Hod* = Glory. [*Zohar*, Part II, fol. 138*b*.] So also Iron is once referred to *Malkuth* and once to *Tiphereth*. I must add that the great text knows little and next to nothing of a connection between the planets and *Sephiroth*, because the planets belong to *Assiah*. The distinctive name of the planetary world is *Galgooleem*, which is here taken as a synonym of *Assiah*, and, as we have seen, this world corresponds to *Malkuth*, the repetition of the Sephirotic decade in each world being a later invention. Our particular author dwells, however, on a mystical interconnection between all the worlds and between the kingdom of metals and the kingdom of heaven. " The mysteries of this wisdom differ not from the superior mysteries of the Kabalah. For the same consideration obtains respecting the predicaments in holiness as respecting those of the impure region. The *Sephiroth* which are in *Atziluth* are the same as those in *Assiah* ". It is added that " their excellency is always greater on the spiritual plane ". It follows from this that the author of *Purifying Fire* recognises that there is a correspondence, not, however, developed, between the metals hidden in the earth and the planets which move in heaven : herein he is at one with alchemical literature, taken as a whole, and, I presume, with certain aspects of astrology. He recognises further that there is a higher, more momentous, correspondence between the metals and *Sephiroth*, extending through all the worlds recognised by Kabalism : herein he is particular to himself, and it is at this point that his thesis begins to emerge, if anywhere, into a mystical light.

The *Sephiroth* in the *Zohar* are a ladder of sanctity by which a man can be united to the Holy One, and the allocation of certain *Sephiroth* to certain metals, though comprehensible in a text belonging to Hermetic literature, which is committed to the Doctrine of Correspondences, is a stretching of that doctrine to breaking point, unless the metals themselves are spiritualised. As much must be said in my opinion, concerning the planets ; and I do not suppose that, on either side, the alternatives can be regarded as lying within the field of legitimate or tolerable discussion. Now, in orthodox Kabalism it cannot be said that there is any trace of symbolism concerning the Metallic Kingdom, save and except in so far as the Sephirotic correspondences which I have mentioned may imply—as I hold that they do—not only a marriage in symbolism, but an uplifting into a spiritual order. The question of planetary allocations is in much the same case. The sun, according to the *Zohar*, is in correspondence with *Tiphereth*, the moon with *Malkuth*, and these luminaries are spiritualised after the same manner as will be found in Holy Scripture. For example, the light which rules the day is the Sun of Justice and of Righteousness that " shall arise with healing in its wings ", according to *Malachi iv, 2*. I must not make myself responsible for the content of a colossal text like the *Zohar* on the face-value of memory, but I do not believe that there are any other express allocations of planets to *Sephiroth* found therein. Yet it would be difficult to affirm that much which passed into expression and extension at a later period is not by implication in the *Zohar*, and at the dawn of the sixteenth century, or some fifty years before the text in question was printed, the following notable attributions are registered by Cornelius Agrippa in his *Three Books of Occult Philosophy*, which was in the hands of Abbot Trithemius in 1510, as appears by his letter prefixed to this work. The planet Saturn is referable to *Binah*, the third *Sephira* ; Jupiter to *Chesed* ; Mars to *Geburah* ; the Sun to *Tiphereth* ; Venus to *Netzach* ; Mercury to *Hod* ; and the Moon to *Yesod* [*Op. cit.*, Book III, Ch. 10]. These ascriptions differ from both tabulations of *Aesh Mezareph*, but the author of this work testifies that " if anyone hath placed these things in another order, I shall not contend with him, inasmuch as all systems tend to the one truth ". Cornelius Agrippa invented nothing on his own part, being only a diligent compiler, and it follows that on this subject he drew from early Kabalists ; but I have no means of identifying them. I regard his scheme as preferable to those of later date, and it assuredly implies that the *Sephiroth* connected with the planets had also an influence on the metals which correspond to these, a correspondence which he develops fully elsewhere in his work. [*Ibid.* Book I, Chapters 23 to 29.]

Let us take, however, the second classification of *Aesh Mezareph* and see what it implies in the light of Zoharic Theosophy.

We have seen that the three alchemical Principles are in the place of the supernal *Sephiroth*, which is the world of Deity. Philosophical Mercury is in analogy with the Metallic Root of the alternative list and belongs to *Kether*, wherein is the Great White Head of the Zoharic Holy Assemblies, being That which resulted from the first movement of the Unknowable God towards the state of being declared and manifest. Out of *Kether*, by a simultaneous development, there proceeded the co-equal *Sephiroth* which are called *Chokmah* and *Binah*, being the Divine Father and Mother of Kabalistic Theosophy, both implied in *Kether* and not in separation therefrom. In *The Book of Purifying Fire* these correspond to Philosophical Salt and Sulphur, which are not in separation from Mercury, for the Principles are a trinity in unity, like the three *Sephiroth* of *Atziluth*. But the triad of these Supernals produces a second triad, being *Chesed, Geburah* and *Tiphereth*, or the world of highest created intelligence. In Alchemy they generate Silver, Gold and Iron, or the perfect metals and what, I suppose, might be called alchemically the first degeneration from these. But Philosophical Iron, according to *Aesh Mezareph*, is the Sun of the Wise, the Male or Bridegroom, as we have seen, in correspondence with the Divine Son, begotten by the Divine Father and Mother. A third triad follows, which is another world of created intelligence, namely, *Netzach, Hod* and *Yesod*, or metallically Tin, Copper and Lead. There is no philosophical Tin—according to *Aesh Mezareph*—but Copper has an influence from Gold, as *Hod* draws from *Geburah*, and Philosophical Lead, according to our text, has the whole system of the universe concealed therein, because *Yesod* represents generation and the Kabalistic organs of sanctity by which this is operated. Hence Lead is called also the Father.

Finally, there is the fourth world of *Assiah* or *Malkuth*, the region of manifest things, in correspondence with the Metallic Woman, Moon-Lady and Medicine for the White, " so-called because she hath received a whitening splendour from the sun." There is only one way to explain this allocation, and it is by recourse to Theosophical Kabalism on its highest mystical side. The Sun is that Divine Luminary which is termed Jehovah in the *Zohar*, but also by other Sacred Names, and the Moon-Lady is Shekinah, connected in her manifestation with *Malkuth*.

We are now in a position to understand something of the entire scheme. The outward development of transcendental *Sephiroth* produced, *ex hypothesi*, a perfect manifest order, which, according to tradition, fell subsequently; but the Divine Presence of Shekinah is still on this earth of ours, and the return journey by which all things are consummated in God is by and in union with her. She is the leader of the human race—or at least the elect therein—into the beatific state of *Atziluth*, and the nature of the travelling is adumbrated by the qualities ascribed in the *Zohar* to the *Sephiroth* above *Malkuth*, up to and including *Chesed*. There is no opportunity here to specify these qualities, but they can be ascertained by a collation of Kabalistic texts.

On the alchemical side it is testified by the entire literature that the intention of Nature was always to make Gold or by inference at least Silver, as an alternative perfect metal; but owing to effective hindrances the so-called inferior metals have been produced instead. In the *Malkuth* of the metallic Kingdom, there is, however, that which *Aesh Mezareph* denominates a certain " field ", a place of " whitening splendour ", a realm of medicine and of healing, wherein is the Moon-Lady, who is also the field. Herein lies the restoration of metals, so that they shall enter into the perfect state, which is to be understood as the free operation within them of the Three Principles in the Supernals of the World of Metals. This analogy constitutes what I termed at the beginning that other Gate of Alchemy which, if opened by the student, might lead into strange places, even to the Heart of the Master.

In conclusion, I think that the little tract on *Purifying Fire* deals, as I have said, with literal and material metals, but is written in the light of its statement that the greater excellence is always in the spiritual world. So far as it puts forward physical processes seriously, it is the dream of a fantasiast, who held that a described order on the spiritual plane is repeatable of necessity on the material. But the greater excellence is also the greater consequence, and it is this—as it seems to me—which mattered to the "adept anonymous" and lover of strange learning, who set out his Tree of Life in Alchemy after such a manner that the Metallic Root and Mercury—desired of the Wise—corresponded in the mineral kingdom with that Crown of the Tree where his peers and co-heirs on the higher side of the Secret Tradition had fixed the supernal dwelling of God and His Shekinah in union. I am disposed to think that, like Jacob Böhme, he had not "proceeded to the *praxis*", but was content rather to dream in Zoharic palaces on endless worlds of symbolism and proclaim their bonds of union in the traditional Tree of Life. In so far therefore as *Aesh Mezareph* is a Kabalistic Light on Alchemy it is such only on the basis of analogy between things above and below, on the part of one whose chief concern was apparently for those which are above. After what manner this speculative and theoretical part can be said to exhibit the possibility of transmuting metals is for those to find who can : the interest begins when it is realised that the metals can be curiously spiritualised in their correspondences with the *Sephiroth* on the Tree ; but this task is not attempted in the text, as now extant, so that the issue is at a loose end, and there remains only the process, veiled heavily as usual, for the composition of the White and Red Tinctures.

III

Recent Editions of the Suggestive Inquiry

WE have seen that the *Suggestive Inquiry* was issued and suddenly withdrawn in 1850. After the lapse of sixty-eight years it was republished posthumously in 1918 from a revised copy of the writer, collated with another in which Mr. Walter Moseley, an occult student, had corrected " errors of translation, quotation and print ", meaning the overlooked misreadings of compositors. A third edition was called for in 1920, to which were added certain " Table Talk and Memorabilia " from the notebook of Mrs. Atwood.[1] Both reissues were carried through the press by Mr. W. L. Wilmshurst, who furnished also an extended introduction, comprising (1) an account of Mrs. Atwood and of the circumstances under which her book was produced originally ; (2) an *apologia* for its reissue ; and (3) an account of Hermetism from the editor's personal standpoint in relation to the text. The last contribution is in part a dogmatic restatement of views expressed in the *Suggestive Inquiry*, as reflected in the editor's mind, and in part an exposition of further assumptions particular to himself. It offers nothing therefore to the defence, elucidation or critical understanding of a peculiarly challengeable work. It will be fair—and serviceable perhaps otherwise—to offer for those who are concerned the warrants of this judgment by condensing the various dogmatic utterances presented in the third section of the introductory discourse.[2] (1) Hermetism " or its synonym Alchemy " is primarily the science of the soul's regeneration. (2) In a secondary sense it is a method of raising metals and other

[1] It is much to be regretted that the editor was not in a position or did not see fit to distinguish Mrs. Atwood's innumerable extracts from Hermetic and other writers by the simple aid of quotation marks. In their absence—as stated already—the reader is beset with needless difficulties over the beginning and end of citations, more especially when they follow one another in rapid succession. It is unpardonable, moreover, to issue a volume of some six hundred pages written in an involved style on an involved subject and provide no index whatever.

[2] See pp. 26–64.

sub-human things to a nobler form. (3) It postulates an event corresponding to the theological fall of man. (4) A supernatural principle submerged in man can be awakened and a way is thus provided for escaping the consequences of this event. (5) The supernatural principle cannot be awakened, however, by evolutionary processes alone. (6) There must be assistance from outside Nature, and this is the office of Religion. (7) The proper function of Religion is to bring about a second birth in man. (8) A " definite and exact science " of rebirth and its process has been always in the world. (9) It was " possessed and administered " by the " Mystery Schools " of antiquity. (10) There was never a time when it could be taught except in secret. (11) Were it known generally now it could not be put in general practice. (12) The reason is " moral unpreparedness ". (13) Personal and general perils are alike involved, " apart from the privacy " which attaches to something termed " sacrosancties ". (14) The process is affirmed to lay open " the most secret recesses and properties of the human organism ". (15) The candidates for the second birth are said to have been " prepared ". (16) They were prepared in order that they might be identified with " the universal substrate of life ", which is the Light termed " Life of men " in the fourth Gospel, the *Azoth*, Magnesia and First Matter of alchemists. (17) It is " primal fire " and " free ether ". (18) Alchemy is the science of this ether, which man also has within himself because he is " the measure and image of the universe ". (19) The antique sanctuaries purified the natural man and set free " the divine ether " within him. (20) By the concentration of his spiritual energies its light became polarised within him, and was thus consolidated into a Philosophical Stone, otherwise a " vehicle of consciousness " and a " body of regeneration ". (21) The process for discovering the Stone " was accomplished in a condition of magnetic trance mesmerically induced . . . by some wise and skilled operator ". (22) The consciousness of the subject was awakened upon the plane of the polarised ether, which was " elicited into objective form " (*sic*). (23) Thus awakened, it beheld " the interiors and causes of things " and could proclaim divine truths. (24) The enlightened masters of the past were experienced in the conditions of experiment and the limits to which it should be carried in different cases. (25) It follows that Hermetism was " a science of applied magnetism ".

But seeing that the evidence for these things, which are largely an alternative presentation of Mrs. Atwood's thesis in outline, is neither more nor less than that which we have found for the *Suggestive Inquiry* itself, there follows also the conclusion that its editor, so far, makes no contribution to the subject. There remains, however, the question of metallic transmutations, and here it would seem that he has supplied something which is left to be inferred by his text when at the end of Part I the " exoteric view " of Alchemy remains at a loose end. The dogmas are (1) that in the magnetic trance contact would be established first and most easily with the mineral kingdom ; (2) that it was possible in this state to explore the physical world from within it " and to manipulate the metaphysical forces determining its normal external guise " ; (3) that some or many of the magnetic subjects went no further than this and that the Alchemy " associated with physical transmutation only " would " seem attributable " to such.

Mrs. Atwood's belief in the reality of metallic transmutation rests on the records. The records exhibit a compressed powder which was carried from place to place and by which the work was done, sometimes by uninitiated persons who obtained possession. The suggestion that this powder was composed by inward exploration of the physical world and manipulation of metaphysical forces belongs to the world of reverie ; but in reality it means that metals were transmuted by magic and not chemically by the addition of something when they were in a molten state. Now, this belongs to faërie. Supposing that her views on the subject concurred with those of her editor, I conclude that if Mrs. Atwood had never been on the side of wisdom previously she was most certainly on that side when she registered the following decision in 1881 : " It is my abiding wish that so crude an attempt to rehearse the old method of philosophy should not be re-issued but allowed to remain in the oblivion it deserves."

IV

The Mutus Liber and Janitor Pansophus

THERE can be nothing more hazardous in the whole field of interpretation than an attempt to fix a defined and ordered meaning on pictorial symbols which are either accompanied by no text whatever or otherwise by letterpress that does not explain fully. It is partly for this reason that I have relegated to an appendix the consideration of two " hieroglyphical " tracts which are not only remarkable in themselves by the fact of their designs but have long impressed me as pregnant with possible meaning. The second reason is because if that which they suggest to my mind is that also which it was intended to convey in the pictures, they are like signs emblazoned on a Gate of Alchemy which has not been opened or indeed descried previously in the long course of our research. They are concerned with another subject, and it is as if two *anonymi* were seeking to present the alchemical subject from a highly individual standpoint. I proceed to some account of the designs and of the suggestions that they have conveyed to myself, the latter to stand at their value as tentative and speculative in the highest possible degree. If I happen to be right about them, it has to be admitted that they are things set apart in the literature, for I know of no other texts which convey the same notions. On the other hand, if I am misled, as the last statement may quite possibly imply, my account of the designs may lead some other student to the tracts themselves, and if he should have the wit as well as the will to do better, I shall not have worked in vain.

There is an old Rosicrucian romance which is called the *Chemical Nuptials of Christian Rosy Cross*, and those who have read it in a quaint English version of the late seventeenth century will remember that a strange marriage was celebrated therein, amidst much joy and the emblazonments of a long pageant. It took place in a Hermetic Temple which was thronged by persons of both sexes, and if it could be regarded as an allegorical story of the Brotherhood and its concerns at the period there might be little question that Rosicrucianism in and about the year 1616 had thrown open its sacred Houses of Initiation to men and women indifferently, as it does in some of its developments at the present day. I am not claiming to put forward a serious thesis in offering this suggestion, for there is sound and unanswerable evidence that the romance is romance simply and was written by Johann Valentin Andreas as a *jeu d'esprit* or fantasy when he was still of tender age. The historical aspects apart, any question of origin matters little enough, for the *Chemical Nuptials* was taken with all earnestness into the hearts of those who believed that early Rosicrucian documents were issued for the instruction of Europe by an Illuminated Secret Order which had been established for more than a century. The fact that on the surface of its fiction it may have received both sexes on apparently the same terms is a pretext for introducing the present consideration, which is of Woman and the Hermetic Mystery.

The hand of womanhood in the traditions of Hermetic practice is to be traced almost from the beginning, and my suggestion is that behind the simple fact, and in view of the things with which I am about to deal, there may be something withdrawn in the hiddenness. The legends of the Art make mention of Semiramis, Queen of Egypt or rather of Nineveh, as the first woman who had attained the secret of transmutation, unless we assign a superior antiquity to Miriam, the prophetess and sister of Aaron, who was also an adept, according to another tradition, and who has indeed bequeathed by attribution a tract on Alchemy to later followers of the quest. Passing from the region of pure myths and coming to the fourteenth century of the Christian era, there is the case of Nicholas Flamel and his wife Peronella or Pernelle, who worked together on the hieroglyphical book of Abraham the Jew—according to their traditional story—and were finally rewarded *ex hypothesi* by attaining the highest secret. Another example, but in this case apparently a worker in solitude, was Leona Constantia, Abbess of Clermont, who—according to a very curious testimony—was received as a Master into the Order of the Rosy Cross in the year 1736. It follows that in any case at this period there were *Sorores Roseæ Crucis*.

The most interesting evidence on the part of woman in Alchemy is contained, however, in the silent corroboration of picture-symbols. In the year 1677 there was published at Rupella—*id est*, La Rochelle—a work entitled *Mutus Liber*, or *Dumb Book*, the *Book of the Silence of Hermes*, wherein—as its title says—the whole *Philosophia Hermetica* is represented by hieroglyphical figures, apart from all letterpress. In the quaint Latin of the title it is consecrated to the Thrice-Greatest and Most Merciful God, while it is dedicated to Sons of the Art by an author or draughtsman whose veiling name is Altus and has been attributed to Jacob Saulat, Sieur des Merz, and to Tollé, a physician of Rochelle. According to Lenglet du Fresnoy, it had great vogue among students, and it was faithfully reprinted by Mangetus in his *Bibliotheca Chemica Curiosa*. He affirms in his analysis of contents that it is most evidently an opening of the Mysteries of Alchemy to the elect of that doctrine and practice. It consists of fifteen fine copper-plates, and the point which concerns us in the present connection is that the alchemist is represented as working throughout in conjunction with a woman of the Art. They begin and they attain together. The stages of the process are delineated in the successive plates, in which various symbolical personages appear to the workers for their encouragement and guidance, but more frequently to the woman than the man, as if it were her task especially. One of them has a moon upon the left breast, another is Mercury manifesting.

The first design represents the symbolical ladder of Jacob, with angels descending thereon. They are in the act of sounding trumpets to awaken one who is asleep on the ground beneath, thus symbolising the quickening of an artist who is called to the Great Work. The second plate shews that he has responded forthwith and has entered into consultation with a female collaborator, who may be regarded as his wife. The symbolical sun of philosophy is shining in the mid-heaven and beneath it are two angels, having one foot on the earth and another on the water, presumably to indicate that dryness and moisture both enter into the work. They are seen supporting a vessel in which the figures of the Sun and Moon appear in human form, with the god Vulcan seated between them. At the bottom are the student of the Art and his wife, kneeling on either side of a furnace and praying for success in their enterprise. A lamp at the base of the furnace indicates the gradual heat applied to the contents of the vessel suspended above. A third plate seems to promulgate the theory of the work. The Alchemical King is shewn in the clouds of heaven far out of human reach, while below is the circle of experiment and the mode of operation therein, having the Sun and Moon like watchers on either side of the circle. It may be noted at this point that wherever these luminaries appear in connection with the man and his helpmate the Sun is on the side of the woman and the Moon on his.

The last design signifies completion, and therein Jacob's ladder, symbolising the path of ascent from the earth of ordinary life to the heaven of philosophy, is seen laid upon the ground, because the work is done. The Alchemical King of the third plate has been brought from heaven to earth, and his flight is restrained by a rope which the adepts hold between them. They are again kneeling, for they behold his glory with their eyes. Alternatively they are interlinked by the rope which he himself has let down. Between them lies a naked human form, from the face of which a lion's mask is lifted.

The *Mutus Liber* belongs to a dubious period of printed books on Alchemy, for there is no question that a trade was being driven in the subject, and it might well seem foolish to waste time over an anonymous book of prints which may signify only the relations between supply and demand. But even on this supposition the knavery would have missed its mark by running counter to the prevalent school of thought and symbolical presentation on the Hermetic subject. Attainment *ex hypothesi* was possible to men and women or fraudulent productions would not have exhibited them taking an equal share in the work and its toils. Could we certify, on the other hand, that *Mutus Liber* was put forth sincerely as an alchemical thesis, the question would arise as to which aspect of Hermetic experiment was represented thereby, and it must be said that it could belong to either. Though I might incline on my own part to its interpretation in the material sense, the collaboration of male and female has nothing authentic behind it throughout the literature, as the Flamel memorials are mythical. On the other hand, I remember one

D d

testimony which can belong only to the Great Work on its
mystical side.   It is on record that an Unknown Master
testified to his possession of the Mystery, but he added that
he had never proceeded to the practice because he had failed
to meet with an elect woman who was necessary thereto.
I suppose that the statement will awaken in most minds
nothing but a vague sense of wonder, and yet it is possible to
indicate in brief words some part of that which may be
discerned behind it.

The general literature of Alchemy offers the following
elements of symbolism, among many others : (1) the Marriage
of Sun and Moon ; (2) of a mystical King and Queen ; (3)
an union between natures which are one at the root but diverse
in manifestation ; (4) a transmutation which follows this
union and an abiding glory therein.   It is a recurring conjunction between male and female in a mystical sense, a
bringing together by art of what is separated in the imperfect
order of things, and the perfection of natures by means of
such conjunction.   But if the mystical work of Alchemy is an
inward work in consciousness, then any union between male
and female, as these are differentiated in manifestation,
must be an union in consciousness ; and if we remember the
traditions of a state when male and female had not as yet
been divided, it may unfold to us that Higher Alchemy
of this kind may have cherished the idea of return into that
ineffable mode of being.   The traditional doctrine is set forth
in the *Zohar* and it is found in writers like Jacob Böhme ;
it is intimated in the early chapters of *Genesis* ; and according
to a legendary saying of Christ, the Kingdom of Heaven will
be manifested when two shall be as one, or when that state
has been once again attained.   In the light of such a
construction we can understand why a mystical adept went
in search of a wise woman with whom the work could be
performed ; but few there be that find her, and he confessed
to his own failure.   The pictured part of woman in the physical
practice of Alchemy would be like a reflection at a distance
of this more exalted process, and there is evidence that some
of those who worked in metals and sought for a material
Elixir were aware that there were other and greater issues of
the Hermetic Mystery.   On the other hand, as already
indicated, the suggestions of material Alchemy in the designs

of *Liber Mutus* may have been adopted as a pretext only, and then the Ladder of Jacob in its two significant positions may intimate the ascent into union, into that state when the male is with the female, " neither male nor female."

An experiment analogous to that of *Liber Mutus*, but appearing to embody more explicit mystical indications, is called *Janitor Pansophus*, and it appeared in the year 1678 as a section in fine of *Museum Hermeticum Reformatum*, an important collection of Hermetic tracts, with an English translation of which I was concerned in 1893. It consists of four folding plates and commentaries thereupon, by way of scriptural passages and extracts from alchemical books. The *All-Wise Door-keeper* affirms in its sub-title that its plates exhibit analytically " the Mosaico-Hermetic science of things above and of things below ". It seems to have been prepared especially for its place in the *Hermetic Museum*, and there is no record of any separate publication.

The first question which arises is after what manner we are to understand its claim as an· exposition of alchemical or indeed any other symbolism. It is easy to see the surface intention of the designs, without even invoking the help provided by their brief annotations. The first represents the Archetypal World, the ineffable abode of the Trinity, encompassed by the Nine Choirs of the Celestial Hierarchy : it is obviously not a Hermetic scheme in any admitted sense of, the expression ; it is representative rather of pseudo-Dionysius, or it might be placed as a frontispiece to John Heywood's *Hierarchy of the Blessed Angels*. Persons who are acquainted with the fact that Four Worlds are recognised in Zoharic and later Kabalism might speculate that they are presented figuratively in the four plates, when the one now under notice would correspond to *Atziluth*, which is the World of Deity, supposing that Kabalism were rectified, as it has been also, in alembics of Christian Theosophy. There is of course a very obvious analogy, even for those who are unversed in the subject, but there is no living correspondence. It should not be necessary to add that—the text itself notwithstanding—this first diagram is no more Mosaic than Kabalistic : it is the Christian and Thomist scheme of the Angelical World, and this world is seen to be encircling that Divine Centre from which emanate the light, glory and rapture of the Blessed Vision. It is the doctrine of St. Thomas Aquinas projected in the form of a symbol. I should explain also that the angelical figures, each shining like a sun, but unquestionably as reflections from the Central Divine Sun, are presented in a number of aspects, the succession of which seems to follow a certain order; though it might be unwise to suggest that a particular emblematic meaning is to be sought in the variations: they may stand merely for the moods and will of the artist.

The second plate represents the Elementary World, as it was understood by old cosmology, and its analogies are numerous enough in writings like those of Robert Fludd. Again, they are surface analogies, while there are also important, almost vital distinctions. The design embodies the hypothesis of concordance between the greater and lesser worlds, and from this point of view its indications are valuable because of their comprehensive character. In the centre of all is a human figure, having an angel on either side, encompassed by a Latin inscription which sets forth the doctrine of celestial guardians. The implicit is that God is the centre of the Archetypal World but Man of that of the Elements, and this is illustrated further by the third plate, which exhibits the development of creation in a symbolism of ten circles, beginning with the Divine—as it passes towards the activity of manifestation—and ending with the two aspects of humanity, male and female. The implicit in this case is that God is the Eternal Source and Man the term of creation. It should be observed that the two figures bear on their middle part the signs of the Sun and Moon, or the alchemical gold and silver, as if the Hermetic Mystery in transcendence were a Mystery behind sex, and as if the Great Work were the generation between them of that most perfect subject which is called Son of the Sun in some allegories of the Art.

The fourth plate furnishes in figurative form the leading hypothesis of Alchemy. The archetypal Adam and Eve appear again and not alone bearing on their bodies the symbols already mentioned but holding them in their hands, as if the work which they were created to accomplish had been carried to its term. To indicate that it is a Divine Work, the Eternal Father, represented by the Hebrew *Tetragram*, is shewn at the apex; on one side is the Eternal

Son, represented by the symbol of His incarnation, a lamb bearing a pennon ; and on the other is the Eternal Spirit in the state of manifestation—that is, a dove flying. Each human figure is held by a rope fastened to one of the wrists, and these bonds signify their attachment to the Divine in the supernal operation which is depicted in summary above. Like *Altus Liber Mutus*, there is thus again depicted a work accomplished between the man and the woman, but whereas in the symbolism of the latter the male and female characters are typical Germans of their period, in *Janitor Pansophus* they are catholic emblems of humanity at large, as if it were intended to exhibit the true purpose of creation and the order which should have obtained therein. The two emblematical books are thus in an undesigned manner like complements one of another, this representing the doctrine of the whole subject and that a particular sense in which it was undertaken and fulfilled by two prepared students.

If the analogy thus instituted be held to fail, or is referred once again to the mere surface only, because the symbols of *Liber Mutus* are perhaps an allegory of the physical work, whereas those of *Janitor Pansophus* are of all things mystical, it should be remembered that the work of metallic transmutation has been compared by alchemists themselves to that of God in the cosmos and that the stages of the one are affirmed to be an exact reproduction or counterpart of the other. We should remember also that Alchemy in all its departments is dealing with subjects—whether spiritual or material—which are *ex hypothesi* fallen, and that this is true indifferently of so-called base metals and of humanity in the base life. The thesis is that regeneration is an analogous process in every kingdom—that metals are reborn, transmuted or redeemed, and that what happens in their case is in correspondence—*mutatis mutandis*—with the higher work of God in the soul.

In the third plate of the *Janitor* Adam and Eve are environed by light of glory, meaning that they are in the state of Paradise : in the fourth their state is sublunary, amidst the animal and vegetable kingdoms, planets and stars of metals. The primary intention of the third plate is to shew after what manner and for what reason man came forth from God : that of the fourth exhibits him still indeed on this earth but as having undone the Fall therein. There is, however, another sense in which the third plate represents stages in the conversion of the inward man, by which he passes from the natural chaos to the perfect order and union—*opus catholicum* indeed, great and catholic work, as Khunrath would term it.

I pass now to the Latin inscriptions which accompany and explain the designs. The first is illustrated by a quotation from Marcellus Palingenius Stellatus, that is to say, from the *Zodiac of Life*. The extract is an appeal to the creator of all things that a given suppliant may be directed in the right way. It reminds us of a Latin aphorism which is also Hermetic : *Laborare est orare*. To the second plate is appended a citation from *Enchyridion Physicæ Restitutæ* by Jean d'Espagnet, a tract which has been held generally as of signal consequence among the records of Alchemy. It regards Nature as a constant expression of Divine Will, it being understood that the paradisical state is the true nature and that its attainment is God's will in respect of humanity. The third plate is accompanied by a moving prayer of George Ripley, to whom Eirenæus Philalethes owed so much of his light and leading. It asks for grace to know the blessedness and goodness of God, this being the only path to " a knowledge of the Blessed Stone". All things were made by God " out of one chaos ", and the true artist seeks to evolve the microcosm of Alchemy out of one substance, having three aspects, these being veiled by the figurative names of Magnesia, Sulphur and Mercury. The annotation to the fourth plate is the *Emerald Tablet of Hermes*, the doctrine of correspondence between things above and below, and the affirmation of that one substance wherein is " the glory of the whole world ".

Alchemy is a secret science, using a veiled terminology, and it is not to be expected that these indications will prove readily intelligible on the surface. The true path or right way of Palingenius in the mystical work is that by which the seeker after eternal life becomes by interior unfolding that which is Nature herself, or an expression of Divine Will, according to Jean d'Espagnet. The purpose is knowledge of God, in the sense that alchemists of both schools spoke of knowledge of the Stone. It is possession in either case. The analogy instituted by Ripley between primeval chaos and the substance of Art makes a harmony between the third and fourth plates of *Janitor Pansophus*. We see in the third how God's work proceeded in the making of the Greater World, with triune man as the outcome : in the fourth we see the same term attained by means of mystical Alchemy. That which is not expressed and yet is implied clearly in the two diagrams is that the transmuted state depicted in Plate IV is reached through successive inward stages corresponding to those of Plate III : it may be summarised in a single aphorism : the work of God in the soul is like that of God proceeding to the creation of Nature. It is old theosophy enough, and will be familiar in its variant terms to many.

The keeper of this particular Door of Wisdom seems to bear the same testimony as other Wardens of the Portal which leads everywhere that a soul can desire to go : he shews forth after his own manner that the intent of Nature is to make gold on all planes of manifestation. He assists us to recognise, with every disciple of Hermes, that the same thing is everywhere—the same truth, the same possibility, the same grace of attainment and the same witness always in the world. The man also is not without the woman in the manifest order of things, and in the state of attainment the instruction of *Janitor Pansophus* is that they are as Sun and Moon spiritualised.

INDEX

Printed in the United States
80445LV00006B/80